Getting the Gospel Wrong

The Evangelical Crisis No One Is Talking About

J. B. Hixson, Ph.D.

Foreward by: Earl D. Radmacher, Th.D.

PRESS

Getting the Gospel Wrong
The Evangelical Crisis No One Is Talking About
by J. B. Hixson, Ph.D.

Printed in the United States of America

ISBN 978-1-60647-098-5

www.xulonpress.com

ENDORSEMENTS

Hixson's work has provided a needed remedy for the doctrine of salvation in our current postmodern climate. First, it has attempted from a balanced grace view to give a clear and precise definition of the gospel of eternal life. In a day weighed down with the absence of clarity and the expansion of uncertainty, this is a welcome breath of fresh air. Second, it provides a keen analysis of varying approaches to the preaching of the gospel of eternal life that dominate so much of North American culture especially involving media personalities. I have not seen this analysis brought together in one place. In light of these two factors, Hixson's book is well worth the effort of a careful read.

> Dr. Mike Stallard, Academic Dean and Professor of Theology
> Baptist Bible Seminary, Clarks Summit, PA

J. B. Hixson's book is not only the most readable, the clearest, and most concise book on what the gospel is and is not that I have read, it continues to serve as a reference work to which I return again and again. It simply refuses to stay on the bookshelf. Hixson accomplishes a rare feat in today's theological world: he is both sharply analytical and interesting. If you want one book on the subject of the gospel which says it all and says it well, this is it!

> Dr. Mike Halsey, President
> Free Grace Seminary, Atlanta, GA

Distortions of the gospel began soon after Paul wrote his first letter (Galatians). He viewed such distortions as a threat to the very core of Christianity. It is our very fallen nature which tempts us to make the gospel more attractive, usually introducing some sort of meritocracy to beef it up or democracy to water it down. Dr. Hixson puts the modern distortions into five categories, all in order to help us identify the true gospel. This is a very valuable work.

> Dr. Dave Anderson, President
> Grace School of Theology, The Woodlands, TX

The gospel you believe will impact your philosophy of ministry as well as determine the content of your evangelism. J. B. Hixson is a friend of the gospel. In this new work, he also seeks to be a guardian of the biblical gospel. Theological analysis and contemporary case studies make *Getting the Gospel Wrong* both thought provoking and readable. Dr. Hixson offers scholarly analysis with pastoral passion. His extensive research and careful exegesis are combined with clearly illustrated analysis. Hixson concludes that definite and dangerous additions to and subtractions from the gospel are prevalent among evangelicals. You may disagree with some of his conclusions, but I believe you will agree the serious discussion is overdue. Hixson gives us a carefully considered place to start.

> Dr. Timothy K. Christian, Professor and Dean of Students
> Mid-America Baptist Theological Seminary, NE Campus
> Schenectady, NY

It is grievous to admit, but this book is absolutely needed today. Hixson takes head on the present confusion about the gospel and cogently, biblically, and logically presents a true gospel. The best presentation I have ever read. It should be required reading for all who are in the ministry or who want to understand what it means to believe the gospel of our salvation.

> Dr. Charlie Bing, President
> Grace Life Ministries, Burleson, TX

The issue regarding the content and clarity of the gospel has been the seminal issue for the Church from the Jerusalem Council of Acts 15 down to this present day. Dr. Hixson provides both theological analysis and pastoral insight for the church. He is to be commended for both his methodology and mindset concerning the scope of this most critical theological topic.

> Dr. Fred Chay, Assoc. Professor of Theology
> Phoenix Seminary, Phoenix, AZ
> President, Grace Line Ministries

"For if the trumpet makes an uncertain sound who will prepare for battle?" (1 Cor 14:8, NKJV) These words should echo deep in our souls as they assert a truism which needs a resurrection if the gospel has any hope of surviving its most recent enemy. The logic is simple—-if one must believe to be saved eternally, then what one must believe is unavoidably the life-giving means through which faith becomes 'saving' in the individual. Said differently, "If the gospel makes an uncertain sound, then who will be prepared for heaven?"

Dr. Hixson offers a detailed analysis of the current climate of confusion which has so many disoriented concerning the gospel by which we are saved. In a case study analysis, with the backdrop of postmodernism's tentacled grip on what can be truly known, Dr. Hixson invites the reader to both re-think and re-affirm his own understanding and expression of The Gospel. The onslaught against the gospel shows up in confusion about what one must believe to be saved, as well as what one must preach to offer salvation. All the major missteps in communicating the gospel are exposed, considered, and properly challenged against the authority of the Scriptures. One could ask for little more, except for greater clarity concerning the content of the gospel. Dr. Hixson provides insight on this matter as well, offering (in summation) that the content of saving faith for the proclamation of the gospel is that: Jesus Christ, the Son of God, who died and rose again to pay the penalty for all sin, gives eternal life to each one who trusts Him, and Him alone, for it.

If you care about a clear gospel, then you will want to add *Getting the Gospel Wrong* to the truth shelf in your library; but only after you've spent the time needed to get the point. And, of course, the point is to share a clear and saving message to a confused world which is groping about in the dark for the light of the gospel.

Dr. Fred R. Lybrand, Author and Senior Pastor
Northeast Bible Church, Garden Ridge, TX

In this important work Hixson stands firm as a champion for the cause of the gospel. First, Hixson stands for the clarity of the gospel. He defines the gospel clearly from the text of Scripture and exposes the so-called gospel messages of many today as inadequate. Second, Hixson stands for the core of the gospel: salvation by grace alone through faith in Christ alone. Hixson's message is greatly needed in our postmodern context of ambiguity and will be heartily welcomed by all who stand on the grace of God in Christ Jesus as the only hope for a lost world in need of salvation.

Dr. Ken Gardoski, Professor of Theology
Baptist Bible Seminary, Clarks Summit, PA

Getting the Gospel Wrong delivers a potent, biblical, and timely message that must be heard and heeded by the evangelical Church of our day. To this bewildered generation that seems to have lost all sense of divine direction, *Getting the Gospel Wrong* offers a desperately needed spiritual compass. Grounded on the authority of God's Word, this well-researched, well-written book issues a clarion call to return to the truth of the gospel of the grace of God. In so doing, Dr. Hixson has effectively shined the light of the knowledge of the glory of God upon the face of our Savior, Jesus Christ. May the Lord greatly use this book to enlighten this generation and especially to stir the hearts of evangelicals to believe solely in the truth of the gospel.

Tom Stegall, Pastor, Word of Grace Bible Church
Milwaukee, WI

Dr. Hixson is addressing a critical concern in the Evangelical Churches of today. Many have taken the wrong fork in the road, and he has directed us back to the original fork, and guided us down the correct path. He is like the watchman on the wall, declaring what is seen, and what needs to be changed.

Andy Anderson, National Sales Manager
Logos Bible Software, Bellingham, WA

Dr. Hixson addresses in this volume the Kadesh-Barnea of evangelical Christianity, namely, "What exactly is the Gospel of eternal salvation?" In doing so, he accurately and clearly not only expounds what the Gospel is based on the Word of God, but also exposes some of the prominent false gospels of our day. If you are passionate about the clarity and purity of the Gospel of grace in our postmodern society that disdains absolute truth, this is a book I recommend that you carefully read.

Dennis Rokser, Pastor-Teacher
Duluth Bible Church, Duluth, MN

Dr. Hixson's clear and incisive work is distinct in its format and presentation. His treatise of the content of the gospel and the nature of faith is worth the read alone. In this day and age of getting the gospel wrong, Dr. Hixson got it right!

Dr. Buck Anderson, Pastor,
Leadership Development Grace
Bible Church, College Station, TX

Hixson's scholarly approach toward these relevant theological matters facing our postmodern milieu make this an important read for all evangelicals. This book sheds light on the errant soteriological assumptions behind much of conventional church growth methodology and its undulating effects that lead to unhealthy congregational growth.

Dr. Mike Ayers, Professor
College of Biblical Studies, Houston, TX

It is refreshing to see such a complex subject covered with such passion and clarity. In this book Hixson has succinctly and effectively reminded the church to keep focus on being true to the true Christian Gospel. I encourage lay people, pastors and professors to take the time to read this exceptional work.

Joseph Parle, Academic Dean
College of Biblical Studies, Houston, TX

Whether from the radio or television or in church, people hear an amazing number of presentations of "the gospel," many of which are in conflict with the simple biblical truth. Dr. Hixson, in this book, takes on most of them. This is a necessary book.

Bill Ball, Retired Bible College professor
Edmond, OK

Even though you might not agree with all of its content, a book like this ought to be read to help you come to your own conclusions. It will certainly challenge your thinking.

Dr. R. Larry Moyer, President and CEO
EvanTell, Inc., Dallas, TX

Dr. Hixson's book answers many questions that are being asked about the gospel that is being so misrepresented throughout our country. Dr. Hixson is well known in the theological circles and brings both a theological and pastoral message addressing these issues. I recommend this book to anyone who is charged with the responsibility of presenting the truth.

Rick Blount, Pastor, First Baptist Church
Jacinto City, TX

Getting the Gospel Wrong is the right book for anyone trying to clear up the confusing "gospel" messages about today. Hixson exposes unclear and unbiblical presentations of the gospel, and helps readers understand how to simply and clearly present the Good News!

Phil Congdon, Pastor
New Braunfels Bible Church, New Braunfels, TX

As I was reading Dr. Hixson's work I was struck with the casual, if not careless, use of words I had lapsed into through the years. All readers will be encouraged by this work and the clear call it makes to stay within the simple but profound presentation of the Gospel.

Les Wright, Prison Chaplain Ministry
Houston, TX

DEDICATION

To Wendy
"There are many virtuous and capable women in the world,
but you surpass them all!"
(Proverbs 31:29)

ACKNOWLEDGMENTS

*G*etting the Gospel Wrong represents the culmination of nearly twenty years of reflection on the topic of evangelical soteriology (the doctrine of salvation). Of course, since systematic theology is a life-long *process*, not a *product*, refinement and reflection are ongoing as I study the Word of God and continually synthesize theological truths from Scripture—the only standard for our beliefs, attitudes and practices. Nevertheless, the present work reflects a comprehensive overview of the biblical doctrine of salvation from a conservative, evangelical perspective, as well as a critique of the various soteriological methods prevalent within postmodern American evangelicalism. Along the way many people have influenced my thinking as I interacted with biblical and theological scholarship on this issue.

First, I wish to acknowledge my immediate and extended families who made significant sacrifices during my academic pursuits at Houston Baptist University, Dallas Theological Seminary and Baptist Bible Seminary. I am grateful for the strong, biblical heritage that my mom and dad provided during my formative years and for their faithful, unconditional support of my ministry to this day. I equally am grateful for my godly wife, Wendy, who never has failed to support whatever ministry endeavors we have pursued together, even when the personal cost was quite high; and has affirmed my passion for the purity of the gospel at every turn. My children have made sacrifices they may not even be aware of as I was away from home four to six weeks a year for several years during my Ph.D. studies. And when I *was* home, the seemingly endless hours of study and writing often kept me from spending time with my wife and children to the degree that I wish I could have. My prayer is that the positive contribution to the body of Christ that is provided by *Getting the Gospel Wrong* will offset any negative effects of the sacrifices made by Wendy and the children.

In addition to my family, I wish to thank the following people for the part they played, whether wittingly or unwittingly, in the development of this book: the members of the churches I have pastored: Community Bible Church in Van Alstyne, TX; Tremont Baptist Church in Tremont, IL; Keeler Baptist Church in Borger, TX; Anchor Bible Church in Cypress, TX; my friends and colleagues at various other ministries where I have served: The College of Biblical Studies, Fairfield Baptist Church, Grace School of Theology, Free Grace Seminary, Free Grace Alliance, Logos Bible Software; my dissertation readers at Baptist Bible Seminary: Dr. Ken Gardoski, Dr. Mike Stallard, and Dr. Robert Lightner. I am especially grateful for Dr. Mike Stallard's profound influence on the development of my theological method. Dr. Stallard helped me to see the importance of being consistent in the synthesis of my hermeneutics, exegesis and systematic theology. A special thank you also is owed to Dr. Ken Gardoski for his patience, grace and editing expertise as he helped me produce the final draft of my dissertation.

It would be difficult to recall and list all of the many other individuals who have helped to shape my thinking through the years on the topic of the purity and accuracy of the gospel. God places people in our lives whose influence often is unrecognized this side of Glory. Thank you to all of my close friends, colleagues, professors, mentors and acquaintances for the sharpening role you have played in my life and ministry.

FOREWARD

God's people are engaged in a war that makes the war in the Middle East pale into insignificance by comparison. It has been going on, not simply for five years, or even five hundred years but thousands of years—ever since "By faith Abel offered to God a more excellent sacrifice than Cain through which he obtained witness that he was righteous" (Gen 4:4–8; Heb 11:4), and he is listed first in the Hall of Faith. Its results are more than temporal. They are eternal. It's a blood sacrifice and its final portrait is the blood sacrifice of God's Son, Jesus Christ, which is sufficient for all and effective for all who receive it Robert Lowry captures its essence in a century old hymn:

> What can wash away my sin?
> Nothing but the blood of Jesus;
> What can make me whole again?
> Nothing but the blood of Jesus.
>
> For my pardon this I see —
> Nothing but the blood of Jesus;
> For my cleansing, this my plea —
> Nothing but the blood of Jesus.
>
> Nothing can for sin atone –
> Nothing but the blood of Jesus;
> Naught of good that I have done –
> Nothing but the blood of Jesus.

This is all my hope and peace –
Nothing but the blood of Jesus;
This is all my righteousness –
Nothing but the blood of Jesus.

Oh! Precious is the flow
That makes me white as snow;
No other fount I know,
Nothing but the blood of Jesus.

In this war our enemy is not other human beings but Satan who in his deceitfulness is crafty and clandestine. The Apostle Paul reminds us of the "wiles of the devil" and that "we do not wrestle against flesh and blood, but against principalities, against powers, against the rulers of the darkness of this age, against spiritual hosts of wickedness in heavenly places" (Eph 6:11–12). And there is nothing that Satan's crowd wants to destroy more than the pure gospel and its presentation. From the beginning of the entrance of sin, Satan has labored to destroy the infinite value of Christ's sacrifice through his blinding and beguiling maneuvers. He sought to use the Scripture to dissuade Jesus from His mission (Matt 4:1–11) but he failed miserably. He sought to keep Jesus from the cross but he could not distract Him. Jesus was focused! And He sets the example for us as recorded in Hebrews 12:2: "Looking unto Jesus, the author and finisher of our faith, who for the joy that was set before Him endured the cross, despising the shame, and has sat down at the right hand of the throne of God."

It is that focus that J. B. Hixson has exercised in this one-of-a-kind book—*Getting the Gospel Wrong*—dealing with a thorough and comprehensive treatment of the most important doctrine in the Word of God, namely, *the pure gospel*. He rightly states: "Amid the cacophony of the evangelical gospel presentations today, there remains a disconcerting indifference to the epidemic of erroneous gospel presentations that fail to meet the standard of Biblical saving faith."

He does not hesitate to call a spade a spade in a gracious but probing examination of some of the most well-known names in

Evangelicalism. And it is about time that we deal with this serious problem. In some cases it may mean the difference between heaven and hell for many well meaning people. And certainly, if it goes uncorrected, it will result in significant loss at the Judgment Seat of Christ (2 Cor 5:10) accompanied by much shame (1 John 2:28).

Little wonder that such carelessness with the Gospel caused Paul the Apostle to confront the Apostle Peter with respect to his hypocrisy in adding to the Gospel: "Now when Peter had come to Antioch, I withstood him to his face because he was to be blamed... And the rest of the Jews also played the hypocrite with him, so that even Barnabas was carried away with their hypocrisy. But when I saw that they were not straightforward about the truth of the gospel, I said to Peter before them all, If you, being a Jew, live in the manner of Gentiles and not as the Jews, why do you compel Gentiles to live as Jews? We who are Jews by nature, and not sinners of the Gentiles, knowing that a man is not justified by the works of the law but by faith in Jesus Christ, even we have believed in Christ Jesus, that we might be justified by faith in Christ and not by the works of the law; for by the works of the law no flesh shall be justified (Gal 2:11, 13–16).

It was this early confrontation with the Apostle Peter that caused the Apostle Paul, in this, his earliest letter to write: "I marvel that you are turning away so soon from Him who called you in the grace of Christ, to a different gospel, which is not another; but there are some who trouble you and want to pervert the gospel of Christ. But even if we, or an angel from heaven, preach any other gospel to you than what we have preached to you, let him be accursed. As we have said before, so now I say again, if anyone preaches any other gospel to you than what you have received, let him be accursed" (Gal 1:6–9).

The Jews understood "blessing" and "cursing" very well (Deut 28–29). We might do well to note that Moses lists 14 verses here on blessing and 83 on cursing. I believe that, if the Apostle Paul were here today, he would call Dr. Hixson "blessed" for the careful, comprehensive, and faithful checkup he has provided for us that, if followed, will bring "well done" from our Lord at the Bema.

Rejoicing in the matchless grace of Christ,
A servant of the Lord, Earl D. Radmacher, Th.D.
President Emeritus and Distinguished Professor of Systematic
    Theology, Emeritus
Western Baptist Seminary

PREFACE

V ince Lombardi is widely recognized as one of the greatest football coaches of all time. On one occasion, after a particularly
tough loss for his team, he gathered his players in the locker room
for the usual postgame speech. In a short but poignant statement,
the coach cut right to the heart of the matter. Holding up a football, Lombardi quipped, "Gentlemen, *this* is a football." His point
was not lost on the players: Their performance in the game that just
concluded had evidenced an utter lack of competency in the very
basic fundamentals of the game.

A survey of the state of American evangelicalism reveals a
similar incompetency when it comes to the basics of the Christian
faith—namely, the Gospel. There is a crisis regarding the nature of
the gospel within evangelical theology today and very little is being
done to address the issue. While most evangelicals agree that Jesus
Christ is the object of saving faith, there is widespread inconsistency regarding the specific content of saving faith. What is it about
Jesus Christ that one must believe in order to have eternal life? Are
there certain non-negotiable truths that must be included in a gospel
presentation in order for it to be considered the pure gospel? An
abandonment of certainty, as well as a general disdain for absolute
truth within the postmodern ideological milieu, have created fertile
ground for erroneous gospel presentations—each competing for
legitimacy within the evangelical church at large.

Perhaps most disturbing is the fact that each of these inherently contradictory gospels is welcomed as a legitimate pretender
to the true biblical gospel and few, if any, evangelical leaders seem

concerned with the transparent incongruity. This suggests at least a couple of possibilities. (1) Either various evangelical pastors, scholars and leaders are not really paying attention to what other evangelicals are saying about the gospel and thus have not noticed the incongruity; and/or (2) each evangelical pastor, scholar, or leader does not hold his or her particular view of the gospel with any degree of conviction and is thus open to embracing competing views on the matter. Either explanation does not speak well of the state of evangelicalism today.

What is needed today is a Lombardi-style critique in which pastors and evangelical leaders confidently raise their Bibles and remind the church, "This is the Gospel!" The present work examines the postmodern evangelical climate and interacts with various gospel claims. Each is evaluated based upon the standard of Scripture and a five-fold standard of the gospel is outlined. The conclusion is both unmistakable and disturbing. Certain core essentials necessary in order for any soteriological method to claim a rightful place within biblical orthodoxy are missing from the vast majority of gospel presentations in postmodern, American evangelicalism.

Necessarily, the present work examines in detail not only the content of the gospel, viz. its core essentials, but also the nature of faith itself. What precisely does it mean to *believe* the gospel? Is there such a thing as defective faith and if so what is it that makes it defective? These questions are fundamental to any examination of the gospel. After establishing the standard of the pure gospel and examining the nature of faith itself, several case studies are undertaken as an example of five broad types of erroneous soteriological methods prevalent in the postmodern era. These include: the purpose gospel, the puzzling gospel, the prosperity gospel, the pluralistic gospel and the performance gospel. Each of these is discussed in detail with various examples cited. The present work concludes with several suggested correctives to the problem of faulty gospel presentations. Although the widespread mishandling of the gospel within contemporary evangelicalism presents a seemingly insuperable threat to the historic Christian faith, the battle is not lost. If the body of Christ will return to the centrality of the Scripture, and the clarity of the simple gospel it proclaims, revival and true evangelistic success will reshape the evangelical landscape.

TABLE OF CONTENTS

Chapter

1. Introduction..27
2.Surveying the Landscape 37
3.Establishing the Standard: What Is the Pure Gospel?.........77
4.The Purpose Gospel 195
5.The Puzzling Gospel 223
6.The Prosperity Gospel..253
7.The Pluralistic Gospel..277
8.The Performance Gospel.......................................301
9.Summary and Conclusion 331
10.Suggested Correctives..343
Appendices..355
Glossary 367
Bibliography 375
Epilogue 403

CHAPTER 1

INTRODUCTION

In matters of principle, stand like a rock; in matters of taste,
swim with the current. –Thomas Jefferson

The present work is a foray into the often complex and murky
realm of evangelical soteriology.[1] The nature of this study
is as much practical as it is theological. This is not a comprehensive exegetical treatise—though a significant amount of exegetical
spade work necessarily is included. Nor is it solely a lament of the
current state of evangelical affairs—though frequently, appropriate
criticisms are expressed. Rather, in examining contemporary evangelical soteriology and the extent to which it has departed from its
biblical standard, it is hoped that readers will be redirected and reenergized to stand like a rock and proclaim the simple, saving message
of Christ in a clear and accurate manner.

The focus of this study is on various case studies arranged
according to five thematic categories representing prevalent evangelical soteriological methods within the present American culture.
It will be demonstrated that the gospel has been deconstructed in
several ways resulting in erroneous gospel presentations.[2] The case
study approach undertaken in the present work is by no means
exhaustive. Indeed, a comprehensive examination of every evangelical gospel presentation in the current culture would be an impossible
undertaking. Instead, selected case studies are critiqued to validate

the present writer's five-fold categorization within American evangelical soteriology. Such an approach requires several preliminary considerations such as a review of the current theological climate and a treatment of the biblical data in an effort to establish a standard against which these soteriological methods may be evaluated.

The Significance and Purpose of this Study

Postmodernism has cultivated a resurgence of interest in spiritual matters.[3] Unlike the rationalism of the modern age, the present age is marked by an acceptance of the supernatural and a desire to connect on some level with this coveted, though misunderstood, "other-worldliness." That is why, as one writer points out, "Eastern mysticism is becoming increasingly popular in Western culture. Indeed, postmodernism claims that an individual must embrace spirituality to become a whole person. And since there is no one true religion, any spirituality will do."[4]

This presents a fertile ground for sharing the gospel with those who recognize that life is about more than what they can see and feel and touch. However, this awareness of the spiritual realm coupled with a rejection of absolute truth constitutes a volatile and dangerous mixture. With no arbiter available to police the quest for truth, people stand ready and eager to accept any individualized truth that is pitched as a means of bringing personal fulfillment or satisfaction. As the Proverb says, "To a hungry soul every bitter thing is sweet.[5]

The secular world has been quick to capitalize on this prevalent gullibility via the pervasive marketing of self-help and quick-fix philosophies. Personalities like Oprah Winfrey and Dr. Phil have exploited this search for significance with their humanistic advice, ungrounded in absolute truth; yet so too have many evangelicals.[6] Often with the best of intentions, many churches and evangelical leaders seek to improve the lives of their parishioners by offering resources that, while motivational and meaningful, nevertheless eclipse the centrality of the Scriptures. No longer is the Bible the foremost core value in evangelical churches. In fact, in many cases, the Bible is absent altogether. It is not uncommon for the typical evangelical megachurch today to market its programs, small groups, children's activities, entertaining weekly services, and a host of other needs-based initiatives as motivations for attendance. Rarely, it seems, is a church's marketing campaign based upon its commitment to the authority of God's Word.

Consider the following ad campaign where the enticement to attend church services is built upon the promise of *comfortable seats*. A prominent megachurch in the Houston, Texas area, *Second Baptist Church*, recently launched an initiative wherein several satellite assemblies were organized in area movie theaters and the Sunday morning services from the main campus were simulcast on the movie screens in high definition digital format. In marketing the grand opening of one of these area movie theater satellites, an E-Newsletter was mass distributed via email with the headline: "Same Experience. Comfier Seats."[7] The posters, billboards and other marketing media around Houston contain the same slogan and Second Baptist has launched similar movie theater satellite campuses throughout the United States. Such an approach to marketing, while creative and perhaps effective in attracting crowds, may run the risk of undermining the biblical authority on which the church's message supposedly is built.

Another prominent megachurch provides additional anecdotal evidence of the neglecting of the centrality of Scriptures by evangelical churches. A postcard marketing campaign advertising a sermon on how to "ensure a lasting love" in your marriage, distributed by *Community of Faith* in Cypress, Texas featured a husband and wife, each members who serve key roles in leadership at the church and identify themselves as close friends with the church's pastor, Dr. Mark Shook. The present writer had a personal conversation with the wife featured on the postcard. The conversation included a discussion of Community of Faith and its core values. When asked why one of the church's staff members recently had left the church after serving less than a year, the woman told the present writer that the staff member left Community of Faith because "he wanted to serve at a church that *emphasized the Bible*.[8] This comment illustrates well the underlying premise of many postmodern evangelical churches today: the Bible is secondary to relationships and community.

In abandoning the centrality of the Scriptures as the only absolute standard of truth, some evangelical churches have, at the same time, jeopardized the gospel. One cannot marginalize the Bible without simultaneously marginalizing its gospel message. The very thing that the world needs most, the gospel, has been downplayed, ignored and redefined with devastating results.

The present work is not primarily a polemic against postmodern ideology, though postmodernism is addressed and critiqued at some length in chapter two. Rather, the present work is a polemic against erroneous gospels that permeate American evangelical Christianity in the *present culture*. To the extent that the present culture is characterized by postmodern thinking, postmodernism necessarily must be addressed to frame this discussion. Yet, it must be kept in mind that not all erroneous gospels being propagated today originated within the postmodern era. That is to say, not all erroneous gospels that are critiqued in the present work are the direct result of postmodern ideology. Some have their roots in a time and cultural setting well before the onset of postmodernism in American society. Nevertheless, all of the soteriological methods critiqued herein take place within a postmodern milieu and thus may be considered in that light.

Approach to This Study

Before evaluating the accuracy of selected gospel presentations, two preliminary matters will be addressed. First, a survey of the current postmodern American landscape will help to contextualize the setting in which the gospel is being proclaimed. This discussion of postmodernism takes place in chapter two. Second, and most importantly, the standard of the pure gospel against which all others will be evaluated will be defined. Chapter three below sets out to accomplish this goal by answering the question, "What precisely must someone believe in order to obtain eternal life?" That is, what is the *pure gospel?* It is an important chapter to the extent that it creates the theological grid through which the case studies in the following chapters must pass for evaluation.

Chapters four through eight apply the standard established in chapter three to various case studies of gospel presentations prevalent within postmodern evangelicalism. The reader should keep in mind that the case studies are not intended as comprehensive treatments of an individual's soteriological method. Rather, the case studies should be viewed as Polaroid snapshots, of sorts, that illustrate how the gospel is communicated erroneously in the present age. The case studies are drawn from such evangelical outlets as books, sermons, gospel tracts, web sites and other common media of the day and classified according to *five broad categories,* one in each chapter. A subject's inclusion in the case studies should not be taken as an indication that he *always* presents the gospel inaccurately. Nor does a subject's inclusion in one particular category indicate that his errors are limited *only* to that category. The case studies are merely isolated examples that serve, when taken together, as cumulative evidence of a crisis of evangelical soteriological method in the present American culture.

The individuals selected by the present writer for further study in each category were selected because of their prominence (i.e., they are well-known) and/or popularity (i.e., they are particularly well-liked) within contemporary evangelicalism. The case study chapters are not intended as an in-depth critique of the particular soteriological method under consideration in each chapter. That is, for each of the five case study chapters, more research could be done and additional or different individuals could be chosen to illustrate a given soteriological method. The case studies should not be read as a detailed soteriological defense as much as an illustrational reportage of the current state of soteriological affairs in American evangelicalism. In choosing a case study approach, the present writer's goal is to validate the premise that erroneous soteriological methods are well-entrenched in postmodern American evangelicalism and to interact with each case study sufficiently to show that it fails to meet the standard of the biblical gospel.

The first erroneous version of the gospel examined below is perhaps the most common: *The Purpose Gospel* (chapter four).[9] In this category are those evangelicals who couch the gospel in terms of personal fulfillment and meaning in this present life with little or no emphasis on sin and its eternal consequences. Of the five types of gospel presentations critiqued in the present work, the *purpose gospel* is second perhaps only to the pluralistic gospel in its reflection of postmodern thought.

In chapter five, *The Puzzling Gospel,* it is suggested that many gospel presentations are faulty because they are either imprecise, vague or in some cases inconsistent (i.e., self-contradictory). Of course, confusing gospel presentations are nothing new. Long before the onset of postmodernism Christianity suffered from poorly articulated gospel presentations. Yet given the ideological distinctives of postmodernity, such inconsistent and self-contradictory gospels are more likely than ever to go unnoticed and perhaps even thrive.

The Prosperity Gospel (chapter six) connects the gospel with the promise of earthly blessings such as wealth and good health. This brand of evangelicalism has been around for decades. But the tendency toward experientialism and subjectivity, as well as self-fulfillment, that characterizes postmodernism seems to have emboldened its adherents such that it remains a serious pretender to the pure gospel of Scripture. In chapter seven, it is suggested that an alarming number of evangelicals are espousing what may be termed *The Pluralistic Gospel* to the extent that they remain open to alternative religions as valid pathways to heaven. Some of these are explicitly pluralistic. Others are more subtly so. In any event, postmodernism's emphasis on diversity rather than sameness as well as its abandonment of objectivity and certainty make the pluralistic gospel particularly appealing to unbelievers and non-discerning believers.

Finally, chapter eight addresses the tendency on the part of some evangelicals to promote a soteriological method that makes man's entrance into heaven contingent to varying degrees upon his own good behavior. *The Performance Gospel* emphasizes man's good works as a either a prerequisite or postrequisite to saving faith. Works-oriented gospels, like the prosperity gospel, are hardly novel. Indeed, the inclination on the part of man to earn his way to eternal salvation is as old as man himself. Yet the trend in postmodern American culture to define deviancy down seems to have reenergized works-based gospels as some well-intentioned evangelicals attempt to stem the tide of moral relativism by placing additional requirements on those who wish to gain eternal life.[10] Whether the prevalence of performance gospels indeed reflects a reaction to postmodern ideology or merely is the continuation of a soterio-logical method that has always flourished is impossible to say with certainty. But in any event, postmodernism's penchant for moral relativism has created a fertile ground for those who are inclined to emphasize works as part of the gospel.

The present work will conclude with a summary in chapter nine and suggested correctives to the problem in chapter ten. In chapter ten it is suggested that in light of (1) a prevalent inconsistency among evangelicals when it comes to the precise definition of the gospel, (2) a lack of awareness of or attentiveness to this inconsistency, and (3) perceived indifference toward accuracy in gospel presentations, evangelicals must strive to combat erroneous soteriological methods by implementing various intentional correctives. The suggested correctives are grouped according to the soteriological method they address.

ENDNOTES
CHAPTER ONE

1. *Soteriology* refers to the doctrine of salvation.

2. Deconstructionism refers in general to the removal of inherent meaning from written texts so that they are made to communicate something other than the original authorial intent. This concept will be defined and discussed at length in chapter two.

3. See chapter two for a detailed discussion of postmodernism.

4. Paul R. Shockley, "Postmodernism as a Basis for Society?" in *The God of the Bible and Other Gods: Is the Christian God Unique among World Religions?* Robert Paul Lightner (Grand Rapids: Kregel Publications, 1998), 201.

5. Proverbs 27:7. Unless otherwise noted, all Scripture quotations are from the New King James Version.

6. Oprah Winfrey's recent collaboration with New Age guru, Eckhart Tolle during a 10-week online course promoted on her television show, as well as her promotion of fellow New Age guru Helen Schucman's "A Course in Miracles" on Winfrey's XM satellite radio station, are just two examples among many of Oprah's encroachment into the pseudo-spiritual world. In recent years Winfrey has invited an increasing number of New Age spirituality experts onto her show, including Marianne Williamson, Barbara DeAngelis, LaVar Burton, Richard Carlson, Betty Eadie, and many others. Oprah has endorsed many of their works, and has featured some of them in her Book Club. See http://www.lifesitenews.com /ldn/2008/mar/08030701. html for more information.

7. From an email sent October 19, 2006 from news@second.org to subscribers of Second Baptist's online newsletter. The subject line was "Cypress Campus Grand Opening."

8. This conversation took place in the present writer's home in March of 2006, emphasis added.

9. The labels attached to each of the five soteriological methods addressed in this work are offered by the present writer as descriptive designations that help articulate each method's primary error. It should be noted that in some cases, those to whom the present writer attaches a particular label would not agree with the characterization it suggests. (For example, few evangelicals would appreciate having their gospel presentation labeled *puzzling*.) In other cases, such as the pluralist gospel, some adherents wear the label proudly.

10. Ron J. Bigalke, Jr. provides a helpful summary of the origin of the phrase *defining deviancy down*. He writes, "Senator Daniel Patrick Moynihan from New York coined the popular alliteration 'Defining Deviancy Down' in his infamous article of the same name, published in *American Scholar* (Winter 1993). Influenced by the propositions of Emile Durkheim, Moynihan suggested, 'the amount of deviant behavior in American society has increased beyond the levels the community can afford to recognize [i.e., the "Durkheim Constant"].' As the amount of deviant behavior increases, deviancy must be redefined 'so as to exempt conduct previously stigmatized.' Behavior formally characterized as abnormal by earlier standards would be quietly raised to the 'normal' level. The outcome of such thinking is that behavior once deemed deviant is now considered normal." See Ron J. Bigalke, Jr., "The Latest Postmodern Trend: The Emerging Church," *Journal of Dispensational Theology* 10, no. 31 (December 2006): 20, n. 4.

CHAPTER 2

SURVEYING THE LANDSCAPE

If we are to communicate the Christian faith effectively we must know and understand the thought forms of our own generation. –Francis Schaeffer

An examination of evangelical soteriological methods in the present era is aided by an understanding of the ideas, mindset, and philosophical trends that characterize the present age. This chapter attempts to frame the discussion at hand in terms of postmodernism and its influence on evangelical thought. It should be pointed out, however, that not all of the negative influences of postmodern thinking have a direct impact on the nature of a given soteriological error discussed later in this work. For instance, much will be said in this chapter about deconstructionism and its prevalence in contemporary thought. Yet not all of the case studies examined herein are examples of deconstructionism in a technical, intentional sense. Indeed, some of the theologians critiqued in this work share the present author's disdain for deconstructionism as an approach to the written text that is growing more and more popular in the present age. It will be suggested in this chapter that even when postmodern thinking is not the direct cause of soteriological error, the postmodern mindset often allows various errors to flourish more easily.

A Crisis of Eternal Proportions

Robert Jensen is a self-professed Christian. Yet, by his own admission, he does not believe Jesus is the Son of God. Nor does he believe that Jesus rose from the dead. In fact, Robert Jensen *does not even believe there is a God.* According to Jensen, a journalism professor at the University of Texas at Austin, he is a Christian because he has *faith.* Not faith in Jesus Christ, however; faith in mankind's ability to achieve a "world in which we can imagine living in peace with each other and in sustainable relation to the nonhuman world."[1] Jensen calls himself a "secular Christian" or "a Christian atheist, perhaps."[2]

One would be hard pressed to find any evangelical scholar, theologian, teacher, or preacher—or any evangelical period, for that matter—who would not declare Jensen's idea of saving faith to be sorely deficient. One presumes that evangelicals, in solidarity, would decry Jensen's kind of faith as non-saving faith—that is, faith that will not result in eternal salvation. After all, eternal salvation requires faith alone in Christ alone for the forgiveness of sins. On this, all evangelicals agree. In fact, it is the *sine qua non* of evangelicalism: belief in a born again experience by faith in Christ.[3]

Jensen's views of saving faith and Christianity are radical departures from the gospel message of the Bible; but what about more subtle departures from the biblical teaching on the gospel? Is there, in actuality, widespread agreement within evangelicalism regarding precisely what it means to believe in Jesus Christ unto eternal life? A closer scrutiny of the postmodern evangelical gospel yields a surprising and disturbing answer.[4]

For centuries, the debate over the gospel has been cast within the framework of the long-standing Pelagius/Augustine debate (c. AD 400): Is eternal salvation a free gift of God or must man earn his eternal salvation by good works?[5] During the Protestant Reformation, the debate re-emerged in the form of Arminianism vs. Calvinism. Today, while this foundational discussion still continues, a different question has arisen. Even among those who believe that the Bible unambiguously teaches eternal salvation is a free gift, wholly apart from any good works on the part of the sinner, there is startling inconsistency over the precise content of saving faith. While it is generally agreed that saving faith has as its sole object Jesus Christ, the question at hand is what *precisely* must someone believe about Jesus in order to obtain eternal life?

Perhaps more troubling is that few people seem to acknowledge the problem. There is a ubiquitous and unsettling indifference about the clarity of the gospel among postmodern evangelicals. One Bible college president, when confronted with the idea that precision in presenting the gospel is vital, dismissed the notion with an imperious wave of the hand—describing those who are concerned with the clarity of the gospel as "purists."[6] To his way of thinking, and many others, it is enough it seems to proclaim Jesus as the way, without explaining *how He is the way.* Indeed, evangelical preachers and writers today seem content to throw open the gates of heaven to anyone who names the name of Christ, regardless of the precise content of their faith.

For instance, noted evangelical theologian Clark H. Pinnock espouses a widening approach to the gospel. Pinnock, who previously taught at such distinguished American evangelical institutions as New Orleans Baptist Theological Seminary and Trinity Evangelical Divinity School, has spent the last twenty-five years at McMaster Divinity College in Hamilton, Ontario, Canada, where he currently serves on the emeritus faculty. It is noteworthy that the marketing tag for McMaster Divinity College is "Canada's *Evangelical* University-Based Seminary."[7] Endorsing the book, *What Does It Mean to Be Saved? Broadening Evangelical Horizons of Salvation*, Pinnock writes, "The essays in this volume helpfully suggest a broadening of the horizons of an evangelical doctrine of salvation. This book will help us not to trivialize the topic in merely private terms, without a holistic vision, but to give more attention to its this-worldly consequences."[8]

Similarly, Neal Plantinga, President of Calvin Theological Seminary in Grand Rapids, Michigan, applauds the same book. "A dozen first-class essayists show us 'how wide and long and high and deep is the love of Christ,' and they do so to wonderful effect. Here, at last, salvation is much bigger than we are."[9] Yet, does the perspective presented by this collection of articles from leading evangelicals really reflect positively on the state of evangelicalism today, vis-à-vis the gospel?

Consider the suggestion of the book's general editor, evangelical theologian John Stackhouse, "[W]e could make an important start simply by teaching that salvation is *not* about 'Christians going to heaven.'"[10] For Stackhouse, and many of the contributors to his book, evangelical soteriology has been oversimplified. In reality, they say, it is more complex than previously assumed.

Salvation is about God redeeming the whole earth. Salvation is about Christians—and perhaps others, also saved by the work of Christ but perhaps not knowing about him in this life—heading home to the God they love and the company of all the faithful. Salvation is about heading for the New Jerusalem, not heaven: a garden city on earth, not the very abode of God and certainly not a bunch of pink clouds in the sky. ... [S]alvation is not only about what is to come but also about what is ours to enjoy and foster here and now....

These essays prompt us to think in larger, more vivid, and more exciting ways. They lead us out of our narrow and rather boring views of salvation into the resplendent landscapes of God's re-creative power and love.[11]

Stackhouse's desire to expand and even *redefine* evangelical soteriology is evidenced by his reference to *others* who are *saved without knowing about Christ in this life* and his characterization of traditional evangelical soteriology as *narrow and rather boring*.

John Webster expresses cautious criticism of the predominant views put forth by Stackhouse and many of his fellow-contributors. In his response to the articles Webster writes,

What's evangelical about evangelical soteriology? In their different ways, the essays in this volume propose that a soteriology that is authentically evangelical—one that is governed by the gospel of Christ—will, of necessity, have a broader range than has been customary in a good deal of evangelical church life and theology. Though they make the point in different ways—some by exegesis, some by historical analysis, some by a rather more informal mix of Christian teaching and cultural comment—the essays, taken together, are a collective suggestion that "evangelical" soteriology covers a great deal more ground than some dominant strands of contemporary evangelicalism are disposed to believe. And, on that basis, they appeal for a revision of thinking, a reorientation of action, and not a little repentance.[12]

Reflecting on the theological methods employed by the contributors to the volume, Webster asks, "Am I alone in worrying whether some more sharply focused judgment about the norms and sources of theology would be helpful here?"[13] He suggests that more debate is needed and wonders whether contemporary evangelical soteriology will "resist the drift into the private, the isolation of the affections from reason and common life" and whether it will "honor its history as a whole."[14] Webster's concern is well founded.

The views expressed by the contributors to *What Does It Mean to Be Saved?* are not isolated exceptions within mainstream evangelicalism. They are representative of a larger epidemic of evangelical ambiguity regarding truth in general and the gospel in particular.[15] And this ambiguity is manifested not just in academic circles. It has moved beyond the classroom, through the pulpit and into the pew. Popular evangelical pastors likewise have adopted a soteriological method that neglects the core essentials of the biblical gospel. The enormously popular Rick Warren, for example, who identifies himself as an evangelical, is well known for framing the gospel in terms of its positive appeal, rather than its negative warning.[16] Although a more detailed treatment of Warren's teaching on the gospel is provided in chapter four, the following quotations should sound an alarm.

Warren told *USA Today*, "Rather than threaten sinners with fire and brimstone, we believe in attraction evangelism. We believe in loving people into the Kingdom."[17] Elsewhere he contends, "It really doesn't matter what your label is. If you love Jesus, we're on the same team."[18] For Warren, the focus of evangelism is on drawing circles of inclusion rather than lines of distinction.[19] Salvation, he insists, requires belief that "God loves you and made you for his purposes," belief that "you're not an accident," and belief that "you were made to last forever."[20]

Warren's gospel formula is chiefly relational and conspicuously focused on the present life. In his now larger than life book *The Purpose Driven Life*, he presents the gospel primarily as a means of improving one's station in *this life*, more so than an opportunity to gain *eternal life*. "It's time to settle the issue," he writes, "*Who are you going to live for—yourself or God? ...Don't worry. God will give you what you need if you will just make the choice to live for him.*"[21] It will be demonstrated in the pages to follow that Warren's soteriological method represents a departure from the biblical standard.

Similarly, Joel Osteen, pastor of the largest evangelical church in America, Lakewood Church in Houston, Texas, espouses a gospel that, among other aberrations, reflects postmodernism's inclusivist ideology.[22] Osteen told Larry King when asked about the exclusivity of Christ for salvation, "I'm very careful about saying who would and wouldn't go to heaven. I don't know."[23] In his best-selling book, *Your Best Life Now*, Osteen writes, "God focuses on the things you're doing right. He sees the best in you. ... [Y]ou can stop obsessing about all your faults and give yourselves a break. Every person has weaknesses."[24] By his own admission, he intentionally avoids using the word *sin* in his preaching and writing, choosing instead to use words such as *imperfections, shortcomings, mistakes, weaknesses*, and *insecurities*.[25] When asked why he avoids using the term "sinners" in general, Osteen told Larry King, "I don't use [the word sinners]. I never thought about it. But I probably don't. But most people already know what they're doing wrong. When I get them to church I want to tell them that you can change. There can be a difference in your life. So I don't go down the road of condemning."[26]

Osteen's soteriological method, although possessing subtle distinctions from that of Warren, is likewise alarming. How far removed, really, is the soteriology of leading evangelical academicians like Pinnock and Stackhouse, as well as popular evangelical leaders like Warren and Osteen, from Robert Jensen's form of "secular Christianity?" It has been suggested that the gospel is like a lion. All the preacher has to do is to open the door of the cage and get out of the way! Yet, if the gospel is inaccurate, the lion resembles more of a harmless kitten. If "the gospel is the power of God to salvation to everyone who believes [it]" (Rom 1:16), then how one defines the gospel is of paramount importance. It is belief in the gospel that secures eternal salvation, not belief in something similar to the gospel. Even the slightest alteration to the biblical gospel renders it impotent to save and opens the door to evangelical inclusivism wherein atheists like Jensen proclaim themselves to be Christians because they have faith in *something*.[27] This prevalent lack of consensus when it comes to the gospel signifies an evangelical crisis of eternal proportions.

The Underlying Problem: Postmodernism

It is not difficult to see how this crisis has developed. The present *Zeitgeist* encourages ambiguity and celebrates diversity. The battle for the clarity and accuracy of the gospel within evangelicalism is taking place within the larger ideological battlefield of postmodernism. The problem of an indefinable gospel is symptomatic of a larger crisis of language in the postmodern age. Paul R. Shockley succinctly defines the essence of postmodern thought when he writes,

Postmodernism really is a simple set of ideas that has complicated repercussions. It hangs on the framework of the belief that (1) absolute or objective truth does not exist. What is true for one individual may not be true for another. Therefore, (2) reality is in the mind of the beholder. Objective reasoning does not exist because (3) humanity is molded or scripted by its own subcultures. If absolute truth is bound in personal biases, then (4) there is no objective, universal authority. Postmodernism is marked by (5) cynicism and (6) decision making on the ethical bases of feelings, emotions, and impressions.[28]

Postmodernism, then, presents a unique and thorny playing field in the battle for the accuracy of the gospel. If, as Shockley writes, "what is true for one individual may not be true for another," then each gospel presentation is allowed to stand on its own even though it may contradict another. Worse, even two substantially similar presentations of the gospel may be *interpreted* differently by the listener or reader since "reality is in the mind of the beholder."[29] In the absence of absolute standards, there is no basis on which to police the accuracy or meaning of the gospel. The realm of acceptability is broad—and growing broader all the time. The gospel in postmodern evangelicalism may be described aptly as a *kaleidoscopic gospel*, emphasizing a shifting variety and diversity of content, rather than a *microscopic gospel*, with an emphasis on precision and biblical accuracy.

One writer correctly describes the present turmoil over truth as a "crisis of epistemology."

[P]ostmodernism is in fact a form of radical skepticism about the knowability of truth. Another way to say this is that we are in a period marked by a crisis of epistemology. The routes taken by so-called modernity to the attainment of knowledge have proved to be dead-end streets. The optimism of modernity about the attainability of universal truth has been replaced by a profound skepticism which amounts to a definitive defeatism. Man can only attain relative knowledge with limited validity for himself and others of his community, but he must abandon the effort to find truth universally applicable to all men.[30]

The result of this "crisis of epistemology" is pervasive religious pluralism in the present culture. Pluralism is a philosophical perspective that demands diversity and difference over unity and sameness. Carson puts it succinctly, "[P]luralism is the view that all religions have the same moral and spiritual value, and offer the same potential for achieving salvation, however 'salvation' may be construed."[31] It is the belief that any absolute view is wrong. Thus, Christianity, Judaism, Islam, and a host of other religions are all equally valid pathways to heaven. No one religion can claim to be the *only* way. Pluralism rejects absolutism.[32]

Of course, it often has been pointed out that pluralism itself is a form of absolutism.

Self-avowed pluralists who espouse this pluralist doctrine thus become the worst form of imperialist—denying to others what they themselves claim to have. That is, epistemological agnosticism is, in fact, a covert claim of knowing the truth about truth. "That no one can or should claim to know the truth" is a truth claim.[33]

Although the logic of this conclusion seems clear enough, the self-contradictory "truth" that "truth cannot be known" persists in this postmodern age. It is axiomatic that such thinking has captured the minds of secular culture today. The evidence is overwhelming when one examines such mainstream establishments as higher education, the news media and Hollywood elitists. Consequently, Carson is correct in fearing that such postmodern thinking may represent "the most dangerous threat to the gospel since the Gnostic heresy in the second century."[34]

For the most part, evangelicalism has resisted breathing the postmodern ether and remains, at face value anyway, opposed to pluralism. Most evangelicals have stood their ground in proclaiming, if only tepidly, the exclusivity of Christ when it comes to eternal salvation. There are, of course, notable exceptions. Reference has been made to prominent evangelical leader Joel Osteen and his repeated refusal to acknowledge that Jesus Christ is the only way to salvation during a televised interview on CNN's Larry King Live. A fuller examination of the exchange between Osteen and King illustrates just how far Osteen has drifted toward full-fledged inclusivism.[35]

King: [We've] had ministers on who said your record don't count. You either believe in Christ or you don't. If you believe in Christ...you're going to heaven. And if you don't....you ain't.

45

Osteen: Yeah, I don't know.....

King: What if you're Jewish or Muslim, you don't accept Christ at all?

Osteen: You know—I'm very careful about saying who would and wouldn't go to heaven. I don't know.

King: If you believe you have to believe in Christ, they're wrong, aren't they?

Osteen: Well, I don't know if I believe they're wrong. ... from the Christian faith this is what I believe. But I just think that only God will judge a person's heart. I spent a lot of time in India with my father. I don't know all about their religion. But I know they love God. And I don't know. I've seen their sincerity. So I don't know. I know for me, and what the Bible teaches, I want to have a relationship with Jesus.

Eventually, King abandoned his attempts to coax Osteen into espousing an exclusivist view of the gospel and moved on to other topics, such as why Osteen does not use the word "sinners" in his sermons. Nevertheless, a caller from Phoenix, Arizona would not let Osteen off so easily.

Caller: Thank you, Joel, for your positive messages and your book. I'm wondering, though, why you side-stepped Larry's earlier question about how we get to heaven. The Bible clearly tells us that Jesus is the way, the truth and the life and the only way to the Father is through Him. That's not really a message of condemnation but of truth.

Osteen: Yes, I would agree with her. I believe that.

King: So then a Jew is not going to heaven?

Osteen: No, [that's not what I am saying]. Here's my thing, Larry, is I can't judge somebody's heart. You know? Only God can look at somebody's heart, and so—I don't know. To me, it's not my business to say, you know, this one is or this one isn't....

King: But you believe your way.

Osteen: I believe my way. I believe my way with all my heart.

King: [So] someone who doesn't share it is wrong, isn't he?

Osteen: Well, yes. Well, I don't know if I look at it like that. I would present my way, but I'm just going to let God be the judge of that. I don't know. I don't know.

King: So you make no judgment on anyone?

Osteen: No. But I—

King: What about atheists?

Osteen: You know what, I'm going to let someone—I'm going to let God be the judge of who goes to heaven and hell. ...I'm not going to go around telling everybody else—if they don't want to believe that that's going to be their choice.[36]

Osteen's equivocation as he attempted to tiptoe around Larry King's question is self-evident. No less than ten times in these two brief interchanges, he used the phrase "I don't know" in keeping with postmodernism's rejection of certainty. Osteen's propensity toward a pluralistic gospel will be discussed in more detail in chapter seven below; but in general such equivocation is rare on the part of evangelical leaders today—and rightly so since the Bible clearly identifies Christianity as the only correct pathway to Heaven.

The Bible claims within its own pages to be the authoritative standard of truth. Consider the following sampling of Scripture references:

The entirety of Your Word is truth, and every one of Your righteous judgments endures forever (Ps 119:160).

Therefore all Your precepts concerning all things I consider to be right... (Ps 119:128).

Every Word of God is pure... (Prov 30:5).

Forever, O Lord, Your word is settled in heaven (Ps 119:89).

Concerning Your testimonies, I have known of old that You have founded them forever (Ps 119:152).

Jesus Christ Himself also claimed to be the only means of obtaining eternal life when He proclaimed, "I am the way, the truth, and the life. No one comes to the Father except through Me" (John 14:6). As Biblicists, evangelicals have long pointed to these and other Scripture passages in support of the exclusivity of the Christian faith.

In evangelical circles, pluralism often manifests itself in subtle ways. It is a stealth enemy. Like so many postmodern ideologies, pluralism creeps in unnoticed. Could it be that, while not labeling it as such, evangelicalism unwittingly has espoused a pluralistic view of the gospel within its own ranks? Evangelicals are comfortable drawing lines where the pluralist is not. That is why most evangelicals draw a clear line when it comes to Jesus Christ being the only means of eternal salvation. But whereas the avowed pluralist rejects *any lines*; many evangelicals reject only *certain lines*. Lines that are deemed inconsequential or unnecessary, as well as those that might cause them to appear harsh or narrow-minded, are often erased or avoided in an effort to attain perceived legitimacy in the intellectual community. One of those lines is the purity of the gospel.

Owing to the influence of postmodern pluralistic thought, many evangelicals are fearful of defining the gospel too narrowly, lest they offend their otherwise like-minded Christian brothers. They are comfortable with affirming the "Christian gospel" as the only true pathway to heaven, but they are content leaving the precise meaning of the gospel open to individual interpretation. Of course, there are basic components that are common to all versions of the evangelical gospel such as *Jesus Christ* and *faith*, but the following pages will demonstrate that *precision* is sorely lacking in the postmodern gospel—and accuracy always suffers when precision is neglected. It is not enough to proclaim the exclusivity of the Christian gospel if that gospel is so imprecise as to be pluralistic itself.

The Abandonment of Certainty

Many postmodern evangelicals are undermining the very ground of truth on which the exclusivity of Christ is built by adopting postmodernism's *abandonment of certainty*. In a transparent contradiction with Proverbs 22:21, "That I may make you know the *certainty of the words of truth...*," even while holding firm to various "truths" that evangelicals have long considered fundamental to the Christian faith, a growing number of evangelical leaders are suggesting that their grip on such "truths" is tenuous at best since, in their minds, nothing can be known with absolute certainty.[37]

Consider the following example. Michael Patton and Rhome Dyck host an Internet radio program entitled, "Theology Unplugged."[38] Patton, a Th.M. graduate of Dallas Theological Seminary in Dallas, Texas, is the Director of *The Theology Program* at Stonebriar Community Church in Frisco, Texas. Dyck is also a Th.M. graduate of Dallas Theological Seminary and, like Patton, also serves on the pastoral staff at Stonebriar Community Church. *The Theology Program (TTP)* is a ministry of Stonebriar.

The Theology Program is a program of Christian theology (study of God) and apologetics (defending the faith) created with all believers in mind. TTP seeks to give people who may never have the time, ability, or circumstances that allow them to attend full-time seminary the same opportunity to study the great and rich Christian heritage of truth. Here, you will learn theology historically, biblically, and irenically (in a peaceful manner). The contents of TTP are created from a broadly evangelical perspective, engaging other traditions in a persuasive yet gracious manner. In short, we seek to help people think theologically by understanding what they believe and why they believe it.[39]

It is noteworthy that TTP identifies itself as representing a "broadly evangelical perspective," in contrast to "other traditions" within Christian history. TTP has been endorsed by a number of notable evangelical leaders such as Chuck Swindoll, past president of Dallas Theological Seminary and current Senior Pastor at Stonebriar Community Church, J.P. Moreland, Distinguished Professor of Philosophy at Talbot School of Theology and Biola University, Roger E. Olson, Professor of Theology at George W. Truett Theological Seminary and Baylor University, and John M. Frame, Professor of Systematic Theology and Philosophy at Reformed Theological Seminary.

In the following partial transcript of a *Theology Unplugged* Podcast, Patton and Dyck, along with the emcee of the program, Greg Cromartie, engage in an exchange that illustrates how evangelicalism is wrestling with, responding to, and perhaps even consenting to postmodernism's abandonment of certainty.[40]

Michael: If you believe in God and you believe in Jesus Christ and it does you good, fine. That is pure postmodernism. A lot of these people are smart in that they really do know better than some of us as Christians that *we can't be as certain as we like to think we are* [emphasis added].

(Later)

Michael: There are a lot of things that we are not going to be so sure about and we need to have some kind of doctrinal hierarchy in our theologies so that whenever we're saying, "Yeah, you're right. You know it's very difficult to come to a conclusion on that passage and there's a lot of valid interpretations out there that could be right." But whenever it comes to this issue, let's say, the resurrection of Christ, the bodily resurrection of Christ, there isn't any doubt.

Greg: So essentially what you're saying is there are some things we can break fellowship over and other things that we're just gonna have to hold in tension and discuss as brothers and sisters in Christ.

Rhome: The words we can use are there are some things that are essential for Christianity and some things that are non-essential. And I think Michael has a very valid point and that's that we don't need to either pit the church against postmodernism or modernism nor do we need to become that to be Christian. My point is that we need to interact with them and we need to understand them to understand our culture. I agree with Michael, postmoderns are asking some very, very good questions. It is very healthy for the church. It is very healthy for theology. How much do we really know? How much can we really say? How knowable is our God? There is an answer to that, but it is helpful to ask those types of questions and engage them with where they are at.

Michael: Let me ask you both, okay. This will be something to demonstrate it and get very unplugged and y'all are going to be mad at me afterward for this, but hey, we're unplugged. How sure are you on a scale of 1 to 10, on a certainty factor, 10 is the surest that you can be, okay, you're as sure as you are about anything in this life. It's kind of like a 10 is "I am sure that I exist," okay? How sure are you that God exists, in your theology on a scale of 1 to 10?

Greg: Rhome's looking at me. He wants me to take the first step. You know, I've actually thought about that lately. It wasn't in relation to God but it was in relation to some other theological issues. It was about the knowability—

Michael: You're dodging man. You're dodging.

Greg: I'm sliding like a baseball player. <laughter> It was about knowing, um, that I'm saved. Can you really know that you are going to heaven?

Michael: That's good. That's good.

Greg: It's a similar question. And I would say—I'm gonna give you a number—I would say it's somewhere between um a 5 and an 8.

Michael: How sure are you, Rhome that God exists?

Rhome: I was going to use the number "7." There are lots of philosophical proofs, but with a gun at my head, I don't bottom line know 100%.

Michael: Guys, I was hoping to get a "10" out of both of you all. But I am gonna, listen, audience, I am gonna have a session with these guys after we go off and really try to convert them so do not worry.

Greg: Let me say it this way. That's intellectual, but I live like it's a ten.

Michael: Okay, okay. That's good. So you've got an intellectual certainty and an emotional certainty on both of them. Emotionally certain you're a "10." Intellectually certain you're a "7," okay. That's a good way to put it. Okay, now let's move down the line. Let's just say that a "10" represents as sure as you can be. Not absolute certainty but as sure as you can be, okay? And there's probably not many things in life that you are more sure of than that God exists. So let's go ahead and put you both at a "10" right now. I'm savin' 'em. <laughter> You're a "10" on this. Let's ask this question now, you're a "10"that God exists, how sure are you that you are saved eternally?

Greg: I'd have to say probably 5 or 6.

Michael: You're not working on the curve that I gave you.

Greg: Oh, you mean start with God as a 10.

Michael: Yeah, yeah.

Greg: Okay, I was back at the first one. Okay, I love curves. So let's go with—let's—it still has to be beyond 50% I would say—uh for me personally, and I certainly live like it's a 10, again, um—boy you know that's a very tough question. Intellectually, you know I'd have to say maybe it is a 5.

Michael: The point is either way it is going to be below that God exists to some degree.

Greg: Sure. Sure.

Michael: And then you move on down the line. Are you sure that Christ is going to come before a great tribulation and rapture us out of the world—the church?

Greg: That's a great story, isn't it? <laughter>

Michael: I mean you might be a zero on that. Or even a negative.

Greg: No. Whenever I have to make a decision I say yeah that's the only thing that I can see intellectually makes reasonable certainty. But if you're going to pin me down on it—and put a gun to my head—I'm gonna say, I don't know, a "2."

Michael: Yeah. And see you're moving down on it and your showing, your showing—

Greg: Hey wait a minute. I'm the only one that's been answering these things. Where's Rhome? <laughter>

Michael: I know. Rhome is just warming up. He left the room and just now came back. He had to go to the bathroom while we were asking these questions.

Rhome: Listen, mark me down one "8" and one "0." <laughter>

Michael: The idea here is a lot of times whenever Christians preach from the pulpit they act as if there's no degree of certainty with all of these things. Whether I'm teaching about the resurrection of Christ, the existence of God, my assurance of salvation, all the way down to things that aren't quite so clear, such as the pretribulationalist rapture I am gonna preach that with the same passion and the same conviction. And in postmodernism they see that as hypocritical. They see right through that. They see the disagreements and they see the separation that causes. And so they not only come to this with a lot of confusion, saying, "Gosh. Why are you so sure about that? The Bible doesn't seem that clear on this?" Then they will start to say, "Maybe you're not that clear about everything." If you're preaching this much about the pretribulationalist rapture, there's a lot of other good people that disagree with you, how much am I gonna trust you about the other things that you say? How much am I gonna trust you about the existence of God and your assurance there? I cannot trust your emotional commitments. That's basically what the postmodern is saying. Your emotional commitments are your emotional commitments. And so unless you show some kind of hierarchy within your intellectual certainty, then you're not going to have a witness to the postmodern today. And so we need to make people understand that. We need to make ourselves understand that. There are some things that are more clear and there are some things that are less clear. Does God exist? "10" Did Christ rise from the grave? "10" Is He coming back? "10" When's He coming back? Well, I don't know. We're going way down the scale on this. What is the nature of man—does he have a true free will or not? You know we gotta go down a little bit on these types of things.

Rhome: I think it's important to understand, Michael that you brought out a characteristic, or what I'd even call a hallmark of postmodernism which is so healthy and that's the fact that more than valuing reason and empiricism, the postmodern values authenticity— that idea that you can't hold everything believing it 100%, even those squirrelly things. The absolutes of the Christian faith we don't waver from them at all. But some of the other things that just aren't clear that we can authentically say, "Hey, I'm not that sure. I'm not totally positive on this. And I want to be open with you, I believe it, but my certainty about my belief isn't a "10.""

Michael: Let me tell you something. And I know we're about out of time. The moment you start to show an uncertainty in issues and you're not so dogmatic about everything—I don't mind if you're dogmatic about a few things—but the moment you start to show uncertainty and you start to show, like Rhome said, this authenticity, your value in my mind goes way up and that's the way the postmodern thinks. The trust factor has just moved up ten notches because it was at zero before you started now it's at nine.

The hesitancy on the part of these evangelical theologians to espouse the notion of absolute certainty is evident. The entire tone for this discussion is established early on by Michael Patton's contention that "we can't be as certain as we like to think we are." His comment illustrates well evangelicalism's capitulation to postmodernism's abandonment of certainty. One wonders how such an ideology would have influenced Job's famous statement, "For I *know* that my Redeemer lives and He shall stand at last on the earth" (Job19:25, emphasis added). Did Job really mean "I am *seventy percent* sure that my Redeemer lives?"

The scientific community's recent conclusion that Pluto no longer be classified as a planet in the solar system serves as a metaphor of sorts for the present challenge to the knowability of truth. If truths long held firmly and taught in textbooks for decades can be summarily dismissed (whether justifiably so or not), it begs the question *can anything be known with certainty?* And when evangelicals express uncertainty about truth, either because they have adopted postmodernism's assumptions or perhaps in a misguided effort to be accepted in the public square, it only serves to undermine confidence in the evangelical gospel as a solution to man's sin problem.

Deconstructionism: A By-Product of Pluralism

Not only has pluralism given rise to the abandonment of certainty in general, but it has led to the deconstruction of language in particular. In days gone by, when one wanted to affirm the certainty of a propositional statement, he might assert, "It's the gospel truth!" Yet, today, such a statement stands as a meaningless redundancy; both "gospel" and "truth" are inherently ambiguous. This dearth of meaning in language is called *deconstructionism* and represents perhaps the most formidable foe for evangelicalism within the present culture. The nineteenth-century German atheistic philosopher Friedrich Nietzsche once remarked, "I fear that we haven't gotten rid of God because we haven't gotten rid of grammar."[41] Could it be that when the lights dim on the postmodern era, grammar may indeed have gone the way of all flesh leaving no empirical mechanism to facilitate communication? One can only hope not.

Deconstructionism is the natural outworking of an ideology that rejects absolute truth. Like constitutional revisionism, deconstructionism is a calculated means to an end.[42] It is an effort to create one's own truth by redefining the plain truth of the written text, thereby justifying one's personal beliefs, attitudes and/or behaviors.

> Deconstructionism strips reality and written texts of inherent meaning. It reduces language to but a social construct mirroring the interpreter's personal perspective. Consequently, every interpreter is free to handle the text selectively, that is, to deconstruct it, and to refashion favored segments into fresh readings that reflect one's own preferences without evident anchorage in the text.[43]

In other words, in a world where *truth* is relative, *words* likewise are relative. Just as truth is a construction, so too is the meaning of words—a plight Kevin Vanhoozer calls "hermeneutic indeterminacy."[44]

Meaning no longer exists as an inherent end in itself. Rather, the search for meaning is like the endless pursuit of a moving target. Vanhoozer writes,

> Deconstruction is not the same thing as destruction. It is not simply a matter of demolishing something through external force, but of disassembling it. Deconstruction is a pains-

taking taking-apart, a peeling away of the various layers—historical, rhetorical, ideological—of distinctions, concepts, texts, and whole philosophies, whose aim is to expose the arbitrary linguistic nature of their original construction. Deconstruction is an intense analytical method, occasionally perversely so, that results in the collapse from within of all that it touches. It is an "analysis" in the etymological sense of the term (Greek: analusis): an "un-loosing" or "un-tying." Deconstruction is thus best understood as a kind of undoing, with all the attendant connotations that the term implies: untying, undermining, and ruining.[45]

Thus, in the absence of authoritative meaning in language, the listener or reader is free to construct his own truth, viz. his own *meaning*.

The result of this ideological framework is chaos; or, as Gene Veith calls it, *cultural chaos*.

According to postmodernism, truth is relative. We can never know some absolute, objective, once-and-for-all truth. What's true for one person may not be true for someone else. Individuals and cultures construct truths that work for them. Since truth is not discovered but constructed, there are many ways of putting together a plausible explanation. Constructing a model that accounts for the evidence is the best that we can do, and one model is just as valid as another. By this way of thinking, spin is literally everything. Since truth is not an absolute, it can be continually revised, without even worrying about contradictions.[46]

This "revision of truth" is perhaps most visibly manifested in the context of the battle over the meaning of the United States Constitution. A recent U.S. Supreme Court case involving the death penalty for minors illustrates the point.

On March 1, 2005, by a 5–4 margin, the Court ruled that it is unconstitutional to execute juveniles who are convicted of capital murder if they were under the age of eighteen at the time they committed the crime. This decision represented a reversal of a decision made by the U.S. Supreme Court just fifteen years earlier. In the dissenting opinion, Justice Scalia laments the Court's handling of the Constitution as a living text, the meaning of which is subject to change over time.

> In urging approval of a constitution that gave life-tenured judges the power to nullify laws enacted by the people's representatives, Alexander Hamilton assured the citizens of New York that there was little risk in this, since "[t]he judiciary... ha[s] neither *force* nor *will* but merely judgment." But Hamilton had in mind a traditional judiciary, "bound down by strict rules and precedents which serve to define and point out their duty in every particular case that comes before them." Bound down, indeed. What a mockery today's opinion makes of Hamilton's expectation, announcing the Court's conclusion that the meaning of our Constitution has changed over the past 15 years—not, mind you, that this Court's decision 15 years ago was wrong, but that the Constitution has changed. The Court reaches this implausible result by purporting to advert, not to the original meaning of the Eighth Amendment, but to "the evolving standards of decency," of our national society.[47]

Scalia's point, well articulated, is that by appealing to "evolving standards" rather than the absolute standard of the "original meaning" of the Constitution, the court has given an opinion built upon shifting sand. This decision (like all decisions for advocates of constitutional revisionism) is not anchored to an unchanging standard, but rather is subject to the interpretive whims of each succeeding Court.

The parallels to the battle for the meaning of the gospel are striking. Whereas the original meaning of the constitution should serve as the standard for all court cases, the stake in the ground for the gospel is the timeless truth of the Bible. The gospel does not change to meet the evolving needs of a postmodern society. Rather, the meaning of the gospel is static. It is the same today as it was in the first century. It is particularly troubling that many evangelicals who seem to reject postmodernism's pluralistic view of religion and truth simultaneously affirm its deconstruction of language, viz. an acceptance (and even celebration) of inherently contradictory evangelical gospel messages.

The Need for Definition

As noted, the crisis in postmodern evangelicalism centers on the definition of the gospel. In trusting Jesus for salvation, what precisely must someone believe about Him in order to obtain eternal life? A mathematical illustration will help clarify the need for definition and the importance of the correct content of saving faith. Assume for the sake of illustration that the pure gospel is represented by "X." Therefore in order to obtain eternal life one must believe "X." "X" represents the precise content of saving faith. So then, if one believes "X+1" or "X-1" or "Y," can he be saved? The logical conclusion is no because $X+1 \neq X$. In the same way, neither "X-1" nor "Y" equal "X." If one believes "X+1" or "X-1" or "Y" it will not result in salvation. Of course, there are those who would argue that the content of saving faith is a matter of degree of accuracy. But this complicates the matter further by begging the question how accurate is accurate enough to secure eternal life?

For those who suggest that the gospel is not as precise as mathematics and that anything in the neighborhood of the pure gospel is close enough to suffice, another illustration will prove helpful. Most evangelicals agree that faith in Jesus is the only requirement for eternal salvation. The operative question is what is the *precise content* of saving faith in Jesus? Suppose "X" is defined as "the Dallas Cowboys will win the Super Bowl next year." That is, in order to obtain eternal life, one must believe that the Dallas Cowboys will win the Super Bowl next year. This being the case, if someone believes "the price of gasoline will exceed $5.00 per gallon by the year 2010," has this person expressed saving faith (i.e., believed "X")? Of course, the answer is no. In no sense is belief that the price of gasoline will rise similar to belief in the future success of the Dallas Cowboys football team. If, as stated for the sake of the illustration, belief "that the Dallas Cowboys will win the Super Bowl next year" is in fact what is required to obtain eternal life, then those who place their faith in the price of gasoline will not be saved. There can be no argument on this point.

When "X" and "not X" are vastly disparate, it is easy to see why evangelicals are quick to agree that "not X" is a false gospel. For instance, most evangelicals readily concur that belief in the five pillars of Islam as a means of obtaining eternal life is erroneous. In no way is it similar to the Christian gospel. Yet, when "X" and "not X" are similar, the lines of distinction quickly become blurred. The question is how disparate must two gospels be before one of them is deemed to be erroneous? More to the point, how far from the standard of "X" can a gospel presentation depart before it is declared false?

Continuing with the previous illustration, suppose someone believes that the Dallas Cowboys will make the playoffs next year. Is that close enough to "X" to be deemed saving faith? (Remember, in the illustration, "X" is defined as belief that "the Dallas Cowboys *will win the Super Bowl.*") The crisis today in postmodern evangelicalism is that many evangelicals, who would readily dismiss belief in the rising price of gasoline as incongruent with the true gospel, nevertheless will accept belief in the Cowboys' playoff hopes as close enough to suffice. Yet, according to the established standard for "X," neither belief about the Cowboys' playoff hopes nor belief about the price of gasoline meets the standard.

There is a certain kernel of salvific truth in the gospel that cannot be expanded, amended or altered in any way if it is to remain viable as the means to eternal life. Keith Davy calls this the "essence of the gospel."

By "the essence of the gospel" I am referring to that core of gospel truth, all of which is essential and must be communicated in gospel presentations regardless of form. The essence of the gospel is that which is left when the gospel is boiled down to its irreducible minimum. Anything less and you no longer have the gospel.[48]

Thus, there are no degrees of accuracy when it comes to the gospel. Given the fact that postmoderns are inherently comfortable with ambiguity and imprecision—indeed, perhaps even thrive on it—evangelicals must strive even harder to define the gospel in tight, clear terms that communicate nothing more and nothing less than the salvific "essence," as Davy calls it.

For those who argue against purity and precision in the gospel and insist that it is merely a matter of degree of accuracy, there still remains, even in their scheme, a line of accuracy that cannot be crossed. Once it is acknowledged that *some* parameters for the accuracy of the gospel do exist, then the question becomes what are those parameters? How close is close enough when it comes to the content of saving faith? What *precisely* must someone believe about Jesus in order to obtain eternal life? Amid the cacophony of evangelical gospel presentations today, there remains a disconcerting indifference to the epidemic of erroneous gospel presentations that fail to meet the standard of biblical saving faith.

A Matter of Semantics?

Some evangelicals might object that all of this is much ado about nothing. After all, they might claim, perhaps the perceived disparity among evangelical gospel presentations is merely a matter of semantics. Yet, Charles Ryrie is correct when he states, "A good choice of words is essential if we are to state the Gospel clearly and accurately."[49] The multiplicity of gospel messages within postmodern evangelicalism cannot be dismissed as a simple matter of semantics. The present crisis over the precise meaning of the gospel owes as much to poor communication skills and the rapidly fading ability of so-called scholars to engage in logical, analytical thinking as it does to the postmodern ideological milieu of pluralism and deconstructionism.

How often I have heard the retort, "It's only a matter of semantics." In my experience it usually came from students using it as a defense mechanism to justify a poor answer to a question. And usually the question involved defining or explaining carefully the meaning of a biblical doctrine or concept. "A matter of semantics" was supposed to excuse fuzzy thinking and a poor, if not wrong, choice of words.

Actually, semantics is not an excuse, nor is it incidental; it is the whole point. Semantics involves the study of meanings of words; so if one uses words which do not convey the meaning he or she is attempting to express, then a different meaning comes across.[50]

Ryrie's point is well-taken. In this age of deconstructionism, it is especially important that evangelicals examine the precise meaning of their words when presenting the gospel. For, as mentioned previously, accuracy suffers when precision is neglected and the gospel must be accurate if it is to lead the hearer to salvation.

Although the biggest enemy of precision within postmodern evangelicalism may be the widespread acceptance of patently contradictory gospel messages, another formidable foe in the quest for clarity is ineffective, careless communication by those who should know better. There are those who, despite acknowledging that the gospel has a quantifiable definition and that any departure from or addition to this identifiable meaning is unacceptable, nevertheless worsen the problem by using sloppy or indiscriminate verbiage and then appealing to semantics in an effort to excuse the resultant false gospel. This issue will be addressed more fully in chapter five below.

Summary of Chapter Two

In this chapter it was suggested that postmodern thinking provides a fertile ground for erroneous gospel presentations. The abandonment of certainty, as well as the corresponding embracement of uncertainty, has fostered ambivalence toward accuracy and purity in evangelical soteriological methodology. It was suggested further that this ideological climate makes the need for definition especially urgent, lest the gospel lose its identity in the midst of a cacophony of vague and inaccurate terminology. The issue at hand is not one merely of semantics; it is substantive. Those who preach the gospel have an obligation to do so clearly and accurately according to the standard of Scripture. It is this standard that is the subject of the next chapter.

ENDNOTES
CHAPTER TWO

1. Robert Jensen, "Getting Religion: Why This Atheist Is a Christian (Sort of)," *Houston Chronicle*, 11 March, 2006.

2. Ibid.

3. Definitions of the term "evangelical" are varied and many. R. C. Sproul suggests that perhaps the word has "suffered the death of a thousand qualifications, to the point that it is no longer a descriptive category." Nevertheless, he endeavors to recapture the historic meaning of the term. He writes, "[W]e must note in passing that the term *evangelical Christian* may be a redundancy. If in its rudimentary form the term *evangelical* means 'gospel-believing,' then it would seem redundant to speak of gospel-believing Christians. This would indicate that there are non-gospel-believing Christians, or Christians who do not believe the gospel, which *prima facie* sounds like a contradiction in terms. It is somewhat like the term *born-again Christian*. If all who are Christians are born again and all who are born again are Christians, the term *born-again Christian* would be redundant, involving the use of a distinction without difference." R. C. Sproul, *Getting the Gospel Right: The Tie That Binds Evangelicals Together* (Grand Rapids: Baker Books, 1999), 29, 32, emphasis original.

The Evangelical Theological Society (ETS), the preeminent assembly of self-proclaimed evangelical scholars today, has the following as its doctrinal basis which must be affirmed by all members: "The Bible alone, and the Bible in its entirety, is the Word of God written and is therefore inerrant in the autographs. God is a Trinity, Father, Son, and Holy Spirit, each an uncreated person, one in essence, equal in power and glory." *Evangelical Theological Society*. <http://www.etsjets.org/> (accessed 2 September 2006). Thus, ETS sees two primary doctrinal assertions as delineating evangelicals: inerrancy and the Trinity.

Another large representative body within evangelicalism is the *National Association of Evangelicals* (*NAE*), representing about sixty denominations and 45,000 churches in America. The NAE lists seven core beliefs in its doctrinal statement: (1) We believe the Bible to be the inspired, the only infallible, authoritative Word of God. (2) We believe that there is one God, eternally existent in three persons: Father, Son and Holy Spirit. (3) We believe in the deity of our Lord Jesus Christ, in His virgin birth, in His sinless life, in His miracles, in His vicarious and atoning death through His shed blood, in His bodily resurrection, in His ascension to the right hand of the Father, and in His personal return in power and glory. (4) We believe that for the salvation of lost and sinful people, regeneration by the Holy Spirit is absolutely essential. (5) We believe in the present ministry of the Holy Spirit by whose indwelling the Christian is enabled to live a godly life. (6) We believe in the resurrection of both the saved and the lost; they that are saved unto the resurrection of life and they that are lost unto the resurrection of damnation. (7) We believe in the spiritual unity of believers in our Lord Jesus Christ. *National Association of Evangelicals.* <http://www.nae.net/index.cfm?FUSEACTION =nae.statement_of_faith> (accessed 28 February 2007).

In the introduction to their book *One Faith: The Evangelical Consensus*, J.I. Packer and Thomas Oden write, "Evangelical Christians, in our definition, are those who read the Bible as God's own Word, addressed personally to each of them here and now; and who live out of a personal trust in, and love for, Jesus Christ as the world's only Lord and Savior. They are people who see themselves as sinners saved by grace through faith for glory; who practice loyal obedience to God; and who are active both in grateful, hopeful communion with the triune God by prayer, and in neighbor-love, with a lively commitment to disciple-making according to the Great Commission. Different people profile evangelicals in different ways in light of their own interests. Historians categorize evangelicals as people who emphasize (1) the Bible as the Word of God, (2) the cross as the place where salvation was won, (3) conversion as a universal need and (4) missionary outreach as a universal task. Theologians dissect evangelicalism as a compound of the classic trinitarianism of Nicaea, the Cappadocians and Augustine; the classic Christology of Chalcedon; the classic soteriology and ecclesiology of the Reformation; the classic pneumatology of the Puritans and Edwards; and the classic missiology of Carey, Venn and Hudson Taylor." J. I. Packer and Thomas C. Oden, *One Faith: The Evangelical Consensus* (Downer's Grove: InterVarsity Press, 2004), 19–20.

Noted evangelical pollster and researcher George Barna suggests a more detailed standard for the label *evangelical*. He writes, "'Evangelicals' is a much-used, little-understood term. To the secular media, it typically means right-wing religious fanatics. In my writings, the term refers to people who meet several criteria. These are people who have an orthodox Judeo-Christian definition of God; rely solely upon the grace of God through the person of Jesus Christ for their salvation; believe that Satan is a real being, not merely symbolic; contend that a person is incapable of earning eternal salvation; believe that the Bible is accurate in all of its teachings; and believe that they personally have a responsibility to share their religious faith with others who believe differently. Currently, evangelicals represent a bit less than 10 percent of the national population, according to this battery of criteria." George Barna, *Evangelism That Works: How to Reach Changing Generations with the Unchanging Gospel* (Ventura, Cal.: Regal Books, 1995), 44, n. 1.

Perhaps representative of the general understanding of the word *evangelical* within postmodern American secular culture is TIME magazine's assertion that it is "a blanket term for the dozens of denominations that emphasize the authority of the Bible, salvation through a personal relationship with Jesus, and the need to share their faith with others." Jackson Dykman and others, "America by the Numbers," *TIME*, October, 30 2006, 50. For an extensive treatment of the changing face of evangelicalism especially as it relates to postmodernism, see D. A. Carson, *The Gagging of God: Christianity Confronts Pluralism* (Grand Rapids: Zondervan, 1996), 443–89.

In the absence of a definitive, delimiting definition of *evangelical*, the present writer will use the term throughout this work in a general sense to refer to those who, among other likely shared theological beliefs (such as belief in the Trinity and inerrancy), believe that faith in Christ is the only means of obtaining eternal life. The very name *evangelical*, from the Greek word εὐαγγελιον, usually translated "gospel" or "good news," suggests that the centrality of the Gospel is the defining mark of evangelicalism.

4. The term *postmodern* will be discussed in more detail later in this chapter. In general, the term *postmodernism* refers to the philosophical mindset and general attitude pervasive throughout the present American culture. This worldview challenges the fundamental underpinnings of historic Christianity as expressed in the Bible. The corresponding term *postmodernity* refers to the present age—an age characterized by the philosophy of postmodernism. The adjective *postmodern* is employed to indicate a person or viewpoint characterized by this worldview. See Carson, *The Gagging of God: Christianity Confronts Pluralism*. See also David S. Dockery, ed., *The Challenge of Postmodernism: An Evangelical Engagement* (Wheaton: Victor Books, 1995). The term *gospel* is discussed at length in chapter three where it will be demonstrated that the term does not carry a strict, technical meaning. It is used in Scripture to refer not only to the particular good news about salvation, but also to good news in general. The focus of this paper is on the *good news* of individual eternal salvation and precisely how one obtains it.

5. Even before Pelagius and Augustine, the *man's merit* versus *God's free gift* debate raged in the early days of the Church. The apostle Paul addressed this concern in his letter to the Galatians where Jewish Christians (called Judaizers) sought to make good works (epitomized by Jewish circumcision) a necessary component of saving faith.

6. This quote was obtained via the present writer's personal communication with the president of a large, evangelical Bible college in the spring of 2005. The president's assertion was repeated on multiple occasions during discussions about the gospel.

7. *McMaster Divinity College*. <http://www.macdiv.ca/home.php> (accessed 20 October 2006), emphasis added.

8. Clark H. Pinnock, in *What Does It Mean to Be Saved? Broadening Evangelical Horizons of Salvation*, ed. John Gordon Stackhouse (Grand Rapids: Baker Academic, 2002), back cover. Pinnock has authored several books in which he espouses a broader view of the gospel. See for example Clark H. Pinnock, *A Wideness in God's Mercy: The Finality of Jesus Christ in a World of Religions* (Grand Rapids: Zondervan, 1992), Clark H. Pinnock, *Most Moved Mover: A Theology of God's Openness*, Didsbury Lectures; 2000 (Grand Rapids: Baker Academic, 2001), Clark H. Pinnock and Robert Brow, *Unbounded Love: A Good News Theology for the 21st Century* (Downer's Grove: InterVarsity Press, 1994).

9. Cornelius Plantinga, in *What Does It Mean to Be Saved*, back cover.

10. John Gordon Stackhouse, "Preface," in *What Does It Mean to Be Saved*, 10, emphasis original. John Stackhouse teaches theology at Regent College in Vancouver, British Columbia. He has written or edited several books on the issue of contemporary evangelical theology. See John Gordon Stackhouse, *Evangelical Futures: A Conversation on Theological Method* (Grand Rapids: Baker Books, 2000), John Gordon Stackhouse, *No Other Gods before Me? Evangelicals and the Challenge of World Religions* (Grand Rapids: Baker Academic, 2001). The tendency on the part of postmodern evangelicals to de-emphasize heaven and overemphasize the present life is a major theme of the present work and one that will be examined more fully in chapters three and four.

11. Stackhouse, "Introduction," in *What Does It Mean to Be Saved*, 10.

12. John Webster, "What's Evangelical About Evangelical Soteriology?" in *What Does It Mean to Be Saved*, 179.

13. Ibid., 183.

14. Ibid., 183–84.

15. D.A. Carson has written a monumental work on the influence of postmodern thinking on the present culture and, more specifically, evangelicalism. In *The Gagging of God*, Carson writes, "The loss of objective truth and the extreme subjectivity bound up with most forms of postmodernism have called forth, in the religious arena, a variety of responses. These are most commonly reduced to three: (1) Radical religious pluralism: ...this stance holds that no religion can advance any legitimate claim to superiority over any other religion....(2) Inclusivism: This stance, while affirming the truth of fundamental Christian claims, nevertheless insists that God has revealed himself, even in saving ways, in other religions. Inclusivists normally contend that God's definitive act of self-disclosure is in Jesus Christ, and that he is in some way central to God's plan of salvation for the human race, but that salvation itself is available in other religions. (3) Exclusivism: This position teaches that the central claims of biblically faithful Christianity are true. Correspondingly, where the teachings of other religions conflict with these claims, they must necessarily be false. This stance brings with it certain views of who Jesus is, what the Bible is, and how salvation is achieved." Carson, *The Gagging of God: Christianity Confronts Pluralism*, 26–27. See also Dennis L. Okholm and Timothy R. Phillips, eds., *Four Views on Salvation in a Pluralistic World* (Grand Rapids: Zondervan, 1996), 7–26.

Those postmodern evangelicals who eschew clarity and purity in the gospel, if not fully committing themselves to an *inclusivist* view of the gospel, are nevertheless embracing incipient forms of it. This contention will be validated in the case studies to follow.

16. In a televised interview, Warren told Rebecca Haggerty of NBC's *Dateline*, "My father was a Baptist pastor. I grew up in little tiny churches of less than 50 people. *I call myself an evangelical.*" Rick Warren, "Dateline," *NBC*, May 23, 2005, emphasis added.

17. Cathy Lynn Grossman, "This Evangelist Has a 'Purpose'," *USA Today*, 21 July, 2003.

18. Ann Rodgers, "Pastor Urges Anglicans to Unite and Care for Poor," *Pittsburgh Post-Gazette*, 12 November, 2005. In the context, Warren is discussing his commitment to an ecumenical approach to helping the poor as part of a broader evangelistic enterprise.

19. The assertion will be validated in the fuller treatment of Rick Warren in chapter four.

20. Rick Warren, *The Purpose Driven Life* (Grand Rapids: Zondervan, 2002), 58.

21. Ibid., emphasis original.

22. In July, 2006, Lakewood Church was ranked among the top five most influential churches in America. The same publication ranked Joel Osteen behind only T. D. Jakes as the second most influential Christian in America. *The Church Report.* <http://www.thechurchreport.com/> (accessed 21 October 2006).

23. Joel Osteen, "Larry King Live," *CNN*, June 20, 2005.

24. Joel Osteen, *Your Best Life Now: 7 Steps to Living at Your Full Potential* (New York: Warner Books, 2004), 65, 67.

25. These words are used frequently throughout *Your Best Life Now*.

26. Joel Osteen, "Larry King Live," *CNN*, June 20, 2005.

27. Some might object to the use of the phrase *impotent to save* when describing a false gospel. After all, the objection goes, isn't salvation the sole work of God and can't God save anyone regardless of the sloppiness or inaccuracy of the gospel presentation? In an absolute sense, this is true. Indeed, God is sovereign over all things. Ultimately those whom God has chosen will be saved and those whom He has not will not, and nothing can change this. But this theological reality does not mitigate man's responsibility to preach a

sound gospel. Nor does the objection properly take into account the fact that God's sovereign plan of salvation includes man's witness to the gospel. Furthermore, the objector's rationale also could be expanded to apply to *any* actions on the part of man. For instance, since God already has chosen who will be saved, and nothing can change this fact, why bother to share the gospel at all? In the end, such an objection is an example of fatalistically overplaying God's sovereignty and ignoring man's responsibility. The present discussion of the clarity and accuracy of the gospel is cast within the framework of man's point of view without intending to suggest that man's efforts, whether accurate or inaccurate, can somehow contravene God's sovereignty.

28. Paul R. Shockley, "Postmodernism as a Basis for Society?" in *The God of the Bible and Other Gods: Is the Christian God Unique among World Religions?* Robert Paul Lightner (Grand Rapids: Kregel Publications, 1998), 198. For an excellent discussion of the abandonment of truth in postmodernity see David F. Wells, *No Place for Truth, or, Whatever Happened to Evangelical Theology?* (Grand Rapids: Eerdmans, 1993), David F. Wells, *God in the Wastelands: The Reality of Truth in a World of Fading Dreams* (Grand Rapids: Eerdmans, 1994).

29. Shockley, "Postmodernism as a Basis for Society?" 198.

30. Zane C. Hodges, "Post-Evangelicalism Confronts the Postmodern Age," *Journal of the Grace Evangelical Society* 9, no. 1 (Spring 1996): 5. The present writer does not share Hodges' view on the content of saving faith. It will be discussed later in this work that Hodges' recent work on the nature of the gospel represents a departure from classical evangelical soteriology. However, Hodges' work on postmodernism provides a helpful contribution to evangelical theology.

31. Carson, *The Gagging of God: Christianity Confronts Pluralism*, 278–79. For a more in-depth definition of pluralism see note fifteen.

32. Netland and Johnson have made the insightful observation regarding the rise of pluralistic thinking in the postmodern age, "The most obvious factor driving pluralism is the increased awareness that we have in the West of religious diversity. No longer are other religions exotic novelties encountered only by the few; they are part of the social and cultural fabric of American life. Immigration has brought different cultures and religions into our neighborhoods.... As the number of religious options multiply, the relative authority of any individual tradition seems to diminish." Harold A. Netland and Keith E. Johnson, "Why Is Religious Pluralism Fun—and Dangerous?" in *Telling the Truth: Evangelizing Postmoderns*, ed. D. A. Carson (Grand Rapids: Zondervan, 2000), 53.

33. C. Ben Mitchell, "Is That All There Is? Moral Ambiguity in a Postmodern Pluralistic Culture," in *The Challenge of Postmodernism: An Evangelical Engagement*, ed. David S. Dockery (Wheaton: Victor Books, 1995), 273.

34. Carson, *The Gagging of God: Christianity Confronts Pluralism*, 10.

35. The following official transcript is provided without alteration. Any grammatical or syntactical errors belong to the original speakers themselves.

36. Joel Osteen, "Larry King Live," *CNN*, 20 June 2005. Osteen later apologized and attempted to clarify his statements from the Larry King interview before a Lakewood Church audience and in a written letter posted on his personal web site. *Joel Osteen Ministries.* <http://www.joelosteen.com/site/PageServer> (accessed 13 July 2005). In the letter, Osteen writes, "It was never my desire or intention to leave any doubt as to what I believe and Whom I serve. I believe with all my heart that it is only through Christ that we have hope in eternal life. I regret and sincerely apologize that I was unclear on the very thing in which I have dedicated my life. ... It wasn't until I had the opportunity to review the transcript of the interview that I realized I had not clearly stated that having a personal relation-

ship with Jesus is the only way to heaven." Osteen's clarification letter leaves one with more questions than answers. Given Larry King's repeated attempts to allow Osteen to affirm the exclusivity of Christ—at times even putting the very words in Osteen's mouth—as well as similar attempts to seek clarification on the part of the caller from Phoenix, Osteen's subsequent clarification is conspicuously unconvincing. One is left with the impression that in front of his hometown congregation Osteen is comfortable espousing the exclusivity of Christ; yet in the public square he is apt to prevaricate and espouse a more politically correct pluralistic view.

In a subsequent appearance on *Larry King Live*, almost two years later, Osteen was given the opportunity to clarify his position on the gospel. King revisited the now infamous exchange with Osteen with the following lead-in, "On this program you angered some evangelicals two years ago when you did not say that accepting Jesus is the only way to heaven. This is the birth of Jesus coming up Monday. You still believe that?" Osteen responded tersely, "No. I believe that Jesus is the only way to heaven." The interview abruptly moved on to other subjects. Joel Osteen, "Larry King Live," *CNN*, 22 December 2006.

37. For an excellent discussion of the abandonment of certainty in postmodern evangelicalism see Robert N. Wilkin, *Why Is Certainty Objectionable among Evangelical Scholars?* (Valley Forge, Pa.: 57th Annual Meeting of the Evangelical Theological Society, 2005). The present writer appreciates very much Wilkin's work on the abandonment of certainty in the postmodern mindset. However, Wilkin's conclusions regarding the content of saving faith are not shared by the present writer. Like the conclusions of Wilkin's mentor Zane Hodges, Wilkin's view on the gospel represents a serious departure from classical evangelical orthodoxy. This issue will be addressed in more detail later in this work.

38. *Reclaiming the Mind Ministries.* <http://www.ttpstudents.com/content/> (accessed 2 October 2006).

39. *The Theology Program.* <http://www.ttpstudents.com/content/ ttp/about> (accessed 2 October 2006).

40. This entire exchange is taken from an audio Podcast of the Theology Unplugged lesson entitled "Epistemology 02." The transcript is reproduced without alteration. Any grammatical or syntactical errors belong to the original speakers themselves. *Theology Unplugged Archives.* <http://www.ttpstudents.com/ content/tup/ archive> (accessed 21 October 2006).

41. This quote is attributed widely to Nietzsche in various writings.

42. See David Barton, *Original Intent: The Courts, the Constitution & Religion* (Aledo, Tex.: WallBuilder Press, 1996), Robert H. Bork, *The Tempting of America: The Political Seduction of the Law* (New York: Collier Macmillan, 1990), Robert H. Bork, *Slouching Towards Gomorrah: Modern Liberalism and American Decline* (New York: Regan Books, 1996).

43. Carl F. H. Henry, "Postmodernism: The New Spectre?" in *The Challenge of Postmodernism: An Evangelical Engagement*, ed. David S. Dockery (Wheaton: Victor Books, 1995), 39.

44. Kevin J. Vanhoozer, *Is There a Meaning in This Text? The Bible, the Reader, and the Morality of Literary Knowledge* (Grand Rapids: Zondervan, 1998), 98. For an excellent discussion of the influence of postmodern thinking on evangelical hermeneutics, see also Robertson McQuilkin and Bradford Mullen, "The Impact of Postmodern Thinking on Evangelical Hermeneutics," *JETS* 40, no. 1 (March 1997): 69–82, Paul R. Shockley, "The Postmodern Theory of Probability on Evangelical Hermeneutics," *Conservative Theological Society Journal* 4, no. 11 (April 2000): 65–82.

45. Vanhoozer, *Is There a Meaning in This Text? The Bible, the Reader, and the Morality of Literary Knowledge*, 52.

46. Gene Edward Veith, "A Postmodern Scandal," *World Magazine*, February 21, 1998, 24.

47. "Donald P. Roper, Superintendent, Potosi Correctional Center, Petitioner V. Christopher Simmons," (United States Supreme Court, 2005), emphasis added.

48. Keith A. Davy, "The Gospel for a New Generation," in *Telling the Truth: Evangelizing Postmoderns*, ed. D. A. Carson (Grand Rapids: Zondervan, 2000), 354.

49. Charles Caldwell Ryrie, *So Great Salvation: What It Means to Believe in Jesus Christ* (Wheaton: Victor Books, 1989), 21.

50. Ibid.

CHAPTER 3

ESTABLISHING THE STANDARD: WHAT IS THE PURE GOSPEL?

> Jesus Christ did not say, "Go into the world and tell the world that it is quite right." The gospel is something completely different. In fact, it is directly opposed to the world. –C. S. Lewis

Charles Ryrie rightly observes, "Confusion abounds with respect to the content and presentation of the Gospel of the grace of God. Some do not present it purely; some do not present it clearly; some do not present it sincerely. But because God is gracious, He often gives light and faith in spite of our imprecise witness."[1] Notwithstanding God's graciousness, precision and accuracy in presenting the gospel should not be abandoned as a hopeless, elusive goal, lest postmodern evangelicals presume too much upon God's grace.

In seeking to identify the pure gospel, several preliminary determinations must be made. First, to what does the term *gospel* refer and how is it used biblically? Is it acceptable to use the term *gospel* as a reference to that which must be believed in order to obtain eternal life? Is not the term used in Scripture to refer to something broader than merely the content (or object) of saving faith?[2]

Additionally, it is necessary to define *faith*. Knowing what must be believed in order to have eternal life is one thing. Knowing what it means to believe it is another. What does it mean to express *saving faith*? Is there a difference between *faith* in general and *saving faith* in particular? What about so-called *spurious faith*? Is there such a thing as faith that does not result in eternal salvation? And if so, what is it about such faith that makes it incapable of securing eternal life? Is there a distinction between *head faith* and *heart faith*, as is often suggested?

Other biblical terms have significant relevance to the current discussion. One of these is the term *salvation*. How is it used in Scripture? Does salvation always refer to *eternal salvation* (i.e., receiving eternal life)? Likewise the term *repentance* bears on this subject. How does it relate to the notion of *faith?* How does it relate to *salvation?*

Clearly defined terms are vital if one is to develop an accurate, biblical standard against which postmodern American evangelical soteriology is to be critiqued. This chapter is divided into two sections: First, *What is the Gospel?* And second, *What Does it Mean to Believe the Gospel?*

What is the Gospel?

In order to determine how much deconstruction the gospel has suffered, one must first establish the identity of the biblical gospel. Three considerations help to identify the pure gospel in Scripture. First, how is the biblical term *gospel* (εὐαγγέλιον) used? This first consideration leads to a second one: what is the good news, broadly speaking, about God's plan of salvation for mankind? Finally, the third consideration concerns the narrow sense of the word gospel: what precisely must someone believe in order to have eternal life?

Exegetical Considerations

Even a casual survey of the usage of the term *gospel* (Gk. εὐαγγέλιον) in Scripture reveals that it is *not* used in a technical sense.[3] There is no inherent, technical meaning of *gospel*. Rather, its meaning is determined by the context in which it is used. Although attempts have been made to demonstrate a technical meaning of the term, such efforts are an example of what D.A. Carson calls *the fallacy of false assumptions about technical meaning*.[4] "In this fallacy, an interpreter falsely assumes that a word always or nearly always has a certain technical meaning—a meaning usually derived either from a subset of the evidence or from the interpreter's personal systematic theology."[5]

Εὐαγγέλιον is used seventy-six times in the New Testament. It is normally translated *gospel* or *good news*. The verb form, εὐαγγελίζω, is usually translated *preach the gospel* or *preach the good news*. It is used fifty-four times in the New Testament. A survey of the New Testament usage helps clarify the various nuances of the word and one quickly concludes that the term *gospel* is not a technical term. The specific *good news* under consideration differs from context to context.

For instance, in Luke 1:19, the angel Gabriel brings Zechariah *good news* about the miraculous birth of John the Baptist. In Luke 2:10 the *good news* pertains to the birth of the Savior as announced to the shepherds in the fields. In Matthew 4:23 Jesus is described as proclaiming the *good news* about the coming Messianic Kingdom to Jews, and so on. Likewise in the Septuagint (the Greek translation of the Old Testament) the term εὐαγγέλιον is used in a generic sense to mean *good news*. In 2 Samuel 4:10, to cite only one Old Testament example, news that Saul had died was described as *good news* by a messenger to David.

When it comes to the *good news* about man's salvation, appeal is often made to 1 Corinthians 15:1–8 as the definitive content of the so-called technical gospel. But even when the term is used in the context of man's eternal salvation, one finds that it seems to have both a broad and narrow sense. For instance, the good news Paul describes in 1 Corinthians 15 appears to be broader than the precise content of saving faith. That is, it includes components that one is not required explicitly to affirm if he is seeking to secure eternal salvation. In the passage below, the underlined portions indicate Paul's detailed description of the good news that he declared.

Moreover, brethren, I declare to you the gospel which I preached to you, which also you received and in which you stand, by which also you are saved, if you hold fast that word which I preached to you—unless you believed in vain. For I delivered to you first of all that which I also received: that Christ died for our sins according to the Scriptures, and that He was buried, and that He rose again the third day according to the Scriptures, and that He was seen by Cephas, then by the twelve. After that He was seen by over five hundred brethren at once, of whom the greater part remain to the present, but some have fallen asleep. After that He was seen by James, then by all the apostles. Then last of all He was seen by me also, as by one born out of due time (1 Cor 15:1–8).

Paul lists nine things (underlined) that elaborate on the *good news* he had proclaimed to the Corinthians.[6] It is self-evident when one compares Scripture with Scripture that Paul does not intend to include all nine of these facts as part of the precise content of saving faith, since nowhere are individuals exhorted, for example, to express faith in the fact that Jesus "was seen by Cephas" in order to be saved. Yet this eyewitness account (and others) is part of the *gospel* as articulated in 1 Corinthians 15.

Sometimes, as with Paul's famous statement in Romans 1:16, εὐαγγελίζω is used with reference to the content of saving faith since it results in eternal salvation to those who believe it.[7] Other times, as with the introductory statement in Mark's gospel, "The beginning of the gospel of Jesus Christ, the Son of God" (Mark 1:1), the *good news* is broader, including not just the narrow content of saving faith but the entire story about Jesus' life, ministry, atonement and resurrection.

A survey of the biblical usage of the term *gospel* suggests that it is not a technical term in Scripture referring exclusively to that which must be believed in order to secure eternal life. It also suggests, however, that the term in fact is used sometimes in this sense and therefore it is acceptable for evangelicals to use *gospel* as a general designation for the content of saving faith. Evangelists are not wrong when they say, for example, "If you believe *the gospel* you can be saved." Such usage is consistent with both historic and biblical uses of the term. What is more important than validating the usage of the word *gospel* is ensuring that the precise content of saving faith, whatever its label, is articulated clearly and accurately.

God's Plan of Salvation

The good news of man's salvation includes three primary aspects. In the first place it emphasizes the bad news that man is a sinner in need of a Savior. Secondly, it presents the good news that God has provided this Savior through His Son, who died and rose again. Finally, a gospel appeal intended to accurately portray the means of securing eternal life must include the condition of obtaining eternal life, namely faith alone in Christ alone. These three points may be characterized as: *the predicament, the provision,* and *the profession.*

The Predicament

Accurate gospel presentations must begin by establishing the need for salvation. The gospel message in the New Testament occurs in the context of man's sinfulness. It begins with a premise: man is a sinner in need of a Savior. Paul sets the example in this regard in the book of Romans by discussing man's predicament in the first three chapters. Romans 3:23 states, "For all have sinned and fall short of the glory of God." If one does not acknowledge he is a sinner, he remains ignorant of his predicament and thus unable to receive salvation.[8] Indeed, what makes the gospel message *good news* is that it solves man's predicament. Man's sinfulness, if not remedied, results in eternal damnation. "For the wages of sin is death…" (Rom 6:23a).[9]

Accordingly, then, the salvation that is offered as part of the gospel message involves deliverance *from hell* and *into eternal life.* It is surprising how many so-called evangelical gospel presentations ignore the discussion of sin, hell and even *heaven.* For many post-modern evangelicals, the appeal in the gospel message is to a life of earthly meaning, purpose, contentment or prosperity and the like.

Salvation is often generically offered but not sufficiently identified. This assertion will be established and explored further in chapter four.

The Provision

The gospel also announces the solution. Jesus Christ, the Son of God, paid the penalty for mankind by dying on the cross. He rose again the third day and offers freely to all deliverance from hell and the gift of eternal life. "...the gift of God is eternal life through Jesus Christ our Lord" (Rom 6:23b).[10] Romans 5:8 states, "But God demonstrates His own love toward us, in that while we were still sinners, Christ died for us." Though a discussion of God's plan for the salvation of mankind can and often does include much more than this, it must at a minimum include the death and resurrection of the Savior, for it is precisely His death and resurrection that identify Jesus Christ as the Savior.

For one to place his faith in Jesus Christ as his personal Savior, he needs to know who Jesus is and what He did for him. Saving faith involves faith in a Person—Jesus Christ. Yet it necessarily involves faith in certain propositional truths about Christ that are essential to the gospel. It is not enough to say merely, "trust in Jesus" when the name *Jesus* has no context or meaning to the hearer.

We must give people something to believe. Since it is the object of faith that saves, there must be meaningful content about that object, which is Jesus Christ Himself. We should present Jesus as the Son of God who died for our sins (John 1:29) and rose again. Content-less emotional appeals are not enough. It will do no good to call people to believe in something empty or erroneous.[11]

As Bing correctly points out, trusting in Jesus for eternal life entails belief in certain propositions about Him. This is an important point that will be expounded further in the pages to follow.

The Profession

Having explained man's predicament and God's solution, an accurate gospel presentation concludes with a *call to faith*. The instrumentality of faith in securing eternal salvation is undeniable in Scripture.[12] Jesus said, "Whosoever *believes* in Me has everlasting life" (John 6:47, et al.). Here is where most gospel presentations go awry. It is typical for evangelistic presentations to include man's predicament and God's solution (although as mentioned, this is not always the case); yet upon coming to the moment of "What must I do to accept God's provision?" many gospel presentations lead the hearer down a dead end street. As the case studies in the following chapters will demonstrate, the call to action in the typical postmodern evangelical gospel is a far cry from *faith alone in Christ alone*—and in many cases, *faith* is absent altogether.

The Content of Saving Faith

The *predicament*, the *provision* and the *profession* aspects of the gospel of salvation all set the stage for the moment when the lost person places his faith in the *correct object* thereby securing eternal life. When one's faith secures eternal life, it may be termed *saving faith*.[13] What is this specific object of saving faith—the "irreducible minimum" of the gospel?[14] Saving faith is actually quite simple. Jesus likened it to the faith of a child (Matt 18:3–4; 19:14). Regarding the simplicity of saving faith, A. T. Pierson writes,

> You have what you take, do you not? It is a very simple thing to take what is given to you, and so to have it. That is, practically, *all there is in faith*. We may make faith obscure by talking too much about it, leading others to infer that there is in it some obscurity or mystery. Faith is very simple: it is taking the eternal life that is offered to you in Christ.[15]

Pierson's statement is a helpful reminder that saving faith entails faith in a Person—Jesus Christ—coupled with faith in what Jesus Christ offers. That is, there is a *personal* as well as a *propositional* component to saving faith. Discussing saving faith in terms of belief in a *proposition* often makes some evangelicals uneasy. It intellectualizes the notion of saving faith too much, they might say. Yet it will be demonstrated below that the object of saving faith necessarily involves both personal trust in Jesus as Savior, as well as acceptance of certain propositional truths about Him.[16]

A profession of saving faith zeroes in on the correct kernel of salvific truth within the broader good news about man's salvation. There are many aspects to God's plan of salvation which, while relevant as a backdrop for salvation in the context of evangelism, are nevertheless not required to be affirmed explicitly by those seeking to obtain eternal life. For example, depending on the audience, one might begin an evangelistic appeal by explaining the grand metanarrative of Scripture. Or, one might focus only on the events surrounding Calvary. Some evangelists might employ evidentiary apologetics; others might use the Romans Roadmap. An evangelistic discussion also might emphasize any one of various non-negotiable truths such as the Trinity, inerrancy, full humanity of Christ, or the hypostatic union of Christ. But one does not have to affirm explicitly these truths in order to receive eternal life.

In the course of explaining the gospel, at some point the moment comes when, having sufficiently addressed man's predicament and God's provision, the sinner is ready for specific instruction on how to appropriate God's free gift of eternal life by professing faith in *something or someone*. It is this precise instruction that is the focus of the present study. Has postmodern American evangelicalism run amuck when it comes to instructing sinners accurately on how to obtain eternal life? Does the precise content of saving faith matter at all to the average postmodern evangelical? In critiquing postmodern American evangelical soteriological method, the following standard of the pure gospel will be applied: *Saving faith is the belief in Jesus Christ as the Son of God who died and rose again to pay one's personal penalty for sin and the one who gives eternal life to all who trust Him and Him alone for it.*[17] Consider more carefully each component of this definition.

(1) "Jesus Christ"

The centrality of Jesus Christ as the object of saving faith is indisputable. "For God so loved the world that He gave *His only begotten Son*, that whoever believes *in Him* should not perish but have everlasting life" (John 3:16, emphasis added). Jesus affirmed this truth many times, "Most assuredly, I say to you, he who believes *in Me* has everlasting life" (John 6:47, emphasis added).[18] Paul inseparably links man's salvation with the person and work of Jesus Christ in Romans 5:8, "But God demonstrates His own love toward us, in that while we were still sinners, *Christ* died for us" (emphasis added). And again in his response to the Philippian jailor, "Believe on the *Lord Jesus Christ*, and you will be saved, you and your household" (Acts 16:31, emphasis added). In his Gospel, John tells his readers, "And truly *Jesus* did many other signs in the presence of His disciples, which are not written in this book; but these are written that you may believe that *Jesus* is the Christ, the Son of God, and that believing you may have life in *His name*" (John 20:30–31, emphasis added). Any gospel presentation that lacks explicit reference to Jesus Christ cannot rightly be considered the pure gospel.

(2) "The Son of God who died and rose again"

Yet, as mentioned, belief in Jesus requires an understanding of *who He is*. It is not belief in an undefined, ambiguous name. It is belief in the *person* behind the name. Saving faith is faith *in Jesus Christ*, which necessarily entails belief in certain propositions about Him.[19] Although the concepts of *person* and *proposition* are not technically identical, there is an inseparable correlation. Belief in a person involves belief in propositions related to that person. As one writer aptly put it, "For sure, I believe that salvation is through faith alone in Christ alone. But my faith is in *the Christ who died in my place, paying the penalty for my sin*."[20] To omit the death and resurrection of Christ from the gospel is to have improperly "bifurcated the person and work of Christ."[21]

In identifying the content of saving faith, it is best to speak of faith in the person of Jesus Christ—viz. the Jesus of the Bible—

and then expand on this idea by addressing which non-negotiable propositions about Him must be included in the kernel of salvific truth. For instance, one must understand that Jesus is the Son of God who died and rose again. To believe in Jesus as the Son of God who died and rose again is to accept Him as uniquely qualified to impart eternal life (cf. John 11:26–27). It is to understand, on some level, that He is the Son of God—a title that distinguishes Him from every other person in the history of mankind. To be sure, saving faith does not require the affirmation of a fully developed doctrine of the deity of Christ. Indeed, the term *deity* may not even come up in an evangelistic encounter. Yet, saving faith involves recognizing—however rudimentary this recognition may be—that Jesus *is God in the flesh.*

John begins his Gospel with a strong affirmation of this fact. "In the beginning was the Word, and the Word was with God, and *the Word was God*" (John 1:1, emphasis added). He then goes on to explain that accepting this premise is necessary if one desires to become a child of God (i.e., to be saved). "He came to His own, and His own did not receive Him. But as many as *received Him*, to them He gave the right to become children of God, to those who *believe in His name*" (John 1:11–12, emphasis added). John equates "receiving Him" (Gk ἐλαβον) with "believing" (Gk. πιστεύουσιν) in His name. To "believe in His name" is to accept that Jesus is who John said He is—the eternal Word of God "[who] became flesh and dwelt among us" (John 1:14a). It is to "welcome the Word in faith."[22] John goes on to explain, "[We] beheld His glory, the glory as of the only begotten of the Father, full of grace and truth" (John 1:14b).

In spite of many who rejected the Word, there were some who received Him. This provides the initial identification of "believe" by equating it with "receive." When we accept a gift, whether tangible or intangible, we thereby demonstrate our *confidence in its reality and trustworthiness*. We make it part of our own possessions. By being so received, Jesus gives to those who receive him a right to membership in the family of God.[23]

By expressing confidence that Jesus has given "membership in the family of God" on the basis of one's faith in Him for it, one of necessity must believe that He is qualified or capable of giving the very gift He promises. At the outset of His gospel (and throughout) John seems to connect Christ's self-identification as the Son of God with His ability to save.

For instance, later in his Gospel, John records an exchange between Jesus and the Pharisees in which Jesus alludes to His own deity. Jesus said, "If you had known Me, you would have known My Father also" (John 8:19). Shortly thereafter, Jesus declares, "[I]f you do not believe that I am He, you will die in your sins" (John 8:24). The New International Version translates this verse, "[I]f you do not believe *that I am the one I claim to be*, you will indeed die in your sins" (John 8:24, emphasis added). Although this is a loose paraphrase of the Greek phrase (ἐὰν γὰρ μὴ πιστεύσητε ὅτι ἐγώ εἰμι, lit. "for if you do not believe that I am"), it nevertheless captures well the sense of Jesus' statement in light of the context. Saving faith involves faith in Jesus as the Son of God—the One who is able to forgive sin and grant eternal life.

In John 11:26, Jesus tells Martha that she must believe in Him if she is to have eternal life. "Whoever lives and believes in Me shall never die. Do you believe this?" Her response in the next verse indicates that belief in Jesus means belief in His ability as the Son of God to impart life: "Yes, Lord, I believe that *You are the Christ, the Son of God*, who is to come into the world" (John 11:27, emphasis added). John reiterates this point in John 20:31, the purpose statement for his entire Gospel, "[B]ut these are written that you may believe that *Jesus is the Christ, the Son of God*, and that believing you may have life in His name" (emphasis added).[24]

In these verses, "Christ" (Χριστός) and "Son of God" (υἱος του θεου) are in apposition to one another, indicating that "Son of God" is a Messianic title denoting not only the Jewish expectation of a King according to the Davidic Promise (cf. 2 Sam 7:12–16), but the divine origin of the King. Tom Constable comments,

That [Martha] truly understood and believed what Jesus revealed about Himself is clear from her reply. She correctly

87

concluded that if Jesus was the One who would raise the dead and impart spiritual life He must be the Messiah. She clarified that what she meant by "Messiah" was not the popular idea of a revolutionary leader but the biblical revelation of a *God-man* whom God promised to send from heaven (cf. 1:9, 49; 6:14).[25]

Constable's use of the phrase "God-man" is instructive. It suggests, as the present writer likewise contends, that identifying Jesus as the *Son of God* meant, on some level, recognizing His transcendence. Certainly, it would be an oversimplification to suggest that the title *Son of Man* is a synonym for *deity* or *God*. But undoubtedly it conjured up in the minds of the original readers Old Testament prophecies that identify the future Messiah as divine.

For instance, Isaiah 9:6–7 connects the promise of a Messianic "Son" with the idea of His deity by referring to Him as *Mighty God* and *Everlasting Father*.

> For unto us a Child is born, Unto us a Son is given; And the government will be upon His shoulder. And His name will be called Wonderful, Counselor, *Mighty God*, *Everlasting Father*, Prince of Peace. Of the increase of His government and peace There will be no end, Upon the throne of David and over His kingdom, To order it and establish it with judgment and justice From that time forward, even forever. The zeal of the Lord of hosts will perform this (Isa 9:6–7, emphasis added).

And the famous prophecy of Daniel 7:13–14 likewise highlights the deity of Christ by speaking of Him as "One *like* the Son of Man" (Dan 7:13, emphasis added).

> I was watching in the night visions, And behold, *One* like the Son of Man, Coming with the clouds of heaven! He came to the Ancient of Days, And they brought Him near before Him. Then to Him was given dominion and glory and a kingdom, That all peoples, nations, and languages should serve Him.

His dominion *is* an everlasting dominion, Which shall not
pass away, And His kingdom *the one* Which shall not be
destroyed (Dan 7:13–14).

This prophecy refers to the Second Coming of Christ at the end
of the Tribulation (i.e., Daniel's seventieth week) to establish the
Messianic Kingdom. The phrase "Son of Man" highlights the fact
that He will be a human offspring, yet the qualifier "like" implies
something more than mere humanity.[26]

In first century Jewish thought, the concepts of *Messiah* and *deity*
were closely linked, though not entirely crystallized.[27] A well-devel-
oped understanding of the doctrine of the deity Christ, and even
more so the Trinity, was lacking. These doctrines did not take shape
fully until later in Church history. Yet saving faith involved the rudimentary affirmation of Christ as uniquely divine or transcendent on
some level. In Jesus' day, this was linked to His identification as
Messiah. Those seeking eternal salvation had to affirm that Jesus
was the long-awaited Messiah and that as such, He was the Son
of God. Today, however, saving faith does not necessarily require
recognition that He is the Messiah, even though affirming Him as
the only One who can forgive sin and give eternal life remains an
essential component of the gospel.[28]

Jesus' death and resurrection, more than anything else, sets Him
apart as unique among men. Ultimately, His death and resurrection
attest to His deity even if early believers did not entirely make this
connection. In fulfillment of Old Testament prophecy, the Son of
God died and rose again to pay man's penalty for sin (cf. Ps 16:9–
11; 68:18; 110:1; Isa 53:4–10). The New Testament further suggests
that His death and resurrection are related to His deity (Matt 12:39–
40; Mark 8:31; Luke 11:29–30; 24:26; John 2:19–21; Acts 2:23–24,
29–32; 1 Cor 15:3–4).

The object of saving faith, then, must include the essential truth
that Jesus Christ is *the Son of God who died and rose again*. This
does not mean that one must affirm a fully developed doctrine of the
deity of Christ with all of its theological intricacies; nor does it mean
that one must explicitly articulate the phrase *deity of Christ* as part
of his profession of faith.[29] Rather, believing in Jesus as the Son of

God means understanding that Jesus is who He said He is: the divine Son of God who alone can forgive sin and grant eternal life (cf. John 11:25–27).[30]

(3) "To pay one's personal penalty for sin"

Identifying Jesus as the object of saving faith necessarily involves understanding not only that He is the Son of God who died and rose again, but also the *significance* of His death and resurrection. It involves recognizing that His death and resurrection serve as the basis for His substitutionary atonement for sin. In John 4:24, the Samaritans affirm that Jesus "is indeed *the Christ, the Savior of the World*" (emphasis added). Just as to be "the Christ" is to be "the Son of God" (see discussion above), likewise to be "the Christ" is to be "the Savior." Jesus said, "I am the good shepherd. The good shepherd *gives His life for the sheep.* Therefore My Father loves Me, because *I lay down My life* that I may take it again" (John 10:11, 17, emphasis added). He also said, "[I]f you do not believe that I am He, you will *die in your sins*" (John 8:24, emphasis added).

At the outset of Jesus' earthly ministry, John the Baptist declared that Jesus is "the Lamb of God *who takes away the sin of the world*" (John 1:29, emphasis added). That Jesus came into the world to rescue man from the penalty of sin is affirmed frequently in the New Testament. For instance, the angel's announcement to Joseph regarding Jesus' birth includes the proclamation, "[Y]ou shall call His name Jesus, for He will *save His people from their sins*" (Matt 1:21, emphasis added). Similarly, the angelic announcement of Jesus' birth to the shepherds refers to Jesus as the "Savior," a reference to His atoning work on the cross (Luke 2:11; cf. Isa 53:4–6). Paul makes Christ's atoning work central to His incarnation, "This is a faithful saying and worthy of all acceptance, that Christ Jesus came into the world *to save sinners*, of whom I am chief" (1 Tim 1:15, emphasis added). And John describes Jesus as "the *propitiation for our sins*, and not for ours only but also for the whole world" (1 John 2:2, emphasis added).

Saving faith includes the specific content that Jesus' death and resurrection involve *personal, substitutionary atonement for sin.*

The general belief that Jesus died and rose again is not, in and of itself, enough to save. Rather, one must believe that Jesus died and rose again *for him personally*. Peter explicitly identified this content when he challenged Cornelius' household, "To [Jesus] all the prophets witness that, through His name, *whoever believes in Him will receive remission [i.e., forgiveness] of sins*" (Acts 10:43, emphasis added). Likewise Paul in his Pisidian Antioch sermon proclaimed, "Therefore let it be known to you, brethren, that through this Man is preached to *you the forgiveness of sins*" (Acts 13:38, emphasis added). There is a personal, substitutionary component to the evangelistic call to saving faith.

Saving faith involves recognizing that Jesus is the answer to one's sin problem. Before being rescued one must first recognize he is in danger. And before one can be saved he must first acknowledge he is a sinner. Absent a proper understanding of sin and its consequence, one cannot express saving faith because he has no impetus to do so. Romans 3:10 establishes the universal fact that all have sinned. "As it is written: 'There is none righteous, no, not one.'" So too does Romans 3:23, "[F]or all have sinned and fall short of the glory of God."

Yet it is further necessary to ensure that the consequence of sin is properly defined. If, in acknowledging his sinfulness, one understands merely that his present life is experientially depreciated or otherwise practically devalued, he has not comprehended the full gravity of sin. To truly comprehend man's sinfulness, one must acknowledge that sin has created a disconnection with God that has eternal ramifications. Acknowledging one's sinfulness includes recognizing the *consequence of sin*, namely, separation from God which results ultimately in eternal damnation in hell. Sin separates man from God (cf. Gen 2:7; Rom 5:1–10; 6:23). But this separation goes beyond mere relational or experiential enmity. It also is much broader than mere temporal, earthly displeasure or discontentment. Ultimately, the separation caused by sin includes eternal, spatial separation if left unremedied.

Jesus' contrast between the unbelieving rich man and the believing beggar named Lazarus illustrates that the eternal consequence of sin is confinement in a place of torment for those who do not believe the gospel (Luke 16:19–31). This place of torment for the unsaved is separated from the dwelling place of believers by a "great gulf" (Luke 16:26). The ultimate result of man's enmity with God because of his sin is *eternal separation from God* in a place of torment. This ultimate place of torment is described in Scripture as a "lake of fire" (Rev 20:15) that involves being "tormented day and night forever and ever" (Rev 20:10).

When Jesus says that those who fail to believe in Him will "die in their sins" (John 8:24), He means that they will die without having remedied their sin problem by believing the gospel and thus will pay the ultimate consequence for their sin. In John 3:16 Jesus describes this as "perishing." "For God so loved the world that He gave His only begotten Son, that whoever believes in Him *should not perish* but have everlasting life" (emphasis added). Perishing (Gk. ἀπό ληται) is thus contrasted with eternal life (Gk. ζωήν αἰώνιον). To perish is to fail to secure eternal life and instead to experience the opposite: eternal torment. Thus, saving faith has as its content belief in Jesus Christ as the Son of God who died and rose again to pay *one's personal penalty for sin* thus rescuing him from hell. To omit the eternal aspect of sin's consequence and focus only on the temporal, earthly consequence is to preach a deficient gospel.

(4) "Gives eternal life to all who trust Him ... for it"

To be rescued *from hell*, though, has a corresponding antithesis. In being rescued from hell, one simultaneously receives *eternal life*. Not only does saving faith require the correct understanding of the consequence of sin, but it also necessitates a proper understanding of the very nature of salvation. *What is it that one secures by expressing saving faith?* The very adjective *saving* in the phrase *saving faith* suggests a definable commodity.

In identifying the nature of *salvation,* one cannot appeal merely to the lexical meaning of the term. Although evangelicals customarily use the term *salvation* to refer to *eternal salvation*, a survey of biblical usage indicates a broader range of meaning. Indeed, most often temporal deliverance of some kind is in view. A brief excursus on the meaning of the term *salvation* is in order.

The terms <u>save</u> (Gk. σώζω) and <u>salvation</u> (Gk. σωτηρία) carry the primary meanings of <u>rescue</u> and <u>deliverance</u>, respectively.[31] The context must determine whether the deliverance in question is temporal in nature—such as deliverance from sickness or danger—or eternal in nature—that is, deliverance from the penalty of sin, namely, hell. For instance, the verb *save* (Gk. σώζω) occurs 109 times in the New Testament.[32] Only forty-one of these occur in the context of eternal salvation. The remaining occurrences refer to temporal deliverance from physical harm, sickness or danger (fifty times); eschatological deliverance into the Messianic Kingdom (fifteen times); or eschatological deliverance at the Bema Judgment (three times). Similar data exist for the noun *salvation* (Gk. σωτηρία).[33]

Thus, in seeking to answer the question, "What is it that one secures by expressing saving faith?" one cannot appeal to a supposed intrinsic meaning of the term *salvation*. Instead, one must examine the context surrounding biblical offers of salvation. In so doing, one finds that the essence of what is provided in eternal salvation is *eternal life*. <u>Saving faith rescues one from eternal torment in hell and secures eternal life in heaven.</u>[34] While there are many additional benefits that accompany eternal salvation—Lewis Sperry Chafer lists thirty-three—the *sine qua non* of eternal salvation is the receiving of eternal life.[35]

The Bible repeatedly characterizes eternal salvation in terms that transcend this present life. Eternal salvation passages in Scripture are rife with terms like "eternal life," "everlasting life," "never perish," "never die," etc. Consider the following passages where references to the eternal nature of eternal salvation have been italicized for emphasis.

Now behold, one came and said to Him, "Good Teacher, what good thing shall I do *that I may have eternal life?*" (Matt 19:16)

And these will go away into *everlasting punishment*, but the righteous into *eternal life* (Matt 25:46).

[T]hat whoever believes in Him should not perish but *have eternal life*. For God so loved the world that He gave His only begotten Son, that whoever believes in Him should not perish but *have everlasting life* (John 3:15–16).

He who believes in the Son *has everlasting life*; and he who does not believe the Son shall not see life, but the wrath of God abides on him (John 3:36).

Most assuredly, I say to you, he who hears My word and believes in Him who sent Me *has everlasting life*, and *shall not come into judgment*, but has passed from death into life (John 5:24).

And Jesus said to them, "I am the bread of life. He who comes to Me *shall never hunger*, and he who believes in Me *shall never thirst*" (John 6:35).

And this is the will of Him who sent Me, that everyone who sees the Son and believes in Him may *have everlasting life*; and I will raise him up at the last day (John 6:40).

Most assuredly, I say to you, he who believes in Me *has everlasting life* (John 6:47).

Whoever eats My flesh and drinks My blood *has eternal life*, and I will raise him up at the last day (John 6:54).

This is the bread which came down from heaven—not as your fathers ate the manna, and are dead. He who eats this bread *will live forever* (John 6:58).

Most assuredly, I say to you, if anyone keeps My word he *shall never see death* (John 8:51).

And I give them *eternal life*, and they *shall never perish*; neither shall anyone snatch them out of My hand (John 10:28).

And whoever lives and believes in Me *shall never die*. Do you believe this? (John 11:26).

[A]s You have given Him authority over all flesh, that He should give *eternal life* to as many as You have given Him. And this is *eternal life*, that they may know You, the only true God, and Jesus Christ whom You have sent (John 17:2–3).

Then Paul and Barnabas grew bold and said, "It was necessary that the word of God should be spoken to you first; but since you reject it, and judge yourselves *unworthy of everlasting life*, behold, we turn to the Gentiles" (Acts 13:46).

Now when the Gentiles heard this, they were glad and glorified the word of the Lord. And as many as had been *appointed to eternal life* believed (Acts 13:48).

[S]o that as sin reigned in death, even so grace might reign through righteousness *to eternal life* through Jesus Christ our Lord (Rom 5:21).

But now having been set free from sin, and having become slaves of God, you have your fruit to holiness, *and the end, everlasting life*. For the wages of sin *is* death, but the gift of God *is eternal life* in Christ Jesus our Lord (Rom 6:22–23).

However, for this reason I obtained mercy, that in me first Jesus Christ might show all longsuffering, as a pattern to those who are going to *believe on Him for everlasting life* (1 Tim 1:16).

Paul, a bondservant of God and an apostle of Jesus Christ, according to the faith of God's elect and the acknowledgment of the truth which accords with godliness, *in hope of eternal life* which God, who cannot lie, promised before time began (Titus 1:1–2).

[T]hat having been justified by His grace we should become heirs according to *the hope of eternal life* (Titus 3:7).

That which was from the beginning, which we have heard, which we have seen with our eyes, which we have looked upon, and our hands have handled, concerning the Word of life— the life was manifested, and we have seen, and bear witness, and *declare to you that eternal life* which was with the Father and was manifested to us (1 John 1:1–2).

And this is the promise that He has promised us—*eternal life* (1 John 2:25).

And this is the testimony: that God *has given us eternal life*, and this life is in His Son. He who has the Son has life; he who does not have the Son of God does not have life. These things I have written to you who believe in the name of the Son of God, *that you may know that you have eternal life...* (1 John 5:11–13).

These passages provide ample evidence to confirm that the essence of eternal salvation is the receiving of *eternal life*. To define eternal salvation in terms that emphasize only earthly hope, meaning, or purpose in this life to the exclusion of the eternal aspect, as many postmodern evangelicals are wont to do, is to eviscerate it, change its essential nature, and transform it into a subjective experience focused entirely on man's feelings, emotions, and present, temporal existence.

Even in eternal salvation passages where the word *eternal* (or its equivalent) is not used explicitly, it can be demonstrated that implicit within the context is the concept of eternality. For instance, Paul's discussion of salvation in Romans often focuses on such words as justification or righteousness. One might ask, how does "being justified" imply "having eternal life in heaven?" The answer is found in the meaning of justification. To be justified (Gk. δικαιόω) means to be declared righteous. Jesus made it clear that man's self-righteousness was not enough to enter the kingdom (Matt 5:20). Paul echoes this thought in Romans 9:30–10:4.

> What shall we say then? That Gentiles, who did not pursue righteousness, have attained to righteousness, even the righteousness of faith; but Israel, pursuing the law of righteousness, has not attained to the law of righteousness. Why? Because they did not seek it by faith, but as it were, by the works of the law. For they stumbled at that stumbling stone. As it is written: "Behold, I lay in Zion a stumbling stone and rock of offense, And whoever believes on Him will not be put to shame." Brethren, my heart's desire and prayer to God for Israel is that they may be saved. For I bear them witness that they have a zeal for God, but not according to knowledge. For they being ignorant of God's righteousness, and seeking to establish their own righteousness, have not submitted to the righteousness of God. For Christ *is* the end of the law for righteousness to everyone who believes.

Paul's reference to Israel being *saved* is in the context of national deliverance into the future Messianic Kingdom. This is indicated by Paul's quotations of Joel 2:32 (Rom 10:13), Isaiah 59:20 (Rom 11:26), and Psalm 14:7 (Rom 11:26)—all Old Testament passages that refer to Israel's deliverance into the promised eternal kingdom. Paul's point in Romans 9–11 is that God has not cast away national Israel forever. A remnant of Jews is experiencing salvation in the present Church Age and one day in the future, all of national Israel (cf. Rom 11:25–26)—not just a remnant as in the present day—will experience national deliverance into the eternal Messianic Kingdom (cf. 2 Sam 7:16). Believing Jews in Paul's day understood that justification makes one righteous enough to enter *the eternal kingdom* and that this justification comes only by faith (Rom 5:1). In any event, justification is not an end in itself, but a means to an end.

Using similar systematic theological linking, the same argument can be made to demonstrate that other salvation terms and phrases likewise carry an implicit eternal aspect.[36] While eternal salvation is described in Scripture using a variety of forensic theological terms, the essence of eternal salvation is the *securing of eternal life*. When one expresses faith in a particular object in order to secure salvation, his expectation of what that salvation actually consists of is an essential component of his faith.

Consider again Jesus' dialogue with Martha in John 11:25–27. As discussed above, Jesus required Martha to believe that *He was who He said He was*—namely, "the Christ, the Son of God"—in order to receive eternal life. But this is not all Jesus required Martha to believe. Jesus also expected Martha to believe that *He would do what He said He would do*. Jesus said, "He who believes in Me, *though he may die, he shall live*. And whoever lives and believes in Me *shall never die"* (John 11:25–26, emphasis added). Then Jesus asked Martha, "Do you believe *this*?" The pronoun *this* (Gk. TOUTO) refers not only to the fact that Jesus is the Son of God (as indicated by Martha's response in v. 27), but that He gives eternal life to those who trust Him for it. Commenting on this passage, Hodges writes,

[T]o believe that Jesus is the Christ is to believe that He guarantees resurrection and eternal life to everyone who believes Him to be the Christ. The Christ is the Guarantor of these things to every believer. To deny that He does this for every believer, or to doubt that He does it, is not to believe what Martha believed. To deny or doubt this, is not to believe what John wants his readership to believe.[37]

Thus, the *goal* of saving faith is part and parcel to the *object* of saving faith. That is, saving faith naturally requires an awareness of what one is receiving as a result of his faith.

The goal of saving faith is not a mystery. It is not ambiguous. Contrary to prevalent postmodern evangelical thought, it is not focused on psychological and emotional benefits in this present life. Indeed, in defending the resurrection of the saved to eternal life, Paul states emphatically, "If *in this life only* we have hope in Christ, we are of all men the most pitiable" (1 Cor 15:19, emphasis added). The goal of saving faith is deliverance from hell and the securing of eternal life beyond the grave. Henry Wadsworth Longfellow captures this important point eloquently in his poem *A Psalm of Life.* The second stanza reads: "Life is real! Life is earnest! And the grave is not its goal; Dust thou art, to dust returnest, was not spoken of the soul."[38] Saving faith, then, is the belief in Jesus Christ as the Son of God who died and rose again to pay one's personal penalty for sin and the one who *gives eternal life to all who trust Him* for it.

(5) "Him alone"

But there is one final yet equally indispensable component of the content of saving faith: the *exclusivity* of faith in Jesus Christ. One cannot be said to have expressed saving faith if, while expressing faith in Jesus Christ for eternal life, he simultaneously has as the object of his faith additional competing interests. That is, if one believes that eternal life is gained by trusting Christ *and* doing good works; or by trusting Christ *and* being baptized, etc.; or if one expressly believes that faith in Christ is just one valid pathway among many to eternal life (e.g. those who espouse evangelical pluralism), then his faith is not in the proper object and thus is not *saving faith.*[39] Faith that does not rest solely on Jesus Christ as the only One who can pay the penalty for sin and give the gift of eternal life is not saving faith.

That Jesus demands exclusivity is indicated by His statement to the disciples in the upper room. "I am the way, the truth, and the life. *No one comes to the Father except through Me"* (John 14:6, emphasis added). Peter likewise affirms the exclusivity of faith in Christ in his address before the Sanhedrin.

[L]et it be known to you all, and to all the people of Israel, that by the name of *Jesus Christ of Nazareth,* whom you crucified, whom God raised from the dead, by Him this man stands here before you whole. This is the "stone which was rejected by you builders, which has become the chief corner-stone." Nor is there salvation in any other, *for there is no other name under heaven given among men by which we must be saved* (Acts 4:10–12, emphasis added).

Similarly, the Apostle Paul leaves no room for alternate routes to eternal salvation.

For this *is* good and acceptable in the sight of God our Savior, who desires all men to be saved and to come to the knowledge of the truth. For there is one God and *one Mediator between God and men, the Man Christ Jesus,* who gave Himself a ransom for all, to be testified in due time (1 Tim 2:3–6, emphasis added).

Saving faith is faith in *Christ alone* for eternal life. Insisting on the exclusivity of Christ is especially important in light of the present postmodern mindset.

Today's evangelist is called to proclaim the gospel in an increasingly pluralistic world. In this global village of competing faiths and many world religions, it is important that our evangelism be marked both by faithfulness to the good news of Christ and humility in our delivery of it. Because God's general revelation extends to all points of his creation, there may well be traces of truth, beauty and goodness in many non-Christian belief systems. But we have no warrant for regarding any of these as alternative gospels or separate roads to salvation.[40]

This soteriological confession captures well the exclusivity saving faith.

Case Studies from the Book of Acts

The establishment of these five core essentials of saving faith— viz. (1) Jesus Christ; (2) the Son of God who died and rose again; (3) to pay one's personal penalty for sin; (4) gives eternal life to all who trust Him and (5) Him alone for it—is a matter of theological synthesis.[41] By linking Scripture with Scripture, one can conclude that these five essentials comprise the kernel of salvific truth that must be believed if one is to receive eternal life. Moreover, a survey of various gospel presentations from the book of Acts validates these essentials.

When examining the evangelistic pericopes in the book of Acts one must keep in mind a key hermeneutical principle of narrative literature. It is a general rule of literal-grammatical-historical hermeneutics that historical narratives in Scripture, such as those in Acts, are not intended to give exhaustive or comprehensive doctrinal details. Thus, not every gospel presentation in Acts explicitly lists all of the content that is necessary for saving faith. Sometimes knowledge of one or more component of the object of saving faith on the part of the target audience is presumed.

> Narratives record what happened—not necessarily what should have happened or what ought to happen every time.... *All* narratives are selective and incomplete. Not all the relevant details are always given (cf. John 21:25). What does appear in the narrative is everything that the inspired author thought important for us to know. Narratives are not written to answer all our theological questions.[42]

For instance, Paul's gospel presentation in reply to the Philippian jailor is quite terse: "Believe on the Lord Jesus Christ and you will be saved" (Acts 16:31). Undoubtedly, implicit within "Jesus Christ" is an awareness of the essentials: His identity as the Son of God, His death and resurrection, His offer of forgiveness of sins and eternal life, and His exclusivity. The alternative is that Paul preached, and Scripture recorded, an incomplete gospel—an alternative that must be rejected.

Similarly, Peter's famous Pentecost sermon in Acts 2 contains implicit references to Jesus Christ as the Son of God (2:36); and the remission of sins (2:38).[43] But Peter does not mention specifically the *eternal destiny* of those who believe nor the *exclusivity of Christ.* Presumably the *exclusivity of Christ* and *eternal life* aspects of the gospel are here bound up in Peter's references to Old Testament

Messianic passages (Joel 2:28–32; Pss 16:8–11; 110:1). The Jewish audience, in acknowledging that Jesus was *the* long-awaited Messiah, thereby affirmed His exclusivity (cf. Acts 4:12) and as the Messiah, they likewise understood that He was the one who would usher in the *eternal* Kingdom as promised in 2 Samuel 7:12–16.[44]

Peter's sermon before members of Cornelius' household comes close to explicitly affirming all five components of the object of faith—and may in fact do so. He introduces Jesus Christ at the outset (Acts 10:36) and implies His divine, transcendent nature as the Son of God by referring to Him as "Lord of all" (Acts 10:36) and the one "ordained by God to be Judge of the living and the dead" (Acts 10:42). Peter proclaims the death and resurrection of Christ (Acts 10:39–40) and explains that He is the source of forgiveness of sins (Acts 10:43). The only one of the five essentials that must be inferred is the exclusivity of Christ, but this inference is not at all strained when one considers Peter's statement that "all the prophets" witnessed to Him—that is, Jesus is *the* fulfillment of the Messianic promise, thus excluding any other pretenders to this claim.

Paul's sermon on Mars' Hill is particularly intriguing (Acts 17:22–34). Of note is the fact that according to the recorded text of his message, Paul does not mention directly the name *Jesus Christ.* Instead he refers to Him as "the Man" whom God has ordained (v. 31). Yet undoubtedly the audience knew precisely to whom Paul was referring (cf. 17:18). Paul clearly refers to Jesus' *death and resurrection* (vv. 31–32) and, like Peter's sermon just discussed, the reference to Jesus as the one who will "judge the world" implies deity.

But conspicuous by their absence in Paul's Mars' Hill sermon are any explicit references to *sin* or *eternal life.* It is possible that his reference to Jesus judging the world "in righteousness" (v. 31), as well as his exhortation to "repent" (v. 30), could be taken as implicit challenges for his listeners to deal with their sin, but more likely the challenge to repent simply represents Paul's call for members of his audience to change their minds about their view of God and Christ in general.[45] One must keep in mind that historical narratives contain only snapshots of what happened at a moment in time. Not everything that happened in a given situation is preserved in the inspired text of Scripture.

Explicit reference to Jesus' substitutionary atonement for sin and the hope of eternal life is evidently not contained in this particular sermon because the broader context already provided such information to the people. Perhaps these topics had been addressed by Paul as he reasoned in the synagogue with Jews and Gentiles alike prior to his climactic address in the midst of the Areopagus (cf. 17:17). Presumably he had presented the gospel more fully and with greater detail during those discussions.

One could examine every evangelistic appeal in the Book of Acts and yet it is difficult to build a theology of the pure gospel from these narrative texts *alone*. This is because the recorded content of the gospel message is necessarily impacted by the context in which it is given, the selectivity of Luke, and the prior knowledge of the audience. Nevertheless as the preceding discussion illustrates the core essentials of the gospel message are validated either implicitly or explicitly by the narrative literature of the New Testament. By means of the systematic study and comparison of various New Testament passages, one can reach a determination regarding the precise content of saving faith with confidence.

Summary of the Content of Saving Faith

The goal of this section has been to demonstrate that saving faith has a clearly definable and non-negotiable content and to articulate that content precisely. The proclamation of the gospel is "in this sense, an intellectual exercise; it is a truth-conveying exercise." It is a "battle for the minds of men and women."[46] Therefore, as Carson emphatically insists, *content* is critical.

American evangelicalism is in desperate need of intellectual and theological input. We have noted that not a little evangelical television is almost empty of content. It is mawkishly sentimental, naively optimistic, frighteningly ignorant, openly manipulative.... [E]ntertainment is not enough; emotional appeals based on tear-jerking stories do not change human behavior; subjective experiences cannot substitute for divine revelation; evangelical clichés can never make up for lack of thought. The mentality that thinks in terms of marketing Jesus *inevitably* moves toward progressive distortion of him; the pursuit of the next emotional round of experience easily degenerates into an intoxicating substitute for the spirituality of the Word. There is a non-negotiable, biblical, intellectual content to be proclaimed. By all means seek the unction of the Spirit; by all means try to think through how to cast his content in ways that engage the modern secularist. But when all the footnotes are in place, my point remains the same: the historic gospel is unavoidably cast as intellectual content that must be taught and proclaimed.[47]

The "intellectual content" that comprises the content of saving faith includes five essential components: (1) Jesus Christ, (2) the Son of God who died and rose again, (3) to pay one's personal penalty for sin, (4) gives eternal life to those who trust Him and (5) Him alone for it. These five essentials, however they may be expressed or articulated, must be included as the content of saving faith and the content of saving faith must *not* include anything that contradicts these five essentials.

Saving faith is the belief in Jesus Christ as the Son of God who died and rose again to pay one's personal penalty for sin and the one who gives eternal life to all who trust Him and Him alone for it. There is nothing magical about these particular English words; nor is it suggested that saving faith necessitates the articulation of a particular formula, verbiage or incantation. What is important to recognize is that saving faith has a *particular, non-negotiable content*. It is against this standard that the case studies in the following chapters will be measured for accuracy.

What Does It Mean to Believe the Gospel?

There remain, however, additional preliminary matters to consider prior to applying this standard to various case studies in postmodern American evangelical soteriology. Chief among these are the definitions of *faith, saving faith,* and *non-saving faith.* It is not enough to quantify the precise content of faith if one does not understand precisely what it means to believe it. Vital to the purity of the gospel is a proper understanding of the nature of faith.[48]

—*H*—

What is Faith?

It is important to note that this first question deals primarily with the definition of *generic faith.* What does it mean to believe *anything*? The question being asked is not, *per se,* "What does it mean to believe the gospel," although these two questions are related. Saving faith is a "species of faith in general."[49] The definition of saving faith will be addressed in greater detail in the next section. This preliminary question is more basic than that: What is faith? The reason so many postmodern evangelicals have misunderstood and miscommunicated the gospel is because they lack a rudimentary understanding of the nature of faith.

Generic faith may be defined as the *assurance or confidence in some stated or implied truth.* As discussed in the previous chapter, this truth may be in the form of a simple *proposition,* or it may be in the form of a *person* with one or more propositions inseparably wrapped up in that person.[50] In either case, when one believes something, by definition he is certain of its truthfulness or reliability at that moment. Of course, it is possible for one to believe something and later change his mind; and it is also possible for one to believe something and be wrong about his belief. But in any event, to believe something or someone (i.e., have faith in it, trust it—see note fifteen above) is to accept it as true.

The biblical usage of the term *faith* validates this basic sense of the word. For instance, the writer of Hebrews states, "Now faith is the substance of things hoped for, the evidence of things not seen" (Heb 11:1). While it would be an overstatement to suggest that this famous verse provides the definition of generic faith, it nevertheless is a good starting point. The more paraphrastic New International Version translates the noun "substance" (Gk. ὑπόστασις) in this verse as "being sure," and the New American Standard, recognized as a more formal translation, translates ὑπόστασις as "assur-

105

ance." These are good translations since one nuance of the noun ὑπόστασις is "confidence or assurance."[51] In fact, the NKJV translates ὑπόστασις as "confidence" in 2 Corinthians 9:4, 11:17, and Hebrews 3:14. The reference in Hebrews 11:1, then, is to confidence or assurance in a future desired reality. The context of the remainder of the chapter indicates that this desired reality pertained to the promises of God. Each person listed in this famous "Hall of Faith," as it has been called, faced unique circumstances in which he or she was called upon to have confidence in God to fulfill specific promises.

A survey of the biblical usage of both the noun *faith* (πίστις) and the verb *believe* (πιστεύω) validates this basic sense of the words.[52] Additionally, a review of the biblical usage makes it clear that not all occurrences of *faith* and *believe* refer to *saving faith*. For instance, in Luke 1:20 Gabriel tells Zacharias, John the Baptist's father, "But behold, you will be mute and not able to speak until the day these things take place, because you did not *believe* my words which will be fulfilled in their own time" (emphasis added). The words that Gabriel had spoken to Zacharias pertained to the birth of John the Baptist, not the gospel; and the indictment against Zacharias was that he had not been confident in Gabriel's promise that Elizabeth would bear a son—he had not *believed it*.

In Luke 8:25, Jesus rebukes the disciples for their fearfulness by asking "Where is your *faith?*" He was not suggesting that they were unsaved because they had failed to believe the gospel; rather he was pointing out that they had demonstrated a lack of confidence (i.e., trust, faith, belief) in His ability to protect them from physical danger during a storm on the Sea of Galilee.

The Apostle Paul frequently uses the words *faith* or *believe* in a context other than eternal salvation. In 1 Corinthians 2:5, Paul speaks of *faith* in the wisdom of men as contrasted with *faith* in the power of God. In 1 Corinthians 11:18 he tells his readers that he *believes* the reports of division in the Corinthian church. In 2 Corinthians 5:7 Paul speaks of walking by *faith* as opposed to sight; that is, living with a daily confidence in God. In 2 Thessalonians 1:4 he refers to *faith* in the midst of persecutions.

As further evidence that faith simply means confidence and that it can have any number of unique objects (whether a simple proposition or a person/proposition), consider the following passages. In each reference cited, the italicized words emphasize the fact that the object of generic faith can be something non-soteriological.

Who has *believed our report?* And to whom has the arm of the LORD been revealed. (Isa 53:1, LXX)

Therefore, when He had risen from the dead, His disciples remembered that He had said this to them; and they *believed the Scripture* and the word which Jesus had said. (John 2:22)

If I have told you *earthly things* and you do not *believe*, how will you *believe* if I tell you *heavenly things*. (John 3:12)

Jesus said to him, "Go your way; your son lives." So the man *believed the word that Jesus spoke to him*, and he went his way. (John 4:50)

But if you do not *believe his [Moses'] writings*, how will you *believe My words?* (John 5:47)

And the prayer of *faith will save the sick*, and the Lord will raise him up. And if he has committed sins, he will be forgiven. (Jas 5:15)

Beloved, do not *believe every spirit*, but test the spirits, whether they are of God; because many false prophets have gone out into the world. (1 John 4:1)

And we have known and *believed the love that God has for us*. God is love, and he who abides in love abides in God, and God in him. (1 John 4:16)

But I want to remind you, though you once knew this, that the Lord, having saved the people out of the land of Egypt, afterward destroyed those who did not *believe* [i.e., God's promises]. (Jude 5)

These passages illustrate that *faith* is not always *saving faith.* That is, not all faith has as its object that which will result in eternal salvation. Sometimes faith is generic and non-soteriological.

Despite the fact that faith quite naturally can have varying objects, some suggest that there is an essential distinction between faith that has as its object a *proposition* and faith that has as its object a *person.* Faith in a person, it is often suggested, involves something more than *confidence* in the truth of what that person is saying.[53] Faith in a person, it is alleged, involves the added components of allegiance and a willingness to obey. But an examination of the biblical evidence disproves this theory. As Clark has demonstrated, the presence of a noun or pronoun object following the verb πιστεύω in Scripture demands no different treatment than when a clausal object follows the verb. That is, the nature of the object (person vs. proposition) does not change the meaning of the verb (confidence). The noun or pronoun objects are simply "linguistic forms that simplify the text by implying without expressing the propositions to be believed."[54]

For instance, in John 4:21 Jesus said to the Samaritan woman, "Woman, believe Me, the hour is coming when you will neither on this mountain, nor in Jerusalem, worship the Father." To "believe Me" is equivalent to "believe what I say."[55] Even when the object is Jesus' name (e.g. in the expression "believe in His name"), the idea is still one of confidence *that what He says about Himself is true.* The Jewish background pertaining to the significance of one's name, viz. an indication about one's character, informs the meaning of such phrases. Believing in Jesus' name means believing in the trustworthiness of His claims. Hence, *believing in Jesus* is inherently *propositional.*

John 1:11–12 illustrates this point. "He came to His own, and His own did not receive Him [i.e., welcome His message, Gk. παρὰ λαμβάνω]. But as many as received Him, to them He gave the right to become children of God, to those who believe in His name."[56] To "believe in His name" is to believe that He is who He said He is—

the Messiah. Martha, for example, understood that when Jesus said "believe in Me" (John 11:25–26), He meant "believe that I am the promised Old Testament Messiah" (cf. John 11:27). In other words, to believe in Jesus is to be confident that the Old Testament propositions about Him are true.

It also has been suggested that attaching a particular preposition to the verb πιστεύω can change the sense of the verb.[57] For instance, appeal is sometimes made to the differing New Testament constructions πιστεύειν εἰς ("believe in") and πιστεύειν ὅτι ("believe that") in support of the mistaken notion that belief in a person is distinct from belief in a proposition. But it can be demonstrated that the two Greek constructions are used interchangeably throughout the New Testament so as to be semantic equivalents.

The fact that πιστεύειν εἰς is equivalent to πιστεύειν ὅτι shows rather that πιστεύειν εἰς arises out of the use of πιστεύειν for "to regard as credible, as true." πιστευ 'ειν εἰς Χπρίστον Ἰησούν (Gal 2:16) ["believe in Christ Jesus"], εἰς αὐτον ["in Him"} and εἰς Εμε ["in Me"] ... etc. simply means πιστεύειν ὅτι Ἰησούς ἀπέθανεν και ἀνέστη ["believe that Jesus died and rose again'] (1 Thess 4:14; cf. Rom 10:9) or ὅτι Ἰησούς ἐστιν ὁ Χρίστος ["that Jesus is the Christ"] (John 20:31), etc."[58]

In short, there is no distinction in the meaning of πιστεύω regardless of whether it is used with a noun, pronoun, person or proposition, and regardless of which preposition might accompany its use. Indeed, the meaning of the word *faith* is not at all complex. When one believes in the truthfulness or reliability of someone or something, he has faith. To *believe*, *have faith*, and *trust* are all ways of expressing the same thing: assurance or confidence in a stated or implied truth.[59] "Surely it is one of the conceits of modern theology to suppose that we can define away simple terms like 'belief' and 'unbelief' and replace their obvious meanings with complicated elaborations."[60]

What is Saving Faith?

Having previously delineated the precise content of saving faith, and having discussed the meaning of *generic faith*, arriving at an accurate description of *saving faith* becomes a rather basic task. Saving faith occurs when *faith meets the right object*—the gospel. "The saving power resides exclusively, not in the act of faith, or the attitude of faith, or the nature of faith, but in the object of faith."[61] Though one can and does believe many things in life, *saving faith* occurs when one believes in Jesus Christ as the Son of God who died and rose again to pay one's personal penalty for sin and the one who gives eternal life to all who trust Him and Him alone for it.[62] Charles Ryrie elaborates on the correct content of faith as the determinative factor in securing salvation:

> You can … believe Christ about a multitude of other things, but these are not involved in salvation. You can believe He is Israel's Messiah, and He is. You can believe He was born without a human father being involved in the act of conception, and that is true. You can believe that what He taught while on earth was good, noble, and true, and it was. You can believe He will return to earth, and He will. You can believe He is the Judge of all, and He is. You can believe He is a Prophet, and He is. You can believe He is a Priest. You can even believe that His priesthood is after the order of Melchizedek, and it is. You can believe He is able to run your life, and He surely is able to do that, and He wants to. But these are not the issues in salvation. *The issue is whether or not you believe that His death paid for all your sin and that by believing in Him you can have forgiveness and eternal life.*[63]

Thus, it all comes down to *what* one believes. Saving faith occurs when faith meets the correct object.

According to some evangelical theologians, however, the correct object of faith is not enough. Saving faith, they say, not only must be quantified (i.e., have the correct object), but *qualified* if it is to produce eternal salvation. That is, it must be the right *kind of faith* if it is going to result in eternal salvation.[64] *Real* saving faith, it is suggested has three components each identified by a Latin designation: A knowledge element (*notitia*), which is understanding the content of truth (i.e., mentally comprehending it); an agreement element (*assensus*), which is the mental assent to the truth (i.e., agreement that it is true); and a volitional element (*fiducia*), which is the personal determination to submit to the truth.[65] Thus, it is said, eternal salvation is gained by acknowledging, accepting and obeying the demands of the gospel.[66] Only when all three components are present can one be said to have expressed true saving faith. This idea will be expounded further in the pages to follow, but first it is helpful to see how the Reformers arrived at such a notion of saving faith.

The Reformers and the Redefinition of Saving Faith

The origin of the confusion regarding the nature of saving faith can be traced to the Protestant Reformation and the reaction to the Roman Catholic understanding of faith.

With respect to the nature of saving faith, the principal ground of controversy was this, that Romanists held that it had its seat in the intellect, and was properly and fundamentally assent (*assensus*), while the Reformers in general maintained that it had its seat in the will, and was properly and essentially trust (*fiducia*). The great majority of eminent Protestant divines have adhered to the views of the Reformers upon this point....[67]

The Reformers were concerned that Roman Catholicism was bestowing eternal salvation upon anyone who desired it even if they expressed no explicit faith in the truths of Scripture. One's self-identification with *The Church* was enough to secure eternal salvation. Often called "the baptism of desire," this Catholic notion taught that anyone who sincerely seeks God as best he can is saved by "implicit faith." This idea was offensive to the Reformers, and rightly so. In Book III of his *Institutes of the Christian Religion,* in a chapter entitled, "Faith Defined and Its Properties Described," John Calvin decries this Catholic notion of implicit faith.

But we must now examine the nature of this faith, by which all who are adopted sons of God enter on the possession of the heavenly kingdom; since it is certain, that not every opinion, nor even every persuasion, is equal to the accomplishment of so great a work. And we ought to be the more cautious and diligent in our meditations and inquiries on the genuine property of faith, in proportion to the pernicious tendency of the mistakes of multitudes in the present age on this subject. For a great part of the world, when they hear the word *faith*, conceive it to be nothing more than a common assent to the evangelical [i.e., Christian] history. And even the disputes of the schools concerning faith, by simply styling God the object of it, (as I have elsewhere observed), rather mislead miserable souls by a vain speculation than direct them to the proper mark....

They not only, by their obscure definition [of faith], diminish, and almost annihilate, all the importance of faith, but have fabricated the notion of implicit faith, a term with which they have honoured the grossest ignorance, and most perniciously deluded the miserable multitude. Indeed, to express the fact more truly and plainly, this notion has not only buried the true faith in oblivion, but has entirely destroyed it. Is this faith—to understand nothing, but obediently to submit our understanding to the Church? Faith consists not in ignorance, but in knowledge ... For we do not obtain salvation by our promptitude to embrace as truth whatever the Church may have prescribed, or by our transferring to her the province of inquiry and of knowledge.... [B]y this knowledge [i.e., of the gospel], I say, not by renouncing our understanding, we obtain an entrance into the kingdom of heaven. For, when the apostle says, that "with the heart man believeth unto righteousness ... [Rom 10:9]," he indicates, that it is not sufficient for a man implicitly to credit what he neither understands, nor even examines; but he requires an explicit knowledge....[68]

One certainly can appreciate Calvin's passion on this issue. The Reformation's battle cry of *sola fide, solus Christus* (faith alone, Christ alone) was much needed given Catholicism's abandonment of personal, individual faith in favor of a works-based soteriological method. But, as is often the case, in seeking to address the error, Calvin, and especially later adherents to Reformed Theology, over-corrected and created a notion of faith that is neither logical nor biblical.[69]

The Reformers were right to reject the Catholic idea of implicit faith. It was not saving faith. But in seeking to make faith in the gospel more *explicit* rather than *implicit*, Reformed Theology histor-ically has appealed not just to a clearly defined, biblical *content* of faith, but to a redefinition of the meaning of *faith* itself. The problem with this approach is that it fails to consider that what makes faith deficient (i.e., unable to save) is its inaccurate content, not the quali-tative nature of the faith itself. Yet this is precisely the suggestion of many evangelical theologians who perpetuate this Reformed notion of saving faith.

The Latin designations for the supposed three-pronged nature of faith are somewhat curious. As discussed in the preceding section, the word normally translated *believe* in the New Testament is the Greek verb πιστεύω, used some 243 times. The related Greek noun is πίστις, also used about 243 times in the New Testament. Noted Greek scholar Art Farstad has pointed out that the common English translation of the noun πίστις has played a role in the Reformed understanding of the nature of saving faith.

The classic English Bible, the KJV, is basically Anglo-Saxon in vocabulary and completely so in structure. But the 1611 translators were not afraid to use some choice Latin-type words, especially in the theological texts: justification, salva-tion, faith, cross, glory, and propitiation, to name a few.

But this dual origin of English vocabulary occasionally poses a problem. Oddly enough, the most important Gospel word-family in the Greek NT is obscured in English. This is because we translate the Greek verb [πιστεύω] by the Anglo-Saxon word *believe*, and the related noun [πίστις] by the totally unrelated word *faith* (from the Latin *fides*, by way of French).

At least partly due to this lack of similarity, many preachers who are weak on grace are able to maintain that the Greek lying behind one or both of the English words includes a whole possible agenda of works, such as commitment, repentance, perseverance, etc.

Actually, *believe* and *faith*, as the Greek shows, are just the verb and the noun for a concept that is really no different in English than in Greek. That concept is *taking people at their word, trusting that what they say is true*.[70]

In other words, in defining saving faith as including the component of *fiducia* the Reformers placed undue emphasis on the Latin translation of πίστις, *fides*. A more natural, and more accurate, rendering of πίστις is *belief*. The question *What is faith?* would be better rephrased as, *What is belief?* or *What does it mean to believe?* Indeed, perhaps the confusion regarding the nature of saving faith could be avoided altogether if the noun πίστις were translated *belief* throughout the New Testament.

The crux of the problem with the popular analysis of faith into *notitia* (understanding), *assensus* (assent), and *fiducia* (trust), is that *fiducia* comes from the same root as *fides* (faith). The Latin *fide* is not a good synonym for the Greek [πιστεύω]. Hence this popular analysis reduces to the obviously absurd definition that faith consists of understanding, assent, and faith.[71]

Clark has summarized the problem well. The alleged distinction between *believing* and *trusting* should never have arisen, for there is nothing mysterious about belief. It is the act of believing.

One easily can see how the first two components of faith made it into the Reformed creed. To believe a proposition one must certainly understand it (*notitia*) and assent to its truthfulness (i.e., accept it as true, *assensus*). But what justification is there for including the idea of volitional willingness to trust or follow (*fiducia*)? In creating a distinction between the alleged "mental assent" and "volitional commitment" aspects of faith, the Reformed view of faith has thus manufactured a new definition of saving faith. This definition is reflected in the writings of many contemporary advocates of the Reformed view.

> [F]aith encompasses obedience…. Modern popular theology tends to recognize *notitia* and often *assensus* but eliminate *fiducia*. Yet faith is not complete unless it is obedient…. The real believer will obey…. A concept of faith that excludes obedience corrupts the message of salvation…. Clearly, the biblical concept of faith is inseparable from obedience…. Obedience is the inevitable manifestation of true faith.[72]

Another advocate of the Reformed notion of saving faith even goes so far as to suggest that saving faith should require a six-month probationary period before it can be validated. Describing what it means to believe the gospel, he writes,

> The issue here is that when one turns *to* something, he must at the same time turn *from* something else…. The New Testament term for this turning away is *repentance*. It means not just remorse, but a turning around so that one goes in an entirely different direction…. Since we cannot read other people's hearts and discern their true status (saved or lost) before God, we need to help them measure themselves by God's standard to see if they are in the faith…. I suggest that six months of turning from sin and fruit-bearing for Christ may be appropriate evidence of genuineness.[73]

Andrus's radical suggestion of a six-month probationary period to validate the genuineness of one's faith not only obscures the essence of faith by making it dependent upon works, it also fails to explain the biblical record which describes frequent occasions when baptism followed *immediately* after one's profession of faith (cf. Acts 2:38, 41; 8:36; 9:18; 10:47; 16:15, 33; 18:8; 19:5; 22:16).

Similar to the contention that *real* saving faith is *obedient* faith is the related view that real saving faith requires repentance of sins. It is somewhat surprising that repentance has worked its way into a discussion of the nature of saving faith given the biblical data on the subject.[74] The New Testament occurrences of the words repent (μετανοέω, thirty-four occurrences) and repentance (μετανοία, twenty-two occurrences) are remarkably scarce as compared to the occurrences of believe (πιστεύω, 243 occurrences) and faith (πίστις, also 243 occurrences); and it has often been pointed out that the one New Testament book written expressly to tell readers how to have eternal life, the Gospel of John, does not use the words *repent* or *repentance* even a single time.[75]

Nevertheless, many evangelicals insist that real saving faith requires repentance of sins. That is, eternal salvation is imparted only to those who are willing to forsake all of their sins and pledge to avoid them in the future.

> Repentance is a critical element of saving faith ... it always speaks of a change of purpose, and specifically a turning from sin. In the sense Jesus used it, repentance calls for a repudiation of the old life and a turning to God for salvation.... It is a redirection of the human will, a purposeful decision to forsake all unrighteousness and pursue righteousness instead.... Repentance is not a one-time act. The repentance that takes place at conversion begins a progressive, life-long process of confession.... Repentance has always been the foundation of the biblical call to salvation.[76]

Another leading evangelical insists "we must respond to this Good News by repenting of our sins and believing the Gospel if we would be forgiven by God, reconciled to Him, and saved from

116

the wrath to come." And when sharing the gospel it is important to "make sure people know that they must persevere in a lifestyle of repentance...."[77]

To require sinners to make the purposeful decision to forsake all unrighteousness and pledge to follow Christ as a condition for receiving eternal life is a bit like asking a child to get cleaned up so that he can take a bath. To the extent that the indwelling of the Holy Spirit is required in order for anyone to experience moral reformation, no one will be able to change his behavior until *after* he has been saved by faith alone. James H. Brookes puts it eloquently,

> [Saving] faith then, is the simple acknowledgment that what God has said is true, and that what Christ has promised is sure. Let there be a heartfelt acceptance of this grace on your part, with calm, unshaken reliance upon Him for your salvation. *You are not to make yourself worthy of the offer in any respect or degree*; for self-righteousness is at the bottom of all these efforts "to make yourself fit," and pride is at the bottom of all this apparent humility that keeps the soul away from the Redeemer. The promise is not to those who have reached a certain degree of fitness to satisfy themselves, for "they that be whole need not a physician, but they that are sick (Matt 9:12)."[78]

As Brookes intimates in the above quote, one reason the Reformed notion of saving faith is to be rejected is that it changes the essence of faith from a "simple acknowledgment that what God has said is true" and "an unshaken reliance upon Him for salvation" to a form of "self-righteousness" in which one's behavior becomes determinative in receiving eternal life.

"Spurious Faith"

Saving faith not only has been redefined to include a pledge of obedience and repentance of sins, but additionally, and by consequence, a new kind of faith altogether has been manufactured: *spurious faith*. Faith that does not meet the three-fold standard of the Reformers is said to be spurious faith. The notion of spurious faith undoubtedly developed out of the best of intentions. Well-meaning and passionate evangelical pastors and leaders understandably decry the prevalence of immorality within the church. It is painful for shepherds to watch their sheep engage in conduct that reflects poorly not only on the church, but more importantly on the Lord of the church, Jesus Christ. In seeking to make sense of such behavior evangelical theologians quite often gravitate toward the position that perhaps such pew-dwellers are not, in fact, saved after all. This would provide an easy explanation for their unchristian-like behavior. Hence, the *spurious faith* classification often is employed to describe the faith of these individuals because it is alleged that their faith lacks the elements of volitional obedience and surrender and thus will not result in eternal salvation—it is *spurious* (or so it is claimed).

The argument goes something like this: *So-and-so claims to have believed the gospel but he is living a life of profound or prolonged carnality. Therefore, he must not have truly believed the gospel. After all, true belief requires surrender and obedience. Since so-and-so is not living an obedient life, his faith must have been deficient.* Spurious faith, then, becomes a kind of escape clause—a label to protect the moral integrity of the church and motivate church members to godliness.[79]

But this approach, while convenient, has a definite, though perhaps unintended, negative implication. It makes good works the focus when validating one's eternal salvation and thus by default, instrumental in securing eternal life.[80] This is a serious charge that will be addressed more fully in the pages to follow. More to the point, however, the spurious faith notion fails the test of theological scrutiny. Notwithstanding the widely-respected and multitudinous opinions to the contrary, especially by many from the Reformed perspective, Scripture does not teach that a prolonged state of carnality proves that one is not in fact a Christian.

Indeed, it is possible—though by no means desirable—for those who believe the gospel, subsequent to expressing saving faith, to live immoral lives without necessarily impugning the validity of the faith they once expressed. When faced with such a parishioner, pastors and fellow believers serve the body of Christ more effectively by rebuking and challenging the sinning brother within the context of Christian sanctification rather than by casting doubt on his salvation and suggesting that his faith is somehow deficient. Immoral conduct is no more a guarantee that one is unsaved than moral conduct is a guarantee that one is saved. Of course, one must always allow for the possibility that those living in a state of carnality are in fact unsaved. But such a determination must only be made on the basis of one's profession (Has he believed the gospel?) and not his behavior (Is he living right?).

John F. MacArthur, perhaps the most well-known contemporary proponent of the spurious faith view, describes so-called spurious faith as follows.

Is it enough to know and understand and assent to the facts of the gospel—even holding the "inward conviction" that these truths apply to me personally—and yet never shun sin or submit to the Lord Jesus? Is a person who holds that kind of belief guaranteed eternal life? Does such a hope constitute faith in the sense in which Scripture uses the term? James expressly teaches that it does not. *Real faith, he says, will produce righteous behavior.* And the true character of saving faith may be examined in light of the believer's works.[81]

MacArthur's elevation of good works to an essential role in saving faith is unmistakable. Referring to the alleged spurious faith of the believers mentioned in John 8:31, another scholar writes, "Clearly they are inclined to think that what Jesus said was true. But they were not prepared to yield Him the *far-reaching allegiance that real trust in Him implies.*"[82] It is this last phrase that encapsulates the essence of saving faith in Reformed thought: Saving faith requires a pledge of allegiance to Christ; it must promise to follow and obey Him. Absent such commitment, faith will not save.

Reformed scholar J. I. Packer contrasts so-called "spurious faith" with true "saving faith."

[*Faith*] *is a whole-souled response*, involving mind, heart, will, and affections.... But if "good works" (activities of serving God and others) do not follow from our profession of faith, we are as yet believing only from the head, not from the heart: in other words, justifying faith (*fiducia*) is not yet ours. The truth is that, though we are justified by faith alone, the faith that justifies is never alone. *It produces moral fruit*; it expresses itself "through love" (Gal 5:6); it transforms one's way of living; it begets virtue. This is not only because holiness is commanded, but also because the regenerate heart, of which *fiducia* is the expression, desires holiness and can find full contentment only in seeking it.[83]

As Packer's statement demonstrates, the Reformed idea of spurious faith is built upon such artificial distinctions as "head faith" versus "heart faith" and "intellectual faith" versus "sincere faith."[84] That is, faith that contains only the first two components of the tripartite notion of faith (*notitia* and *assensus*) is not real faith; it is spurious and it will not save. Only when faith includes the component of *fiducia* (personal determination to commit and obey) can it rightly be called saving faith.[85]

"Easy-Believism?"

Those who espouse the classic Reformed view of saving faith often label the opposing view *easy-believism*. This is because to them, it seems too easy that salvation can result from simple faith in the gospel, apart from any commitment to good works or abandonment of sin or pledge of obedience, or surrendering of the will, etc. Saving faith should be *hard*, they insist. Consider the following assertion by a leading evangelical who holds to the Reformed notion of saving faith.

Don't believe anyone who says it's easy to become a Christian. Salvation for sinners cost God His own Son; it cost God's Son His life, and it'll cost you the same thing. *Salvation isn't the result of an intellectual exercise. It comes from a life lived in obedience and service to Christ* as revealed in the Scripture; it's the fruit of actions, not intentions. There's no room for passive spectators: words without actions are empty and futile. Remember that what John saw was a Book of Life, not a Book of *Intellectual Musings. The life we live, not the words we speak, determines our eternal destiny.*[86]

It appears that the intellectual aspect of saving faith is downplayed (if not rejected entirely) in favor of a personal determination to obey. Indeed, this particular quotation almost makes it sound as if good works are the explicit cause of eternal salvation. Note: "Salvation ... comes from a life lived in obedience;" and "The life we live ... determines our eternal destiny." The very title of the book from which the quotation is taken, *Hard to Believe: The High Cost and Infinite Value of Following Christ*, suggests that something more than simple faith is necessary in order to be saved ... something *harder*. Faith is too easy, it seems, for this leading evangelical.

Easy-believism is described by this same scholar as faith "that makes no moral or spiritual demands." *Easy-believism*, he claims, "has unsanctified the act of believing and made faith a nonmoral exercise."[87] Such a charge implies that saving faith in fact possesses some inherent *moral* demands that must be met by the one expressing faith, and that by omitting such demands from the content of saving faith, adherents of so-called *easy-believism* are propagating a deficient gospel.[88] In reality, just the opposite is true. To add moral demands to the gospel and make them a mandatory part of saving faith is to create a false definition of saving faith.

The label *easy-believism* can come across as pejorative; it implies that those who reject the Reformed notion of saving faith have somehow compromised the gospel and opened the gates of heaven to anyone for any reason. Of course this is not at all the case. Opponents of the Reformed notion of saving faith simply contend that the Bible conditions eternal salvation solely upon simple faith alone in Christ alone, and that to express faith in Jesus is to be convinced that He has given eternal life to the one who simply believes in Him for it. No act of obedience, preceding or following faith in Jesus Christ, such as a promise to obey, repentance of sin, pledge of obedience or surrendering to the Lordship of Christ, may be added to, or considered part of, faith as a condition for receiving eternal life.

If the label *easy-believism* is intended merely to identify those who contend that faith in the gospel is an *easy concept to comprehend*, then the label may be appropriate. After all, saving faith *is* a simple equation—simple enough for a child to understand (cf. Matt 18:3–5; Luke 18:15–17). But as far as the present writer knows, those tagged with the label *easy-believism* have never suggested that gaining eternal life is *easy* in and of itself because unfortunately human pride often makes it very difficult for people to believe that something as valuable as eternal life can be obtained merely by faith. Therefore, like the rich young ruler (Luke 18:18–23), many find it very difficult to abandon their misplaced trust in self, or riches, or works, or baptism, etc. and trust only in Christ for eternal life. Remember, saving faith must be exclusively in Christ alone. In this sense, it is by no means easy to believe the gospel. "[I]t is not easy to believe that Someone whom you and every other living person has never seen did something nearly 2,000 years ago that can take away sin and make you acceptable before a holy God. But it is believing that brings eternal life."[89]

> Salvation is a free gift. You simply lay hold of what Christ has provided. Period. And yet the heretical doctrine of works goes on all around the world and always will. It is effective because the pride of men and women is so strong. We simply *have* to *do* something in order to feel right about it. It just doesn't make good humanistic sense to get something valuable for nothing.[90]

For this reason the *easy-believism* label is misleading and unfair to those who, while affirming the simplicity of faith, nevertheless acknowledge the difficulty of letting go of one's misplaced trust.

Yet, it is not the difficulty of letting go of one's misplaced trust that is normally in view when Reformed theologians decry what they call *easy-believism*. Rather it is faith that, in their view, lacks sufficient good works and obedience to be rightly called *saving faith*.

For this reason, it is unfortunate that the *easy-believism* charge is so often made for in so doing, one fears that it may serve to advance the mistaken notion that one must engage in difficult, diligent good works in order to obtain eternal life.

Sometimes those against whom the *easy-believism* charge is made are mischaracterized as suggesting that mere comprehension of facts is enough to secure eternal salvation. But one is hard-pressed to find any opponent of the Reformed notion of saving faith who suggests that saving faith involves only *comprehension of facts*.[91] As discussed above, the Reformers were correct to delineate two components of faith: *notitia* and *assensus*. The former involves mental comprehension of the facts—understanding the words of the gospel and what they mean. The latter involves *assenting to their truthfulness*—confidence that they are true. It is this second step that is the essence of saving faith. The component of the Reformed notion of saving faith that is rejected by those often labeled as espousing *easy-believism* is the third element, *fiducia*—the idea that one must commit his will in full surrender and obedience to the Lordship of Christ in order to be saved. Thus, when advocates of the Reformed view of saving faith suggest that their opponents support a notion of saving faith that is "merely the acknowledgement of facts," they are creating a straw man.

For example, John F. MacArthur, claims that by omitting *fiducia*, "Proponents of no-lordship evangelism [i.e., easy-believism] take the reductionist trend to its furthest extreme.... [T]hey render faith utterly meaningless by stripping it of everything but its *notional aspects*."[92] Notice that he claims his opponents include only the *notional aspects* [i.e., *notitional*] of saving faith. This is simply not true. It is axiomatic that *understanding* the gospel and *believing* the gospel are two entirely different matters. Saving faith requires both.

Alleged Biblical Support for the Notion of "Spurious Faith"

The biblical review of the term *faith* already undertaken in the preceding section indicates that saving faith should not involve a pledge of moral obedience, as suggested by many Reformed theologians. To believe something (i.e., trust it, have faith in it) simply means to be certain that it is true. Nevertheless, several additional passages are worthy of special consideration in light of the Reformed position. Those who contend that the Bible teaches two kinds of faith, genuine and spurious, have a common list of passages, which they claim support their view. A detailed exposition of these passages is outside the scope of this present work, but a brief treatment of each text, in order to demonstrate that plausible alternatives to the classic Reformed interpretations exist, is instructive.

James 2:14–26

By far the most famous passage cited in support of the notion of spurious faith is James 2:19.[93] The argument goes like this: Demons have "intellectual faith" and they are clearly not saved; therefore, all "intellectual faith" is spurious faith. But the entire argument is framed incorrectly at the outset. The demons never claim to have saving faith; nor does the context imply that this was their expectation. The object of their faith—the proposition they believe—is *the unity of God*. No one, demons or otherwise, receives eternal salvation by believing in the unity of God.

Furthermore, such argumentation fails to properly consider the context. James is not contrasting *faith that leads to heaven* with *faith that does not lead to heaven* in this passage. He is contrasting vibrant, healthy faith of believers with useless, ineffective faith. Indeed, it is not even James that makes the famous statement about the faith of demons. A closer scrutiny of the passage reveals that 2:19 contains the words of an interlocutor—a hypothetical objector. James takes on the voice of an objector to anticipate what might be on the minds of his readers and then refute it. Although consensus is lacking on precisely where the words of the objector end and the words of James resume, when one considers the objector/reply formula it appears that the objector's words comprise all of verses eighteen and nineteen.[94] This rhetorical device is used elsewhere in the New Testament by Paul (cf. Rom 9:19–20; 1 Cor 15:35–36). The words of the imaginary objector are characteristically introduced by the phrase "but someone will say" (or similar) and the original speaker's reply to the hypothetical objector usually commences with the phrase, "Do you want to know, O fool (or O man)...."

This being the case, the reference to the faith of demons is made by the objector, not James, which begs the question, what objection is the interlocutor putting forth? To answer this question, one must first identify James' argument in the broader passage (2:14–26). James says that faith and works naturally go together. It is neither normal nor healthy for Christians to eschew good works. Believers who do not perform good works have a *dead* faith (2:17), James says. Elsewhere he describes their faith as *useless* (2:20).[95] It is not necessary to identify "dead faith" with so-called spurious faith.[96] Indeed, James begins this argument by referring to his readers as *brothers*, indicating his confidence in their salvation. He is writing to an audience whom he describes as born from above and "firstfruits of His creatures" (Jas 1:17–18). To suggest that James' intended audience is unbelievers within the church is at best an argument from silence.

Because James insists that faith without works will not *save* (2:14), the majority of commentators assume that James means that faith must produce good works or it will not result in eternal life.[97] But it has been discussed already that *save* does not always refer to eternal salvation.[98] In fact, most of the time it refers to something other than eternal salvation (62% of the occurrences in the NT). There is no reason for the hasty conclusion that James is here talking about eternal salvation—especially in light of his four other uses of the verb *save* in this letter, which refer to physical deliverance from harm, sickness or death (cf. Jas 1:21; 4:12; 5:15; 5:20).[99] Furthermore, the immediate context indicates that James is talking about the believer's practical deliverance at the day of judgment (i.e., the Bema Judgment, cf. 1 Cor 3:10–15; 2 Cor 5:9–11) when he will be rewarded based on, among other things, whether he has shown compassion and mercy to others (Jas 2:12–13). It is not necessary to import eternal salvation into the context of this passage.

Returning, then, to the objector's words in 2:18–19, one sees that the objector is reacting to James' contention that believers must produce good works if they are to have a healthy, useful faith; that is, if they are to experience both present blessings (cf. 1:25) and eschatological rewards (2:13).[100] The objector disagrees that faith and works have a corresponding relationship. Paraphrasing, the objector asserts, "You might be able to show me your faith *without* works and I might be able to show you my faith *with* works (v. 18). See, works and faith do not *have* to go together!" But it is not enough for the objector simply to state his assertion that two people can each have faith while only one has works; following James' earlier lead of providing illustrations (cf. "the naked brother" in 2:15–16), the objector likewise illustrates his point in an attempt to make his case. The objector continues in 2:19 (again, paraphrasing), "Okay, James. Let's say you have faith in the unity of God and you do good works. The demons believe the same thing, but they do *not* do good works—they tremble. See, I've proven that two people can share a common belief while only one of them produces good works."[101] And with that the objector sits down, supposing to have made his case.

James will not give up so easily, however. He responds by restating his premise: "Do you want to know, O foolish man, that faith without works is useless" (2:20)? He then proceeds to bring in other arguments in 2:20–23 directed specifically at the objector (note the second person *singular* verbs in this section: θέλεις, βλέπεις). Finally, he returns to addressing the audience at large and concludes by reasserting that "faith without works is dead" (2:26) (note the return to the second person *plural* verb "you" in 2:24 [ὁράτε]).

The preceding exposition, though brief, suggests that James 2:19 does not support the notion of spurious faith. Even if one assumes that the objector's statement about the faith of demons represents actual demon belief, and is not merely an illustration with no corresponding reality, then the most that can be inferred from this verse is that demons, like many others, believe in monotheism. But belief in monotheism is not saving faith. The reason demons are not saved (or anyone else for that matter) is because their belief is in a non-saving object, not because it lacks volitional commitment. Furthermore, it is worth pointing out that any comparison between the faith of demons and saving faith is tenuous at best since demons are incapable of securing eternal salvation to begin with. "There is no redemption for the evil angels. It is illogical to compare faith of the spirit world with faith in the human realm."[102]

John 2:23–25

In this passage, it is often alleged that those who "believed in [Jesus'] name" (v. 23) must have had spurious faith because "Jesus did not commit Himself to them" (v. 24). For instance William Hendriksen writes, "Many trusted in his name; i.e., because of the manner in which his power was displayed they accepted him as a great prophet and perhaps even as the Messiah. This, however, is not the same as saying that they surrendered their hearts to him. *Not all faith is saving faith.*"[103]

But this conclusion is by no means certain. The Greek construction πιστευειν εἰς το ὀνομά ("believed in His name") is exclusively Johannine and in every other case seems to refer to saving faith. Indeed, John begins his Gospel with the unwavering assertion that anyone who believes in His name is a child of God (1:12–13). It would be unusual for John to employ the phrase just a few paragraphs later in his Gospel to refer to those who are *not* children of God. One Greek expert has pointed out that "there is nothing in the usage in 1:12 that in any way prepares the reader to understand 2:23 as most commentators understand it [i.e., as referring to spurious faith]."[104]

Furthermore, the suggestion that the faith of these believers was spurious simply because it was based upon Jesus' signs flies directly in the face of John's stated purpose in his Gospel. "And truly *Jesus did many other signs* in the presence of His disciples, which are not written in this book; but *these are written* that you may believe that Jesus is the Christ, the Son of God, and that believing you may have life in His name" (John 20:30–31, emphasis added).

More natural is the conclusion that Jesus' refusal to "commit Himself" to these believers referred to His unwillingness to reveal Himself more intimately to these new believers because He knew that they were untrustworthy—i.e., prone to secrecy about their faith and shy about confessing Jesus to others (cf. John 19:38–39).

It is frequently overlooked that an important subtheme in the Gospel of John is the subject of intimacy with the Lord Jesus. The full flowering of this significant motif is found, of course, in the so-called Upper Room Discourse (John 13–17). While a full treatment of this theme is not possible here, some basic points must be made about it.

Although in the Fourth Gospel eternal life is presented as a gift freely given to every believer, an intimate experience of fellowship with Christ is offered on the condition of obedience to His commands. This is plainly expressed in the Lord's words to the Eleven in John 15:14—"Ye are my friends, if ye do whatsoever I command you...." If the question is raised as to what it might mean for the Lord Jesus to "commit Himself" to people who have believed in His name, the answer ought to be given in Johannine terms. Obviously, His friends are those to whom He commits Himself (as we do to ours!), for it is to them that He unfolds all that He has heard from His Father. It is, in fact, this "commitment" of God's thoughts to them that raises them above the level of mere servants and admits them to a true intimacy with Himself.

When, therefore, it is asserted in John 2:24 that "Jesus did not commit himself" to those who had just believed in His name, it is by no means necessary to draw the radical conclusion that these people were therefore unregenerate. That would be to violate John's normal use of the πιστεύειν εἰς construction. Rather, much more simply, it ought to be concluded that these new believers were not ready for fuller disclosures from the One they had just trusted. Looking with supernatural discernment into their hearts, Jesus did not regard them as truly prepared—just then at least—for friendship with Himself.[105]

As Hodges suggests, the key to understanding John 2:23–25 lies in properly identifying what it means for Jesus to "commit Himself" to those who believe in His name. Admittedly, this determination is a matter of theological synthesis rather than exegesis, but given the near reference to "believe in His name" (1:12), which can only

128

refer to true believers, and given John's purpose statement in John 20:30–31, it is quite plausible that the ones to whom Jesus did not commit Himself in this passage are genuine believers.

John 6:60–66

Following Jesus' extended metaphor about the "Bread of Life," many of His disciples were offended (v. 61). Jesus responded by asserting that some of His disciples did not believe (v. 64). That these followers of Christ were in fact unbelievers (i.e., non-saved) is reasonably clear from the context, because of the references to Judas (vv. 65, 71). John tells us that from that time on many of Jesus' disciples "went back and walked with Him no more (v. 66)." This statement by John has led many commentators to assume that those who "walked with Him no more" had spurious faith.[106] That is, they had "believed" the gospel but their subsequent lack of obedience and commitment "proved" their faith to be only "spurious faith." But it is not necessary to draw this conclusion from the context.

The "spurious faith" view of this passage is built upon the erroneous idea that "disciple" and "believer" are synonymous in the New Testament. But, as J. Dwight Pentecost has pointed out, there are three categories of disciples in the New Testament: the *curious—* those who only followed Christ out of curiosity but never believed the gospel; the *convinced—*those who followed Him and believed the gospel; and the *committed—*those who not only believed in Him for eternal salvation but also were faithful in following Him and obeying His commands.[107] That some of Jesus' followers in John 6 turned out to be only curious non-believers should not be surprising.

Contrary to the common contention, John 6:60 does not support the notion of spurious faith. Tom Constable articulates well this view of the passage.

The term "disciple" is not synonymous with "believer," as should be patently clear in the Gospels. In verse 64 Jesus said that some of these "disciples" did not believe. Some of Jesus' disciples were believers, but many of them were following Him to learn from Him and to decide if He was the Messiah or not. This teaching persuaded many in this seeker category to abandon their Rabbi. Some of them undoubtedly wanted the physical benefits of Jesus' messianism but had little interest in spiritual matters (cf. vv. 14–15, 26, 30–31). Others could not see beyond Jesus' humanity to His true identity (vv. 41–46). Others probably could not accept Jesus' claim to be greater than Moses (vv. 32–33, 58). Still others may have found Jesus' language offensive, particularly His references to eating flesh and drinking blood (vv. 53–54).[108]

In other words, those who turned back were disciples who had *never believed the gospel*. Whatever belief they possessed, it was not belief in the gospel. Thus, those from the Reformed perspective who identify the offended disciples in this passage as unbelievers are correct to identify them as unbelievers; however, they are incorrect to suggest that what made them unbelievers was a spurious faith. Rather, what made them unbelievers was their failure to believe the correct object of saving faith—namely, the gospel.

John 8:30–31

Those who claim that this passage supports the spurious faith notion are guilty of the same interpretive error mentioned in the preceding discussion. The text indicates that in response to Jesus' teaching "many believed in Him (v. 30)." In the next verse, Jesus tells those who believed, "If you abide in My word, you are My disciples indeed." Many commentators read this as if it says, "If you faithfully obey My word, it proves that you have *really believed*."[109] But it has already been pointed out that the word *abide* (Gk. μένω) simply means to remain in close fellowship.[110] Jesus is here speaking about the condition for discipleship—not the condition for so-called "real saving faith."[111]

Acts 8:9–25

Luke's description of the profession of faith by Simon the sorcerer in Acts 8:9–25 has been the subject of much debate. Those who hold to the existence of spurious faith point to Simon as a classic example of one who *believed* but did not *really believe*.[112] But this conclusion is drawn only from the fact that subsequent to Simon's belief, he evidenced behavior that was abhorrent for a Christian and quite deserving of the strong rebuke given by Peter (8:20–23). Simon attempted to profit from his newfound faith in Christ by purchasing miraculous powers from the Apostles, who refused Simon's request. Nothing in the text itself explicitly states that Simon was unsaved.

Indeed, Peter's specific rebuke—viz. that Simon's "money perish" with him—suggests that temporal discipline is in view, since money cannot perish eternally. The English word *perish* (Gk. ἀπωλεία, lit. "destruction"), although often carrying the sense of eternal destruction (cf. John 17:12; 2 Pet 3:7; Rev 17:8, 11), can also have a temporal sense. For example, in Hebrews 10:39—another passage which admittedly is the subject of much interpretive debate—the word ἀπωλεία appears to describe believers whose faith is weak when tested and thus face God's discipline (cf. 10:35–39). And in Matthew 26:8 it is used to describe the loss of costly oil. Furthermore, Paul uses the verb form (ἀπολλύμι) in 1 Corinthians 8:11 to describe what may happen to a "weaker brother" if he is made to stumble.

In addition, it is often suggested that Peter's call for Simon to *repent* indicates he was not a true believer. This is because those holding the spurious faith position see repentance of sins as a vital component to saving faith.[113] But Peter states that if Simon repents (i.e., changes his mind about his evil behavior), God "perhaps" may forgive him; and it is "difficult to imagine that there is any 'perhaps' in the gospel offer to the unregenerate."[114] The appeal to Acts 8:9–25 in support of the spurious faith idea is by no means definitive. It is quite plausible that Simon was a Christian.

131

Matthew 13:20–21 and Luke 8:13

These verses are part of Jesus' parable about the sower and the soils. Some suggest that the ones who "receive the word with joy," "believe for a while" but later "fall away" represent those who expressed spurious faith.[115] But such is by no means the only plausible explanation of this parable. Consider the following exposition of the passage:

Today true believers sometimes stop believing because of information they receive that convinces them their former faith was wrong (e.g., youths who abandon their faith in college). Luke's treatment of this passage shows his concern for apostasy (i.e., departure from the truth) under persecution.

Those of us who have grown up in "Christian" countries sometimes fail to appreciate the fact that genuine Christians have renounced their faith in Jesus under severe persecution (e.g., Peter). We may tend to think that people who do this were never genuine believers. That may be true in some cases. However we need to remember that for every Christian martyr who died refusing to renounce his faith there were other believers who escaped death by renouncing it. To say that their behavior showed that they never truly believed is naive and unbiblical (cf. Luke 19:11–27; 2 Tim 2:12; 4:10a).

The people in view in [Luke 8:13] stop believing because of adversity, but those in verse 14 do so because of distractions (cf. Matt 6:19–34; Luke 11:34–36; 12:22–32; 16:13). Notice that Jesus said that these "believers" (v. 13) produce no mature fruit (cf. John 15:2). In the light of this statement we need to examine the idea that every true believer produces fruit and that if there is no fruit the person must be lost. Fruit is what appears on the outside that other people see. It is what normally, but not always, manifests life on the inside. It is possible for a fruit tree to produce no fruit and still be a fruit tree.[116] Today the testimony of many Christians would lead onlookers to conclude that they are not believers because they do not produce much external evidence of the divine life within them. However, Jesus allowed for the possibility of true believers bearing no mature fruit because they allow the distractions of the world to divert them from God's Word (cf. John 15:2). Luke alone mentioned the pleasures of this life, which were a special problem for his Greek readers.[117]

As Constable correctly points out, the fact that one's faith in Christ can waver, or perhaps even disappear altogether, does not mean that he never expressed saving faith to begin with. Thus, support from the parable of the sower and the soils for the Reformed notion of spurious faith is tenuous at best.

1 Corinthians 5:9–13

Paul's teaching about how to deal with immorality in the church (1 Cor 5:9–13) is another passage that has drawn the attention of those attempting to demonstrate that the New Testament includes a category of spurious faith.[118] Of note is the phrase "anyone named a brother" (Gk. τίς ἀδέλφος ὀνομαζόμενος) in verse eleven. The New American Standard translates this phrase as "so-called brother," implying that he is not really saved. But this conclusion is quite tenuous.[119] The context indicates that Paul's use of the phrase τις ἀδέλφος ὀνομαζόμενος is employed explicitly to designate *believers* as contrasted with those *outside the church* (i.e., unbelievers; cf. v. 10). Furthermore, Paul's later exhortation to forgive and restore this person indicates that a believer is in view (cf. 2 Cor 2:5–11).[120]

Even if it could be demonstrated that Paul was referring to unbelieving church members here, the passage says nothing about *why they are unbelievers*. There is no reference to spurious faith here. If the "brothers" in question are not really Christians, it is because they never believed the gospel, not because they believed it but failed to subsequently obey.

Matthew 7:15–23

It also has been suggested that Jesus' warning during His Sermon on the Mount that "Not everyone who says to Me, 'Lord, Lord,' shall enter the kingdom of heaven" (Matt 7:21a), indicates that there is a category of those who believe the gospel, but nevertheless are unsaved.[121] The fact that they do not do good works (i.e., "the will of the Father," v. 21b), it is alleged, shows that their faith was only spurious. In the broader context, Jesus is warning against false prophets, whom, He says, can be known by their fruits. Many commentators assume that by "fruits" Jesus is referring to outward behavior in spite of the fact that the context suggests *just the opposite*.[122]

According to Jesus, the false prophets appear outwardly to be like sheep (7:15). They do all of the things that one would expect a believer in that day to do (7:22). In other words, it is not their behavior that proves they are not saved; it is their profession itself. The "fruit" of a prophet is his words. How else can prophets be judged, if not by what they say? Furthermore, Jesus' subsequent teaching in Matthew 12:33–37 likewise suggests that *fruit* refers to *words*. It is natural when testing the genuineness of a prophet that one would look to the content of his message. There is no question that the false prophets in this passage are not saved. But the text says nothing about their faith being spurious.[123]

Galatians 2:4 and 2 Corinthians 11:26

In these two passages Paul uses the word ψευδαδέλφος, "false brother." These are the only two uses in the New Testament and understandably the word is not used in the Septuagint, since it has a distinctly First Century Christian context. As the prefix ψευδο suggests, it means quite simply *one who claims to be a Christian brother, but is not*. Yet, without warrant, some lexicons supply an *inherent reason* that the brother is not actually a Christian. For instance, one respected lexicon defines ψευδαδέλφος as "one who pretends to be a fellow-believer, but whose claim is belied by *conduct toward fellow-believers*."[124] Nothing in the context of the word's two NT occurrences indicates that the person's *behavior* is the basis for concluding he is not saved.

The fact that false brothers—those who claim to be Christians but are not—exist in the church today is undisputed. No one suggests that everyone who claims to be a Christian really is one. But nothing in these passages supports the notion that the people so-described are non-Christians *because of the spurious nature of their faith*. They are false brothers because they never believed the gospel. Perhaps they claimed to be Christians for selfish, manipulative reasons, knowing full well they were not. That is, perhaps they lied about being a Christian. Or, perhaps they really thought they were "Christians" because they kept the Law. That is, they had the wrong object of their faith. They were, perhaps, trusting in their works rather than the gospel. Whatever the reason, Paul clearly identifies them as non-Christians; but he says nothing to indicate that they were unsaved because their faith lacked an element of surrender, obedience and commitment.[125]

The Faulty Logic of the "Spurious Faith" View

Not only does the notion of *spurious faith* lack undisputed biblical support, it suffers from logical fallacies as well. That is, the traditional three-pronged approach to faith is not only the result of deficient theological construction; it is logically unsustainable. Logically a person *believes* what he *believes* whether or not he ever acts on that belief. Faith is faith. It is to trust (i.e., believe, have faith) with assurance and certainty that something is true. To suggest that faith is not real unless it produces consistent behavior is to make the very existence of faith (i.e., the *actuality* of faith) indiscernible until time and distance have transpired. At the moment one expresses faith, he can never be sure whether or not he is *really* expressing faith. He must wait and see. The best that can be said when he believes the gospel is that he has expressed *latent saving faith* or *potential saving faith* but it cannot be said to be actual saving faith, since it is alleged that *real* faith must produce corresponding behavior.

Yet such reasoning is flawed because it is a phrenic impossibility to believe something and not really know whether you believe it at the same time. When it comes to faith, there are only two options: belief or disbelief. Reflecting on the Apostle John's description of saving faith in his Gospel, Charlie Bing writes,

> It is extremely significant that we do not see qualifiers with the word believe. John does not condition salvation on whether one "really believes" or "truly believes." Neither does he speak of "genuine faith," "real faith," or "effectual faith." There is only one kind of faith. One either believes in something or he does not. Therefore, those who speak of "spurious faith" … are psychologizing faith as the Scripture neither does, nor provides the basis for doing.[126]

One either believes something or he does not believe it (or he has not made up his mind on the matter yet, which is by its nature disbelief). Belief and disbelief in the same object cannot exist simultaneously. Consequently, one cannot believe something and then subsequently have his actions prove that he really did not believe it.

In seeking to refute this premise, several objections have been raised. Some point out that one might believe something and then subsequently change his mind and no longer believe it. But this does not constitute belief and unbelief *at the same time*. Remember, the premise of the Reformed notion of saving faith is that someone can believe the gospel, really think he believes it, but discover *ex post facto* that he really did not. To believe something and then change one's mind, is not the same thing as believing but not really believing.[127]

Others have pointed out that one might *say* he believes something when he really does not. That is, he might lie about his belief. But again, this is not simultaneous belief and disbelief. Rather it is *dishonesty* and disbelief. It goes without saying that people often profess belief in something that they do not really believe. There is any number of motivations to do so: peer pressure, personal embarrassment, fear of appearing ignorant, manipulation, even outright deceit for personal gain, etc. In these cases, despite the person's professed belief, *he really knows that he does not believe it*. He knows he is lying. The fact that one may lie about his belief does not prove that he can believe something and not believe it at the same time.

Finally, some have suggested that belief in a falsehood is not real belief. But this confuses the ideas of *incorrect* vs. *correct* belief and *real* vs. *non-real* belief. Whether what someone believes is *actually true* or *not*, has no impact on whether or not he *really believes it*. In the case of incorrect belief, the faith itself is not spurious, it is just misplaced.[128] Faith does not have to be well-founded to be real. People often believe things that are untrue. A child's belief in Santa Claus is no less real than his parent's belief that Santa Claus is a myth. When it comes to salvation, however, saving faith is, in fact, faith in a *correct* object: the gospel.

The idea that a person can believe something but discover later that he really did not believe it simply does not hold up under logical scrutiny. Faith is the assurance that something is true. The fact that actions are sometimes inconsistent with belief is not unusual. People often act in a manner inconsistent with what they believe. For example, if one believes that smoking cigarettes will lead to cancer, he is not obligated to quit smoking in order to validate his belief. There are millions of people who believe that smoking is dangerous, yet choose to continue smoking, thereby acting in a manner inconsistent with what they believe. In fact, if belief and actions necessarily must correspond in order for belief to be *real*, then there is actually no such case as "actions that are inconsistent with belief," for in that case, there is nothing for actions to be inconsistent with since belief supposedly never existed in the first place. Belief does not have to be validated by actions to be real.

It is belief in the correct object that is the condition for receiving eternal life—not consistent belief or proven belief. It is faith *alone* that saves. More than 160 times the New Testament conditions eternal life upon faith alone.[129] Neither the *quality* of faith nor the *evidence* of faith affects the *reality* of faith. The only relevant factor when it comes to securing eternal salvation is the *object* of faith. The idea that intellectual assent must be married to volitional commitment in order for faith to be real is "semantically flawed."[130]

Implications of the "Spurious Faith" View

One of the most significant implications of this idea of *spurious faith* is that it minimizes or eliminates the possibility of assurance.[131] The doctrine of assurance may be defined as *the personal certainty that one has received the gift of eternal life*. It is distinct from the doctrine of eternal security in that eternal security (sometimes called perseverance of the saints) deals with whether or not one can lose his salvation.[132] The doctrine of assurance relates to whether or not *one can know that he is saved to begin with*.

Today, owing to the pervasiveness of Reformed thought on the nature of saving faith, the doctrine of assurance, when discussed at all, is couched in terms that are at best confusing and at worst unbiblical. Indeed, so foreign to the average Christian is the clear, biblical doctrine of assurance that when confronted with the notion that a believer can know with absolute certainty that he is going to heaven when he dies, many people today react in one of two ways. Either they invoke the prevalent postmodern mantra that certainty about *anything* is presumptuous and impossible, or they react defensively as if promoting assurance of salvation destroys any motivation for holiness.[133] But assurance of salvation is the birthright of every believer. Jesus said, "I give them *eternal life* and they shall *never perish*."[134]

The doctrine of assurance involves both actuality and potentiality. The actuality of assurance is that the very essence of saving faith is being assured that Jesus Christ alone, the Son of God, who died and rose again, has paid one's personal penalty for sin and given him eternal life. Thus, *at the moment of conversion*, saving faith involves confidence in eternal life. To put it another way, at the precise moment that he expresses saving faith, the sinner must be certain (i.e., believe, trust, have faith) that Jesus has given him eternal life. If one is not confident that he has eternal life at the moment he trusts Jesus Christ for it, then he has not in fact trusted Jesus Christ for eternal life. In this sense, assurance is of the essence of saving faith.

But the doctrine of assurance also involves potentiality. Assurance is not only an actual, integral part of saving faith at the moment of conversion; it is also the continual birthright of all believers. Unfortunately, and for many reasons, but especially because of the prevalent false teaching about the nature of saving faith, many believers, who at one time expressed faith in Jesus Christ for eternal life, subsequently doubt their salvation. The presence of doubt does not mean, of course, that they are not saved, provided at one time in their life they did in fact express confident assurance in Jesus Christ as the only one who could save them. But such doubt about one's eternal destiny is not healthy—indeed it is never healthy to doubt the promises of Christ. Believers can and should have assurance. Assurance of eternal salvation is based upon the objective promise of God in His Word that everyone who trusts in Jesus Christ alone possesses eternal life (John 5:24; 1 John 5:9–13).

The Reformed notion of spurious faith often invites unnecessary personal introspection on the part of the believer who wonders, due to sin in his life, whether perhaps he has not really believed the gospel. It makes "faith in one's faith" the issue, rather than faith in the gospel.[135] Yet, as Chafer indicates,

> It is quite possible for any intelligent person to know whether he has placed such confidence in the Savior. Saving faith is a matter of personal consciousness. "I know whom I have believed." To have deposited one's eternal welfare in the hands of another is a decision of the mind so definite that it can hardly be confused with anything else. On this deposit of oneself into His saving grace depends one's eternal destiny.[136]

This personal introspection regarding one's faith is hailed by some evangelicals as a normative, healthy part of the Christian life.[137] Quite the contrary, however, for a person to question whether or not his belief is real is evidence of serious psychological confusion. It is "the product of years of theological brainwashing. We have been told so many times that some people have spurious belief and that we should check out our own faith to make sure it is true saving faith, that we almost believe [it]. The Bible knows nothing about this sort of thing."[138]

But not only does the Reformed notion of spurious faith invite believers to question the very validity of the saving faith they expressed; it also encourages them to look at their actions as the basis for assurance. All *true* believers, it is said, of necessity will persevere in consistent good works until the end of their lives. Faith, absent good works, cannot rightly be considered *saving* faith. It is defective faith. The natural outgrowth of this alleged indefectibility of saving faith is commonly referred to in Reformed circles as the doctrine of *perseverance of the saints*.[139]

D.A. Carson puts it this way: "[The] failure to persevere [in good works] serves to undermine assurance."[140] But it has been pointed out that Carson ought to have said, "The *possibility of a failure* to persevere undermines assurance."[141] After all, one cannot know whether or not he has persevered until the end of his life. Therefore, how can one have assurance since he must always allow for the possibility of a failure to persevere in the future? If perseverance in good works is required to validate one's eternal salvation, then it also must be required as a basis for assurance. And if perseverance is required as a basis for assurance, assurance is unattainable since perseverance can only be verified *after death*—at which point one needs no assurance, though he may desire a change of residence!

One of the clearest statements of this troubling view of assurance within evangelicalism is given by John F. MacArthur: "Genuine assurance comes from seeing the Holy Spirit's transforming work in one's life, not from clinging to the memory of some experience."[142] Elsewhere, MacArthur writes,

How can you tell genuine Christians from the imposters? There are a number of criteria, but among the most important is the matter of obedience. A person may profess faith in Christ, yet live a life of disobedience to the One he professed as Lord. Something is wrong—terribly wrong. Our Savior asked the sobering question, "Why do you call Me, 'Lord, Lord,' and do not do what I say?" (Luke 6:46). People have a right to be suspicious of one who says he believes in Jesus but fails to live up to that claim. James declared that genuine faith must result in a life of good works (James 2:14–26). If you really believe God, then there should be evidence of it in the way you live, in the things you say, and in the things you do. There is an inseparable relationship between obedience and faith—almost like two sides of a coin. It is impossible to detach one from the other, though many today are trying very hard to devise a doctrine of "faith" that is disjointed from obedience.[143]

In other words, harkening back to a moment in time when one believed the gospel is not a valid basis for assurance. According to MacArthur, assurance is derived from an examination of one's actions. If visible good works are present, one can be relatively sure he is saved. But absent any visible, tangible good works, one can have no confidence that he has received the gift of eternal life.[144]

The problem with this approach is that it makes a subjective evaluation of one's works the determining factor in knowing whether one is really saved or not. How much sin in the life of a believer is permitted before the believer's faith is deemed spurious? At least one defender of this premise admits that believers may fall; they just cannot fall "the whole way."[145] But what does this mean, exactly? How much sin constitutes falling *the whole way?* Similarly, the contention is made that "*true* faith never remains passive. From the moment of regeneration, faith *goes to work*."[146] This begs the question how much work is needed to validate that one's faith is *true faith?* The quagmire of subjectivity created by this Reformed notion of saving faith makes assurance of salvation impossible.

Good works, which can and should follow saving faith, are not a valid basis for assurance of eternal life since evaluating one's good works is an inherently subjective exercise and therefore inconclusive.[147] Good works may have a secondary, encouraging value (Eph 2:10; Titus 3:8). They may serve as a "smell test" of sorts for one's salvation, but they must never be seen as the definitive ruling on the matter.[148]

The theory that the absence of good works or the prevalence of sin in the life of a believer proves that his faith is spurious and thus, that he is not a Christian, is quite common in evangelical Christianity today. Evangelical pollster George Barna uses this line of reasoning when he reflects on the alleged "half of all adults who attend Protestant churches on a typical Sunday morning [who] are not Christian[s]." He suggests that although some people have "complied with the biblical mandate to ask for [the Lord's] forgiveness and to acknowledge that He, and He alone, is able to dismiss our failings and gain us entry into God's presence for eternity," this acknowledgement is only *"in their own minds*[!].*"*[149] In other words, Barna claims that a person who has believed the truth of the gospel as the only means of obtaining eternal life may not really be saved because he only believed it *in his own mind.* Since his commitment level is low and his actions are inconsistent, Barna deems this person to be a "non-believer." It is hard to imagine how Barna feels qualified to peer into the mind of the believer and declare that he really does not believe what he says he believes.

The problem with this view of doubt and assurance is that contrary to the assertions of Packer, Sproul, MacArthur and others, faith is in fact capable of great defect.[150] This is not healthy, by any means, but it is a reality. This defect may manifest itself in two ways. First, true believers might not persevere in good works. Galatians 5:16–25 indicates that believers are capable of looking very much like unbelievers if they cater to the flesh. Indeed, there is not a single sin that an unbeliever can commit that a believer cannot also commit if he caters to his fleshly nature. Hymanaeus and Alexander fall into this category. Their faith was "shipwrecked" (1 Tim 1:18–20).

Secondly, believers may experience defective faith because they actually stop believing. According to the New Testament, it is possible for true believers to:

Believe only for a while (Luke 8:13)
Become unfruitful (Matt 13:22)
Not remain in the Word of Christ (John 8:31)
Become disqualified (1 Cor 9:24–27)
Stray from the faith (1 Tim 1:5–6; 6:9–10, 20–21)
Experience shipwrecked faith (1 Tim 1:18–20)
Depart from the faith (1 Tim 4:1–3)
Deny the faith (1 Tim 5:8)
Become faithless (2 Tim 2:13)
Turn aside to follow Satan (1 Tim 5:12–15)

Furthermore, the faith of Christians is variously described in Scripture as:

Weak (Rom 4:19; 14:1)
Steadfast (1 Pet 5:9; Col. 2:5)
Established (Col 2:7)
Sound (Titus 1:13; 2:2)
Standing fast (1 Cor 16:13)
Rich (Jas 2:5)
Growing (2 Thess 1:3)
Great (Matt 8:10)
Little (Matt 8:26)
Absent (Mark 4:40; Luke 24:11, 41; John 20:27; Cf. Luke 8:25)
Increasing (Luke 17:5; 2 Cor 10:15)
Full (Acts 6:8; 11:24)
Continuing (Acts 14:22)
Strengthened (Acts 16:5)
Abounding (2 Cor 8:7)
Living (Gal 2:20)
Dead (Jas 2:14, 17)
Incomplete (1 Thess 3:10)
Persevering (2 Tim 4:7)
Abandoned (1 Tim 4:1)
Exemplary (1 Tim 4:12)
Denied (1 Tim 5:8)
Strayed from (1 Tim 6:21)
Pursued (1 Tim 6:11; 2 Tim 2:22)
Overthrown (2 Tim 2:18)
Confident (Heb 10:22)
Tested (Jas 1:3)
Genuine (1 Pet 1:7)

The above references suggest that neither the *quality* of a believer's faith nor the *evidence* of his faith have a bearing on the *saving nature* of his faith. Faith of varying qualities does not invalidate the presence of saving faith.

The popular notion of spurious faith is dangerous and unhealthy. It fosters doubt. It logically leads to the conclusion that one cannot be 100% confident of his eternal destiny because he must leave open the possibility that his faith in the gospel was not *real* saving faith. It gives rise to the following hypothetical conversation with oneself: "I thought I believed the gospel, but now I am not sure if I really did because there is sin in my life. Maybe I really did not believe the gospel after all." To suggest that one cannot know whether or not he has really believed the gospel is irrational. Of course one can know what he has or has not believed. If one cannot know whether or not he has believed something, how can he know *anything*? The reality of belief, in anything, is not dependent upon how consistently one acts upon his belief.[151]

What is Non-Saving Faith?

Dave Anderson summarizes well the distinction between saving faith and non-saving faith.

No conclusive New Testament evidence supports different categories of faith. Different levels, yes; different categories, no. Faith is faith, real faith, genuine faith, through and through. It is true that not all faith in the New Testament is saving faith. Faith as small as a grain of the mustard seed is enough to move a mountain (because it is real faith), but that is not saving faith. The faith that "makes you whole" is also real faith, but not necessarily faith in an eternally saving object. The faith of the demons in James 2 is real faith … but they did not believe a message offering eternal life. Saving faith is *only* that faith tethered to the person and work of Jesus Christ alone for eternal life. Such faith is always saving faith.

We do not take issue with the assertion that some expressions of faith in the New Testament are not saving faith, that is, do not involve believing salvific content. The notion that in the New Testament believing in Jesus as Savior is not saving faith is simply wrong. The New Testament knows of no sub-level or insufficient faith in Christ as Savior that does not save. Even Simon Magus of Acts 8:13 had saving faith. There is nothing in the text to indicate that his belief and baptism are to be distinguished from the other believers in Samaria.

Though saving faith begins as an assessment of certain facts about Jesus Christ [i.e., *notitia*], it consummates when a person believes that Christ has died for *his* sins on the cross and has given him the gift of eternal life [i.e., *assensus*].[152]

Although, as Anderson correctly asserts, there is no such thing as spurious faith, it does not follow that everyone who claims to be a Christian really is saved. There is a category of non-saving faith. That is, there are people, undoubtedly many people, who have expressed faith in something but are not saved. Yet what makes their faith non-saving has nothing to do with the intrinsic nature or quality of their faith; rather, what makes their faith non-saving is that it is misplaced. It is not in the correct object of saving faith. Non-saving faith describes those who, despite earnestly believing that they are saved, are not, because they have never believed the gospel.

Summary of Chapter Three

In this chapter, a biblical examination of the Gospel has been set forth and defined first in terms of God's larger plan of salvation—including man's predicament, God's provision, and the profession of faith necessary to secure salvation—and second, in terms of the precise content of saving faith. What precisely must someone believe in order to obtain eternal life? It was suggested that saving faith includes five essential components: (1) Jesus Christ; (2) the Son of God who died and rose again; (3) to pay one's personal penalty for sin; (4) gives eternal life to all who trust Him and (5) Him alone for it. These five essentials, however they may be expressed or articulated, must be included in the content of saving faith and the content of saving faith must *not* include anything that contradicts these five essentials.

It was then suggested that to believe the gospel requires nothing more than confidence that what Jesus has promised is true. Generically speaking, *faith* is assurance or confidence in the truth of some object. *Saving faith* occurs when faith meets the right object— the gospel. Though one can and does believe many things in life, saving faith occurs when one believes in Jesus Christ, the Son of God, who died and rose again to pay his *personal* penalty for sin, as the only One who can give him eternal life.

In following chapters selected versions of the gospel in post-modern American evangelicalism will be examined and critiqued according to the five-fold standard set forth above. Upon review, it will be suggested that these represent distortions of the pure gospel and that there is a profound inconsistency and indifference among evangelicals when it comes to the precise definition of the gospel.

ENDNOTES
CHAPTER THREE

1. Charles Caldwell Ryrie, Basic Theology: A Popular Systemic Guide to Understanding Biblical Truth (Chicago: Moody Press, 1999), 387.

2. In the present work, the phrases "object of faith" and "content of faith" sometimes are used interchangeably. Although some scholars have sought to establish a theological distinction between the "object of faith" and the "content of faith," viz. "object" meaning God and "content" meaning specific truths about God's plan of salvation (cf. Charles Caldwell Ryrie, *Dispensationalism*, rev. and expanded. ed. [Chicago: Moody Press, 1995], 115.), such distinctions are subtle and unwarranted insofar as the two aspects of saving faith are inseparable. That is, although there is a semantic distinction in identity between the *object* and *content* of faith, it is a distinction without separation. One cannot trust in a person (i.e., "object") without believing specific propositional truths made by or about that person (i.e., "content"). For example, if one trusts in Jesus as the *object* of his faith, but the specific *content* of his faith is that Jesus is the Easter Bunny, his faith will not result in eternal salvation. For this reason, the present writer prefers to see "object of faith" and "content of faith" as distinct but inseparable elements of saving faith, and thus usually both components are implied when reference is made to one or the other. See discussion of saving faith below.

3. H. A. Ironside gives a helpful seven-fold categorization of the *gospel* in the New Testament in chapter two of his classic book, *God's Unspeakable Gift*. See H. A. Ironside, *God's Unspeakable Gift* (London: Pickering & Inglis, 1908).

4. Cf. Jeremy D. Myers, "The Gospel Is More Than 'Faith Alone in Christ Alone'," *Journal of the Grace Evangelical Society* 20, no. 2 (Autumn 2006): 33–56. Myers concedes that the term *gospel* has various referents throughout the New Testament, yet he argues that there is one "broad New Testament *Gospel*" that includes various

truths related to salvation. In so doing, he creates a *de facto* technical meaning of the term. One implication of this conclusion is that since, in his view, the term *gospel* refers technically to the broad message of salvation, Myers is uncomfortable applying the term in a narrow sense to refer specifically to the kernel of salvific truth that must be believed to be saved. He writes, "saying that one has to believe the gospel to be saved is like saying that one has to believe the Bible to be saved. Such a statement is not wrong; it's just too vague" (p. 51). But if, as the present writer contends, the term *gospel* has no technical meaning, but rather refers simply to contextually-determined *good news*, why cannot the term be used to refer to the specific good news that must be believed in order to be saved? Additionally, it should be noted that Myers' article is written from the perspective that saving faith requires no particular content other than Jesus' guarantee of eternal life. In other words, Myers suggests that one does not necessarily need to know anything about Jesus' work on the cross or relationship to the Father in order to be saved—a point with which the present writer strongly disagrees. This issue will be addressed more fully later in this work.

5. D. A. Carson, *Exegetical Fallacies*, 2d ed. (Grand Rapids: Baker Books, 1996), 45.

6. Some might point out that the post-resurrection appearances of Christ could be combined into one category, thus creating only four components of the gospel here: (1) Christ died; (2) was buried; (3) rose again; (4) and was seen by witnesses. Nevertheless, the point is that belief in Christ's burial and post-resurrection appearances, whether specifically or generally identified, are nowhere listed as components of saving faith.

   Some also might suggest that Paul's description of the gospel in 1 Corinthians 15 is actually too *narrow,* rather than too *broad,* in that it omits certain content that is necessary as the object of saving faith. They might point out, for instance, that there is no explicit mention of "forgiveness of sins." Yet upon careful scrutiny, it can be concluded that in fact Christ's substitutionary atonement for sin is addressed in verse three: "Christ died for our sins;" and the fact that *belief* in this reality is necessary for eternal salvation is seen in verse eleven: "so we preach and so you *believed* [emphasis added]." Furthermore, if the context is expanded to include the remainder of chapter fifteen, the "forgiveness of sins" issue is covered in verse seventeen. Indeed, all of the components of saving faith, which will be quantified in the next section, are contained in 1 Corinthians 15.

It also has been noted that the repeated phrase "according to the Scriptures" (vv. 3, 4) may well mark out the core essence of the gospel, thus relegating the post-resurrection appearances to a place of supporting material as distinguished from the components that are a required part of the content of saving faith. That is, the death and resurrection of Christ are part of the explicit content of saving faith; whereas the burial and post-resurrection appearances of Christ are merely supporting evidences of His death and resurrection.

7. See also Mark 1:15; Acts 15:7; Rom 10:16; 2 Cor 4:3–4; 9:13; 11:4; Eph 1:13; Col 1:5; 1:23; 2 Thess 1:8; 2:14; 1 Pet 4:17. The suggestion that *salvation* in Romans 1:16 refers to *sanctification* and not *justification* is utterly unwarranted and out of step with the context. The gospel Paul desired to preach in Rome, which to that point he had been unable to do in person (cf. 1:15), is the good news about how to obtain eternal salvation. This fact is indisputable when one considers Romans 15:20, where Paul claims that his target audience for the gospel proclamation in Rome are those who have never before heard about Christ. "And so I have made it my aim to preach the gospel, *not where Christ was named*, lest I should build on another man's foundation" (emphasis added).

8. Ignorance about sin does not excuse one from believing the gospel. According to Scripture all men are without excuse when it comes to salvation because of God's general revelation (cf. Rom 1:18–32; Ps 19:1; Acts 14:17). Yet before one can receive salvation by faith alone in Christ alone he must first acknowledge the specific nature of his predicament—namely, that his personal sinfulness has consigned him to hell.

9. It is acknowledged that this famous verse occurs within a broader section of Romans in which Paul is addressing the believer's sanctification and on-going struggle with sin. Yet this does not preclude the use of this verse as a proof-text for the consequences of sin in the life of the unbeliever. The point Paul is making in Romans 6 is that the believer has been set free from both the *penalty* and *power* of sin and that he should no longer behave as if he is a slave of sin. Romans 6:22 assures the believer that he has been set free from sin and has received everlasting life. Romans 6:23 then serves as a summary statement (note the explanatory *for*) contrasting the unavoidable consequence for those who are still in positional bondage to sin with the gracious end that awaits those who have received the "gift of God," namely, "eternal life in Christ Jesus." Paul's point is that the believer has been set free from sin (which if left unremedied would have resulted in eternal damnation; 6:23a) and has received the gift of God (which is the present possession of eternal life; 6:23b).

10. See previous note.

11. Charles C. Bing, "The Condition for Salvation in John's Gospel," *Journal of the Grace Evangelical Society* 9, no. 1 (Spring 1996): 34.

12. See *Appendix A: 160+ Verses Demonstrating Justification by Faith Alone.*

13. The distinction between what may be termed *generic* faith and *saving* faith is discussed at length later in this chapter. See section entitled, *What Does it Mean to Believe the Gospel?*

14. Keith A. Davy, "The Gospel for a New Generation," in *Telling the Truth: Evangelizing Postmoderns*, ed. D. A. Carson (Grand Rapids: Zondervan, 2000), 354. The present writer is borrowing Keith Davy's term "irreducible minimum," even though Davy does not share the present writer's view on the content of saving faith. The term "irreducible minimum" is helpful in that it frames the discussion of the content of saving faith in terms of its precision.

Some evangelical scholars, especially some who share the present writer's concern over the infusion of works and other performance–oriented components into the gospel, dislike the term "minimum" when referring to the content of saving faith. Yet, it is difficult to see why this phrase would be a concern. Perhaps the concern reflects the influence of postmodernism's celebration of imprecision.

The issue at hand is: Is it possible for one to know what he has to believe in order to receive eternal life? The answer to this question *has to be yes*, otherwise no one could ever be saved. And since it is in fact possible to know what one has to believe in order to receive eternal life, then the natural and necessary follow–up to that question is: "What *is* it?" What is the precise content of saving faith? The issue is *precision*. At a time when postmodern evangelicalism is comfortable with ambiguity and uncertainty, it is crucial that the church quantify accurately the biblical content of saving faith.

15. Arthur T. Pierson, *The Heart of the Gospel: Sermons on the Life-Changing Power of the Good News* (Grand Rapids: Kregel Publications, 1996), 46–47, emphasis added.

16. See section below entitled, *What is Saving Faith?*

17. The respective meanings of *faith* and *saving faith* are discussed at length in subsequent sections of this chapter. Detailed attention is given to the tendency on the part of some, particularly some from the Reformed tradition, to create a distinction between *belief* and *trust* wherein *trust* is said to involve elements of personal obedience or a pledge of allegiance to the object of one's faith. Those who hold this view suggest that *believing* in Jesus is not enough; one must *trust* in Him (i.e., promise to obey Him) in order to be saved. It is the contention of the present writer, however, that *saving faith* does not require elements of obedience or a personal pledge of allegiance. See section below entitled, "What is Saving Faith?"

Other evangelicals who likewise reject the notion that *saving faith* requires obedience still prefer to see a semantic distinction between *belief* and *trust*. For them, *belief* more naturally relates to *propositional* truths and *trust* more appropriately relates to a *person*.

While the semantic distinction between faith in a person and faith in a proposition is worth noting (as discussed above), it is the present writer's contention that the terms *faith, belief* and *trust* (along with their corresponding verb forms) are synonymous, referring to "the assurance or confidence in some stated or implied truth." The fact that this truth may relate to a *person* or to *propositions about that person* does not alter the meaning of faith. Furthermore, given the popular Reformed delineation of *belief* and *trust* wherein *trust* is said to require obedience, it is probably best to avoid making sharp distinctions between such English words as *belief, trust* and *faith*. The pertinent issue when quantifying saving faith is the *content of faith*, not the *kind of faith* (i.e., belief versus trust). This issue is addressed in greater detail later in this chapter.

18. See also John 6:35; 7:38; 11:25–26; 12:46, et al.

19. In recent years, some theologians have departed from the biblical view of the gospel by suggesting that one can believe in Jesus for eternal life without explicit knowledge that He died and rose again for one's sins. For these theologians, knowledge of Christ's death and resurrection as a payment for one's sins is optional as part of the content of saving faith.

The view that one can believe in Jesus for eternal life without knowing that He died and rose again has been variously termed the "crossless gospel," the "promise-only gospel," the "content-less gospel," the "minimalist gospel," and the "refined gospel." This view is being propagated primarily by the Grace Evangelical Society (www.faithalone.org) and such notable theological scholars as Zane Hodges, Bob Wilkin and John Niemela (www.mol316. com), to name a few. Their self-labeled view of the gospel is termed the "refined view," indicating that the accepted view of the gospel throughout two thousand years of church history has been incorrect and that they have now provided a long-overdue corrective. Hodges refers to the traditional view of the gospel, as including the death and resurrection of Christ, as "flawed." Cf. Zane C. Hodges, "How to Lead People to Christ, Pt.2," *Journal of the Grace Evangelical Society* 14 (Spring 2001): 9–18. Hodges elsewhere states, "The simple truth is that Jesus can be believed for eternal salvation *apart from any detailed knowledge of what He did to provide it.*" Ibid., p. 12. See also Zane C. Hodges, "How to Lead People to Christ, Pt.1," *Journal of the Grace Evangelical Society* 13 (Autumn 2000): 3–12, emphasis added.

For Hodges and others who hold this view, the gospel is limited to: "Belief in Jesus Christ as the guarantee of eternal life." Hodges writes, "People are not saved by believing that Jesus died on the cross; they are saved by believing in Jesus for eternal life, or eternal salvation." Hodges, "How to Lead People to Christ, Pt.2," 10. According to Hodges, details such as who Jesus is (i.e. the Son of God) and His work on the cross are not relevant to the precise content of saving faith. To be clear, proponents of this view believe Christ died and rose again; *they just do not believe one has to believe in the death and resurrection of Christ to be saved.*

The present writer applauds the quest for precision in the content of saving faith by those who hold this view; yet, in a tragic example of a theological method gone awry, they have gone too far. Their theological method manifests several errors such as [1] an unbalanced appeal to the priority of the Johannine Gospel (Consider Hodges' statement, "All forms of the gospel that require greater content to faith in Christ than the Gospel of John requires are flawed." Hodges, *How To Lead a Person To Christ,* Part 1, p. 8. And, "Neither explicitly nor implicitly does the Gospel of John teach that a person must understand the cross to be saved." Ibid., p. 7.); [2] A failure to acknowledge and correctly handle the progress of revelation in Scripture (See the present writer's discussion of this issue in note twenty-eight below.); [3] A failure to acknowledge the changing content of saving faith within each dispensation (In support of their position that saving faith today does not require knowledge of Christ's work on the cross, adherents of this view often will appeal to the fact that Abraham and other OT saints did not believe in the death/resurrection of Christ. Such an argument evidences a departure from the foundational dispensational understanding regarding the changing content of saving faith. It is self-evident that OT saints did not believe explicitly in the death and resurrection of Jesus Christ, since the events of Calvary had not occurred yet. But it does not follow from this observation that someone *today* could be saved without knowledge of Christ's work on the cross. See note twenty-eight below.); [4] An improper theological synthesis when comparing Scripture with Scripture; and [5] The tendency to read a presupposed theological conclusion into a given passage, thus obscuring the plain, normal sense of the passage.

Sadly, in their commendable effort to eliminate any elements of works or human effort from the gospel, they have stripped it of key salvific components. One proponent of this view stated that it is possible for a person to get saved in the present age by believing in Jesus, and then die and go to heaven, whereupon he is surprised to learn that the Jesus who saved him also died and rose again for his sins. (Bob Wilkin, Question & Answer time during Wilkin's presentation at the 2007 Meeting of the Evangelical Theological Society in San Diego, CA, entitled, "Our Evangelism Should Be Exegetically Sound," November 15, 2007.) According to Wilkin, as long as one believes that Jesus guarantees him eternal life, he can be saved, even if he does not know that Jesus is the Son of God and even if he knows nothing about Jesus' work on the cross.

Yet, several New Testament passages indicate that explicit knowledge of Jesus' death and resurrection *is* necessary for eternal salvation. A detailed critique of the so-called "crossless gospel" is beyond the scope of this present work, but a couple of passages are worth noting here. In 1 Corinthians 1:17–18 Paul references the gospel he preached and refers to the "cross of Christ" and the "message of the cross." Three verses later in 1:21, he states that one is saved by believing the message he preached. Two verses after that, he affirms once again the content of his message, which, when believed, results in salvation. He states, "we preach Christ crucified…" (1:23). This passage inseparably links the work of Christ on the cross to the content of saving faith. Later in 1 Corinthians 15, in a passage previously discussed in this present work, Paul states that one is saved by believing the gospel, which he then defines as including the death and resurrection of Christ. Galatians 1:8–9 also is instructive here. In Galatians 1:8–9, Paul states plainly that any gospel other than the one he had preached to the Galatians during his visit to them is a false gospel. Scripture provides a record of the precise gospel that Paul preached to the Galatians during his first missionary journey. That record is contained in Acts 13. There, one finds that the gospel Paul preached included quite naturally the death and resurrection of Christ (cf. Acts 13:28–30; 38–39). When synthesizing Galatians 1 with Acts 13, the conclusion can only be that any gospel that omits the death and resurrection of Christ is a *false gospel.* Many additional passages could be cited that affirm the centrality of the cross in the gospel message, but these should suffice to render the view discussed above as warrantless and unbiblical.

For a detailed treatment of this erroneous view of the content of saving faith, see Tom Stegall's 5-part series in *The Grace Family Journal.* Tom Stegall, "The Tragedy of the Crossless Gospel, Parts 1–5," *The Grace Family Journal* (2007). Available online at http://www.duluthbible.org/246451.ihtml. See also Gregory P. Sapaugh, "A Response to Hodges: How to Lead People to Christ, Parts 1 and 2," *Journal of the Grace Evangelical Society* 14 (August 2001): 21–29.

20. Sapaugh, "A Response to Hodges...," p. 29, emphasis added.

21. Ibid.

22. George R. Beasley-Murray, "*John,*" in *Word Biblical Commentary,* vol. 36 (Dallas: Word, 1998), 12.

23. Merrill C. Tenney, "The Gospel of John," in *The Expositor's Bible Commentary,* vol. 9, ed. Frank E. Gaebelein (Grand Rapids: Zondervan, 1981), 32, emphasis added.

24. See also John 1:49, "Nathanael answered and said to Him, 'Rabbi, You are the Son of God! You are the King of Israel!'"

25. Thomas L. Constable, *Expository Notes on John* (Garland, Tex.: Sonic Light, 2005), 178, emphasis added. Leon Morris concurs with Constable, "[Martha's] faith is not a vague, formless credulity. It has content, and doctrinal content at that.... First, Jesus is 'the Christ' i.e., the Messiah of Jewish expectation. Secondly, He is 'the Son of

God.' It is an expression that can mean little more than that the person so described is *a godly man*, but it can also point to a specially close relation to God. It is in the latter sense that it is used throughout this Gospel, and, indeed, John writes explicitly to bring men into faith in Jesus as the Son of God (20:31). There can be no doubt that Martha is giving the words their maximum content." Leon Morris, *The Gospel According to John: The English Text with Introduction, Exposition and Notes* (Grand Rapids: Eerdmans, 1971), 551–52, emphasis added.

26. Cf. Renald E. Showers, *The Most High God: A Commentary on the Book of Daniel* (Bellmawr, N.J.: The Friends of Israel Gospel Ministry, Inc., 1982), 80–81. Showers suggests that the identification of the Son of Man in this passage as "coming with the clouds of heaven" further implies His deity. He writes, "Several Old Testament passages declared that the clouds are the chariot of God (Ps 104:3; Isa 19:1). Thus, the fact that this Son of Man was coming "with clouds of heaven" indicated that He also was deity. Daniel was seeing a person who was deity incarnated in human form. Who was this unique person? Ancient Jewish writers believed that He was the Messiah. Jesus Christ believed the same, for, when He presented Himself as the Messiah during His first coming, He frequently claimed to be the Son of Man who would come with the clouds of heaven (Matt 24:30; 25:31; 26:64). The Apostle John recognized Jesus as this person (Rev 1:7, 13; 14:14)." John F. Walvoord agrees, "The expression that He is attended by 'clouds of heaven' implies His deity.... Clouds in Scripture are frequently characteristics of revelation of deity (Exod 13:21–22; 19:9, 16; 1 Kgs 8:10–11; Isa 19:1; Jer 4:13; Ezek 10:4; Matt 24:30; 26:64; Mark 13:26)." John F. Walvoord, *Daniel: The Key to Prophetic Revelation* (Chicago: The Moody Bible Institute, 1971), 167.

27. Jesus' interaction with Philip in the Upper Room (John 14:7–11) indicates that while the disciples believed Jesus to be the Messiah, they were not entirely clear on the concept of His deity.

28. Although a detailed defense of dispensational theology, vis-à-vis the distinction between God's program for the Church and God's program for Israel, is beyond the scope of this present work, it should be pointed out that the precise content of saving faith changes with each new dispensation in human history. That is, although sinners in all ages have been saved by grace through faith alone, the object of saving faith is not the same in each age. Abraham, for example, was saved by faith but his saving faith did not have as its specific object a Redeemer named "Jesus" as required in the present age (cf. Gen 15:6). During Jesus' earthly ministry, saving faith required the affirmation that Jesus was Messiah. Today, during the present church age, characterized among other distinctions by a "blindness" for Israel (Rom 11:25), saving faith does not have Christ's Messiahship as part of its core essence.

Recognition of the distinction in the unique content of saving faith within each dispensation is a hallmark of dispensational theology. Consider the following quote from the doctrinal statement of Dallas Theological Seminary, widely acknowledged as the dispensational standard-bearer since its foundation in the 1920s. "We believe that according to the 'eternal purpose' of God (Eph. 3:11) salvation in the divine reckoning is always 'by grace through faith,' and rests upon the basis of the shed blood of Christ. We believe that God has always been gracious, regardless of the ruling dispensation, but that man has not at all times been under an administration or stewardship of grace as is true in the present dispensation (1 Cor. 9:17; Eph. 3:2; 3:9, asv; Col. 1:25; 1 Tim. 1:4, asv). We believe that it has always been true that 'without faith it is impossible to please' God (Heb. 11:6), and that the principle of faith was prevalent in the lives of all the Old Testament saints. *However, we believe that it was historically impossible that they should have had as the conscious object of their faith the incarnate, crucified Son, the Lamb of God* (John 1:29), and that it is evident that they *did not comprehend as we do that the sacrifices depicted the person and work of Christ.*" (From Point 5 of the Dallas Theological Seminary doctrinal statement, available at http://www.dts.edu/about/ doctrinalstatement/, emphasis added.) n.b. The statement explicitly acknowledges the fact that the precise content of saving faith in the present age (viz. the "person and work of Christ") differs from the precise content of saving faith for Old Testament saints, for whom it was impossible for the crucified Son of God to be the "conscious object of their faith."

For further study on dispensational soteriology see Lewis Sperry Chafer, *Salvation* (New York: C. C. Cook, 1917), 42–53, Robert Paul Lightner, *Sin, the Savior, and Salvation: The Theology of Everlasting Life* (Nashville: T. Nelson Publishers, 1991), 158–77, Earl D. Radmacher, *Salvation*, Swindoll Leadership Library (Nashville: Word, 2000), 113–28, Ryrie, *Dispensationalism*, 105–22.

29. Appeal often is made to 1 John in support of the contention that explicit belief in the deity of Christ is a necessary component of saving faith. Passages such as 1 John 4:2, 15; 5:1, and 5:20 are interpreted as requiring a belief in the deity of Christ in order to be a Christian. A closer examination of the context of these passages, however, reveals that they are not referring to the essence of saving faith but rather to the requirement for believers to maintain right fellowship with God. 1 John is written to encourage believers to maintain fellowship with God through the Son. This concept of *fellowship* is expressed through the Greek word μένω (lit. "remain"), usually translated "abide." To abide in Christ is to remain in right fellowship with Him. See Joseph C. Dillow, "Abiding Is Remaining in Fellowship: Another Look at John 15:1–6," *BSac* 147, no. 585 (1990): 44–53.

In this context of abiding in close fellowship with Christ, John cautions believers, "Whoever confesses *that Jesus is the Son of God*, God abides in Him and he in God" (1 John 4:15, emphasis added), and "Whoever believes *that Jesus is the Christ* is born of God..." (1 John 5:1, emphasis added). While these verses often are taken as indicating that denial of Christ's deity indicates that one is not a Christian, this is not John's point. John's point is that believers cannot abandon their belief in the deity of Christ, as the false teachers of that day were encouraging them to do, and yet remain in *right fellowship* with Him.

John's use of μένω in John 15:1–8 (The Upper Room Discourse) helps clarify its use in 1 John and further demonstrates that "abiding in Christ" is not equivalent to "being a Christian" since in the

Gospel of John context Jesus commands the Eleven (Judas was no longer present) to "abide in Me" in order to *bear much fruit*. That the Eleven are already believers at the time of Jesus' statement is beyond dispute. Jesus' command to "abide in Him" was not an evangelistic appeal but rather a call to the disciples to walk in close fellowship with Him in order to bear fruit and glorify God (John 15:8). For an excellent discussion of John's use of the word "abide" see Gary Derickson and Earl Radmacher, *The Disciplemaker* (Salem, Ore.: Charis Press, 2001), 332–35, Zane C. Hodges, *The Epistles of John: Walking in the Light of God's Love* (Irving, Tex.: Grace Evangelical Society, 1999). For a helpful exposition of John 15:1–8 see Gary Derickson, "Viticulture and John 15:1–6," *Journal of the Grace Evangelical Society* 18, no. 1 (Spring 2005), Derickson and Radmacher, *The Disciplemaker*, 149–95, 326–29.

30. It should be noted that even though explicit affirmation of the doctrine of the deity of Christ may not be a necessary aspect of saving faith, if one explicitly *denies* or *rejects* Christ's deity at the time of his profession of faith, such a denial likely indicates that his belief is misplaced. That is, one cannot trust in Jesus alone as the giver of eternal life while simultaneously denying His deity. Simply put, saving faith must not deny the deity of Christ though it is not necessarily required to affirm it explicitly in so many words.

31. Cf. *BDAG*, 3d ed. (Chicago: University of Chicago Press, 2000), 982, 985.

32. See *Appendix B: 109 NT Occurrences of Σώζω*. For a more thorough discussion of σώζω see Joseph C. Dillow, *The Reign of the Servant Kings* (Hayesville, N.C.: Schoettle Publishing Co., 1992), 111–33, Radmacher, *Salvation*, 3–14. Although the present writer is not always comfortable with Dillow's handling of individual biblical passages—especially when it comes to his conclusions about some of the implications of the believer's rewards at the Bema Judgment—his work in *the Reign of the Servant Kings* is an excellent resource.

33. See for example Radmacher, *Salvation*, 3–14.

34. While it is the *eternal* aspect of salvation that is essential in the gospel, it is worth noting that the biblical phrase *eternal life* has both a *present* and *future* reality. At the moment of conversion, one receives (present possession) eternal life. John's gospel often highlights the present reality of one's newly obtained eternal life, at times even shortening the reference to life (i.e., omitting the qualifier eternal). E.g. "The thief does not come except to steal, and to kill, and to destroy. I have come that they *may have life*, and that they may have it more abundantly" (John 10:10, emphasis added). By contrast, Paul's epistles often emphasize the future reality of eternal life. E.g. "…having been justified by His grace we should become heirs according to *the hope of eternal life*" (Titus 3:7, emphasis added).

Eternal life ultimately involves spending eternity with God in the new heavens and new earth during the eternal state (cf. Rev 21:1–27). When the present writer refers to a believer "going to heaven," *heaven* serves as a metonym for the afterlife for believers. It is understood that during the first one thousand years following Christ's return believers will not be in heaven *per se*, but rather on the old earth where they will serve with Christ during His millennial reign.

35. Lewis Sperry Chafer, *Systematic Theology*, vol. 3 Soteriology (Dallas: Dallas Seminary Press, 1948), 234–66.

36. For example, "peace" (Rom 5:1), "reconciliation" (2 Cor 5:17–21), "forgiveness' (Acts 13:38), "redemption" (Gal 3:13), and others.

37. Zane C. Hodges, "Assurance: Of the Essence of Saving Faith," *Journal of the Grace Evangelical Society* 10, no. 1 (Spring 1997): 7.

38. Henry Wadsworth Longfellow, "A Psalm of Life," in *One Hundred and One Famous Poems*, ed. Roy J. Cook (Chicago: The Reilly & Lee Co., 1958), 123.

39. See discussion of pluralism in chapter two. See also a more detailed case study of the *Pluralistic Gospel* in chapter seven.

40. From Chapter Six of *The Amsterdam Declaration, 2000: A Charter for Evangelism in the 21ˢᵗ Century*, cited in J. I. Packer and Thomas C. Oden, *One Faith: The Evangelical Consensus* (Downer's Grove: InterVarsity Press, 2004), 137.

41. This is an important point that must not be passed over too quickly. One arrives at the essence of the gospel via theological synthesis, not arbitrary proof-texting. That is, there is no single verse that states in so many words, "Thus saith the Lord: the precise content of saving faith is..." As with all doctrine, the content of saving faith is determined based upon a comparison of Scripture with Scripture that takes into account the progress of revelation. Some within evangelicalism, who have rightly been termed "minimalists," have stripped the gospel of some of its essential elements based upon an improper hermeneutic that fails to acknowledge the role of theological synthesis in the Bible study process. For instance, a small minority of evangelical theologians now suggest that knowledge of Christ's work on the cross is optional when it comes to saving faith.

This view is based upon, among other things, the naïve observation that nowhere does Scripture call man to "believe in Christ's death and resurrection" in order to be saved. But if the same theological method were to be applied to other doctrinal matters, several foundational standards of Christian orthodoxy would come under question. For instance, doctrines such as the Trinity, the hypostatic union, and the inerrancy of Scripture are all matters of theological synthesis and not based upon a single proof-text. To be clear: These doctrines are true and indispensable. The point is, however, that they are developed through a proper hermeneutic that takes into account the literal-grammatical-historical context of a given passage, and then synthesizes the meaning of one passage with the meaning of other passages, thus resulting in a comprehensive statement of biblical doctrine. For a more in depth critique of the view that one can be saved apart from knowledge of Christ's work on the cross, see note nineteen above.

42. Gordon D. Fee and Douglas K. Stuart, *How to Read the Bible for All It's Worth: A Guide to Understanding the Bible*, 2d ed. (Grand Rapids: Zondervan, 1993), 84, emphasis original. See also Walter A. Henrichsen and Gayle Jackson, *Studying, Interpreting, and Applying the Bible* (Grand Rapids: Lamplighter Books, 1990), Elliott E. Johnson, *Expository Hermeneutics: An Introduction* (Grand Rapids: Academie Books, 1990).

43. Although Peter does not use the term "believe," his exhortation that his listeners "know assuredly [v. 36]" (Gk. ἀσφάλως γινωσκέτω) is semantically similar. BDAG defines the qualifier ἀσφαλως when used with the verb γινώσκω ("know") as "pertaining to being certain, assuredly, certainly" (*BDAG,*147). It will be demonstrated later in this chapter that this is the essence of belief: to know with certainty. Thus, Peter's audience in Acts 2 experienced saving faith in Acts 2:37 when, according to Luke, they were convinced (Gk. Κατανύσσομαι) of the truthfulness of Peter's gospel message. Understood in this way, Acts 2:38 then becomes not an evangelistic appeal but a call to discipleship (repent and be baptized). See discussion of the meaning of *faith*, as compared with *saving faith*, below.

44. That the Messianic/Davidic promise of a Kingdom for Israel included the idea that this Kingdom would be *eternal* is clear in the Old Testament. Cf. 2 Sam 7:13, 16; 1 Kgs 9:5; 1 Chr 17:14; 22:10; 28:7; Ps 45:6; 89:34–37; 145:10–13; Is 9:6–7; Dan 4:3, 34; 7:14, 27; 9:24; 12:2.

45. See *Appendix C: A Survey of the Biblical Usage of the Words Repent and Repentance.*

46. D. A. Carson, *The Gagging of God: Christianity Confronts Pluralism* (Grand Rapids: Zondervan, 1996), 507.

47. Ibid., 508, emphasis original. Carson rightly insists that saving faith is an intellectual exercise and that the gospel has a definable content that must be believed. However, for Carson this is not all there is to saving faith. Carson suggests that the gospel also has an "affective element" that requires an "appeal to the will" (Ibid., 507). According to this view, saving faith occurs only when the sinner has both assented to the truth of the gospel's content and, by an act of his will, volitionally consented to follow and obey Christ. This view of saving faith is quite common and owes to the influence of the Reformed tripartite view of faith as *notitia, assensus, and fiducia*. This definition of saving faith is discussed at length and critiqued later in this chapter.

48. For a helpful, recent contribution to the discussion of the nature of saving faith, see Fred Chay and John Correia, *The Faith that Saves: The Nature of Faith in the New Testament* (Scottsdale, AZ.: Grace Line, Inc., 2008).

49. Gordon Haddon Clark, *What Is Saving Faith?* (Jefferson, Md.: Trinity Foundation, 2004), 17. Clark was a staunch defender of Reformed Theology who nevertheless opposed the standard Reformed notions of saving faith versus spurious faith. The work cited is a reprint of two of his previous works, *Faith and Saving Faith* (1983) and *The Johannine Logos* (1972) here combined into one volume. Although his conclusions regarding the precise object of saving faith are questionable, his delineation of the differences between faith and saving faith and his critique of the notion that faith requires a determination to obey are outstanding.

50. It is impossible to have faith in a person without also understanding and believing certain propositions associated with that person. For instance, the isolated statement, "I believe in Jim," absent any corresponding propositional assertions, is meaningless. Such an ambiguous statement immediately begs such questions as,

"What do you believe about Jim?" or *"What* do you believe Jim will *do?"* In this sense, it is pointless to separate faith in a person from faith in a proposition. Ultimately, all faith is propositional since faith in a person demands corresponding propositions. On the other hand, faith in an isolated proposition does not necessarily demand the presence of a person. E.g. "I believe the earth is round" is a simple proposition with no related personhood attached. This discussion of person versus proposition will be taken up in more detail under the discussion of *What Is Saving Faith?* below. For now it is enough to clarify that generic faith may be defined simply as confidence or assurance in the accuracy or reliability of some stated or implied truth.

51. W. E. Vine, Merrill Frederick Unger, and William White, *Vine's Complete Expository Dictionary of Old and New Testament Words with Topical Index* (Nashville: T. Nelson, 1996), 43, 120. See also Rudolf Bultmann, "Πιστεύω, etc." in *TDNT*, vol. 6 (Grand Rapids: Eerdmans, 1985), 173–228. BDAG suggests the meaning of "reality" in Hebrews 11:1, which while slightly different from the suggestions of other lexicons, nevertheless is consistent with the sense of confidence or assurance. For something to represent reality it must be true—in contrast with false reality which is not true. See BDAG, 1040.

52. It will be demonstrated in the pages to follow that this idea of *confidence* or *assurance* is the essence of the words πίστις and πιστεύω in every New Testament usage with the exception of those instances where the noun πίστις is used in a special sense to refer to the *body of Christian truth* (cf. Acts 13:8; 14:22; 16:5; Gal 1:23; 6:10; 1 Tim 1:19; 4:1; 6:21; Jude 3).

53. E.g. Louis Berkhof, *Systematic Theology*, 2d rev. and enl. ed. (Grand Rapids: Eerdmans Publishing Co., 1941), 493–509. Berkhof suggests, "If the object is a person, it is ordinarily employed in a somewhat pregnant sense, including the deeply religious idea of a *devoted*, believing trust." Berkhof, *Systematic Theology*, 494, emphasis added. Elsewhere, he contends that in certain Greek

constructions faith "includes the idea of *moral motion*, of mental direction towards the object" and "a complete *self-surrender* to God." Berkhof, *Systematic Theology*, 495, emphasis added.

54. Clark, *What Is Saving Faith*, 143.

55. Cf. John 5:38, 46; 8:31, 45–46; 10:37, et al.

56. Note that John here uses παραλαμβάνω ("receive" or "welcome/ embrace") as a synonym for πιστεύω ("believe"). To believe in Jesus is to embrace (i.e., express confidence/assurance in) the truthfulness of His message in John's Gospel about how to have eternal life.

57. Again see Berkhof, *Systematic Theology*, 494–95.

58. Bultmann, *TDNT*, 6:203. It is equally unconvincing to suggest that πιστεύω when used alone, absent either εἰς or ὅτι, (e.g. John 8:31) denotes non-saving faith. See also Charles C. Bing, "The Cost of Discipleship," *Journal of the Grace Evangelical Society* 6, no. 1 (Spring 1993): 49, n. 50.

59. Whether the object of one's faith is *actually* true or not is beside the point. Faith in an untrue or incorrect object is still faith, though of course it is not saving faith. This idea will be expounded further in the pages to follow.

60. Zane C. Hodges, *Absolutely Free! A Biblical Reply to Lordship Salvation* (Grand Rapids: Academie Books/Zondervan, 1989), 29. As discussed previously, Hodges' assertions regarding the precise content of saving faith are seriously misguided. However, his discussion of the intrinsic nature of faith itself is helpful.

61. Benjamin B. Warfield, "Faith," in *Biblical and Theological Studies*, ed. Samuel Craig (Philadelphia: Presbyterian and Reformed Publishing, 1952), 425. See also Charlie Bing, "Why Lordship Faith Misses the Mark for Salvation," *Journal of the Grace Evangelical Society* 12, no. 1 (Spring 1999): 29.

62. It is critical to observe the *personal* aspect of this definition of saving faith. Saving faith occurs when one accepts as true the proposition that Jesus Christ alone, the Son of God, who died and rose again, paid his penalty for sin and has given him eternal life. Comprehending the component parts of the gospel, such as the death and resurrection of Christ, is not enough to save someone. Many unbelievers believe that these facts are true. But they do not believe that Jesus died for them *personally* and that He is the *only hope for their personal salvation*. It is in this way that the *personal* and *propositional* aspects of saving faith unite. For example, someone might suggest that Roman Catholics in general accept as true (believe) the proposition that Jesus is the Son of God who died and rose again. However, most do not believe that He is their *only* hope of *personal* salvation. Rather they rest their hope in additional sacramental components thus violating the essential components of the content of saving faith discussed above.

63. Charles Caldwell Ryrie, *So Great Salvation: What It Means to Believe in Jesus Christ* (Wheaton: Victor Books, 1989), 119, emphasis added.

64. For an excellent response to this concept of saving faith see Bing, "Why Lordship Faith Misses the Mark for Salvation," 28–30, Dillow, *The Reign of the Servant Kings*, 271–91.

65. E.g. Berkhof, *Systematic Theology*, 503–6. There is universal agreement on the first component of the Reformed definition of saving faith. It goes without saying that before someone can believe a proposition he must first comprehend it (*notitia*). The point of disagreement involves the relationship between the second and third aspects of the Reformed notion of saving faith. Berkhof's articulation of *fiducia* is inconsistent and confusing. At times he seems to define it in such a way that it is essentially indistinguishable from the Reformed notion of *assensus*. For instance, regarding *assensus* he writes, "When one embraces Christ by faith, he has a deep conviction of the truth and reality of the object of faith, feels that it meets an important need in his life, and is conscious of an absorbing interest

in it, — and this is assent." Ibid., 504–5. Then he defines *fiducia* as "a personal trust in Christ as Savior…." Ibid. How is "personal trust in Christ" distinguishable from "a deep conviction that Jesus meets an important need in his life"?

66. Well-known reformed theologian R.C. Sproul puts it this way, "The Reformers delimited three essential elements of saving faith: *notitia* (knowledge of the data or content of the gospel), *assensus* (the intellectual acceptance or assent to the truth of the gospel's content), and *fiducia* (personal reliance on or trust in Christ and his gospel)." R. C. Sproul, *Getting the Gospel Right: The Tie That Binds Evangelicals Together* (Grand Rapids: Baker Books, 1999), 168. But again, if the content of the gospel is that "Jesus will save you" how is assent to this truth any different from "trusting" this truth? The subtle distinctions between the Reformed notions of *assensus* and *fiducia* result in two primary problems. First, for those who define *fiducia* as mere trust or reliance on Christ as the only One who can provide eternal salvation, then the distinction between it and *assensus* is non-existent and therefore the tripartite definition of faith proposed by the Reformers is redundant and unnecessary. Second, and more problematic is the fact that some Reformed theologians — perhaps aware that *fiducia* must involve something more if it is to retain legitimacy — define it as the personal determination to obey and follow Christ's commands. As such, saving faith thus takes on the added component of good works and obedience. It is this second problem that is the primary focus of the following section entitled, *The Reformers and the Redefinition of Saving Faith.*

67. Clark, *What Is Saving Faith*, 150. Clark is quoting William Cunningham in William Cunningham, James Buchanan, and James Bannerman, *The Reformers and the Theology of the Reformation* (London: The Banner of Truth Trust, 1967), 122.

68. John Calvin, *Institutes of the Christian Religion*, trans. John Allen, 7th American ed., vol. 1 (Philadelphia: Presbyterian board of Christian education, 1928), 595–98.

69. It is conceded that the Reformers were not always clear on their articulation of saving faith. Cf. R. T. Kendall, *Calvin and English Calvinism to 1649* (New York: Oxford University Press, 1979). Less forgiving of Calvin's imprecision on the nature of saving faith is Stephen Thorson. See Stephen Thorson, "Tensions in Calvin's View of Faith: Unexamined Assumptions in R.T. Kendall's *Calvin and English Calvinism to 1649*," *JETS* 37, no. 3 (September 1994). For an excellent discussion of the evolution of the meaning of faith from Calvin to the Westminster Confession, see Dillow, *The Reign of the Servant Kings*, 245–69.

As discussed in note sixty-six, the issue relates to the definition of *fiducia*. Sometimes *fiducia* is expressed in terms of simple trust or reliance. Cf. Charles Hodge, *Commentary on the Epistle to the Romans* (Grand Rapids: Eerdmans, 1967), 29. But, as is often pointed out, if that is all that is meant by *fiducia*, then the tripartite definition of saving faith is reduced to a tautology. Faith becomes: knowledge of facts, assent to their truthfulness, and belief (i.e., trust/ faith) that they are true. How is assent to truthfulness any different than belief in truthfulness? At other times *fiducia* is said to include the idea of a personal determination to obey or commit oneself to the demands of the gospel. Acknowledgement of this inconsistency has led some scholars to speak in terms of "Calvin's Calvinism" (citing those passages where he avoids the volitional obedience language) versus "Classical Calvinism" (fully permeated with the aspects of volitional obedience). Cf. Zane C. Hodges, "Calvinism Ex Cathedra: A Review of John H. Gerstner's Wrongly Dividing the Word of Truth," *Journal of the Grace Evangelical Society* 4, no. 2 (Autumn 1991), William Young, "Historic Calvinism and Neo-Calvinism (Part One)," *WTJ* 36, no. 1 (Fall 1973), William Young, "Historic Calvinism and Neo-Calvinism (Part Two)," *WTJ* 36, no. 2 (Winter 1974). See also W. Stanford Reid, "Justification by Faith According to John Calvin," *WTJ* 42, no. 2 (Spring 1980).

A detailed appraisal of the Reformers' teaching on saving faith would be tedious and largely inconclusive. Indeed, both supporters and opponents of the view of saving faith being critiqued here have appealed to Calvin and Luther for support. For example, see Thomas G. Llewellen, "Has Lordship Salvation Been Taught Throughout

Church History?" *BSac* 147, no. 55 (1990): 54–68. Some have even suggested that the contemporary notion of Reformed saving faith actually has more in common with the Roman Catholic understanding of saving faith than with the Reformers'! For instance, Earl Radmacher laments, "I fear that some current definitions of faith and repentance are not paving the road back to Wittenberg but, rather, paving the road back to Rome. Justification is becoming 'to make righteous' rather than 'to declare righteous.' Repentance is becoming 'penitence' (if not 'penance') rather than 'changing the mind.' And 'faith' is receiving more analysis and scrutinizing rather than the 'object of faith.'" Earl D. Radmacher, "First Response to 'Faith According to the Apostle James' by John F. Macarthur, Jr.," *JETS* 33, no. 1 (March 1990): 40–41. For the purpose of this present work, it is enough to point out only that the popular notion of saving faith under consideration has its roots in the Protestant Reformation.

For a more detailed treatment of this issue, see Philip F. Congdon, "Evangelical/Roman Catholic Agreement on the Doctrine of Justification and Its Ramifications for Grace Theologians," *Journal of the Grace Evangelical Society* 13, no. 1 (Spring 2000): 11–23, Paul Holloway, "A Return to Rome: Lordship Salvation's Doctrine of Faith," *Journal of the Grace Evangelical Society* 4, no. 2 (Autumn 1991): 13–21, Mike Stallard, "Justification by Faith or Justification by Faith Alone?" *Conservative Theological Society Journal* 3, no. 8 (April 1999): 53–73.

70. Art Farstad, "The Words of the Gospel: Believe/Faith," *Grace In Focus*, June 1991, emphasis original.

71. Clark, *What Is Saving Faith*, 47.

72. John MacArthur, *The Gospel According to Jesus: What Does Jesus Mean When He Says "Follow Me"?* rev. and exp. ed. (Grand Rapids: Zondervan, 1994), 173–75. MacArthur plainly states that it is this third component of faith that is at issue in the debate over the essence of saving faith. Elsewhere he writes, "Commitment is the disputed element of faith around which the lordship controversy swirls." John MacArthur, *Faith Works: The Gospel According*

to the Apostles (Dallas: Word Pub., 1993), 43. For a review of MacArthur's *The Gospel According to Jesus*, see Darrell L. Bock, "A Review of The Gospel According to Jesus," *BSac* 146, no. 581 (Jan 1989): 21–40, J. Kevin Butcher, "A Critique of The Gospel According to Jesus," *Journal of the Grace Evangelical Society* 2, no. 1 (Spring 1989): 27–43, Homer A. Kent, "Review Article: The Gospel According to Jesus," *Grace Theological Journal* 10, no. 1 (Spring 1989): 67–77. For a review of MacArthur's *Faith Works*, see Robert A. Pyne, "Review of Faith Works: The Gospel According to the Apostles," *BSac* 150, no. 600 (October 1993): 497–99.

73. Michael P. Andrus, "Turning to God: Conversion Beyond Mere Religious Preference," in *Telling the Truth: Evangelizing Postmoderns*, ed. D. A. Carson (Grand Rapids: Zondervan, 2000), 159–61, emphasis original. Andrus's premise is that churches today are baptizing converts too hastily. Many people who profess faith in Christ are not really saved, he contends, and thus should not be allowed to experience believer's baptism. His conclusion is that churches should emphasize obedience as a fundamental component of the gospel (Ibid., 162).

74. There are at least three broad ways in which repentance has been understood by theologians: (1) *A willingness to stop sinning and surrender to the Lordship of Christ as an inseparable part of saving faith.* Saving faith, it is suggested, must include repentance as so defined. Adherents of this view include John Gerstner, J. I. Packer, John F. MacArthur, James Montgomery Boice, John R. W. Stott and most Reformed scholars who view faith as requiring obedience to be valid. Stott provides a good summary statement of this view: "Repentance is a definite turn from every thought, word, deed and habit which is known to be wrong.... It is an inward change of mind and attitude *towards sin* which leads to a *change of behavior*." John R. W. Stott, *Basic Christianity* (London: Intervarsity Press, 1971), 110, emphasis added. Notice the emphasis on sin and behavior. This view is the subject of the present critique. For a more detailed critique of the notion that repentance of sins is a necessary component of saving faith see Robert N. Wilkin's six-part series in *The Journal of the*

Grace Evangelical Society beginning with the Autumn, 1988 issue. See also David R. Anderson, "Repentance Is for All Men," *Journal of the Grace Evangelical Society* 11, no. 1 (Spring 1998): 3–20, Hodges, *Absolutely Free! A Biblical Reply to Lordship Salvation*, 143–63, Lightner, *Sin, the Savior, and Salvation: The Theology of Everlasting Life*, 167, 212, Ryrie, *So Great Salvation: What It Means to Believe in Jesus Christ*, 89–100, Robert N. Wilkin, *Confident in Christ: Living by Faith Really Works* (Irving, Tex.: Grace Evangelical Society, 1999), 199–210, and Robert N. Wilkin, "Does Your Mind Need Changing? Repentance Reconsidered," *Journal of the Grace Evangelical Society* 11, no. 1 (Spring 1998): 35–46.

(2) *A complete change in one's thinking about God and Christ.* This is the classic dispensational view of Lewis Sperry Chafer and H. A. Ironside and the view of the present writer. Ironside describes repentance as "a complete reversal of one's inward attitude.... To repent is to change one's attitude toward self, toward sin, toward God, and toward Christ." Harry A. Ironside, *Except Ye Repent* (New York: American Tract Society, 1937), 5. This view of repentance has some merit since the lexical meaning of the biblical term repent (μετανοέω) is "to change one's mind" and the words repent and repentance occasionally *do* refer to the process of salvation as whole viz. "a change of mind about God, Christ and the means of salvation" (cf. Luke 24:47; Acts 11:18; 17:30; 20:21; 26:20; Rom 2:4; Heb 6:1). Yet, it may be an oversimplification of the issue since there are times when repentance clearly involves a call to change one's actions (i.e., stop sinning). Most often, the terms in Scripture carry the connotation of *a change of mind about sin* with the result that one stops sinning (cf. Luke 13:3, 5; Acts 8:22; 2 Cor 7:9, 10; 12:21; 2 Tim 2:25; Heb 6:6; 2 Pet 3:9; every occurrence in the book of Revelation). When used in this way (i.e., change your sinful behavior), Scripture never indicates that repentance is a *condition for eternal life* (as adherents to the first view suggest). Rather, it is a generic call upon all men, saved and unsaved alike, to stop sinning or face the consequences (either temporally or eternally). For an overview of the biblical usage of the terms *repent* and *repentance*, see *Appendix C: A Survey of the Biblical Usage of the Words Repent and Repentance*.

(3) *The Roman Catholic view* wherein repentance is defined in terms of confession and doing acts of penance. This view is based upon Roman Catholic tradition rather than sound biblical exegesis and therefore may be rejected.

For further discussion of the issue of repentance from a perspective that differs from the present writer's view see R. N. Wilkin, "Repentance as a Condition for Salvation" (Th.D. diss., Dallas Theological Seminary, 1985). See also Zane C. Hodges, *Harmony with God: A Fresh Look at Repentance* (Dallas: Redencion Viva, 2001).

75. Hodges, for example, writes, "The fourth gospel says nothing at all about repentance, much less does it connect repentance in any way to eternal life. This fact is the death knell for lordship theology. Only a resolute blindness can resist the obvious conclusion: *John did not regard repentance as a condition for eternal life.* If he had, he would have said so. After all, that's what his book is all about: obtaining eternal life (John 20:30–31)." Hodges, *Absolutely Free! A Biblical Reply to Lordship Salvation*, 148, emphasis original. It should be noted, however, that Hodges is addressing specifically the classic Reformed view of repentance wherein it is claimed that one must be willing to stop sinning and surrender to the Lordship of Christ in order to be saved. Insofar as *repentance* sometimes refers to a general change of mind about God, Christ and self when used in the context of receiving eternal salvation, this particular nuance of repentance may indeed be present in John's gospel even though the terms repent and repentance are not themselves used (cf. John 12:37–41, esp. v. 40). As mentioned in the previous note, the present writer does not share Hodges' view on repentance as it relates to eternal salvation.

76. MacArthur, *The Gospel According to Jesus*, 162–67.

77. Mark Dever and Paul Alexander, *The Deliberate Church: Building Your Ministry on the Gospel* (Wheaton: Crossway Books, 2005), 44.

78. James H. Brookes, *How to Be Saved or the Sinner Directed to the Saviour* (Grand Rapids: Baker Book House, 1967), 53–54, emphasis added.

79. It is important to note that the *spurious faith* label is not normally employed to refer merely to those whose faith is in the wrong object. That is, spurious faith is not simply a synonym for *non-saving faith*. It is axiomatic that not all faith saves. What makes faith non-saving, however, is its content, not some inherent deficiency in the faith itself.

For example, someone who believes in the five pillars of Islam as the means of obtaining eternal life has expressed non-saving faith, but it would not be considered *spurious faith* under the normal usage of the phrase. Spurious faith is a label usually reserved for those who have believed the Christian gospel, but whose faith lacks the elements of obedience and surrender that allegedly are required to make such faith "real." It is this idea of spurious faith that is being critiqued in this present section.

80. In response to the charge that their notion of saving faith makes works instrumental in securing eternal life, Reformed scholars are often quick to point out that the required good works in their system do not originate with man himself, but rather are the guaranteed product of regeneration. This is because many who hold this view (though not all) contend that regeneration precedes faith in the *ordo salutis*. For example, R. C. Sproul writes, "Regeneration is not the fruit or result of faith. Rather, *regeneration precedes faith* as the necessary condition for faith…. God chooses to regenerate us before we will ever choose to embrace Him. To be sure, *after* we have been regenerated by the sovereign grace of God, we do choose, act, cooperate, and believe in Christ." R. C. Sproul, *Essential Truths of the Christian Faith*, paperback ed. (Wheaton: Tyndale House, 1998), 172, emphasis original. Elsewhere, Sproul writes, "In regeneration, God changes our hearts. He gives us *a new disposition, a new inclination*." R. C. Sproul, *Chosen by God*, paperback ed. (Wheaton: Tyndale House Publishers, 1994), 215, emphasis added.

81. John F. MacArthur, "Faith According to the Apostle James," *JETS* 33, no. 1 (March 1990): 16, emphasis added.

82. Morris, *The Gospel According to John: The English Text with Introduction, Exposition and Notes*, 454, emphasis added.

83. J. I. Packer, *Concise Theology: A Guide to Historic Christian Beliefs* (Wheaton: Tyndale House, 1993), 160, emphasis added. It is somewhat puzzling that Packer would invoke Galatians 5:6 to make his point that saving faith requires good works. The context of Galatians 5:6 says nothing about how to obtain eternal life. Rather, Paul is speaking about the believer's sanctification and the principle that neither Jewish believers nor Gentile believers can grow in their faith if they place themselves under the bondage of the law (cf. Gal 3:3; 4:9; 5:1). To suggest that "faith working through love" (Gal 5:6) means that one's faith must produce good works in order to be *real* saving faith is an example of reading one's theology into the passage.

84. The frequent reference by Reformed theologians to "head faith" versus "heart faith," such as the reference by Packer in the preceding quote, is unfortunate and does not advance their argument. It has been shown definitively by more than one study that the references to "heart" and "mind" throughout Scripture are used interchangeably. Cf. "Thus my heart was grieved, And I was vexed in my mind" (Ps 73:21; note the synonymous parallelism); "Then I will raise up for Myself a faithful priest *who* shall do according to what *is* in My heart and in My mind. I will build him a sure house, and he shall walk before My anointed forever" (1 Sam 2:35); "I, the LORD, search the heart, *I* test the mind, Even to give every man according to his ways, According to the fruit of his doings" (Jer 17:10); "Oh, let the wickedness of the wicked come to an end, But establish the just; For the righteous God tests the hearts and minds" (Ps 7:9); "Jesus said to him, *'You shall love the LORD your God with all your heart, with all your soul, and with all your mind'*" (Matt 22:37); "Draw near to God and He will draw near to you. Cleanse *your* hands, *you* sinners; and purify *your* hearts, *you* double minded" (Jas 4:8); "I will kill her

children with death, and all the churches shall know that I am He who searches the minds and hearts. And I will give to each one of you according to your works" (Rev 2:23); "For as he thinks in his heart, so *is* he. 'Eat and drink!' he says to you, But his heart is not with you" (Prov 23:7); et al.

Though this is only a partial list, "the Scriptural evidence that the term heart means the mind, the intellect, the understanding, is ... tedious in length." Clark, *What Is Saving Faith?* 59. Indeed, "The three terms—heart, soul, and mind—are synonymous, joined together for emphasis. They do not separate the heart and the mind: They identify them" (Ibid., 61). Since heart and mind are usually synonymous in Scripture, there can be no distinction between so-called "heart faith" and "head faith." In advancing their view of spurious faith, Reformed scholars would do well to abandon this terminology. For a detailed examination of the biblical data on "mind" versus the "heart" see Clark, *What Is Saving Faith?* 55–62. See also Bob Wilkin, "Head Faith, Heart Faith, and Mind Games," *Grace In Focus*, May-June 2001: 1.

85. For a good summary of the *spurious faith* view from one of its proponents, see Walter J. Chantry, *Today's Gospel: Authentic or Synthetic?* (Carlisle, Pa.: Banner of Truth Trust, 1970).

86. John MacArthur, *Hard to Believe: The High Cost and Infinite Value of Following Christ* (Nashville: Thomas Nelson, 2003), 93, emphasis added. For an excellent response to this book see Robert N. Wilkin, "A Review of John Macarthur's *Hard to Believe: The High Cost and Infinite Value of Following Jesus*," *Journal of the Grace Evangelical Society* 17, no. 33 (Autumn 2004): 3–9. It has already been noted that Wilkin's view of the content of saving faith represents a departure from classical evangelical orthodoxy. Nevertheless, his critique of works-based gospel models is helpful and his work in clarifying salvation as a free gift has had a profound positive impact on evangelicalism.

87. MacArthur, *Faith Works: The Gospel According to the Apostles*, 199. For a full-length review of this book see Robert N. Wilkin,

"The High Cost of Salvation by Faith-Works: A Critique of John F. Macarthur, Jr.'s 'Faith Works: The Gospel According to the Apostles'," *Journal of the Grace Evangelical Society* 6, no. 2 (Autumn 1993): 3–24.

88. Elsewhere, MacArthur explains that this gospel is deficient precisely because it "encourages people to claim Jesus as Savior yet defer until later the *commitment to obey* Him as Lord.... By separating faith from faithfulness, it leaves the impression that intellectual assent is as valid as *wholehearted obedience* to the truth." MacArthur, *The Gospel According to Jesus: What Does Jesus Mean When He Says "Follow Me"*, 15–16, emphasis added. This insistence that obedience is a vital component of faith is a prevalent theme in MacArthur's writings.

89. Ryrie, *So Great Salvation: What It Means to Believe in Jesus Christ*, 123.

90. Charles R. Swindoll, *The Grace Awakening* (Dallas: Word Pub., 1990), 87, emphasis original.

91. Indeed, usually opponents of the Reformed notion of saving faith explicitly deny that saving faith is only the comprehension of facts. E.g. "[M]ental acquiescence to the fact of Christ's death, without any conviction of personal sin, is inadequate." Livingston Blauvelt, Jr., "Does the Bible Teach Lordship Salvation?" *BSac* 143, no. 569 (January 1986): 37.

92. MacArthur, *Faith Works: The Gospel According to the Apostles*, 194, emphasis added.

93. For example, "There are people who teach that it is possible to be a Christian, to be saved by faith, and yet not be committed to Jesus.... The answer to this error is to point to the devil, who knows the doctrines of the gospel and believes they are true, but who certainly has not committed himself to follow Christ. James was speaking of this false faith, contrasting it with true faith, when he wrote that

the devils also 'believe' but 'shudder.'" James Montgomery Boice, *The Glory of God's Grace: The Meaning of God's Grace—and How It Can Change Your Life* (Grand Rapids: Kregel Publications, 1999), 87. "My question is, what kind of faith is it that permits a person, having affirmed Jesus Christ as Jehovah God, to continue in an unbroken pattern of sin and rebellion? Is that not demonic faith (James 2:19), orthodox but not efficacious?" MacArthur, *The Gospel According to Jesus: What Does Jesus Mean When He Says "Follow Me"*, 74, n. 1. See also Mark Proctor, "Faith, Works, and the Christian Religion," *The Evangelical Quarterly* 69, no. 4 (1997): 307–32.

94. E.g. NKJV: But someone will say, "You have faith, and I have works." Show me your faith without your works, and I will show you my faith by my works. You believe that there is one God. You do well. Even the demons believe—and tremble (Jas 2:18–19).

NASB: But someone may *well* say, "You have faith and I have works; show me your faith without the works, and I will show you my faith by my works." You believe that God is one. You do well; the demons also believe, and shudder (Jas 2:18–19).

Good News: But someone will say, "One person has faith, another has actions." My answer is, "Show me how anyone can have faith without actions. I will show you my faith by my actions." Do you believe that there is only one God? Good! The demons also believe—and tremble with fear (Jas 2:18–19).

Living Bible: But someone may well argue, "You say the way to God is by faith alone, plus nothing; well, I say that good works are important too, for without good works you can't prove whether you have faith or not; but anyone can see that I have faith by the way I act." Are there still some among you who hold that "only believing" is enough? Believing in one God? Well, remember that the demons believe this too—so strongly that they tremble in terror (Jas 2:18–19)!

95. The Majority Text has *dead* (Gk. νέκρα) in verse twenty rather than *useless* (ἀργη) as found in the older manuscripts. If the original word was *dead*, and a scribe later changed it to *useless*, it indicates

that early in church history it was assumed that by *dead* James meant that the faith of believers, absent works, is useless or ineffective. If, rather, the original word was in fact *useless*, then the contention that James' was speaking of ineffective, unproductive faith of believers is even stronger. In any event, neither textual variant supports the view that *dead faith* is *non-saving faith* (i.e., faith that does not result in eternal salvation).

96. Cf. Paul's reference to sin being "dead" (Gk. νέκρα) before the law came (Rom 7:8). This, of course, does not mean that sin was not *real*, only that upon the introduction of the Law to Jewish life, sin became more emboldened and vivid. The Law highlighted sin just as good works highlight one's faith.

97. The Greek construction of James' question "Can faith save him?" demands a "no" answer.

98. See *Appendix B: 109 NT Occurrences of Σώζω ("Save")*.

99. James' illustration of "a brother or sister [who] is naked and destitute of food" (2:15–17) also is in keeping with his theme of the practical value of the believer's faith when it is accompanied by works.

100. The word profit (2:14) is the Greek noun ὄφέλος, which means "that which is heaped up, accumulated or increased." It is sometimes translated "advantage" (Cf. 1 Cor 15:32; Job 15:3, LXX). It is only used three times in the NT, twice in this passage (vv. 14, 16) and once by Paul in 1 Cor 15:32. The related verb form (ὀφελέω) is used fifteen times and means "to benefit or gain." In the immediately preceding verses (vv. 12–13), James warned his readers that they should behave properly because they will be judged one day. Since the only future judgment awaiting Christians is the Judgment Seat of Christ, this must be what is in view here. In verse 13, James urges his readers to show mercy so that they will be shown mercy at the Judgment Seat themselves. *Immediately after saying that,* he asks them "What does it profit, my brothers, if you do not have good

works?" It is likely that James is alluding to the profit of "accumulating" particular eschatological benefits at the Judgment Seat (cf. the similar idea in Heb 4:2 where ὀφελέω is used). Note also the connection between "speaking" and "doing" in verse 12 and "saying" and "works" in verse 14. Verse twelve says, "speak and do" in such a way that you will be judged favorably. Verse fourteen asks what value is it if one only "speaks" his faith but does not "do" it (cf. Jas 1:21–25)?

101. The phrase καλως ποιεις ("do well") in verse nineteen though given the sense "Good for you!" in most English translations, can also be translated "you do good." Hodges writes, "The Greek phrase (*kalos poieis*) is here taken in the sense of 'do good,' 'do right,' which seems the most appropriate sense in Matt 5:44; 12:12; Luke 6:27. It is also viable in Acts 10:33 ('you did the right thing to come') and even in James 2:8 ('If you keep the royal law … you are doing what's right.')." Zane C. Hodges, *Dead Faith: What Is It?* (Dallas: Redencion Viva, 1987), 31, n. 26. Although Hodges' more recent view on the content of saving faith represents a serious doctrinal aberration, his status as a renowned Greek scholar is without dispute.

102. John F. Hart, "The Faith of Demons," *Journal of the Grace Evangelical Society* 8, no. 2 (Autumn 1995): 54. For a fuller treatment of James 2:19–26 from a similar perspective see Thomas L. Constable, *Expository Notes on James* (Garland, Tex.: Sonic Light, 2006), 27–37, Hart, "The Faith of Demons," 39–54, John F. Hart, "How to Energize Our Faith: Reconsidering the Meaning of James 2:14–26," *Journal of the Grace Evangelical Society* 12, no. 1 (Spring 1999): 37–66, Hodges, *Dead Faith: What Is It*, Zane C. Hodges, *The Epistle of James: Proven Character through Testing: A Verse by Verse Commentary* (Irving, Tex.: Grace Evangelical Society, 1994), 58–72, Zane C. Hodges, "Light on James Two from Textual Criticism," *BSac* 120, no. 480 (October 1963): 341–50, Robert N. Wilkin, "Another View of Faith and Works in James 2," *Journal of the Grace Evangelical Society* 15, no. 2 (Autumn 2002): 3–21.

103. William Hendriksen, *A Commentary on the Gospel of John*, 3d ed. (London: Banner of Truth Trust, 1964), 127, emphasis added. See also Edwin A. Blum, "John," in *The Bible Knowledge Commentary, vol. 2*, ed. John F. Walvoord and Roy B. Zuck (Wheaton: Victor Books, 1983), 280, William MacDonald and Arthur L. Farstad, *Believer's Bible Commentary: A Complete Bible Commentary in One Volume* (Nashville: Thomas Nelson, 1995), 1476–77, Elmer Towns, *The Gospel of John: Believe and Live*, ed. Mal Couch and Ed Hindson, Twenty-First Century Biblical Commentary Series (Chattanooga, Tenn.: AMG Publishers, 2002), 23–24. Although most commentators would agree with the ones cited here that this passage supports the notion of spurious faith, one should keep in mind that an interpretation is not proven accurate merely because it is the majority view.

104. Zane C. Hodges, "Problem Passages in the Gospel of John Part 2: Untrustworthy Believer—John 2:23–25," *BSac* 135, no. 538 (April 1978): 140. However, note the present writer's critique of Hodges' view of the content of saving faith contained earlier in this present work.

105. Ibid., 146–48.

106. E.g. Gerald L. Borchert, *John 1–11*, The New American Commentary, vol. 25a (Nashville: Broadman & Holman, 1996), 274, Morris, *The Gospel According to John: The English Text with Introduction, Exposition and Notes*, 386–87, Rodney A. Whitacre, *John*, ed. Grant Osborne, The IVP New Testament Commentary Series, vol. 4 (Downer's Grove: InterVarsity Press, 1999), 175–76.

107. J. Dwight Pentecost, *Design for Discipleship* (Grand Rapids: Zondervan Publishing House, 1971), 8–16.

108. Constable, *Expository Notes on John*, 115–16.

109. E.g. Everett F. Harrison, *John the Gospel of Faith*, Everyman's Bible Commentary (Chicago: Moody Press, 1962), 54–55, Merrill C.

Tenney, *The Gospel of John*, in The Expositor's Bible Commentary, vol. 9, ed. Frank E. Gaebelein, (Grand Rapids: Zondervan, 1981), 94–95, Whitacre, *John*, 218–219.

110. See note twenty-nine in the present chapter.

111. For a similar treatment of this passage see Bing, "The Cost of Discipleship," 48–50, Bing, "The Condition for Salvation in John's Gospel," 36, Dillow, *The Reign of the Servant Kings*, 150–52. In response to the contention that those who "believed in Him" (v. 30) are distinct from those who "believed Him" based upon the context of verses thirty-three and following, it should be noted that a contextual break occurs in verse thirty wherein Jesus turns His attention to the hostile Jews who had been confronting Jesus with accusations and questions throughout this entire pericope. For example, in 8:13 the Pharisees exclaim "Your witness is not true." In 8:19, they retort "Where is Your Father?" In 8:22, they ask, "Will He kill Himself, because He says, 'Where I go you cannot come'?" In 8:25, they ask disparagingly "Who are You?" John juxtaposes these periodic interjections from the hostile Jews throughout this narrative selection. In verse thirty-three, another one of these interjections occurs when the Jews state emphatically, "We are Abraham's descendants, and have never been in bondage to anyone. How can you say, 'You will be made free'?" The Jews speaking in verse thirty-three are not the same ones whom John indicates believed in Jesus in verses 30–31. Rather, they are unbelievers as the continuing context makes clear (cf. 8:37–47).

112. E.g. William J. Larkin, *Acts*, in the IVP New Testament Commentary Series, ed. Grant Osborne, vol. 5 (Downer's Grove: InterVarsity Press, 1995), 125–27, Richard N. Longenecker, "The Acts of the Apostles," in *The Expositor's Bible Commentary*, vol. 9, ed. Frank E. Gaebelein and J. D. Douglas (Grand Rapids: Zondervan Pub. House, 1981), 358–60, Stanley D. Toussaint, "Acts," in *Bible Knowledge Commentary*, vol. 2, ed. John F. Walvoord and Roy B. Zuck (Wheaton: Victor Books, 1983), 373–74.

113. See the discussion of repentance at note seventy-four.

114. Dillow, *The Reign of the Servant Kings*, 328. For a similar treatment of this passage see ibid., 327–328.

115. E.g. Robert Stein insists that since "they only hold this faith 'for a while' … this text and the full canonical message suggest, this faith is not saving faith." Robert H. Stein, *Luke*, The New American Commentary, vol. 24 (Nashville: Broadman & Holman, 1992), 246. Likewise, John Martin writes, "The fact that they believe for a while but fall away means that they only accept the facts of the Word mentally and then reject it when 'the going gets rough.' It does not mean they lose their salvation, *for they had none to lose*." John A. Martin, "Luke," in *Bible Knowledge Commentary,* vol. 2, ed. John F. Walvoord and Roy B. Zuck (Wheaton: Victor Books, 1983), 225, emphasis added.

116. In a footnote Constable adds, "Most fruit trees bear no fruit for the first few years after their planting, some stop bearing fruit after a while, and others never bear fruit."

117. Thomas L. Constable, *Expository Notes on Luke* (Garland, Tex.: Sonic Light, 2005), 103–4.

118. E.g. C. K. Barrett, *The First Epistle to the Corinthians* (Peabody, Mass.: Hendrickson Publishers, 1993), 131.

119. See Thomas L. Constable, *Expository Notes on First Corinthians* (Garland, Tex.: Sonic Light, 2005), 53–54, MacDonald and Farstad, *Believer's Bible Commentary,* 1760–61, Robert N. Wilkin, "The So-Called So-Called Brother—1 Corinthians 5:11," *The Grace Evangelical Society News*, October 1991: 1.

120. Admittedly, this line of reasoning assumes that the person in 2 Cor 2:5–11 is the same one being discussed in 1 Cor 5:9–13—an assumption that, while common, is not universally accepted.

121. E.g. Frederick Dale Brunner, *Matthew: Volume 1 the Christbook Matthew 1–12* (Dallas: Word, 1987), 287, D. A. Carson, "Matthew," in *The Expositor's Bible Commentary*, vol. 8, ed. Frank E. Gaebelein and J. D. Douglas (Grand Rapids: Zondervan, 1984), 192, MacArthur, *Faith Works: The Gospel According to the Apostles*, 143, 154, 161–62, John F. MacArthur, *Mathew*, MacArthur New Testament Commentary (Chicago: Moody, 1989), 459–80.

122. For example, Craig Blomberg writes, "Verses 21–22 enumerate some of the ways in which individuals can masquerade as Christians. They may verbally affirm that Jesus is their Master, perhaps even with great joy and enthusiasm, *but such claims must issue in lives of obedience.*" Craig Blomberg, *Matthew*, The New American Commentary, vol. 22 (Nashville: Broadman and Holman, 1992), 132, emphasis added.

123. For a similar treatment of this passage see Dillow, *The Reign of the Servant Kings*, 194–99.

124. E.g. *BDAG*, 1096, emphasis added.

125. Furthermore, the Galatians context implies that the reason they were false brothers is because they were still trusting in the Jewish law and not the gospel. Their non-Christian state had nothing to do with their works. Cf. Ronald Fung, "It thus emerges that the interlopers were sham-Christians *precisely because they had not really grasped the fundamental principle of the gospel—justification by faith apart from works of the law.*" Ronald Y. K. Fung, *The Epistle to the Galatians*, International Commentary on the New Testament (Grand Rapids: Wm. B. Eerdmans Publishing Co., 1988), 94, emphasis added.

126. Bing, "The Condition for Salvation in John's Gospel," 32. It is worth noting that in contemporary English language, the phrase "I believe" is sometimes used in the sense of "I think, but I am not sure." For instance, someone might say, "If we leave now *I believe* we might make it home before noon." But this is a special use of the

English word *believe* and one that is not the subject of the present discussion.

127. Some adherents to the Reformed notion of saving faith create a subcategory of *spurious faith* called "temporary faith." The suggestion is that if someone believes the gospel for a while, but then stops believing it, his faith was spurious. *Real* saving faith, it is suggested, never stops believing the gospel. MacArthur, for example, insists that saving faith cannot be "transient" but must have an "abiding quality that guarantees endurance to the end." MacArthur, *The Gospel According to Jesus: What Does Jesus Mean When He Says "Follow Me"?* 173. Support for this view often comes from the contention on the part of some New Testament Greek scholars that ὁ πιστεύων ("the one who believes") refers to *continuous* belief (an unwarranted appeal to the *habitual present* tense), and thus should be translated, "the one who continues to believe has eternal life." E.g., Daniel B. Wallace, *The Basics of New Testament Syntax: An Intermediate Greek Grammar* (Grand Rapids: Zondervan Pub. House, 2000), 224.

But this use of the present tense is highly disputed among Greek grammarians and fails to explain how similar constructions with other verbs clearly *cannot* carry the "continuous" nuance. For example, ὁ βαπτίζων in Mark 1:4; John 3:23; and 10:40 (cf. John 3:26) surely does not mean that John "continues to baptize." Just as John is called "the Baptist" whether or not he continues to baptize; likewise believers in Christ are referred to as "believers" whether or not they continue to believe. Eternal life is given to those who *believe*, not to those who believe *and keep on believing* (cf. John 6:47; 11:25–26; et al.). That is, at the moment one believes, he receives eternal life. And since it is *eternal,* by definition, it can never be lost—even if the person stops believing years later. Furthermore, if *continuous belief* is required in order to gain eternal life, then one is never truly saved until he dies in a state of continuous belief. For a critique of the "continuous belief" view of saving faith, see Charles Stanley, *Eternal Security: Can You Be Sure?* (Nashville: Oliver Nelson, 1990), 73–83, Robert N. Wilkin, "How Deep Are Your Spiritual

Roots? Luke 8:11–15," *Journal of the Grace Evangelical Society* 12, no. 1 (Spring 1999): 3–19.

128. This is the case with those who profess to be Christians but have never believed the gospel. Often proponents of the Reformed view of saving faith mischaracterize their opponents as not having a category of professing (but unsaved) believers. This is not the case. There exist, undoubtedly, many individuals who profess to be Christians but are not. What makes them unsaved, however, is not some inherent defect in their faith, but the fact that they have never believed the *right content* of saving faith. They think they are saved based on their belief, but because their belief is in a false gospel, they are sadly mistaken. This idea will be expounded later in this chapter in the section entitled "What is Non-Saving Faith?" Cf. note seventy-nine in the present chapter.

129. See *Appendix A: 160+ Verses Demonstrating Justification By Faith Alone.*

130. Hodges, "Assurance: Of the Essence of Saving Faith," 5.

131. Carson articulates well the relationship between so-called *spurious faith* and the doctrine of assurance. See D. A. Carson, "Reflections on Christian Assurance," *WTJ* 54, no. 1 (Spring 1992): 13–21.

132. Regarding perseverance of the saints, see note 139 below.

133. See discussion in chapter two regarding the abandonment of certainty in the postmodern age.

134. John 10:28, emphasis added. Cf. John 5:24; 1 John 5:9–13.

135. Bing, "Why Lordship Faith Misses the Mark for Salvation," 29, Zane C. Hodges, "We Believe In: Assurance of Salvation," *Journal of the Grace Evangelical Society* 3, no. 2 (Autumn 1990): 6.

136. Chafer, *Salvation*, 45.

137. Those who hold to the Reformed notion of spurious faith view doubt as a healthy aid to assurance. In other words, doubt might help some "alleged believers" whose faith is only "spurious" come to realize that they are not really saved. Perhaps John Murray, one of the most well-respected Reformed theologians of the previous century, best articulates the Reformed notion that doubt is healthy and absolute assurance is not the entitlement of all believers: "… the absence of full assurance is due to … disobedience to the commandments of God, backsliding, unwatchfulness, prayerlessness, excessive care for the things of this life, and worldliness. There are many sins which believers are prone to indulge and cause to stumble, with the result that their Father's displeasure is manifest in the withdrawing of the light of his countenance, so that they are bereft of the joy of their salvation. Those who at one time enjoyed this assurance may lose it." John Murray, *Collected Writings of John Murray*, vol. 2 (Carlisle, Pa.: Banner of Truth Trust, 1978), 266. See also Ron Kilpatrick, "Assurance and Sin," in *Doubt and Assurance*, ed. R. C. Sproul (Grand Rapids: Baker Book House for Ligonier Ministries, 1993), 69.

Os Guiness is representative of this common understanding. He writes, "[I]f we doubt in believing, we nevertheless also believe in doubting." Os Guiness, "I Believe in Doubt: Using Doubt to Strengthen Faith," in *Doubt and Assurance*, ed. R. C. Sproul (Grand Rapids: Baker Book House for Ligonier Ministries, 1993), 35. Elsewhere he writes, "Faith is not doubt-free, but there is a genuine assurance of faith that is truly beyond a shadow of a doubt." Os Guinness, *God in the Dark: The Assurance of Faith Beyond a Shadow of Doubt* (Wheaton: Crossway Books, 1996), 15. R. C. Sproul, also a defender of doubt as a healthy component to Christian living, suggests that doubt "has the power to sort out and clarify the difference between the certain and the uncertain, the genuine and the spurious." R. C. Sproul, "The Anatomy of Doubt," in *Doubt and Assurance*, ed. R. C. Sproul (Grand Rapids: Baker Book House for Ligonier Ministries, 1993), 16.

The premise that doubt somehow aids assurance is puzzling. As discussed above, belief and disbelief in the same object cannot co-exist simultaneously. Doubt, by definition, is the *absence* of belief. Therefore, to suggest that doubt fosters assurance is a bit like suggesting that heat strengthens ice. Doubt and assurance are mutually exclusive—they do not *help* one another. And if they did help one another, then the best remedy for a lack of faith would be more doubt! This could lead to ridiculous pastoral implications. When someone comes to a pastor expressing doubt about his salvation, the pastor—following this line of reasoning—should counsel the person, "If you want to have assurance that you are saved, keep doubting your salvation. The more you doubt the more sure you will become because doubt strengthens your faith!" Of course, this is not what proponents of the positive nature of doubt are suggesting. They likely would not encourage doubt. Yet, a logical fallacy exists. If in fact, as they suggest, doubt aids assurance, why *not* encourage doubt?

Appeal often is made to Mark 9:24 to support the notion that faith and doubt in the same object can coexist simultaneously. In the context, a father brings his demon-possessed son to Jesus and asks Jesus to heal him. Jesus responds, "If you can believe, all things are possible to him who believes." The father of the boy then cries out, "Lord, I believe; help my unbelief!" One must be careful not to oversimplify and over-apply this passage. To suggest that the father's statement proves that faith and doubt in the same object can co-exist is unwarranted. In the first place, the faith in question is not an issue of *saving faith*. That is, the issue at hand was not eternal salvation but physical healing. Secondly, in saying "I believe" the man was expressing his general faith in Jesus' claims (he was apparently a believer—a Christian); yet, in saying "help my unbelief" he was expressing doubt about the specific situation at hand, namely, his son's potential for healing. This is not faith and doubt in the same object. All believers, at times, have doubts about God's provision or other specific issues in their Christian life. But it does not follow that such doubts should alert the person to the fact that he may be unsaved.

Although, as mentioned, the Reformers themselves were not always clear on the precise nature of saving faith, it appears that at least Calvin himself disagreed with the notion of doubt and assurance articulated by many contemporary Reformed theologians. Cf. Calvin, *Institutes of the Christian Religion*, 615–19.

138. Hodges, "Assurance: Of the Essence of Saving Faith," 7. Hodges concludes, "It is one of the great absurdities of theology that I can't really know whether I believe God's saving truth or not" (ibid., 8). Hodges' work on the logical fallacies related to the notion of spurious faith represents a helpful contribution to the discussion of the nature of saving faith. However, as mentioned earlier, his conclusions regarding the precise content of saving faith are problematic to say the least.

139. Contrary to the common understanding, the doctrine of the perseverance of the saints (the fifth point in Classic five-point Calvinism) does not refer only to the fact that once one is saved he can never again be lost—a view commonly phrased, *once-saved-always-saved*. Rather, historically the doctrine has included the notion that believers will persist in visible good works throughout their lives. A failure to do so "proves" that their faith was spurious, since, according to this view, God's salvation necessarily brings with it the guarantee of both positional justification and practical sanctification.

The view articulated by famous Reformed theologian Louis Berkhof is representative of this doctrine: "The doctrine of the perseverance of the saints is to the effect that they whom God has regenerated and effectually called to a state of grace, can neither totally nor finally fall away from that state, but shall certainly persevere therein to the end and be eternally saved. This doctrine was first explicitly taught by Augustine, though he was not as consistent on this point as might have been expected of him as a strict predestinarian. ...The doctrine of perseverance of the saints requires careful statement, especially in view of the fact that the term 'perseverance of the saints' is liable to misunderstanding. It should be noted first of all that the doctrine *is not merely to the effect that the elect will certainly be saved in the end*, though Augustine has given it this form, but teaches very specifically that they who have once been regenerated and effectually called by God to a state of grace, can never completely fall from that state and thus fail to attain to eternal salvation, though they may *sometimes* be overcome by evil and fall into sin. *It is maintained that the life of regeneration and the habits that develop out of it in the way of sanctification can never entirely disappear.*" Berkhof, *Systematic Theology*, 545–46, emphasis added. See also Jay E. Adams, "Perseverance of the Saints," in *Distinctives of Reformed Theology: After Darkness, Light: Essays in Honor of R. C. Sproul*, ed. R. C. Sproul Jr. (Phillipsburg, N.J.: P&R Publishing Company, 2003), 173–88, Boice, *The Glory of God's Grace: The Meaning of God's Grace—and How It Can Change Your Life*, 231–45.

140. Carson, "Reflections on Christian Assurance," 29. Elsewhere, Carson writes, "Jesus gives a criterion that establishes who are *genuine* disciples: 'If you hold to my teaching, you are really my disciples' [John 8:31]" (ibid., 17, emphasis original). That Carson equates the terms *disciple* and *Christian* is seen in his conclusion that "genuine faith, by definition, perseveres; where there is no perseverance, by definition the faith cannot be genuine" (ibid.). Carson attempts to ground assurance in such objective standards as "the character of God, the nature of the new covenant, the finality of election, [and] the love of God," but at the same time he insists that fruitlessness creates an "implicit challenge" to one's claim of salvation (ibid., 29).

141. Hodges, "Assurance: Of the Essence of Saving Faith," 11, emphasis original.

142. MacArthur, *The Gospel According to Jesus: What Does Jesus Mean When He Says "Follow Me"*, 23.

143. John MacArthur, *Keys to Spiritual Growth*, Rev. and expanded ed. (Tarrytown, N.Y.: F.H. Revell, 1991), 64–65.

144. After defining repentance of sins as a non-negotiable and mandatory component of saving faith, MacArthur states: "Where there is no observable difference in conduct, there can be no confidence that repentance has taken place." The "lack of confidence" to which MacArthur refers is a lack of assurance that one is saved. MacArthur, *The Gospel According to Jesus: What Does Jesus Mean When He Says "Follow Me"*, 163.

145. Boice, *The Glory of God's Grace: The Meaning of God's Grace—and How It Can Change Your Life*, 238. Boice describes perseverance as "resisting and overcoming the world, the flesh, and the devil, and thus being ready for Jesus when he comes" (ibid., 232).

146. MacArthur, *Faith Works: The Gospel According to the Apostles*, 53, emphasis added.

147. Notice the distinction between "can and should" versus "must." (Cf. "genuine faith *must* result in a life of good works." MacArthur, *Keys to Spiritual Growth*, 65.) It is acknowledged that all believers *should* produce good works. This is what Christians are created to do (Eph 2:10). But to suggest that they *must* do good works or they are not saved gives the impression that good works are an instrumental cause of eternal salvation.

148. For an excellent survey of the major views on assurance see Ken Keathley, "Does Anyone Really Know If They Are Saved? A Survey of the Current Views on Assurance with a Modest Proposal," *Journal of the Grace Evangelical Society* 15, no. 1 (Spring 2002): 37–60. See also Robert N. Wilkin, "When Assurance Is Not Assurance," *Journal of the Grace Evangelical Society* 10, no. 2 (Autumn 1997): 27–34.

The common view that 2 Corinthians 13:5 enjoins believers to examine their works as a basis for assurance is refuted by at least two plausible alternative interpretations. The first is best represented by James H. Brookes, "[T]he context [of 2 Cor 13:5] clearly shows that the question under discussion was about the apostle's right to exercise his high office, and not at all about personal salvation. 'Since you seek a proof of Christ speaking in me,' he says, 'examine yourselves, whether ye be in the faith': for the fact that they were in the faith was conclusive proof that Christ had owned his ministry, and therefore that he was not an imposter in claiming to be an apostle." James H. Brookes, *The Way Made Plain* [*Reprint from Philadelphia: American Sunday-School Union, 1871*], (Grand Rapids: Baker Book House, 1967), 294. Brookes goes on to conclude, "Self-examination as conducted in the manner and to attain the ends for which it is usually urged is the most painful and profitless exercise that can engage the soul, and I would confidently appeal to the experience of every conscientious and intelligent Christian to testify whether this is not true. If you expect to get assurance in this way, you might as well expect to get health by looking at disease, to get light by looking at darkness, to get life by looking at a corpse" (ibid., 294–95).

Similarly, J. N. Darby writes regarding 2 Cor 13:5, "But am I not desired to examine myself, whether I am in the faith? No. What then says 2 Cor 13:5: 'Examine yourselves, whether ye be in the faith?' etc. Why, that if they sought a proof of Christ speaking in Paul, they were to examine themselves, and by the certainty of their own Christianity, which they did not doubt, be assured of his apostleship. The apostle's argument was of no value whatever, but on the ground of the sanctioned certainty that they were Christians." "Operations of the Spirit of God," in *The Collected Writings of J. N. Darby,* edited by William Kelly. Reprint, 1972 (Winschoten, Netherlands: H. L. Heijkoop), 3:76. See also James H. Brookes, "A Voice from the Past: Self-Examination as It Relates to Assurance," *Journal of the Grace Evangelical Society* 6, no. 2 (Autumn 1993): 54, n. 3.

Alternatively, 2 Cor 13:5 may be merely a challenge to the Corinthian readers to examine the quality of their faith to see if they are truly living by faith in a manner that will enable them to stand the test (i.e., avoid "disqualification," v. 5b; cf. 1 Cor 9:27) at the Bema Judgment. This view is probably preferred and is supported by Paul's frequent exhortations elsewhere for believers to remain steadfast in the faith (cf. 1 Cor 16:13; Col 1:23; 2:7). In this sense, Paul's command in 2 Cor 13:5 is for the Corinthian believers to examine themselves to see if they are in the faith *at that moment* (i.e., walking by faith, cf. 2 Cor 5:7).

Another passage to which appeal sometimes is made in support of the view that believers should look to their works for assurance of their salvation is 1 John 2:3. "Now by this we know that we know Him, if we keep His commandments." But such an interpretation fails to recognize that John's purpose in this epistle is to encourage believers to remain in right fellowship (i.e., abide; Gk. μένω) with the Lord. As such, the verb *know* (Gk. γινώσκω) is used in the sense of *know intimately* or *know well*. Cf. John 14:9, "Jesus said to him, 'Have I been with you so long, and yet you have not known Me, Philip?'" Clearly, Jesus was not accusing Philip of being an unbeliever. The same argument applies to other passages throughout 1 John that are often taken as tests of whether one is a Christian or not (cf. 2:9–11; 3:4–9; 3:15; 3:24; 5:18). Cf. the discussion of 1 John in note twenty-nine in the present chapter. Regarding self-examination as it relates to 2 Pet 1:10–11 and Hebrews 6:11–12 see Dillow, *The Reign of the Servant Kings*, 293–99.

149. Barna, *Evangelism That Works: How to Reach Changing Generations with the Unchanging Gospel*, 38–39, emphasis added.

150. For an instructive discussion on the possibility of failure in the Christian life see Dillow, *The Reign of the Servant Kings*, 209–43.

151. For a true story illustrating the practical consequences of the Reformed notion of spurious faith see J. B. Hixson, "Dan's Dilemma," *Grace In Focus*, Jan-Feb 2002: 1.

152. David R. Anderson, "The Nature of Faith," *Chafer Theological Seminary Journal* 5, no. 4 (September 1999): 25–26, emphasis original. For an excellent discussion of the distinction between *faith* and *saving faith* see also Clark, *What Is Saving Faith*, 16–90, 141–60. Other helpful resources include Radmacher, *Salvation*, 113–28, Fred Chay and John Correia, *The Faith that Saves: The Nature of Faith in the New Testament*, and Robert N. Wilkin, "Beware of Confusion

About Faith," *Journal of the Grace Evangelical Society* 18, no. 1 (Spring 2005).

CHAPTER 4

THE PURPOSE GOSPEL

The trouble with our age is that it is all signpost and no destination. —Louis Kronenberger

Perhaps the most prevalent erroneous gospel being promulgated within postmodern evangelicalism may be termed the *purpose gospel*. This label is not intended solely as a reference to the ubiquitous purpose driven movement advanced by Rick Warren, although clearly Warren epitomizes this soteriological method.[1] Rather, the phrase *purpose gospel* is a descriptive term intended to denote the primary message of this popular approach to the gospel. Before examining a few case studies on the purpose gospel, and critiquing them based upon the five-fold standard of the gospel outlined in chapter three, a general overview of this soteriological method is in order.

Underemphasizing and Redefining Sin

One of the chief characteristics of the purpose gospel is a notable downplaying of the notion of sin. Sin is at best redefined and at worst absent from the discussion altogether. When it is discussed, personal responsibility and guilt are often overlooked. Commenting on this tendency, D. A. Carson laments, "[In] our efforts to make Jesus appear relevant *we have cast the human dilemma in merely contemporary categories, taking our cues from the perceived needs of our day.*"[2] It is difficult to fathom how one can present the gospel without addressing the sinfulness of mankind. As Colin Smith has pointed out, "We cannot have a gospel without sin any more than we can have a gospel without Jesus. If we replace the message of sin and atonement with a message of fulfillment and satisfaction in Jesus, we are preaching a different gospel."[3]

Yet this is precisely the approach of the purpose gospel. John Portmann, Assistant Professor of Religious Ethics, Philosophical Ethics, History of Western Philosophy, and Philosophy of the Emotions at the University of Virginia recently compiled a collection of essays promoting sin as a healthy aspect of life. Although Portmann could scarcely be considered an evangelical, his book, entitled, *In Defense of Sin*, nevertheless speaks to the prevailing view of sin in the postmodern culture — a view that has been adopted by evangelicals who espouse the purpose gospel. Portmann compares moralists who see sin as a corrupting influence on society to a wide-eyed *Chicken Little* who mistakenly thought the sky was falling. He writes, "Quite a few people have gone on record over the course of the last two thousand years as feeling frightened by the moral decay they perceived around them. If the sky is indeed falling, it is taking a long time to reach the ground. The world keeps turning."[4]

For Portmann, and others like him (including the contributors to his book), the Ten Commandments should be considered merely "good ideas," not "eternal verities."[5]

It seems that sins, like radioactive substances, have half-lives, some of which last longer than others. The most lethal chemicals require the most time to lose their sting, and the same is true of sin. Those sins with the longest half-lives will take the most time to recede from our consciousness. The biggest sins are those targeted in the Ten Commandments.[6]

Portmann is convinced that sin is not nearly as bad as it has been made out to be. "Sin wouldn't frustrate us," he writes, "if it didn't stand in the way of something we really would like to do." Given the softening influences of sin in the present age, Portmann concludes,

"If the sky does one day fall, it will likely land on a world surprised by sin."[7]

Not unlike Portmann, many evangelicals who espouse the purpose gospel focus on the softer side of Jesus, who, as Portmann is quick to point out, cautions against casting the first stone.[8] But such a selective appeal to the teachings of Christ in Scripture makes no attempt to reconcile other statements of Christ such as, "If your right eye causes you to sin, pluck it out and cast it from you; for it is more profitable for you that one of your members perish, than for your whole body to be cast into hell" (Matt 5:29), or "Therefore I said to you that you will die in your sins; for if you do not believe that I am He, you will die in your sins" (John 8:24), or "And I say to you, My friends, do not be afraid of those who kill the body, and after that have no more that they can do. But I will show you whom you should fear: Fear Him who, after He has killed, has power to cast into hell; yes, I say to you, fear Him!" (Luke 12:4–5).

Most evangelicals who espouse the purpose gospel do not eviscerate sin completely the way Portmann does. Instead, perhaps recognizing that the wholesale abandonment of the doctrine of sin would be viewed as a complete departure from orthodoxy, they redefine it. "For most people in our society, the word *sin* has been emptied of its true meaning and filled with another meaning that renders it harmless."[9] But it is no less damaging to the pure gospel to redefine sin than it is to leave it out altogether. Sin is mankind's greatest predicament. Sin is not an inconvenience or temporal hindrance to fulfillment and purpose in life. It is a part of every individual's very composition. Mankind is by nature sinful and that sinfulness is what condemns men to hell. As Mark Dever points out, "People need to grasp not only the theoretical concept of evil and wrong, but also the fact that *they* are evil and wrong."[10] Apart from an accurate awareness of sin, there can be no salvation, for "without sin, what need is there of a Savior?"[11] The purpose gospel fails to meet the standard of biblical accuracy because it fails to adequately address man's predicament: sin.

Overemphasizing the Present

The purpose gospel is further marked by a magnification of the *present*. It downplays or ignores entirely the eternal aspect of salvation. In the purpose gospel, man's predicament relates primarily to a present sense of discontentment or despondency rather than to eternal punishment in hell as a consequence of sin. The need for salvation is couched in terms of the need to find meaning or purpose in *this life*. The result of salvation is not so much the gaining of ultimate *eternal* life in heaven, but rather a newfound sense of fulfillment and direction in the *present life*.[12] Since very little, if anything, is said about sin in general, it is easy to see how its eternal consequences are similarly overlooked.

David Wells suggests that "evangelicals have turned from focusing on God's transcendence to focusing on his immanence and then they took the further step of interpreting his immanence as friendliness with modernity."[13] He describes the postmodern obsession with the present as follows:

> This rearrangement of meaning around the self, around its moods, needs, intuitions, aches, and ambiguities, has entered the church. Its presence is signaled wherever there are those who think, or act, as if the purpose of life is to find ways of actualizing the self, realizing it, and crafting it through technique or purchase, instead of restraining it out of moral considerations and in this sense putting it to death. Where Christian faith is offered as a means of finding personal wholeness rather than holiness, the church has become worldly.
>
> There are many other forms of worldliness that are comfortably at home in the evangelical church today. Where it substitutes intuition and feelings for biblical truth, it is being worldly....
>
> What I have been describing is, of course, the loss of the church's needed otherworldliness and its consuming preoc-

cupation with its this-worldly life. That is a posture that becomes increasingly at home in its culture, and therefore the enemies of Christian faith slowly fade from view. Soon there is very little that cannot be incorporated into the faith or even become the center around which that faith gets reorganized. As it becomes worldly in these ways, it also becomes anthropocentric, its God more horizontal than vertical, its piety more psychological than moral, its gospel more self-focused than cross-centered.[14]

Illustrations of this trend toward what Wells calls *this-worldliness* as it relates to the gospel are not difficult to find. Several significant examples are addressed later in this chapter. For now, though, one example will suffice to illustrate the problem. The ministry of *Child Evangelism Fellowship* (CEF) published a gospel tract in 1962 entitled *Heaven...How to Get There.*[15] The CEF tract begins with the statement "Heaven is a wonderful place!" and proceeds to explain at the very outset that there is "only one way to heaven." A gospel tract published by the same organization in 2004 is entitled *How To Have a Very Special Friend* and begins with the question, "Have you ever wondered how to have a very special friend?" Although the 2004 version goes on to adequately explain sin, hell and heaven, the shift toward a more present-life emphasis is unmistakable.

As another example, consider the gospel presentation promulgated by a well-known law firm in Houston, Texas where the senior partners are Christians. This firm has the praiseworthy tradition of sending a thank you letter to its clients after a case has closed in which they explain the gospel—a unique idea and one no doubt born out of a passion for sharing Christ with others.[16] The thank you letter begins: "Thank you for allowing us to represent you. It has been our privilege and honor. We'd like to show our appreciation to you by telling you something that is of great value. It is simply that the greatest gift in the world can be yours for the asking."[17] Certainly such an opening line garners the attention of the reader! Unfortunately, the well-intentioned efforts of the authors go awry with the next sentence: "That gift is the friendship of our best friend

Savior—Jesus Christ." The letter then makes an ambiguous al to Matthew 11:28, "Come unto Me, all you who are weary and burdened, and I will give you rest" in an attempt to explain how to be saved. Nothing at all is said about heaven, hell, eternal life or even *faith*. The gospel presentation seems focused on the experiential and relational aspects of knowing Christ.

The purpose gospel is appealing because it is positive by nature, meets people where they are, and promises to fulfill deep inner longings that while amorphous are nevertheless real. "In an environment where entertainment is a primary motivation in programming, it is easy to neglect the hard truths of the gospel, because they are not usually attractive or entertaining."[18] Yet in so doing, the purpose gospel treats only one *symptom* of man's sin problem without addressing the *root problem* itself. God did not send His Son to die in man's place primarily so that man may be happy and fulfilled. He sent His Son to rescue mankind from the ultimate penalty of sin: hell. Salvation by definition is deliverance or rescue from *something*. The identification of that *something* is vital to the purity of the gospel.

The Bible repeatedly characterizes salvation in terms that transcend this present life. Salvation passages in Scripture are rife with terms like "eternal life," "everlasting life," "never perishing," etc.[19] If one omits the eternal aspect of salvation in presenting the gospel, he has deconstructed the gospel to a point where it is no longer pure. Telling someone to believe the gospel in order to find meaning and purpose in life is like telling someone who is drowning, "Grab hold of my hand and I'll help you get dry!" While it may be true that the drowning swimmer is wet, and it also may be true that he prefers to be dry, the primary matter of importance at the moment is saving his life! That he also receives a dry towel and a warm change of clothes pales in comparison to being rescued from death. Similarly, the Christian life brings with it many temporal blessings. But the essence of the gospel relates to how one deals with the problem of sin and its *eternal* consequence.

A Lack of Urgency

One of the outgrowths of underemphasizing *sin* and overemphasizing the *present* is a lessening of the urgency surrounding the gospel. With its obsession on the present life, the purpose gospel fails to create in the hearer a decisive sense of crisis or exigency. The purpose gospel capitulates to postmodernism's inherently subjective outlook on life. After all, a sense of contentment and meaning in life is fleeting and unreliable. It comes and goes with each new life experience. And since postmodernism is characterized by "decision making on the ethical bases of feelings, emotions, and impressions," purveyors of the purpose gospel are content to let the lost person *feel his way* to salvation no matter how long it takes.[20]

Churches that preach a purpose gospel are famously non-threatening. Rather than presenting the pure gospel and challenging the hearer to respond to it, the preacher in these seeker-driven environments attempts to coax the lost person into making a commitment to better his life by associating with Jesus Christ only after a comfortable period of personal reflection. Consider the following case in point.

In the atrium of one large, purpose driven church in the suburbs of Houston, there are two large bowls resting on a table. One is labeled *seeker* and the other is labeled *follower*. An attendee who considers himself to be a seeker (i.e., non-Christian) is encouraged to write his name on an index card and place it in the "seeker" bowl. The pitch is, "No pressure …. no commitment. No one will contact you. Just put your name in the bowl and give our church a try." After attending the church for awhile, the theory is, the seeker will experience a period of soul-searching and personal introspection wherein he becomes convinced that Jesus is the only one who can bring meaning and purpose to his life. When this happens, he is encouraged to move the index card with his name on it from the *seeker* bowl to the *follower* bowl. Meanwhile, the pastor and staff point to the increasing number of cards in the *follower* bowl as a validation of the church's soteriological method.[21]

In true postmodern form, the entire equation is hazy, individually defined and subjectively experienced. There is no definitive line-in-the-sand drawn whereby the lost person is warned of the eternal consequences sin and its singular solution through faith alone in Christ alone. There is no urgency—no sense that "today might be the day" or "what if you died today?"

Reflecting on this lack of urgency, Ajith Fernando comments,

Traditionally, Christians have been motivated to evangelism through their belief that the gospel is absolutely true and is the only hope for salvation. However, the aptness of thinking in such categories as "absolutely true" and "only hope for salvation" is being question by today's pluralistic thinking. The postmodern mood is thus hostile to the idea of urgency as it is portrayed in the Bible.[22]

In other words, *seekers* in a postmodern age dismiss out of hand any notion of a universally applicable salvation message. "Who are you to tell me that your way is the only way to eternal life?!" they exclaim.

In response, self-styled, enlightened postmodern evangelicals have devised a way to counteract this rejection of an all-encompassing metanarrative for salvation by repackaging the gospel in a misguided and unnecessary effort to make it appear softer, friendlier and more appealing. Fernando continues,

I would go so far as to say that entertainment has replaced urgency as a primary means of attracting people to the gospel. Therefore, we do not strive to let the truth shine forth in all its glory, an enterprise that calls for dedication and hard work. Instead, the hard work goes to producing an entertaining program. We often find that Christian worship is characterized by an entertaining and technically excellent program of music, drama, worship, and sharing, followed by a ministry of the Word that is comparatively inferior and unimaginative....

As a result of this focus on entertainment, people come to worship looking to have an entertaining time. Songs and stories and humor are chosen so that the people might be entertained. In the process, truth is subordinated to an inferior position. So today when many Christians inquire about the value of a worship service they ask, "Did you enjoy the worship there?" But what they really mean is, "Did you get an emotional lift from the spiritual entertainment provided there?"[23]

Thus, in endeavoring to convince the lost person that what Christianity has to offer is more fulfilling and meaningful than the emptiness of a life without Christ, entertainment becomes the primary tool. The gospel is no longer articulated as the *only solution* to a serious problem with eternal ramifications, but rather merely a *better option* than what the seeker is already experiencing.

In abandoning the eternal aspect of the gospel and focusing instead on a *meaning-in-this-life* approach, the purpose gospel has removed urgency from the gospel. If salvation is nothing but a better life now, a lost person may be content to hold on to his present life as long as he can until his discontentment and despondency become unbearable. Only then will he pursue spiritual avenues in hopes of finding a better present life. Sadly, if those avenues lead him to the purpose gospel, he will find no hope for the real problem in his life: *sin.*

Case Study: Rick Warren (Part One)

A case study on the purpose gospel appropriately begins with a critique of Rick Warren and his enormously popular Purpose Driven movement. Warren founded Saddleback Church in the living room of his small condo in Saddleback Valley, California in 1980. Since that time it has grown to more than 50,000 names on the church roll and a weekly worship attendance of over 22,000. One out of nine people in the area attends Saddleback Church.[24] But the influence of this megachurch extends far beyond the immediate neighborhood.

Warren also leads the Purpose Driven Network of churches, a global coalition of congregations in 162 countries. More than 400,000 ministers and priests have been trained worldwide, and almost 157,000 church leaders subscribe to Ministry Toolbox, his weekly newsletter. His previous book, *The Purpose Driven Church* is listed in "100 Christian Books That Changed the 20th Century." Forbes magazine called it, "The best book on entrepreneurship, management, and leadership in print."[25]

The Purpose Driven Life, published in 2002, is hailed by the publisher as "a groundbreaking manifesto on the meaning of life."[26] It certainly has been well received by the Christian community in particular and secular culture at large. According to one source,

The book has been on the *New York Times* Bestseller list for advice books for 174 weeks (as of May 2006). The book offers readers a 40-day personal spiritual journey, and presents what Warren says are the five Biblical purposes of life on Earth. As of November 2005, *The Purpose Driven Life* has been translated into 56 languages and was the bestselling book in the world for 2003, 2004, and 2005. It has won numerous literary awards.

Since September 2002, over 30,000 congregations, corporations, and sports teams across the United States have participated in a "40 Days of Purpose" emphasis. A May 2005 survey of American pastors and ministers conducted by George Barna asked Christian leaders to identify what books were the most influential on their lives and ministries. The *Purpose Driven Life* was the most frequent response. *The Purpose Driven Church*, Warren's previous book, was the second most frequent response. The book has sold over 24 million copies (as of November, 2005).[27]

Warren's web site proclaims, "*The Purpose Driven Life* is the best-selling hardback book in American history, according to Publisher's Weekly."[28]

In chapter seven, Warren presents the reader with God's plan of salvation. This is the final chapter in the foundational section of the book, in which Warren prepares the reader for the five main purposes to follow. Before the reader can embrace the five purposes, he must first have a relationship with God. Thus, in chapter seven Warren presents the gospel and calls on the reader to respond. The potential for evangelistic impact is enormous given the widespread readership of the book (twenty-four million copies sold and still counting).

The pivotal discussion of the gospel is introduced by the exhortation, "It's time to settle the issue. *Who* are you going to live for— yourself or God? ... Don't worry. God will give you what you need if you will just make the choice to live for him."[29] Warren adds, "Real life begins by committing yourself completely to Jesus Christ. If you are not sure you have done this, all you need to do is...." What follows is a clear outline of what Warren suggests the reader must do if he hopes to gain eternal life and become part of "the family of God."[30]

According to Warren, those who hope to gain eternal life must: (1) believe God loves you and made you for his *purposes*; (2) believe you're not an accident; (3) believe you were made to last forever; (4) believe God has chosen you to have a relationship with Jesus, who died on the cross for you; and (5) believe that no matter what you've done, God wants to forgive you. In addition to believing these things, one must also (6) receive Jesus into your life as your Lord and Savior; (7) receive his forgiveness for your sins; and (8) receive his Spirit, who will give you the power to fulfill your life *purpose*.[31] Thus, for Warren, the gospel begins and ends with an emphasis on God's *purpose* for your life.

How does Warren's eight-part soteriological method measure up to the five-fold standard set forth in chapter two? It was established in previous chapters that the pure gospel contains five essential components: (1) Jesus Christ; (2) the Son of God who died and rose again; (3) to pay one's personal penalty for sin; (4) gives eternal life to those who trust Him and (5) Him alone for it. These five essentials, however they may be expressed or articulated, must be included as the content of saving faith and the content of saving faith must *not* include anything that contradicts these five essentials.

The fact that Warren's list includes eight items does not in and of itself preclude it from being accurate provided that all of the five established essentials are present in his list and provided that none of his eight items contradicts the five established essentials.

Regarding the first essential, certainly Warren's gospel is Christocentric, which is commendable. At first glance Warren appears to cover the second and third essentials in part four of his eight-part plan of salvation when he mentions "Jesus, who died on the cross for you." Yet, notably absent is an explanation of the death and resurrection of Christ. Also missing is an emphasis on the penalty for sin and Christ's payment for that penalty. By mentioning "for you," Warren implies Jesus' personal sacrifice for sins, but the reader must make this connection on his own. There is a passing reference to forgiveness but only an implicit emphasis on man's sinfulness.

The most significant weakness of Warren's gospel in *The Purpose Driven Life* is the complete omission of *eternal life* from the discussion (essential #4). In its place, Warren emphasizes the achieving of man's purpose as the goal of salvation. Furthermore, the suggestion that one "believe you're not an accident" in order to receive eternal life so deconstructs the gospel as to create a requirement for eternal life that is completely foreign to Scripture and therefore violates the fifth essential: exclusivity. The same can be said of Warren's requirement that one "believe you were made to last" in order to be saved. Warren's gospel presentation fails to meet the standard of the simple good news of the pure gospel. It reflects the characteristic approach of the purpose gospel that is commonplace in today's consumer-oriented, needs-based culture.

Case Study: Rick Warren (Part Two)

In a twelve-minute video entitled "What Does It Mean to Follow Christ" Warren demonstrates a soteriological method that differs in some ways from that evidenced in *The Purpose Driven Life*. For the purpose of evaluating Warren's approach to the gospel, the video is especially helpful as it articulates in a quantitative, concise format his understanding of precisely how someone can have eternal life. In the twelve-minute video presentation, produced by *PurposeDriven.com* and made available free of charge for distribution via the Internet, Warren explains the gospel and invites listeners to follow his instructions in order to "begin a personal relationship with Jesus Christ."[32] The video is entitled, "What Does It Mean to Follow Christ?" In a mass emailing to faithful disciples of the Purpose Driven movement, Warren writes,

> I recently created a short video to explain exactly what it means to be a follower of Jesus Christ and posted it on our Purpose Driven Web site. It's a simple presentation you can pass on to anyone you care about. You can place this link on your own Web site http://www.purposedriven.com/salvation and copy and paste it at the bottom of all your e-mails, like I do below. You also can download it and place it on your Web site, too. http://www.purposedriven.com/salvation.zip. My only desire is to help you share the Good News with the people in your life.[33]

Not surprisingly, Warren's video gospel presentation suffers from some of the same errors that one finds in *The Purpose Driven Life*.

Here, as in the book, the first two essentials of the gospel are present: Jesus Christ who died and rose again. Although Warren correctly identifies man's root problem as sin, he frames the issue incorrectly from the outset by failing to accurately identify the results of man's sin problem.[34] To Warren, man's problem is primarily *relational*. Man is lonely and "feels separated from God's love." But sin brings more than broken fellowship. The wages of sin is death and eternal damnation in a literal place called *hell*. Conspicuous by its absence is any reference to hell or the eternal consequence of sin in the video, which begs the question, "From what is man being saved?"

Warren is correct in suggesting that sin leads to failed relationships and enmity with God. But are there not many adverse effects of sin? Sin is ultimately the cause of physical disease, natural disasters, thorns on rose bushes, smog, poor eyesight, and pain in childbirth—just to name a few. Why single out the relational aspect? The fundamental issue in salvation is that sin leads to *hell* and salvation brings *eternal life*. The essence of salvation is eternal life and Warren's gospel fails to emphasize this vital point. Instead of warning his listeners that the punishment for sin is hell, Warren emphasizes the existential, experiential consequences of sin in this present life. And because Warren incorrectly identifies man's problem, he also mischaracterizes the results of salvation. According to Warren's gospel, salvation from sin results in the reclaiming of *purpose* and *meaning* in life and a newfound friend in God.

Finally, Warren's gospel in the twelve-minute video is deficient for its failure to emphasize the exclusivity of Christ. His presentation is not explicitly inclusivistic or pluralistic, but neither does he make it clear that it is faith *alone* in Christ *alone* that saves. And in light of his tendency elsewhere to include various superfluous requirements for salvation that are not a part of the essence of the gospel, one is left wondering if the soteriological method articulated in the video is the *only* pathway to salvation or simply the latest rendition.

Case Study: Kerry Shook

Kerry Shook and his wife, Chris, founded Fellowship of The Woodlands with eight people in 1993. In twelve years the church has grown to 13,000 in average attendance each Sunday.[35] Visitors to the church's web site are greeted with the following welcome message:

> Welcome to Fellowship of The Woodlands (FOTW). We invite you to experience "The best hour of your week." Come enjoy great music, creative videos, drama and relevant, life-changing messages from Pastor Kerry Shook that will help you throughout your week. Fellowship of The Woodlands is a community church for everyone. *We have exciting things going on for people at every stage of life* from infants, toddlers, preschoolers, teens, singles, married and up. Come *experience* Fellowship of The Woodlands.[36]

This welcome message is indicative of the church's well-established emphasis on relationships and experience. The "What We Believe" section of the FOTW web site articulates the church's belief about salvation.

> We believe that Jesus, through His death on the cross, provided salvation for all. However, to receive salvation one must repent of sin and trust Jesus Christ alone. The true believer is eternally secure and cannot lose his salvation. He may, however, lose his joy by sin and bring the loving discipline of the Father upon himself.[37]

FOTW is to be commended for addressing doctrinal beliefs in general on its site and particularly for discussing God's plan of salvation. However, the site does not contain a specific *How to* section for those desiring to be saved. In other words, the FOTW site explains what the church believes about salvation without providing site visitors with specific instructions on how to obtain eternal life. This is a common oversight for churches in the purpose driven arena. Seldom do they emphasize the gospel on their sites, choosing instead to focus on relationships and relegate matters pertaining to salvation to a secondary level of importance.[38]

Another doctrinal distinction listed on the FOTW web site merits positive comment. FOTW proclaims that the Bible is their sole authority.

> "The whole Bible was given to us by inspiration from God and is useful to teach us what is true and make us realize what is wrong in our lives; it straightens us out and helps us to do what is right" (2 Tim 3:16). Since God's Word is the only completely reliable and truthful authority, we accept the Bible as our manual for living. Our first question when faced with a decision is "What does the Bible say?" We practice daily Bible reading, Bible study and Bible memorization. The Bible is the basis for all we believe.[39]

Such a commitment to the centrality of Scripture is encouraging, especially given FOTW's transparent purpose driven approach to ministry. Yet, the absence of a clear gospel presentation on the site demonstrates a disturbing inconsistency in implementing their commitment to the centrality of Scripture. The present writer inquired via email about this omission of the gospel from the FOTW site and received an explanation from a church staff member who wrote, "[The gospel] can be found on our website at www.fotw.org. Click on the link 'About FOTW' and then 'Our Mission' and finally 'What we believe.'"[40] Additionally, the staff member included in his email response a suggested prayer that one can pray if he desires to be saved.

> Dear God, thank you for loving me. Thank you for loving me so much you gave your very own son to die for my sins. I ask you to forgive me of my sins and to *come into my heart and life*. I want to *follow you the rest of my life* and do the things that please you. Thank you for saving me. I receive you now! Thank you for forgiving me of my sin and accepting me. Help me to grow now as your child and *be all that you want me to be*. In Jesus name, Amen![41]

Two points are worth noting from this email exchange. In the first place, as discussed above, the section on the FOTW web site to which the staff member refers *does not* explain adequately *how* to be saved, but merely *what* salvation is. It is a doctrinal statement, not a gospel presentation. The staff member's answer is like responding to someone who asks, "How can I be saved?" by handing them a systematic theology book. It would be better if the FOTW site had a clear presentation of the gospel for those seeking eternal life. The staff member did not respond to a follow up email regarding this matter.

Secondly, when evaluated according to the five-fold essence of the gospel, the suggested prayer of salvation fails the test. It is dominated by an emphasis on this present life with no mention at all of heaven, hell or the eternal ramifications of salvation (essential number four). It also implies that good works are a component part of the gospel by using such language as "I want to follow You the rest of my life and do things that please You." The potential convert may be left wondering, "Is this a requirement? *Must* I do this in exchange for salvation? What if I do not follow God the rest of my life?" The language of the suggested prayer does not make it clear that faith *alone* in Christ *alone* is the only means of obtaining eternal life, and thus it fails to meet the standard of exclusivity (essential number five).

Case Study: Gotlife.org

Gotlife.org epitomizes the purpose gospel in that its sole purpose as a web site is to present the gospel to today's culture through an interactive online video. [42] Many evangelical ministries link to this site on their home sites as a means of communicating the gospel. A close scrutiny of the soteriological method employed by the Gotlife. org site, however, demonstrates a serious departure from the standard of the pure gospel as articulated in chapter three above.

Upon viewing the interactive video, one is struck from the outset with the emphasis on *this life*. The video begins with the teaser, "Get the most out of what you have left. Got life?" This sets the tone for a marked emphasis on the here and now throughout the presentation. To its credit the online presentation does invoke the phrase *eternal life*, but the overarching theme is that of getting the most out of *this* life.[43] Questions such as, "What is the meaning of life?" and "Why do you feel isolated?" and "How can we get past the isolation and get in good with God?" highlight man's psychological needs rather than his spiritual need of forgiveness of personal sin.

Gotlife.org suggests that while many "search for the purpose of their very existence," the answer can only be found in Jesus Christ. Thus, the first essential of the gospel is clear: Jesus Christ. Yet beyond a clear statement about Jesus Christ, little else is on target. Not only does Gotlife.org neglect the eternal aspect of salvation (essential number four), it downplays man's sinfulness by emphasizing *isolation* rather than guilt and personal responsibility.[44] While it is true that sin isolates man from God this is not the primary nuance of the term *isolation* as used by Gotlife.org. In the video, *isolation* has the connotation of personal, experiential and relational feelings of lone-liness and dissatisfaction with life.

What precisely must one do with Jesus to achieve meaning in life? The narrator proclaims, "The ability to have the life you've always dreamed about is within your grasp.... Want life? It's as easy as A-B-C." The "A" is: *Admit that you are a sinner and you are willing to turn 180 degrees from your sin, that is, repent.* True, admitting one's sin is a necessary precursor to receiving salvation. After all, if one does not recognize his problem he will have no reason to seek a solution. But sin is not sufficiently described in terms of man's personal guilt in the video. It is more of an unhappy circumstance. Furthermore, the requirement that man must *repent* (i.e., *turn from his sin*), makes good works an implicit component to the gospel in violation of the fifth essential (exclusivity).[45]

The "B" is: *Believe Christ died for your sin and rose again.* This sufficiently covers the first essential of the gospel but not the second because it lacks clarity on precisely who Jesus is (a clarity that is lacking throughout the video), namely, the Son of God. The "C" is: *Confess verbally and publicly your belief in Jesus Christ.* One wonders how this requirement made its way into the video (except perhaps to round out a clever three-step acronym: A-B-C). After all, nowhere does Scripture demand verbal declaration of one's faith as a requirement to gain eternal life.[46] Thus, once again, with point "C" Gotlife.org violates the fifth essential of the gospel.

Never mind the fact that the three-step approach to salvation (A-B-C) suggested by gotlife.org is fraught with theological problems. The larger question is, *Is salvation really about obtaining the life you've always dreamed about?* Gotlife.org frames the soteriological discussion in the context of this life. Consistent with the prevalent purpose driven soteriology of the present culture, salvation is not about being rescued from hell and delivered ultimately to heaven. It is about "getting the most out of this life."

Summary of Chapter Four

The case studies in this chapter illustrate a prevalent soterio-logical method within postmodern American evangelicalism. In keeping with postmodernism's emphasis on ambiguity and personal experience, over and against the acceptance of universally true standards, the purpose gospel seeks to impact lives through an inherently individualized, introspective approach. One person's spiritual need is not precisely the same as another's and one person's solution is likewise customized to fit his or her personal felt-needs.

Certainly it would be an unfair characterization to suggest that all purpose driven ministries reject the centrality of Scripture. Indeed, many ministries characterized by a purpose gospel express a respect for the Bible as the standard for their beliefs. But in practice, the soteriological method employed by those of this ilk represents a departure from the pure gospel standard contained in the Bible they claim to respect.

The purpose gospel underemphasizes the universal problem of sin vis-à-vis one's personal guilt and responsibility. When it is addressed, sin is often redefined and recast solely in terms of its relational impact rather than its eternal implications. It likewise overemphasizes the present life with its meaning, purpose, and fulfillment of dreams. There is a lack of urgency in sharing the gospel, with many purpose driven ministries avoiding explicit gospel presentations in their marketing and promotional materials. Even Gotlife. org, which at least calls for a decision on the part of viewers, downplays urgency by suggesting that the only consequence of failing to *get life*, is continued lack of personal fulfillment and a prolonged feeling of isolation. Based on the standard established in chapter three, the purpose gospel lacks the essential elements to be considered *the gospel* (cf. Gal 1:6–7).

ENDNOTES
CHAPTER FOUR

1. Cf. *Purpose Driven.* <http://www.purposedriven.com/en-US/Home.htm> (accessed 15 September 2006).

2. D. A. Carson, *The Gagging of God: Christianity Confronts Pluralism* (Grand Rapids: Zondervan, 1996), 221, emphasis original.

3. Colin S. Smith, "The Ambassador's Job Description," in *Telling the Truth: Evangelizing Postmoderns*, ed. D. A. Carson (Grand Rapids: Zondervan, 2000), 185.

4. John Portmann, *In Defense of Sin* (New York: Palgrave Macmillan, 2003), 2.

5. Ibid., 4.

6. Ibid.

7. Ibid., 11–12.

8. Cf. Mike Stallard, "The Tendency to Softness in Postmodern Attitudes About God, War, and Man," *Journal of Ministry and Theology* 10, no. 1 (Spring 2006): 92–114.

9. Smith, "The Ambassador's Job Description," 185, emphasis original.

10. Mark E. Dever, "Communicating Sin in a Postmodern World," in *Telling the Truth: Evangelizing Postmoderns*, ed. D. A. Carson (Grand Rapids: Zondervan, 2000), 148, emphasis original.

11. Ibid., 142.

12. It is acknowledged that eternal life has both a present reality and a future reality (see note thirty-four in chapter three). It is the future reality that is often neglected in the purpose gospel.

13. David F. Wells, *No Place for Truth, or, Whatever Happened to Evangelical Theology?* (Grand Rapids: W.B. Eerdmans, 1993), 300.

14. David F. Wells, "Introduction: The Word in the World," in *The Compromised Church: The Present Evangelical Crisis*, ed. John H. Armstrong (Wheaton: Crossway Books, 1998), 31–32. See also David F. Wells, *No Place for Truth*, David F. Wells, *God in the Wastelands: The Reality of Truth in a World of Fading Dreams* (Grand Rapids: Eerdmans, 1994).

Wells has long been a leading critic of the collapse of evangelical theology in the face of postmodernity. He rightly laments, among other things, the "rise of the everyperson" and the concomitant dearth of evangelical conviction and leadership. Cf. David F. Wells, *No Place for Truth*, 187–217. To Wells, it seems, the greatest consequence of this trend is a profound increase in worldliness within the church. In his view, postmodern evangelicalism has capitulated to the "present worldliness" of the culture, with the result that the church is characterized by a glaring lack of morality and virtue. Although one appreciates Wells's accurate characterization of the present culture, his focus on worldliness as the most significant consequence is misguided. Worldliness may be on the rise (indeed the Apostle Paul predicted this would be the case in the present age—cf. 1 Tim 4:1–3; 2 Tim 4:1–4), but the more serious problem with the postmodern worldview is its destructive impact on the gospel. According to Wells, evangelicals can stem the tide of ungodliness in the church by emphasizing repentance of sin and a moral commitment to personal godliness as part of the gospel on the front end.

Yet such an approach to the gospel is just as problematic as the postmodern "purpose of life" approach itself. Wells is hoisted by his own petard when he emphasizes individual moral behavior as a prerequisite for eternal life, since such an emphasis on works is no less anthropocentric than the prevailing emphasis on individual purpose or contentment that Wells passionately decries (cf. Wells, "Introduction: The Word in the World," 32.) Thus, Wells's suggested solution to the present crisis in evangelicalism does not address the root issue of a deconstructed gospel; it only compounds the problem.

15. *Child Evangelism Fellowship.* <http://www.cefonline.com/> (accessed 19 September 2006). This illustration is not intended as a broad-brushed criticism of CEF's approach to the gospel but rather as one example of the changing face of gospel presentations. In general, CEF is known for presenting a clear and accurate gospel.

16. This custom is particularly noteworthy when one considers that it is a personal injury law firm sharing the gospel!

17. Letter from Simmons and Fletcher law firm dated 11 February 2004.

18. Ajith Fernando, "The Urgency of the Gospel," in *Telling the Truth: Evangelizing Postmoderns*, ed. D. A. Carson (Grand Rapids: Zondervan, 2000), 373.

19. Cf. John 3:15–16, 36; 5:24; 6:40, 47, 54; 8:51; 10:28; 11:26; 17:2; Acts 13:46; Romans 5:21; 6:22–23; 1 John 2:25; 5:11–13; et al. See the discussion of the third core essential of the content of saving faith in chapter three.

20. Paul R. Shockley, "Postmodernism as a Basis for Society?" in *The God of the Bible and Other Gods: Is the Christian God Unique among World Religions?* Robert Paul Lightner (Grand Rapids: Kregel Publications, 1998), 198.

21. This methodology was described and explained to the present writer by a member of this church who experienced it firsthand.

22. Fernando, "The Urgency of the Gospel," 371.

23. Ibid., 377.

24. For more information about Saddleback Church see the church's official website: www.saddleback.com.

25. *Purpose Driven Life.* <http://www.purposedrivenlife.com/rick-warren.aspx> (accessed 15 November 2006).

26. For a detailed review of *The Purpose Drive Life* see the present writer's article, J. B. Hixson, "Review of The Purpose Driven Life by Rick Warren," *Journal of Ministry and Theology* 8, no. 1 (Spring 2004): 134–39.

27. *Wikipedia, Purpose Driven Life.* <http://en.wikipedia.org/wiki/The_Purpose_Driven_Life.> (accessed 15 November 2006).

28. *Purpose Driven Life.* <http://www.purposedrivenlife.com/rick-warren.aspx> (accessed 15 November 2006).

29. Rick Warren, *The Purpose Driven Life* (Grand Rapids: Zondervan, 2002), 58, emphasis original.

30. Ibid., 58–59.

31. Ibid., 58, emphasis added.

32. See http://www.purposedriven.com/salvation to view a copy of the online video.

33. From an email sent to selected *PurposeDriven.com* subscribers on May 31, 2006. The subject line was "Let's get the Good News out!"

34. A recurring problem with Warren's theological method concerns his faulty hermeneutic. Warren often takes Scripture passages out of context to "prove" his point. This tendency manifests itself in the video during his discussion of sin. When discussing man's universal

sin problem, Warren appeals to Isaiah 59:2, "But your iniquities have separated you from your God; And your sins have hidden *His* face from you, So that He will not hear." While it is true that mankind is sinful (and Warren correctly cites Romans 3:23 on this point), the Isaiah passage is not speaking about mankind in general. Contextually, Isaiah 59:2 refers to Israel's specific sins which have aroused Yahweh's displeasure at a particular moment in history.

35. *Fellowship of the Woodlands.* <http://www.fotw.org/> (accessed 1 October 2006).

36. *Fellowship of the Woodlands, About Us.* <http://www.fotw.org/aboutus/whatwepractice.asp> (accessed 1 October 2006), emphasis added.

37. *Fellowship of the Woodlands, What We Believe.* <http://www.fotw.org/aboutus/

whatwebelieve.asp> (accessed 1 October 2006).

38. A common characteristic among purpose driven churches is the absence of doctrinal matter in general, and the gospel in particular, from their promotional materials including web sites, brochures, welcome packets, membership manuals, etc. Admittedly, not all churches that fail to communicate the gospel on their web sites are purpose driven in their soteriological method. Some churches, which otherwise preach a sound gospel, for whatever reason have chosen not to capitalize on the tremendous evangelistic opportunity that the Internet affords them. In and of itself, the absence of a clearly stated gospel presentation on a church web site is no indicator of a church's soteriological accuracy, nor should it be assumed that such churches are not passionately evangelistic. They may be. Yet, from the present writer's perspective, it is difficult to see how any evangelical church with a web site would not make the gospel a priority in the development of their site.

39. *Fellowship of the Woodlands, About Us.* <http://www.fotw.org/ aboutus/whatwepractice.asp> (accessed 1 October 2006).

40. Email from Alan Splawn (asplawn@fotw.org) received October 3, 2006.

41. Ibid., emphasis added.

42. *Gotlife.Org.* <http://www.gotlife.org/intro.html> (accessed 14 November 2006). According to the parent web site, www.gotlifeministries.org, an average of seven people per day fill out the online reply form indicating they have "gotten life" by viewing the evangelistic interactive video and following its instructions. *Gotlife Ministries.* <http://www.gotlifeministries.com/index.cfm> (accessed 14 November 2006).

43. At one point in the video a loose paraphrase of John 10:10 appears on the screen: "Jesus came to give us the most incredible life possible." Eternal life is certainly incredible, yet the phrase *most incredible life possible*, without any clarifying biblical/doctrinal context, lends itself to a sense of something experientially wonderful like winning the lottery or living one's dream life. Indeed, later in the video the narrator proclaims, "The ability to have the life you've always dreamed about is within your grasp."

44. It should be pointed out that at one point text on the screen *does* define sin as *rebellion against God*, but the overall tenor of the video contravenes this cursory definition and no further audio or video elaboration on man's rebellion is offered in the presentation.

45. By suggesting that salvation is gained by believing *and* repenting of sin, the video gives the impression that one must trust not exclusively in Jesus Christ, but also his own good works to be saved. See discussion of repentance at note seventy-four in chapter three.

46. The suggestion that one must confess Christ publicly in order to gain eternal life is usually based upon a misunderstanding of

two particular passages of Scripture. Most often, appeal is made to Romans 10:9–10. "That if you confess with your mouth the Lord Jesus and believe in your heart that God has raised Him from the dead, you will be saved. For with the heart one believes unto righteousness, and with the mouth confession is made unto salvation." Here, Paul uses the terms *mouth* and *heart* to parallel the Old Testament passage he has just quoted in verse eight (Deut 30:14). His point in verse eight is that faith is not too hard for Jews to understand or to obtain (cf. Deut 30:11). Paul does *not* use *mouth* and *heart* to indicate two distinct actions necessary for eternal salvation. The terms *righteousness* and *salvation* refer to two separate realities. In Romans, Paul's favorite way to describe man's eternal salvation is with the words *justification* (δικαιώσιν) or *righteousness* (δικαιοσύνη). In this passage and throughout Romans, Paul explains that *righteousness* (i.e., individual eternal salvation) comes by faith: "It is with the heart man believes unto righteousness" (Rom 10:10; cf. 5:1).

The salvation Paul speaks of in this passage refers to temporal deliverance, specifically national deliverance for Israel into the future Messianic kingdom. This is in keeping with the meaning of the term σώζω (See *Appendix B: 109 NT Occurrences of Σώζω*) and seems clear when one examines the broader context of Romans 9–11, in which Paul is answering the question, "What about Israel?" Paul's quotation of Joel 2:32 in verse thirteen helps frame the discussion. Ultimately, Paul says, all Israel will *call upon* (i.e., confess) the name of the Lord and be *delivered* (i.e., saved) into the Kingdom (cf. Rom 11:26). But before Jews can experience national deliverance, they must first experience individual justification by faith. "How can they call on Him in whom they have not believed?" (Rom 10:14). Thus, *righteousness* (i.e., individual eternal salvation) comes by faith; *salvation* (i.e., national deliverance) comes by corporate confession.

If Paul intended for *believing* and *confessing* to be two separate actions—each necessary for the impartation of eternal life—then why does he put confession before belief? Would not belief naturally come before confession? (cf. 2 Cor 4:13–14). "Confess with your mouth" is the semantic equivalent of "call upon the Lord" in this context and refers to Israel's ultimate confession, "Hosanna, Hosanna, blessed is He Who comes in the name of the Lord," which Israelites will proclaim in unison at the second advent of Christ (cf. Matt. 23:39; Joel 2:32; Ps 118:22–26; etc.). Given everything Paul had taught to this point in Romans, it would be unlikely for his original readers to have missed the point that justification is *solely by faith.* Paul's quotation of Isaiah 28:16 in verse eleven reiterates this point. In summary, Romans 10:9–10 does not teach that public *confession* is a required companion of faith in order to receive individual justification. Rather, it is required for temporal deliverance, which in this context is viewed primarily from the national perspective of Israel.

The second passage to which appeal is often made in an attempt to support the view that public confession is necessary in order to receive eternal life is Matthew 10:32–33 where Jesus tells His disciples, "Therefore whoever confesses Me before men, him I will also confess before My Father who is in heaven. But whoever denies Me before men, him I will also deny before My Father who is in heaven." Once again, the context of this passage precludes the notion that public confession is required of all believers in order to enter heaven. Jesus is here speaking to the Twelve and sending them out for ministry. After warning that persecutions will come (vv. 16–31), He challenges them to stand strong and not cower in the face of intense persecution. Those disciples who follow Christ faithfully even in the midst of persecution will receive Jesus' special commendation before the Father one day in heaven (cf. Rev 3:5). Those who do not boldly confess Jesus when faced with threats and persecution will not receive such special commendation before the Father one day. The passage says nothing about the requirements for receiving eternal life and presupposes that those to whom Jesus is speaking are in fact already saved.

CHAPTER 5

THE PUZZLING GOSPEL

I have made this letter longer than usual, only because I have not had the time to make it shorter. —Blaise Pascal, 17ᵗʰ Century French Philosopher

"A mist in the pulpit is a fog in the pew. If some lack of clarity exists in a gospel presentation, the listener may well be in a fog."[1] This chapter examines the fog of confusion surrounding many gospel presentations, which serves only to compound the already difficult task of evangelism in the postmodern age. The common desire to see the unsaved come to faith in Christ should compel evangelicals to work together toward eliminating the mist of inconsistent, imprecise, and inaccurate gospel presentations thereby causing the fog of ineffectiveness and confusion to lift. Unfortunately, this is seldom the case.

Many gospel presentations are puzzling because they invoke such generic phrases as "Come to Jesus," "Give your life to Him," "Invite Him into your heart," "Turn your life over to Christ," etc., which are vague and unhelpful in the absence of sufficient clarifying explanation. What does "Come to Jesus," mean, precisely? Charlie Bing points out that sometimes gospel presentations are imprecise because they say either *too little* or *too much*.[2] He adds,

Clear communication is an art. When it comes to telling the Gospel it is an art worth refining. We must work to tell the Gospel as clearly as possible. Not always will we succeed. But isn't it a wonderful fact of life that God can still use us in spite of the misplaced approaches and methods that we use? We know, however, that He can accomplish more through us according to how clear and biblical our message and our methods are. And that means that we are clear in our motives, in our Gospel content, in our statement of the condition for salvation, and in our invitation to believe. Given all that is at stake, we want to share the Good News as clearly as possible in a way that is pleasing to God, not just convenient to men.[3]

In this chapter, it will be demonstrated that many gospel presentations are faulty because they are imprecise or in some cases inconsistent (i.e., self-contradictory). Of course, confusing gospel presentations are nothing new. Long before the onset of postmodernism, Christianity suffered from poorly articulated gospel presentations. Yet given the ideological distinctives of postmodernity, such imprecise and self-contradictory gospels are more likely than ever to go unnoticed and perhaps even thrive.

This is because, as Kevin Vanhoozer has pointed out, *meaning* in language has become "demeaned" to the point of irrelevancy.[4] What is more important, it seems, than the propositions behind the words is the experience of the reader or listener. Since "reality is in the mind of the beholder,"[5] and objective reasoning is eclipsed by subjective feelings, imprecision in communication becomes celebrated for its alleged ability to connect with a greater number of people in a greater number of ways. What matters most is the response of the *community*, not whether or not the response is the precise one intended by the *communicator*. In such an ideological climate, gospel presentations that are unclear or self-contradictory are par for the course, even when such lack of clarity and self-contradiction is not evidence of intentional deconstructionism.

The first two case studies in this chapter are a critique of two famous and widely-used gospel tracts. Although these tracts originated prior to the onset of postmodernism in America they continue to grow in popularity. Indeed, the electronic version of one of them has become a common way for churches and other Christian ministries to present the gospel on their web sites. What makes these tracts relevant as an illustration of puzzling gospel methodology, is the fact that despite originating from the same author, *there are substantive contradictions in their content.*

The third case study in this chapter focuses on more than one hundred and fifty gospel presentations collected from upper-level theology students at a large, evangelical Bible college. Over a period of five years, the present writer conducted an exercise in a course entitled, *Issues in Contemporary Theology,* which he taught to junior and senior level baccalaureate students. In the exercise, students were asked to write a succinct answer to the following question: "What precisely would you tell someone if they asked you how to have eternal life?" Students' answers were then collected and compared/contrasted in front of the class by the instructor for the benefit of all. *Every time* this exercise was conducted, students reacted with utter amazement upon hearing the substantive disparity between various gospel presentations submitted by themselves and their classmates. The instructor likewise was dismayed, but not surprised. Such evidence further validates the crisis of unclear gospel presentations within contemporary evangelicalism.

The fourth and final case study in this chapter provides the consummate illustration of what happens when objectivity and meaning give way to experience and community. Where the first three case studies illustrate inconsistency and imprecision in the gospel, the soteriological method under consideration in the fourth case study truly exemplifies postmodernism's celebration of ambiguity and deconstructionism.

Case Study: Billy Graham (Part One)

The Billy Graham Evangelistic Association (BGEA) is perhaps the best known evangelical ministry in the world. Although affiliated with the fervently evangelistic Southern Baptist denomination, Graham's influence goes well beyond one denomination. As David

Dockery points out, "The evangelical movement in America during the past four decades has basically been a transdenominational movement. Billy Graham … [is] more *evangelical* than Baptist."[6] For more than fifty years BGEA has been preaching the gospel through crusades, conferences, books, tracts, audio/video tapes and various other means. Any review of the gospel in print is incomplete without analyzing a sample from the Billy Graham Evangelistic Association.

Steps to Peace with God is a well-known gospel tract published by BGEA. It may well be one of the most famous gospel tracts ever published. It has been used by individuals and ministries for decades and today, many ministries have incorporated this tract into their Internet web sites.[7] Famous Baptist evangelist and Dallas Seminary alumnus Sumner Wemp is known for his use of gospel tracts in sharing the gospel over the last several decades. It would not be an overstatement to say that few Christians, if any, have distributed more gospel tracts than Sumner. When asked about their effectiveness, Rev. Wemp conjectured, "One half of the tracts in print do not present the gospel clearly."[8] Although Wemp's statement represents a general characterization, the first two case studies below validate his speculation.

Steps to Peace with God communicates the gospel using a four-step outline. The first step deals with "God's Purpose: Peace and Life." This section explains that God loves man and desires for man to be at peace with Him. Romans 5:1 and John 3:16 are cited for support. The tract goes on to explain that God wants man to have an abundant life (John 10:10).

Step two is titled "The Problem: Our Separation." Romans 3:23 and 6:23 make this point for the reader that man's sin has separated him from God. A helpful diagram showing the classic *gulf* or *chasm* between man and God is depicted. Step two also addresses "Our Attempts to Reach God." Proverbs 14:12 and Isaiah 59:2 are listed to support the contention that man has tried such vain resources as good works, religion, philosophy, and morality to reach God, but all have failed to bridge the gap. Proverbs 14:12 gives a general principle: "There is a way that seems right to a man, but in the end it leads to death." Relating this principle to man's quest for spiritual peace is an appropriate application. The Isaiah passage, by contrast, refers in the context to Israel's rebellion against God through disobedience and the subsequent need for national confession and repentance in order to experience physical peace in the land once again. Prophetically, this points to the future Messianic kingdom. The "iniquities" that "have separated you from God" refer to specific sins of Israel in the eighth century BC such as murder, lying and injustice (Isa 59:9, 11, 14–15). The separation is not a spiritual, eternal one but rather an experiential one in which God's blessings are removed. Earlier, the prophet wrote, "'There is no peace,' says the Lord, 'for the wicked'" (Isa 48:22). To apply this verse to man's universal, spiritual separation from God stretches the original meaning of the text. Alternative verses that have a more direct application are Ephesians 2:14–18 and Proverbs 15:29. Nevertheless, the discussion of man's various attempts to reach God is helpful as it prepares the reader for the later discussion of Jesus Christ as the only solution to man's sin problem.

Step three is titled, "God's Bridge: The Cross." The accompanying diagram shows a cross with the word *Christ* on it bridging the gap between man's sinfulness and God's holiness. 1 Timothy 2:5, 1 Peter 3:18, and Romans 5:8 are the supporting texts. Each of these verses is an excellent choice in communicating the substitutionary atonement of Christ. This section is clear, concise and biblically true to the text.

Unfortunately, step four is where the tract begins to get confusing. After laying a fairly effective foundation, and preparing the reader for the solution to man's sin problem, step four presents a puzzling and self-contradictory gospel message. The section is titled, "Our Response: Receive Christ." The title in and of itself is not bad (though perhaps *Trust Christ* would be better). What gets confusing is that right beneath the title the reader is instructed to (1) "trust Christ as Lord and Savior" and (2) "receive Him by personal invitation."[9] The implication is that receiving God's gift of salvation involves two steps, rather than the singular step of *faith*. The supporting Scriptural text only adds to the confusion. Revelation 3:20 is cited to support the notion that one must "receive Christ by personal invitation." It often has been pointed out, however, that the context of Revelation 3:20 relates to fellowship with believers, not the means by which one receives eternal life.[10] While this hardly can be considered a serious error (Undoubtedly—and thankfully—God has used untold numbers of gospel presentations over the centuries in spite of such instances of improper hermeneutics!), one unintended problem with the use of this verse and the corresponding terminology is that it may prompt readers of the tract to search for some type of vague and indefinable *knock*.

A second supporting Scripture in this section is John 1:12. If the author prefers to use the term *receive* in his presentation of the gospel—which is an acceptable biblical synonym for faith in the context of John 1:12—then this is an excellent supporting reference. However, in light of the fact that the tract appears to distinguish between the acts of *trusting* and *receiving*, the appeal to this verse only clouds the issue. A third supporting Scripture under the heading of "Our Response: Receive Christ" is Romans 10:9. "That if you confess with your mouth the Lord Jesus and believe in your heart that God has raised Him from the dead, you will be saved." This citation is listed in the tract without commentary and given the common misunderstanding of the phrase "confess with your mouth the Lord Jesus," it lends itself to confusion.[11] At this point the reader might easily assume that obtaining eternal salvation involves (1) trusting, (2) receiving, and (3) confessing.

Step four of the tract next includes a second copy of the cross diagram in which the gulf between man and God is depicted as being bridged only by Christ. The tract then poses the questions, "Where are you?" and "Will you receive Jesus Christ right now?" Immediately following these two questions, the reader is instructed, "Here is how you can receive Christ [i.e., gain eternal life]." Four action items are listed and numbered sequentially one through four. They are: (1) Admit your need (I am a sinner); (2) Be willing to turn from your sins (repent); (3) Believe that Jesus Christ died for you on the cross and rose from the grave; (4) Through prayer, invite Jesus Christ to come in and control your life through the Holy Spirit (Receive Him as Lord and Savior).

How does this formula for obtaining eternal life measure up to the essence of the gospel outlined in chapter three? Certainly, in the earlier sections of the tract, sufficient explanation is given that Jesus Christ is the Son of God who died and rose again to pay one's personal penalty for sin. Thus the first three essentials of the gospel are present. Additionally, the tract explains that eternal life (the fourth essential) is the goal, though not in the most clear manner. Yet in explaining what to do with this content, viz. the specific response that one must make to Jesus if He is to be saved, the tract is unclear. Consider the four action items.[12]

The first action is to *admit your need*. This statement seems out of place and unnecessary since any desire on the part of the reader to take these actions as a means of *making peace with God* presupposes that he has recognized his sinfulness. Having previously established the reader's need for salvation in the previous three sections of the tract, one wonders why, in this *how to* section, this first action item is necessary.[13]

Assuming for the sake of argument that a sequentially ordered list of action items is necessary in order to be saved (a point which the present writer suggests is not the case), why not start with step two: *Believe that Jesus Christ died for you on the cross and rose from the grave?* The first action item has already been done by the sinner seeking salvation. Is the reader now supposed to verbalize his need once more? Nevertheless, one might overlook this deficiency if the tract merely said (1) admit your need and (2) trust Jesus alone to solve it. However, the second and fourth action items listed in the *how to* section of the tract render it thoroughly perplexing.

The second action item is *be willing to turn from your sins (repent)*. This violates the fourth and fifth essentials of the gospel by making something other than faith alone in Christ the means of securing eternal life. It is one thing to recognize one's sinfulness. It is quite another to make a personal commitment to turn from it. The former is required for salvation; the latter is not.[14] The fourth action item is equally confusing: *Through prayer, invite Jesus Christ to come in and control your life through the Holy Spirit. (Receive Him as Lord and Savior.)* As already discussed, to separate the biblical notions of trusting and receiving is unnecessary. Furthermore, the reference to Jesus *controlling one's life*, like the earlier action item of *repentance of sins*, implies some self-initiated works of obedience on the part of the reader—something that again undermines the exclusivity of faith alone in Christ alone.

Is it possible for someone to be saved after reading this gospel tract in spite of its inaccuracies and lack of clarity? Of course it is. As someone has said, "God is able to hit a homerun with a crooked stick." But such glib appeals to God's sovereignty in an effort to excuse poor or unclear semantics do not discharge evangelicals from the duty to present the gospel clearly, accurately and biblically.[15]

Case Study: Billy Graham (Part Two)

How to Become a Christian is another popular gospel tract written by Billy Graham and published by the American Tract Society in Garland, Texas. Yet, there is significant disparity between its content and that of the Billy Graham tract examined in the previous case study. *How to Become a Christian* is clear, concise and meets the standard of the five-fold essentials established in chapter three. Given Billy Graham's renowned status as one of the greatest evangelists of all time, the lack of consistency between these two gospel presentations is startling.[16]

The tract begins with the following introductory paragraph:

The central theme of the New Testament is God's love for you as an individual. This love was revealed through Christ's coming into the world and living among men, His dying on the cross, and rising from the dead. Through Christ's death God offers you forgiveness for your sins, and through His resurrection the promise of everlasting life. Christ died and rose again for the whole world, but for you to become a Christian is an individual matter. The only way to establish a personal relationship with Jesus Christ is to accept His offer of forgiveness and everlasting life. The following Scripture passages show God's part and yours. Read each verse and believe it, for it is the Word of God speaking to you.[17]

The subsequent pages elaborate on this well-stated introduction. The first section is titled, *God's Love is Revealed.* Citing John 3:16, the reader is told that God offers "not only an abundant life here and now, but a life which is *eternal*" (emphasis added). The next section states, *Man is Sinful* and is supported by Romans 3:23. The third section declares, *Sin Has a Penalty*. Graham calls this penalty "separation from God *forever*" (emphasis added). He goes on to explain, "The alternative is to personally receive God's free gift, which is pardon for sin and provision of life everlasting."

This is an excellent, succinct statement of the problem and the solution. Next Graham includes a section titled, *Christ Paid the Penalty*. He cites Romans 5:8 for support and explains, "[God] sent Christ to die in your place and to pay the penalty for your sin so that you can be reconciled to Him." Again, this is an outstanding explanation of the substitutionary atonement of Christ. The next section proclaims, *Salvation is a Free Gift* and provides a helpful explanation of God's grace. After citing Ephesians 2:8–9, the author accurately explains,

> Grace means undeserved favor. God graciously offers to you what you could never do for yourself. God's gift to you is free. You do not, and cannot, work for a gift. *All you need to do is receive it.* Believe with all your heart that Jesus Christ died for you to provide deliverance from your sins.[18]

Graham systematically brings the reader to the place where he realizes there is nothing he can do to overcome his predicament. He must rely wholly and solely on Jesus Christ. In the next section, Graham tells the reader, "We Must Receive Christ." He then quotes John 1:12. Unlike the *Steps to Peace with God* tract, here Graham avoids any reference to Revelation 3:20. He explains *receiving Christ* as "accept[ing] what he has done for you." This is an accurate way of explaining the concept of faith, as John 1:12 equates *receiving* with *believing*.

The tract *does* employ similar *invitation* language as does the *Steps to Peace with God*. "Picture, if you will, Jesus Christ standing at the door of your life. Invite Him in. He is waiting to be received into your life," but without any appeal to Revelation 3:20. Here, in contrast to the *Steps to Peace with God*, the reader would naturally understand the *door* analogy as just that: an *analogy* of what it looks like to trust Christ for everlasting life. Note again the terminology: "*Picture*, if you will, Jesus Christ standing at the door of your life." Given the wording, the reader naturally understands the *door of his life* as figurative and the *invitation* as a mere call to trust Christ and receive His gift.

Finally, in the concluding *how to* section, Graham encourages the reader to "Receive Christ Now." Note the absence of a sequentially order task list. He simply suggests that the reader who wants to be saved pray "something like the following." He then gives the following suggested prayer without labeling it as such:

Dear Lord, I know that I am a sinner and that I need Your forgiveness. I believe that Christ died in *my* place to pay the penalty for *my* sin and that He rose from the dead. I now invite Jesus Christ to come into my life as my personal Savior. Thank you for making me Your child. Help me learn to please You in every part of my life.[19]

This suggested prayer is commendable on several points. First, it addresses the responsibility of the reader to acknowledge his need for a Savior without listing this as a separate action item among several others. Second, there is a clear emphasis within this prayer on *faith*. The reader is encouraged to tell the Lord that he "believes" Christ died in his place and for his sin. He then asks Jesus to save him (implicit within "[be] my personal Savior"). The element of trust is further seen in that after asking Jesus to be his Savior, the reader is immediately encouraged to thank Jesus for "making me Your child." Thanking someone for doing something presupposes belief that he did it.

The final sentence in the prayer, in which the reader is encouraged to ask for God's general guidance in life, comes only *after* the issue of his salvation has already been settled. That is, the one praying this prayer has already acknowledged his need for a Savior; asked Jesus to be that Savior; and thanked Him for saving him. Then, as a clear addendum to the *salvation* portion of the prayer, the new believer now asks his Savior for help in living the Christian life. This prayer stands in stark contrast to many other "sinners prayers," including the one in Billy Graham's *Steps to Peace with God*, in that it does not lead the reader to believe that his willingness to "turn from sins" or "live a good life" are an efficacious part of the prayer.

Following the suggested prayer there is a space for the new believer to make a note of his name and the date on which he trusted Christ. This is a helpful exercise in anticipation of those future times when the believer may have doubts about his conversion experience. Marking the moment with a date and signature can be helpful because it drives home the point that the person has received eternal life *at that moment* and does not have to wait to see if his life gives evidence of repentance and surrender. The tract closes with a section entitled *Promises From the Word of God*. Romans 10:13 is quoted as a springboard for the author's comments on assurance that follow. Graham lists several things that took place in the life of the reader the moment he placed his faith in Christ, each with a supporting reference in parenthesis.[20] He then directs the new believer to base his assurance on the promise and authority of God's Word. When doubts arise, the reader is instructed to review the passages discussed. The tract opens by directing the reader to "read each verse" listed in the tract and it closes by directing the reader to "review the above passages" from God's Word to counter any doubts about his salvation that may arise in the future. Thus, from cover to cover, God's Word has a central place in this tract.

The differences in content between *How to Become a Christian* and *Steps to Peace with God* illustrate well the kind of inconsistency that exists in many puzzling gospel presentations today. The chart on the following page contrasts the two tracts:

Steps to Peace With God Billy Graham	**How to Become a Christian** Billy Graham
The reader is told he must "repent of sins" in order to be saved.	Repentance of sins is never mentioned. (In fact, the words "repent" and "repentance" are never used in the tract.)
The reader is told he must be willing to "turn from his sins" in order to be saved.	No reference to "turning from sins"
The reader is told he must "invite Jesus Christ to come in and control his life" in order to be saved.	No reference to Christ "taking control"
The reader is told he must "receive Christ by personal invitation."	No reference to "personal invitation."
Receiving eternal life is a 4-step process.	Receiving eternal life is a 1-step process.
Revelation 3:20 is prominent.	No mention of Revelation 3:20.
A suggested prayer encourages the reader to invite Jesus Christ "to come into my heart and life."	Suggested prayer encourages reader to invite Jesus Christ "to come into my life as my personal Savior."
The word grace is never mentioned in the tract. (aside from within the text of one quotation of Ephesians 2:8)	The tract contains a lengthy paragraph explaining the meaning of grace under the heading "Salvation is a Free Gift."

It is difficult to believe that these two gospel presentations have the same author. Notwithstanding Graham's legendary status among evangelicals, these differences cannot be dismissed as insignificant or inconsequential. Nor can they be excused as a matter of semantics. As Charles Ryrie points out, "Actually, semantics is not an excuse, nor is it incidental; it is the *whole point*. Semantics involves the study of meanings of words; so if one uses words which do not convey the meaning he or she is attempting to express, then a different meaning comes across."[21] At a time when inconsistency in language is thriving, evangelicals must do a better job of presenting the gospel with consistent accuracy.

Case Study: Bible College Students

"What precisely would you tell someone if they asked you how to have eternal life?" This was the question posed to junior and senior level theology students at a large, conservative, evangelical Bible college during a class exercise. It would be a reasonable assumption that these students would be able to articulate the gospel clearly and accurately and with substantial doctrinal agreement, especially since the successful completion of basic Bible and theology courses (or the equivalent from another college) was required for enrollment in this class. Yet, as the following sampling of data collected over a five year period demonstrates, such is not the case.[22] While some of the more than one hundred and fifty gospel presentations collected articulated key essentials of the gospel such as an emphasis on Jesus Christ, His death and resurrection, His substitutionary atonement, and eternal life, not all of them did.

Before examining some of the faulty answers that were given, a few general observations are in order. First, often some of the students were unable to answer the question in a timely manner. Students were normally given three to five minutes (sometimes longer) to write their answers and the instructor prompted them to keep it simple and focus on the essentials. That some students were unable to articulate the gospel in a timely manner likely indicates that the gospel was not crystallized clearly in their minds—a cause for concern in and of itself. Second, the responses varied considerably in length. In light of the time constraints, most were appropriately short—one paragraph or less. Yet, some were more than a page. However, the focus of the exercise was not to evaluate the length, style or format of the students' gospel presentations, but primarily their *content*. Are they consistent, clear and accurate? Third, it is worth noting that few of the gospel presentations *explicitly* empha-sized the exclusivity of Christ as the only hope of eternal life, though it was implied in many of the answers. Fourth, the interpretation of the gospel presentations is not a matter of conjecture on the part of the instructor. Rather, on each occasion after collecting the answers, the next two hours of class time were dedicated to discussing the answers, during which time the instructor was able to clarify with a good degree of confidence what students meant by their answers. Finally, from the instructor's perspective, the intended goal of the exercise was not so much to expose erroneous gospel presentations, but rather to raise the students' awareness to the fact that there is a prevalent lack of consistency when it comes to the precise nature of the gospel. To that end, the exercise was extremely effective. The following are some of the more common erroneous or unclear answers received during this exercise. They are grouped by common theme.

An emphasis on commitment

Many of the gospel presentations emphasized personal commit-ment to one degree or another. For instance, the instructions, "Surrender your life to Jesus," or "Commit your life to Christ and follow Him," were prevalent. This terminology, while common in personal evangelism, sermons and gospel tracts, is inconsistent with the biblical call to believe in Jesus Christ alone. It violates the essence of the gospel in that, as discussed in chapter three above, no act of obedience, preceding or following faith in Jesus Christ, such as a promise to obey, repentance of sin, pledge of obedience or surrendering to the Lordship of Christ, may be added to, or consid-ered part of, faith as a condition for receiving eternal life.

An emphasis on repentance

Similar to the emphasis on commitment is the requirement that one repent of his sins in order to be saved. It has already been discussed at length that *repentance*, as it relates to salvation, is limited to a *change of mind about God, Christ and salvation*.[23] But in many cases, the students' answers indicated an obligation on the part of the potential convert to change his behavior as a prerequisite for receiving eternal life. Phrases such as "repent of all your sins," and "repent of all known and unknown sins," may give the impression that one must *stop sinning* in order to be saved. Furthermore, regardless of how one defines repentance, the obligation to repent of all *unknown* sins, as suggested by some respondents, is impossible! In many of the student's responses, the command to repent was simply attached to believe without further comment (e.g. "Repent and believe the gospel."). But such terminology is inconsistent in that it implies that repentance is a necessary first step, distinct from faith.[24] This emphasis on repentance is at best confusing and at worst inconsistent with the essential call of the gospel, namely, faith alone in Christ alone as the Son of God who died and rose again to pay one's personal penalty for sin and the one who gives eternal life to all who trust Him and Him alone for it.

An emphasis on confession

Still other students chose to emphasize the language of *confession*. For example, "confess Jesus as Lord," "confess that God is Lord," "confess Jesus Christ with your mouth," or "confess your sins." These responses are inconsistent with the essence of the gospel because they may imply (1) that verbal testimony is necessary for eternal life or (2) that one must swear allegiance to Christ as Lord of his life in order to have eternal life, or both. The phrase "confess your sins," admittedly, is less puzzling than the others in that most would understand such language to mean, "admit you are a sinner." Nevertheless, the context in which such phrases were employed suggests an emphasis on man's own actions as meritorious in securing salvation.

A generally vague emphasis

Some responses did not fall into any of the previous three categorizations, yet nevertheless were inconsistent with the essence of the gospel, or at least, may have been taken in such a way as to be inconsistent. Many students invoked the popular phrase, "ask Christ into your heart," which in and of itself does not provide enough information to communicate accurately the essence of the gospel.[25] So too with the similar phrases "ask God to come into your heart," or "receive Jesus Christ into your life." Even in cases where the student's prelude to this instruction explained key components of the gospel, such as sin, eternal life, and the death and resurrection of Christ, the pivotal *how to* moment is clouded by the ambiguity of these phrases.

Other students opted for the term *accept,* as in, "accept Jesus by personal invitation" or "accept Christ's sacrifice." This language, too, lacks clarity and consistency. One can easily see how such phrases could be taken as semantic equivalents to *trust in Jesus Christ for eternal life*, but it would be better for such a connection to be made explicitly by the evangelist if this terminology is to be effective.

A couple of times, the terminology "pray that God will have mercy on your soul," occurred in the students' responses. Such language is woefully inadequate and ignores the instrumentality of faith in securing eternal salvation. Yet, this anomaly can be dismissed as likely reflecting a Roman Catholic influence and should not be considered commonplace among evangelical gospel presentations.[26]

A misapplied emphasis on faith

Finally, many students appropriately emphasized *faith* but did so in a manner that misapplied it, either due to an incorrect object or the implied notion that one's faith itself has inherent worth unrelated to its object. For instance, one student wrote, "believe in the virgin birth, death and resurrection of Christ," and several included "belief in the Trinity" as part of the object of saving faith. Yet as discussed in chapter three above, while there are many aspects to God's plan of salvation that may serve as a backdrop in the evangelistic discussion, not every foundational truth of Christianity is required to be affirmed explicitly by those seeking to obtain eternal life. The doctrines of the Trinity and the virgin birth fall into this category.

Several students chose to qualify faith with phrases like "whole-heartedly," or "all your heart." For example, "Believe in Jesus with *all your heart* and you will be saved." What does this mean, exactly? If one believes in Jesus Christ alone as the Son of God who died and rose again to pay his personal penalty for sin and the one who gives him eternal life, but he does so with something less than his *whole heart* does he remain unsaved? What percentage of one's heart must be involved in saving faith? Such terminology likely reflects the Reformed notion of saving faith in which both personal commitment to obey *and* faith are required. Even if this implication is not intended by the student, the terminology is unclear.

Case Study: Leonard Sweet

One of the more puzzling and obscure expressions of the evangelical gospel in recent times comes from Leonard Sweet, noted leader within the Emergent Church movement.[27] In his book *The Gospel According to Starbucks*, Sweet recasts the gospel as an "EPIC spiritual experience."[28] The book adopts a clever style with Starbucks coffee as a running metaphor throughout. The acronym *EPIC* reflects the four major tenets of Emergent theology: *Experiential, Participatory, Image-rich,* and *Connecting*.[29] That Sweet elevates experience over propositional truth is unmistakable in his book. "Right belief" should not hold the "upper hand over a believer's authentic experience."[30] Christianity should not be viewed as a "belief system with a distinct worldview," but as an experiential "conversation" with God and others.[31] And the content of faith, viz. non-negotiable truths about Christ, is a matter of polemics best reserved for "divinity schools" not churches.[32]

Sweet's approach is heavily reflective of the perspective espoused by Brian McLaren in his celebrated book, *A Generous Orthodoxy*.[33] McLaren, widely considered the father of the Emergent Church movement, celebrates his pluralistic approach to theology by self-identifying with seemingly *all* theological perspectives. In the book, he asserts quite bluntly: "To be a Christian in the generous orthodox way is not to claim to have the truth captured...."[34] In other words, anyone who claims to know the absolute Truth, and criticizes others whose beliefs are in opposition to the Truth, is *unorthodox*. The only standard of orthodoxy, according to McLaren, is one that affirms *all standards*. Perhaps that is why he considers himself a "Missional, Evangelical, Post/Protestant, Liberal/conservative, Mystical/poetic, Biblical, Charismatic/contemplative, Fundamentalist/Calvinist, Anabaptist/Anglican, Methodist, Catholic, Green, Incarnational, Depressed-Yet-Hopeful, Emergent, Unfinished Christian."[35]

Similarly, Sweet eschews the propositional/doctrinal component of orthodoxy in favor of a more experiential and relational approach to theology. While admitting that faith has a rational component, Sweet insists it is much more than that. One's real "confession of faith" is his "expression [i.e., experience] of life."[36] *Faith* is "not primarily a matter of belief," but rather "immersion and engagement, a full-on experience of life."[37] After all, faith without experience is only a "theory."[38] In Sweet's methodology, "Christian faith is designed to be lived in experiences of beauty."[39] He suggests that churches should spend less time focusing on "what they believe" and "official statement[s] of faith" and more time creating an environment that will foster "multisensory experiences."[40] The gospel, in his view, needs less propositional content and more existential mysticism. In fact, the Christian gospel might learn something from such eastern religions as Buddhism! Sweet wonders with Amos Yong, "what the gospel might look like if its primary dialogue partners are not Plato, Aristotle, Kant, Hegel or Whitehead, but rather Buddha, Confucius, Lao-tzu, Chuang-tzu, Nagarjuna, Shankara, Ramanuja, Chu His, Dogen, Wang Yang Ming, and so on."[41] Such a suggestion evidences a radical departure from the centrality of the Scriptures as Christianity's only standard for the gospel.[42]

Sweet's soteriological method has a built-in defense mechanism, since, in his view the category of *heresy* does not exist. After all, in a world where propositional truth is irrelevant *there can be no heresy*. In fact, Sweet redefines *heresy* as "choosing one truth to the exclusion of other truths."[43] He redefines *truth* as "when a body holds together its various parts in conversation and harmony … when opposites become not a battleground but a playground."[44] And he redefines *absolute* to mean "set free [i.e., from the restrictive confines of absolutism!]."[45] The definitive authority, according to Sweet, is not *the object of one's faith* but *the authority* of *community*.[46] Sweet insists, "The basic question of the Christian life is this: is Christ a living force to be experienced or a historical figure to be reckoned with?"[47] *Experience* is the "engine room" of the "spiritual enterprise" and the "authority of the Scriptures" is placed on equal footing with the "authority of the Christian community."[48]

Not only is the *Gospel According to Starbucks* vague and amorphous, but it disintegrates when examined in light of the five-fold essence of the gospel established in chapter three. Sweet's gospel does introduce *Jesus Christ*, but only *barely*.[49] Jesus' earthly life and experience are elevated above His substitutionary atonement. There is no mention of guilt and sin, nor the consequence of sin. There is no reference to eternal life. And as enumerated above, *faith in Christ* has little to do with the assurance or confidence in Him to provide eternal salvation. Given the degree of departure from the essence of the biblical gospel, it is somewhat surprising to see that some leading evangelicals have endorsed Sweet's brand of a deconstructed gospel, thus helping to further its ascendancy to a place of mainstream acceptance within the church. For example, Ben Young, Associate Pastor at the largest Southern Baptist Church in the world, Houston's Second Baptist Church, writes, "Cultural barista Leonard Sweet serves up a triple venti cup of relevant insights to wake up decaffeinated Christians. Careful, the book you're about to enjoy is extremely hot."[50] Tony Campolo calls Leonard Sweet, "One of the seminal Christian thinkers in the postmodern era."[51] Notwithstanding the unqualified endorsements from these popular, mainstream evangelical leaders, according to the standard of Scripture, *The Gospel According to Starbucks* is far from commendable.

Summary of Chapter Five

The case studies in this chapter focused on the *puzzling* gospel: those gospel presentations that lack precision, accuracy and consistency. The two Billy Graham tracts, as well as the gospel presentations collected from students at an evangelical Bible college, demonstrate a startling *inconsistency* in evangelical soteriological methodology. Additionally, the student responses and at least one of the Billy Graham tracts (i.e., *Steps to Peace with God*) evidence a significant degree of *imprecision and inaccuracy* when it comes to the essence of the gospel. The fourth case study, *The Gospel According to Starbucks,* represents the most profound example of a puzzling gospel. Not only does it lack clarity in communicating exactly what one must believe in order to have eternal life, it celebrates this lack of clarity in favor of a nebulous, experiential conversation with God, ungrounded in propositional truth.

The fog of confusion surrounding many gospel presentations manifests itself in various ways such as imprecision, inconsistency, inaccuracy, and ambiguity. Given the ideological distinctives of postmodernity, such puzzling gospels are more likely than ever to go unnoticed and perhaps even thrive. But such confusion easily gives way to clarity when one communicates the gospel as Scripture defines it: Jesus Christ, the Son of God, died and rose again to pay one's personal penalty for sin and offers eternal life to all who simply trust Him and Him alone for it.[52]

ENDNOTES
CHAPTER FIVE

1. Robert N. Wilkin, "Does Your Mind Need Changing? Repentance Reconsidered," *Journal of the Grace Evangelical Society* 11, no. 1 (Spring 1998): 45.

2. Charles C. Bing, "How to Share the Gospel Clearly," *Journal of the Grace Evangelical Society* 7, no. 1 (Spring 1994): 58–59.

3. Ibid., 65.

4. Kevin J. Vanhoozer, *Is There a Meaning in This Text? The Bible, the Reader, and the Morality of Literary Knowledge* (Grand Rapids: Zondervan, 1998), 99.

5. Paul R. Shockley, "Postmodernism as a Basis for Society?" in *The God of the Bible and Other Gods: Is the Christian God Unique among World Religions?* Robert Paul Lightner (Grand Rapids: Kregel Publications, 1998), 198.

6. David S. Dockery, "Millard J. Erickson: Baptist and Evangelical Theologian," *JETS* 32, no. 4 (December 1989): 519, emphasis added.

7. A few examples include: fishthe.net; wheaton.edu; cbn.org; fletcherbaptist.org; wwcw.org; americanmissionary.org.

8. Personal interview with Sumner Wemp, 21 April 2002.

9. The numbers in parenthesis are not actually printed in the tract. They have been added to highlight that two distinct actions arc implied, if not directly set forth.

10. Cf. "It would be wrong to take this famous statement as a simple gospel invitation, though that has often been done. Here our Lord is addressing a Christian church and, clearly, anyone in the church

is invited to respond." Zane C. Hodges, *Absolutely Free! A Biblical Reply to Lordship Salvation* (Grand Rapids: Academie Books/ Zondervan Pub. House, 1989), 129.

11. See comments on Romans 10:9–10 at note forty-six in chapter four.

12. These four actions may rightly be considered sequential *action items* because by numbering them one through four, the author of the tract clearly intends for the reader to perform them in order, one after the other. This is unfortunate because in so doing the tract leads the reader to believe that obtaining salvation involves performing multiple actions in a particular order as if there were some official equation that must be followed. The reality is there is only one action item necessary to receive eternal life: faith.

13. One might respond that such a critique is quibbling. Yet, consider again the point being made. In the evangelism process there are, generally speaking, three steps (See *God's Plan of Salvation* in chapter three). First, one establishes the need. Second, one explains the provision. And third, one encourages the listener or reader to respond in faith. In the *Steps to Peace with God* tract, the first two steps are sufficiently addressed in the first three sections. The tract intends to offer in the fourth section *specific instructions on how to respond*. By making the *admission of need* the first action item, the tract gives rise to the following potential conversation: Q. Do you need to be saved? A. Yes. I need to be saved. Q. Good. Here is what you must do. First, you must need to be saved. Do you need to be saved? A. Yes. As I said, I need to be saved. In fact, that is what I am trying to do right now. Q. Oh. You are trying to be saved? Good. Let me show you how. The first step is to recognize that you need to be saved. Do you need to be saved? … and so on.

14. See discussion of repentance at note seventy-four in chapter three.

15. See discussion of this issue at note twenty-seven in chapter two.

16. The BGEA web site describes Billy Graham this way: "Mr. Graham has preached the Gospel to more people in live audiences than anyone else in history—over 210 million people in more than 185 countries and territories—through various meetings, including Mission World and Global Mission. Hundreds of millions more have been reached through television, video, film, and webcasts. Since the 1949 Los Angeles mission vaulted Mr. Graham into the public eye, he has led hundreds of thousands of individuals to make personal decisions to live for Christ, which is the main thrust of his ministry. ... Mr. Graham is regularly listed by the Gallup organization as one of the 'Ten Most Admired Men in the World,' whom it described as the dominant figure in that poll since 1948—making an unparalleled 44th appearance and 37th consecutive appearance. He has also appeared on the covers of *TIME, Newsweek, Life, U.S. News and World Report, Parade,* and numerous other magazines and has been the subject of many newspaper and magazine feature articles and books." *Billy Graham Evangelistic Association.* <http://www.billygraham.org> (accessed 1 March 2007).

17. See *How To Become a Christian,* American Tract Society, Garland, Texas, Tract #B75.

18. Ibid., emphasis added.

19. *How To Become a Christian,* emphasis original. It is significant that in *Steps to Peace with God,* prayer was explicitly listed as a requirement in the list of action items. In *How to Become a Christian,* it is not. The Scripture nowhere commands men to pray in order to be saved. Yet, prayer is the most natural way to express one's faith in Christ, and thus it is not inappropriate for gospel presentations to offer a suggested prayer as a means of expressing one's saving faith.

20. Graham says that upon trusting Christ for salvation: your sins were forgiven (Col 1:14); you became a child of God (John 1:12); you were made an heir to all of God's blessings (Rom 8:16–17); you now possess eternal life (1 John 5:12–13).

21. Charles Caldwell Ryrie, *So Great Salvation: What It Means to Believe in Jesus Christ* (Wheaton: Victor Books, 1989), 21, emphasis added.

22. The exercise was conducted between the spring semester of 2001 and the fall semester of 2005.

23. See discussion of repentance at note seventy-four in chapter three.

24. It is acknowledged that when some evangelists and Bible scholars use the language *"repent* and *believe,"* they intend to connote only one act. The mantra, *"Repent* and *believe* are two sides of the same coin," is common. Cf. "It has often been said that repentance and faith are two sides of the same coin.... Repentance turns from sin to Christ, and faith embraces Him as the only hope of salvation and righteousness." John MacArthur, *Faith Works: The Gospel According to the Apostles* (Dallas: Word, 1993), 77. Yet in the students' responses to this exercise, not a single student who invoked the phrase "repent and believe," clarified in writing that he intended the two words to be understood as synonyms. When asked about the inconsistency between calling on someone to *repent to be saved* and calling on someone *to believe in Jesus* to be saved, students usually responded with the Reformed notion that by repent, they meant that one must be willing to forsake his sin in order to be saved.

25. For a helpful discussion of the problems with this terminology, see the booklet by Dennis Rokser, *Seven Reasons Not to Ask Jesus into Your Heart* (Duluth, Minn.: Duluth Bible Church, 1998).

26. One isolated response was so off-the-wall that it merits special comment. A student who had been heavily influenced by a hyper-

Calvinist theological mentor answered with one simple sentence that said only: "If you are chosen, you will go to heaven." While most evangelicals would quickly dismiss this approach (or *non-approach?*) to evangelism as extreme, it does bring up the point that for hyper-Calvinists who see man as utterly and completely passive in the soteriological equation, the entire emphasis on clarity in presenting the gospel is irrelevant and unnecessary. See the present writer's response to this line of reasoning at note twenty-seven in chapter two.

27. The Emergent Church (sometimes called the *Emerging Church*) is a movement within postmodern evangelicalism whose adherents seek to reach the unchurched by adopting many of the ideological and philosophical tenets of secular, postmodern thinking. In many ways, it is built upon the principles and methodologies first popularized by the seeker-sensitive and purpose driven movements. But whereas these movements targeted the so-called baby-boomer generation and encouraged the church to focus on sensitivity to felt-needs, entertainment and an excellence in the weekly worship service (which often resembles more of a production), the Emergent movement targets *Generation X* and is much less corporate in its focus. For advocates of the Emergent Church movement, the primary focus is on the relational *conversation*. Every attempt is made to connect with the unchurched on their level via an emphasis on dialogue rather than propositional beliefs. The Emergent Church methodology is characterized by the noteworthy influence of Eastern Mysticism, the blending of Roman Catholic and evangelical traditions—especially the worship of the Eucharist and the Virgin Mary, a heavy use of candles and other sensory-driven worship aids, and a marked disdain for anything that resembles propositional doctrine.

In addition to Sweet, other notable leaders in this movement include Brian McLaren, Dan Kimball, Tony Jones, and Doug Pagitt. For more information about the Emergent Church, see www.emergentvillage.org. For a discussion and critique of the Emergent Church movement see Ron J. Bigalke, Jr., "The Latest Post-Modern Trend: The Emerging Church," *Journal of Dispensational Theology* 10, no. 31 (2006), 19–39.

Although a detailed foray into the Emergent Church movement is beyond the scope of this present work, Sweet's book was chosen as a focus in this chapter because it illustrates well the celebration of ambiguity and vagueness that characterizes much of postmodern evangelical soteriology. See discussion of the abandonment of certainty in chapter two.

28. Leonard Sweet, *The Gospel According to Starbucks* (Colorado Springs: WaterBrook Press, 2007).

29. Sweet, *The Gospel According to Starbucks*, 20.

30. Ibid., 171.

31. Ibid., 172.

32. Ibid., 5.

33. Brian D. McLaren, *A Generous Orthodoxy: Why I Am a Missional, Evangelical, Post/Protestant, Liberal/conservative, Mystical/poetic, Biblical, Charismatic/contemplative, Fundamentalist/Calvinist, Anabaptist/Anglican, Methodist, Catholic, Green, Incarnational, Depressed-Yet-Hopeful, Emergent, Unfinished Christian* (Grand Rapids: Zondervan, 2004). The very phrase "generous orthodoxy" in the book's title unmasks McLaren's agenda. Historic Christian orthodoxy, according to McLaren, has been too narrow and restrictive. It is time to open the door to a broader more accepting theological outlook. A couple of chapter titles from the book are particularly revealing: *The Seven Jesuses I Have Known* and *Would Jesus Be a Christian?* As if anticipating the reaction of conservative, evangelical scholars, McLaren provides a caveat at the outset: his book is for "mature audiences" only, and those who are troubled by what they are reading are encouraged to "return the book" and get their money back. But such a caveat does little to assuage the fears of traditional evangelicals and in fact makes the contents of his book even more alarming and offensive. The implication of his caveat is that spiritual maturity is only achieved when one becomes open-

minded enough to broaden his standard of orthodoxy and embrace others of opposing views! Many "immature" conservative theologians would disagree vehemently.

34. Ibid, inside front cover.

35. Taken from the subtitle of Mclaren's book, *A Generous Orthodoxy*.

36. Ibid., 46.

37. Ibid., 17.

38. Ibid., 50–51.

39. Ibid., 53. This premise underlies much of the Emergent movement's emphasis on icons, imagery and ecclesiastical relics in worship.

40. Ibid., 56.

41. Ibid., 173. Sweet's statement reflects the influence of evangelical inclusivism and its positive outlook on pagan religions as representing valid spiritual pathways. E.g. Clark Pinnock writes, "I welcome the Saiva Siddhanta literature of Hinduism, which celebrates a personal God of love, and the emphasis on grace that I see in the Japanese Shin-Shu Amida sect. I also respect the Buddha as a righteous man (Matt 10:41) and Mohammed as a prophet figure in the style of the Old Testament." Clark H. Pinnock, "An Inclusivist View," in *Four Views on Salvation in a Pluralistic World*, ed. Timothy R. Phillips and Dennis L. Okholm (Grand Rapids: Zondervan, 1995), 110.

42. Even more troubling than Sweet's suggestion that evangelicals can learn something from Buddha or Confucius, are the activities of Sweet's colleague and fellow-leader in the Emergent Church movement, Doug Paggit. Pagitt and popular evangelical leader Rob Bell joined Muslims, Sikhs, Buddhists, Episcopalians, Catholics

and the United Nations (UNESCO) at the *Seeds of Compassion Interspiritual* event in Seattle, WA on April 15, 2008. Astonishingly, the lineup of speakers with Paggit and Bell included the Dalai Lamaand Desmond Tutu! See http://www.freerepublic.com/focus/ f-religion/ 1987848/posts and http://www.sliceoflaodicea.com /? p=489 for more details.

43. Sweet, *The Gospel According to Starbucks*, 92. Sweet's terminology sounds dangerously close to what D. A. Carson deems "radical religious pluralism." D. A. Carson, *The Gagging of God: Christianity Confronts Pluralism* (Grand Rapids: Zondervan, 1996), 26. Note also the correlation between Sweet's definition of heresy and McLaren's definition of orthodoxy. See note thirty-three above.

44. Sweet, *The Gospel According to Starbucks*, 92. Elsewhere he adds, "The truth of Christianity is the relationships" (p. 144).

45. Ibid., 30. Sweet's penchant for redefining words is illustrative of one of postmodernism's most notable hallmarks: deconstructionism. Indeed, Sweet favorably quotes Derrida's famous axiom, "All the world's a text," and then suggests that "we can read all of our experiences as textual signs" (p. 7). Jacques Derrida suggested that the locus of meaning is the reader. For Derrida, the moment a writer puts words on paper, he "abandons them to [an] essential drift." Jacques Derrida, "Signature Event Context," *Glyph* 1 (1977): 182. Sweet represents a prime example of this perspective on meaning.

46. Sweet, *The Gospel According to Starbucks*, 152.

47. Ibid., 45.

48. Ibid., 46, 53.

49. Sweet writes, "The evangelists of the biblical world announce that Jesus is the center of the experience" (p. 16).

50. From the endorsement page inside the front cover of *The Gospel According to Starbucks*.

51. Ibid.

52. For helpful suggestions on how to share the gospel effectively see Bing, "How to Share the Gospel Clearly," 51–65. See also the outstanding evangelistic training ministry of Dr. Larry Moyer with EvanTell Ministries at www.evantell.org.

CHAPTER 6

THE PROSPERITY GOSPEL

In the day of prosperity be happy, but in the day of adversity
consider— God has made the one as well as the other....
–Ecclesiastes 7:14

The American evangelical movement known variously as
Prosperity Theology, Word of Faith, Health and Wealth, and
Name-It-and-Claim-It, has its origins in the first half of the last
century. Its proponents usually refer to E. W. Kenyon (1867–1948)
as the patriarch of the movement. Kenyon was a New England Bible
teacher whose teaching greatly influenced several later prosperity
preachers such as Kenneth Hagin, Kenneth Copeland, Benny Hinn,
Paul Crouch, Frederick K. C. Price, and Charles Capps.[1]

The *prosperity gospel* connects the gospel with the promise of
earthly blessings such as wealth and good health. Although this soteriological method predates the onset of postmodern ideology, the
tendency toward experientialism and subjectivity that characterize
postmodernism seems to have emboldened its adherents such that it
remains a prevalent force within evangelical thought. A recent *TIME*
magazine article suggests that disciples of the prosperity gospel are
on the rise.

Does God want you to be rich? A growing number of
Protestant evangelists raise a joyful *Yes!* ... It is one of

the New Testament's hardest teachings, yet generations of church-goers have understood that being Christian, on some level, means being ready to sacrifice—money, autonomy or even their lives. But for a growing number of Christians … the question is better restated, "Why *not gain* the whole world *plus* my soul?" For several decades, a philosophy has been percolating in the ten million-strong Pentecostal wing of Christianity that seems to turn the Gospel's passage on its head: certainly, it allows, Christians should keep one eye on heaven. But the new good news is that God doesn't want us to wait…. Its emphasis is on God's promised generosity in this life and the ability of believers to claim it for themselves.[2]

The article's authors have captured well the essence of the prosperity gospel. Postmodern manifestations of this approach to the gospel may be found in such popular current evangelical leaders as T. D. Jakes, Joel Osteen, Joyce Meyer, Creflo Dollar, Kirbyjon Caldwell, and others. Though not all of these trace their lineage to the Pentecostal, Word of Faith movement, they nevertheless espouse a soteriological method that elevates personal prosperity to a place of centrality in the gospel.[3] Osteen, Jakes and Caldwell are considered in more detail in the case studies that follow.

Case Study: Joel Osteen

Joel Osteen is the senior pastor of Lakewood Church in Houston, Texas. Lakewood Church is considered America's largest and fastest growing church with more than forty thousand in attendance at their worship services each weekend.[4] Joel Osteen assumed the pastorate after the death of his father, John Osteen, founding pastor, on October 3, 1999. Not surprisingly, Joel Osteen is uncomfortable being branded a prosperity preacher. Perhaps the negative reputations of some of the more extreme proponents of this view have motivated him to distance himself from the label.[5] When asked about this label on CNN's *Larry King Live*, Osteen responded:

You know, Larry? That's something I kind of get tagged with that I don't even like. I'm not a prosperity preacher, quote. My message is very balanced. I preach about forgiveness and hope, as a matter of fact, I've never preached a message on money.

I think that I—you know, people put me into that sometimes, because I do believe God wants us to be blessed, he wants us to prosper, but to me prospering is not all about money, it's about good health, good relationships. We both know people with—people that have money, but are as lonely as can be or can't get along with somebody. So I do think God does want us to be blessed and it goes back to—when I think about my father, when he was seventeen, he came out of the Depression, they had no money, a rags to riches type of story, where he said my children are not going to be raised like this. He didn't have money to go to school. He had holes in his pants, stuff like that. He made that decision to rise above that. That's my whole message: is no matter where you are, you can rise higher, you can be a better father, be a better husband, you can break an addiction. That's what it's all about. If money is the only thing that we're searching for, that's very shallow.[6]

Yet as Biema and Chu have noted, a common theme in Osteen's sermons is prosperity that relates either directly or indirectly to money, such as how the right attitude can "save your job" or "get you a promotion."[7] Biema and Chu continue,

[Joel] and Victoria meet with *TIME* in their pastoral suite, once the Houston Rockets' locker and shower area but now a zone of overstuffed sofas and imposing oak bookcases. "Does God want us to be rich?" he asks. "When I hear that word *rich*, I think people say, 'Well, he's preaching that everybody's going to be a millionaire.' I don't think that's it." Rather, he explains, "I preach that anybody can improve their lives. I think God wants us to be prosperous. I think he wants us to be happy. To me, you need to have money to pay your bills. I think God wants us to send our kids to college. I think he wants us to be a blessing to other people. But I don't think I'd say God wants us to be rich. It's all relative, isn't it?" The room's warm lamplight reflects softly off his crocodile shoes.[8]

Osteen's desire to distance himself from the significance of money in his theological approach seems disingenuous when one considers that the topic of sowing and receiving financial seeds of blessing is a repeated theme throughout his enormously popular book *Your Best Life Now*—with one entire chapter dedicated to this topic.[9] Notwithstanding his assertions to the contrary, Osteen appears to value money as a central part of the prosperity he preaches.

The tendency on the part of Joel Osteen to equivocate on the gospel has been addressed briefly in previous chapters. The focus of this section is on his articulation of the gospel in his best-selling book, *Your Best Life Now*. Though not nearly as popular as Rick Warren's *The Purpose Driven Life*, Osteen's book is nevertheless a huge hit in the public square. Its sales have eclipsed four million and it has received high praise from a number of leading evangelicals. For instance, Pat Robertson writes, "If you truly want to live your best life now, Joel's book is for you. Take it from one of this generation's most inspiring leaders, enlarge your vision and start believing in what you can become today!"[10] And Max Lucado states, "Our Lord uses Joel Osteen to lift my eyes, lighten my step, and brighten my heart. May God use this book to do the same for you."[11]

Osteen opens with a succinct statement of the book's theme:

To live your best life now, you must start looking at life through the eyes of faith, seeing yourself rising to new levels. See your business taking off. See your marriage restored. See your family prospering. See your dreams coming to pass. You must conceive it and believe it is possible if you ever hope to experience it.

To conceive it, you must have an image on the inside of the life you want to live on the outside. This image has to become a part of you, in your thoughts, your conversation, deep down in your subconscious mind, in your actions, in every part of your being.[12]

In this way, Osteen sets the stage for the development of his seven steps to reaching one's full potential.[13] The entire journey toward personal prosperity is built upon *thinking, dreaming* and *visualizing* a better life. Osteen's emphasis on self-help is seen in his stressing of themes like "discover the power of your thoughts and words," and "choose to be happy." According to Osteen, "Our thoughts and expectations wield tremendous power and influence in our lives."[14] One *becomes* what he believes and one *receives* what he believes. "It's our faith that activates the power of God," Osteen insists.[15] But as Ken Sarles has pointed out, "The value of faith is *extrinsic*, not *intrinsic*."[16]

Perhaps the most difficult concept in the prosperity gospel to understand is human faith. It has been divested of its biblical foundation and given an entirely new meaning. Faith is defined as a positive force.... According to this definition, human faith has intrinsic value apart from its object. Faith becomes a power exerted by individuals. By contrast the Bible teaches that faith is a confident reliance on and trust in another. Instead of being something that is exerted, biblical faith constitutes a resting or repose.... The significance of faith is found in its *object*, namely, God.[17]

Yet rather than emphasizing the proper *object* of faith, for Osteen the emphasis seems to be on one's faith itself. Appealing to the story of the healing of two blind men (Matt 9:27–31), Osteen suggests, "It was their *faith* that turned the situation around. It was their *believing* that brought them healing."[18] For Osteen, "You *become* what you *believe*."[19]

This emphasis on the positive force of faith, as a power inherent within oneself, influences his soteriology as well. Because reaching one's *full potential* is couched in terms of a declarative attitude of the heart, the reader is inclined to think that eternal salvation is likewise built upon the power of positive thinking. According to Osteen, one can find *peace* and *happiness* in life simply by *asking Jesus to come into his heart* and *making Him his Lord and Savior.*[20] Osteen's brief articulation of the plan of salvation on the last page of the book is so truncated as to be lacking key essentials. The essence of the gospel as defended in chapter three is that eternal life is gained solely by faith alone in Jesus Christ alone as the Son of God who died and rose again to pay one's personal penalty for sin. The *object* of faith is the key to saving faith. Although Osteen mentions Jesus in his short gospel presentation, he does not mention His death and resurrection at all. And given the paucity of any detailed discussion of Christ throughout the book, the reader cannot be expected to fully identify *who this Jesus even is* that he is told to make the Lord of his life.

Furthermore, Osteen fails to describe sin adequately in terms of one's personal guilt and responsibility. Throughout the book Osteen minimizes one's personal responsibility regarding sin by describing sin as *imperfections, shortcomings, mistakes, weaknesses,* and *insecurities.*[21] By his own admission, he intentionally avoids using the word *sin* in his preaching and writing. When asked why this is the case, Osteen told Larry King, "I don't use [the word sinners]. I never thought about it. But I probably don't. But most people already know what they're doing wrong. When I get them to church I want to tell them that you can change. There can be a difference in your life. So I don't go down the road of condemning."[22] He writes, "God focuses on the things you're *doing right.* He sees the *best* in you.... [Y]ou can stop obsessing about all your *faults* and give yourselves a break. Every person has *weaknesses.*"[23] But such a softening of sin fails to meet the standard of the essence of the gospel because it does not adequately communicate the nature of the substitutionary atonement of Christ.

Another deficiency in Osteen's gospel is the failure to speak of *eternal life.* As the title of his book indicates, Osteen is more concerned with living life *now*, not what awaits individuals on the other side of the grave. In his brief evangelistic appeal at the conclusion of the book, Osteen casts salvation in terms of finding "peace and happiness" and having "your dreams come to pass."[24] In keeping with the theme of the entire book, *salvation* is about reaching one's full potential in *this* life, not about being rescued from hell in the life to come. Truly, a reader could follow Osteen's simple plan of salvation and then later, when asked, "Are you certain you will go to heaven when you die," respond, "Heaven? What's *heaven?*"

Finally, one of the more glaring deficiencies of Osteen's gospel when examined in light of the pure gospel's five-fold essence, is his mischaracterization of faith. In the first place, *faith* is not mentioned in his brief evangelistic appeal. But even if one grants the benefit of the doubt in assuming that by "I ask You to come into my heart" Osteen means "I *trust* in You," his understanding of *faith* makes the quality of one's faith the key rather than the *object of faith*. As discussed above, Osteen makes faith intrinsic rather than extrinsic. He writes, "Friend, please stop limiting God with your narrow-minded thinking. Learn how to *conceive*. Keep the image of what you want to become in front of you. You're going to become what you believe."[25] Thus, faith is a conception that originates in one's mind, rather than transference of trust from any and all non-saving objects to the only saving object: Jesus Christ. For all of these reasons, Osteen's gospel fails to measure up to the standard of the pure gospel delineated in Scripture.

Case Study: T. D. Jakes

Bishop T. D. (Thomas Dexter) Jakes is an evangelical pastor, author and conference speaker. His church, The Potter's House in Dallas, Texas, is considered one of the largest churches in America.[26] According to the church's web site, Bishop Jakes founded The Potter's House in 1996 with about fifty families and presently the church boasts more than 28,000 members.[27] He is described as "a beloved pastor, a successful entrepreneur, a global advocate and philanthropist, and shepherd to millions around the globe."[28] Jakes's popularity is so widespread that *TIME* magazine ran a cover story featuring him on September 17, 2001 asking, "Is this man the next Billy Graham?"

Yet some leading theologians are not quite ready to pass the evangelical mantel. At issue is Jakes's questionable view on the doctrine of the Trinity. The church's web site expresses his view on the doctrine of God as follows: "There is one God, Creator of all things, infinitely perfect, and eternally existing in three *Manifestations*: Father, Son, and Holy Spirit."[29] Elsewhere on the church site, the Father, Son and Holy Spirit are referred to as "three *dimensions* of one God."[30] Jakes's use of the terms *manifestations* and *dimensions*, coupled with his past association with the Oneness Pentecostal movement, has led some to conclude that he is a modalist.[31]

Another troubling aspect of Jakes's broader theology is his insistence that God imparts new special revelation on an individual basis in the present age. He writes, "God imparts to you a revelation of His plans for your life. That is how vision begins. Then in some cases, God confirms that word *He spoke personally to you* through a prophecy given to you by another man or woman of God."[32] Jakes makes this claim in part based upon an appeal to Proverbs 29:18, "Where there is no revelation, the people cast off restraint; But happy is he who keeps the law." But this tired argument, oft-repeated by proponents of prosperity theology, fully misses the original context. In the Hebrew culture, *revelation* referred to revelatory messages from the Lord (Yahweh) as communicated through human prophets. Prior to the completion of God's written revelation in the form of Scripture, it was such prophetic admonitions that provided guidance and order. Without them, God's people would languish in unrestrained disorder. The antithetical parallelism of the Hebrew couplet informs the meaning. If one keeps God's law (i.e., God's revelation), he is blessed. If he does not, he will suffer. The best that can be said by way of application is that this famous proverb encourages the adherence to God's revelatory standards. It does not suggest that individuals may receive new revelation today.

Jakes connects one's individual "prophetic word" with the walk of faith which results in personal success and fulfillment. "If we continue to walk by faith, believing in the prophetic word that God has spoken over our lives, things that may seem impossible to realize in the natural shall come to pass."[33] According to Jakes, the journey of faith begins not with confident trust in Jesus Christ as the only hope of salvation but with the discernment of a personal vision from God and the inner will power to claim and follow that vision.[34]

Regardless of Jakes's questionable view on the doctrines of the Trinity and the availability of new revelation, it is his soteriological views that are the subject of this present case study. How does his soteriological method measure up to the standard established in chapter three, namely, *that anyone who believes in Jesus Christ alone as the Son of God who died and rose again to pay his personal penalty for sin may have eternal life?*

Not unlike Joel Osteen, Jakes's view of *faith* is expressed in terms of an inner quality rather than simple confidence or assurance in the correct object. He writes,

Regardless of the excesses and some erroneous teachings that have been associated with the "Word of Faith" and charismatic movements, Christians must forever remember and be mindful of the fact that the Word of God declares that anything in our life that is not rooted or brought about by faith in the Almighty, is sin.... It (*faith in God and confidence in self*) is what fuels our lives and gives motivation, inspiration, and *eternal hope for our existence.*[35]

It is noteworthy that Jakes connects *faith in God* and *confidence in self* and that this two-fold combination *gives eternal life*. Jakes elaborates on this thought in the very next paragraph:

Within you lies the power to seize the hour and live your dreams. Faith is the oil that takes the friction out of living. Faith will enable you to turn liabilities into assets and stumbling blocks into stepping stones. When you begin to have faith, your load will get heavy but your knees won't buckle, you'll get knocked down but you won't get knocked out. You've got to have faith if you are going to make it in life. You must *believe in yourself and in a power greater than yourself*, and do your best and don't worry about the rest.[36]

Again one discerns a blurring of the distinction between the *intrinsic* quality of faith and the *object* of one's faith. This error is tantamount to self-salvation in that it depends to some extent upon the earnestness of one's faith. Elsewhere Jakes proclaims, "You, my brothers and sisters, are indeed what God's Word says you are. You are to appropriate what the Word says you are and what the Word says you have. It involves *more* than just 'believing' and 'receiving!'"[37] In Jakes's soteriological method, finding God requires "the right *kind* of faith."[38]

For Jakes, this *declarative faith* is holistic. It involves every area of life. What Osteen calls the path to one's *full potential* Jakes refers to as the *road less traveled* to a place called *there*—different terminology but the same idea.[39] Jakes writes, "The path to true spiritual, moral, physical and economic success is the road less traveled. It's the straight and narrow road."[40] This suggests the connecting of spiritual blessings and financial blessings—a foundational tenet of prosperity theology. According to the prosperity gospel, salvation is a package deal that involves not only spiritual salvation, but good health and increased wealth as well. Yet the pure gospel is narrower than that. The gospel is about how lost man can avoid hell as a consequence for his sin and instead gain eternal life. To import issues of economics, health and other life issues into the salvation equation is to create a soteriological method that violates the essence of the gospel.

Not only is Jakes's gospel deficient because of its improper view of faith, it also lacks an adequate articulation of sin. In another similarity to Joel Osteen, Jakes appears to be soft on sin. For example, in his book *Loose That Man and Let Him Go*, Jakes refers to sinful lust as "little boy thoughts."[41] Elsewhere in the same book he approaches sin from a highly humanistic psychology perspective, referring to dysfunctional men as being "wounded" and manifesting "the child within."[42] Jakes does not adequately address man's personal guilt and responsibility when it comes to sin.

He also violates the established standard of *faith alone*. He states plainly that "unless the believer is willing to *lose his life for Christ's sake, he cannot ever attain everlasting life*. If the Master must suffer to the point of death, so likewise must the servant."[43] In the context,

Jakes's exhortation is much more than an appeal to faith. Rather, Jakes believes that the journey to heaven is paved with self-sacrifice and perhaps even martyrdom! In appealing to a discipleship passage such as this one (i.e., Matt 16:24–27), Jakes's soteriological method resembles that of the performance gospel.[44] It confuses *discipleship* with *salvation*. The ones to whom Jesus issues the call to "lose one's life for His sake" are believers and the call is to a deeper commitment to Him. The passage says nothing about how to have eternal life as Jakes suggests.

One further aberration in Jakes's soteriological method is worthy of mention. Jakes asserts that salvation does not bring with it the automatic identification as a child of God. "Scripture teaches that receiving Christ as your personal Savior *does not necessarily make you a son of God*, but if you choose to do so, the power (authority) and right to do so is present.... Just being saved does not make you a son of God ... only those who are willing to be led by the Spirit actually *realize* and manifest the sonship of God."[45] Yet this flies directly in the face of John 1:12, "But as many as received Him, to them He gave the right to become children of God, to those who believe in His name." Jakes suggests that the "right" or "power" promised in this verse is the right of the believer to do amazing things on his own, not the power of God to make him part of His family. 1 John 3:1 also argues against Jakes's premise: "Behold what manner of love the Father has bestowed on us, that we should be called children of God," as does Galatians 3:26, "For you are all sons of God through faith in Christ Jesus." In the end, T. D. Jakes's gospel, like that of Joel Osteen, fails to meet the biblical standard by, among other deficiencies, redefining faith, failing to adequately address man's sinfulness, adding additional requirements to the sole requirement of faith, and overemphasizing the present blessings of salvation.

Case Study: Kirbyjon Caldwell

Kirbyjon Caldwell is pastor of Windsor Village United Methodist Church in Houston, Texas. Windsor Village boasts more than fifteen thousand members and is known for its impact on the Houston community via social reform and economic initiatives. Caldwell is the author of two books and is an occasional advisor to President George W. Bush.[46] The church's web site describes Windsor Village as "the largest United Methodist Church in the nation" and credits the church's effectiveness to "Pastor Caldwell's belief that the church must embrace theology, identify societal problems and deliver solutions holistically."[47] The web site markets Caldwell's books as "a roadmap to spiritual and emotional wholeness" and a "powerful message of wholistic salvation."[48]

In a manner consistent with other prosperity gospel proponents, including those in the two previous case studies, Caldwell merges emotional, financial and spiritual issues into one salvific equation. His entire ministry is built around the premise that "God has called us into action to help establish (build) on earth the kingdom He has already ordained in Heaven for our personal lives and for the life of our community. Salvation isn't just about the hereafter. God wants us to prosper holistically today and help others go and do likewise."[49] He contends, "Jesus did not die and get up off the Cross so we could live lives full of despair and disappointment," and even suggests, "It is unscriptural not to own land."[50] Caldwell seems uneasy being grouped with other purveyors of the prosperity gospel and yet seeks to justify his emphasis on financial prosperity as a prevalent theme in his teaching. "I am not a proponent of saying the Lord's name three times, clicking your heels and then you get what you ask for. But you cannot give what you do not have. We are fighting what we call the social demons. If I am going to help someone, I am going to have to have something to help them with."[51] Thus, his emphasis on wealth and financial prosperity is evident.

An emphasis on experience rather than simple confidence or trust in Christ alone is evident in Caldwell's soteriology. He too, like Osteen and Jakes, views the Christian life primarily in terms of fulfilling one's purpose and realizing one's potential.

I believe we are all born for a reason and it is our responsibility to discover that reason and redirect our lives toward God's optimal purpose for our lives.... I'm talking about a total reawakening, a calling to realize your full potential in every aspect of your life.... It's an instinctive, gut-level spiritual experience.[52]

Reaching one's maximum potential is what Caldwell refers to as *holistic salvation*. In an obvious example of the exegetical fallacy *illegitimate totality transfer*, Caldwell seeks to justify his concept of holistic salvation by appealing to the range of meaning of the Greek word σωτηρία.[53] "The word salvation comes from the Greek word *soteria*, which means *saved, healed, delivered, pardoned, rescued, protected, preserved, made whole, cured, set free, and restored*.... When we receive Jesus as Lord, all that He is becomes ours."[54] While it is true that the term *salvation* in Scripture is much broader than merely *rescuing from hell*, it does not follow that all of these nuances are included when the term is used in the context of eternal salvation. Caldwell seems to import into the notion of eternal salvation many aspects that are not the focus of the pure gospel—in particular *wealth* and *circumstantial, experiential blessings*.[55]

The journey toward this maximum potential in Caldwell's holistic salvation is called a "faith walk," which has four main legs: (1) faith, (2) focus, (3) action, and (4) prayer and praise.[56] *Faith* is "the audacity to put God's promise into action."[57] *Focus* involves "constructing a mission statement" and "giving your vision a name." Then, keep your eyes on the vision (unlike Peter on the Sea of Galilee) and don't allow "decoy demons" to distract you.[58] *Action* is the "walk" of the faith walk. It is stepping out and taking the first step.[59] *Prayer and Praise* represent the "continuous power of faith." They are what keeps faith operable.[60] Caldwell's view of faith suffers from the same pitfall as many other prosperity preachers. It is based upon a power within rather than an object outside oneself. Regarding one's calling in life—the journey toward maximum potential—Caldwell writes, "You'll *feel it* in your heart before you *know it* in your head."[61]

Beyond a misunderstanding of *faith*, Caldwell's soteriological method suffers from additional significant errors. In response to the question, "How do I get saved?" Caldwell's web site has the following instructions:

God has made it really simple. Answer these four questions: Do you want to be forgiven and saved (1 John 1:8)? Do you believe Jesus Christ, God's son died for you (1 John 1:7)? Are you willing to repent of sin and follow the Lord Jesus Christ for the rest of your life (Acts 2:21; 3:17-19; 16:31; 1 John 1:9)? Do you believe in your heart and confess with your mouth that God does forgive you of your sins and that He does cleanse you from all unrighteousness (Romans 10:9-10; 1 John 1:9)? If you answer yes, you are ready to pray.[62]

These instructions pose several problems when examined in light of the standard established in chapter three. While Caldwell clearly points to Jesus Christ, the Son of God, and His death and resurrection—a key essential of the gospel—he suggests that one must repent of his sins as a requirement for eternal life. That Caldwell views repentance as a matter of behavioral change is clarified by his inclusion of the additional requirement, *follow the Lord Jesus Christ for the rest of your life.* Thus, two behavioral qualifications are placed upon the reader: (1) stop sinning and (2) follow Christ for the rest of his life. Each of these requirements violates the standard of *faith alone* as the only requirement for eternal life.

The added requirement of confessing with the mouth likewise places requirements on the reader that are outside the core essentials of the gospel. As discussed in the previous chapter, verbal confession of Christ is not a requirement for salvation. Furthermore, Caldwell's appeal to 1 John 1:9 in support of the notion that one must confess that he is "cleansed from all unrighteousness," ignores the context of the passage by applying it to the salvation of unbelievers rather than the restoration of fellowship for believers.

Caldwell's suggested prayer only adds to the confusion created by his four questions. He prefaces the sample prayer with a restatement of his holistic salvation theme. "Remember God loves you. He wants you to be whole and complete or saved—spiritually, emotionally, physically, mentally, financially, and socially (3 John 2)." And he makes yet another appeal to the intrinsic *quality* of one's faith when he states, "Pray this prayer, *mean it*, and you will be saved, right where you are sitting."[63] He then offers the following suggested *prayer of salvation:*

Father in heaven, thank you for sending your Son, Jesus, to die on the cross for me, and for His blood that was shed to redeem me and to cleanse me from my sins.

Lord, I am sorry and I repent of my sins. Forgive me. I understand that I must change the course of my life. I am determined in my heart to follow you.

I invite you to become the Lord of my life from this point forward, forever. I openly proclaim and confess that you are the Lord of my life.

I believe in my heart that You have been raised from the dead. Therefore I am saved. I am a new creature. The old things have passed. All things have become new. I am a child of God.

In the Name of Jesus, AMEN![64]

The prayer is commendable for its clear statement of Christ's substitutionary atonement and reference to sin, but an emphasis on man's behavior and commitment to change is pervasive thus negating the exclusivity of faith *alone* in Christ *alone*. One cannot simultaneously place his faith in Jesus Christ *alone* for salvation while also resting his hope of salvation upon his own ability to *change the course of his life*. Thus Caldwell's gospel presentation falls well short of the acceptable standard.

Summary of Chapter Six

Although the *prosperity gospel* traces its lineage to the *word of faith* movement that originated in the mid-twentieth century, it has experienced a resurgence in the postmodern age that is recognized even by secular commentators. Biema and Chu write,

In the past decade ... the new generation of preachers, like Osteen, [Joyce] Meyer and Houston's Methodist mega-pastor Kirbyjon Caldwell, who gave the benediction at both of George W. Bush's Inaugurals, have repackaged the [prosperity] doctrine.... What remains is a materialism framed in a kind of Tony Robbins positivism.[65]

Whether one calls it positivism or prosperity, its emphasis is unmistakable. This soteriological method includes components that lie outside the scope of the pure gospel, such as the promise of present, peripheral benefits accompanying eternal salvation. These benefits usually include financial, physical and emotional well-being, in addition to spiritual salvation. Additionally, the prosperity gospel includes components that violate the essence of the gospel, such as a focus on faith as an intrinsic quality rather than an emphasis on the saving object of faith and a notable absence of the mention of sin.

Three prime examples of this contemporary version of the prosperity gospel were evaluated in this chapter. Joel Osteen's soteriological method suffers from a failure to emphasize the proper meaning of sin, an overemphasis on the present life to the almost complete exclusion of the eternal aspect of salvation, an elevation of material blessings to a place of centrality in the gospel promise, and an improper definition of faith.

Similarly, T. D. Jakes casts faith in terms of its intrinsic quality and suggests that salvation is available only to those with the right *kind* of faith. In so doing, he moves the focus off of the correct object of faith and onto man and his inherent self-will and self-determination. Jakes also downplays *sin* and manifests a number of other theological aberrations such as a troubling view of the Trinity, belief that not all Christians are children of God and a belief in new, individual, prophetic revelation.

Kirbyjon Caldwell's soteriological method likewise contains the characteristic view of faith as a positive, internal force rather than confident assurance in a stated object. His discussion of *holistic salvation* imports non-essential elements into the salvation equation on the front end such as one's emotional and economic well-being. And his gospel presentation is fraught with difficulties such as the requirement that one follow Christ for the remainder of his life and the insistence upon public, verbal confession of Christ. Based on the standard established in chapter three, the prosperity gospel, as illustrated by these three case studies, lacks the essential elements required of the pure gospel.

ENDNOTES
CHAPTER SIX

1. See Hank Hanegraaff, *Christianity in Crisis* (Eugene, Ore.: Harvest House, 1993), 29–39.

2. David Van Biema and Jeff Chu, "Does God Want You to Be Rich?" *TIME*, September 18, 2006, 48–50, emphasis original.

3. For a comprehensive critique of the Word of Faith movement see Robert M. Bowman, *The Word-Faith Controversy: Understanding the Health and Wealth Gospel* (Grand Rapids: Baker, 2001), Gordon Fee, *The Disease of the Health and Wealth Gospels*, 3d paperback ed. (Beverly, Mass.: Frontline Publishing, 1985), Hanegraaff, *Christianity in Crisis*, D. R. McConnell, *A Different Gospel*, updated ed. (Peabody, Mass.: Hendrickson Publishers, 1995), Ken L. Sarles, "A Theological Evaluation of the Prosperity Gospel," *BSac* 143, no. 572 (October 1986): 329–52.

4. *The Church Report*. <http://www.thechurchreport.com/> (accessed 21 October 2006).

5. E.g. Robert Tilton and Peter Popoff

6. Joel Osteen, "Larry King Live," *CNN*, December 22, 2006.

7. Biema and Chu, "Does God Want You to Be Rich," 53.

8. Ibid.

9. Joel Osteen, *Your Best Life Now: 7 Steps to Living at Your Full Potential* (New York: Warner Books, 2004), 258–66. Throughout the book, Osteen refers frequently to financial blessings, in some form or another, as a manifestation of personal prosperity. E.g. "We've got to eliminate this barely-get-by mentality. 'God, if You'll just give me a fifty-cent raise, I think I'll make it this year....' Get rid of that small-minded thinking and start thinking as God thinks.

Think big. Think increase. Think abundance" (p. 11). "Too often, we get comfortable with where we are, and we use that as an excuse to remain in mediocrity. 'My parents were poor,' we say with a pout. 'Before them, my grandparents were poor. Nobody in my family has ever amounted to much, so I guess I won't either....' Make a decision to rise out of the rut. Don't simply settle for what your parents had. You can go further than that. You can do more, have more, be more" (pp. 24–25). "Will you dare to start believing God for greater things? God doesn't want you to drag through life, barely making it. He doesn't want you to have to scrimp and scrape, trying to come up with enough money to pay for food, shelter, transportation, to pay your bills, or to worry about how you are going to send your children to college" (p. 76). "If you are struggling financially, instead of talking about the problem, you need to boldly declare, 'Everything I put my hands to prospers and succeeds!'" (p. 130). "Perhaps you have a big dream in your heart ... a dream to own your own business ... but like David, you don't really see any human way your dream could happen. I have good news for you! God isn't limited to natural human ways of doing things. If you will trust God and keep a good attitude, staying faithful right where you are and not getting in a hurry and trying to force things to happen, God will promote you at the right time ..." (p. 198). "Go out and sow some seeds. If you need a financial miracle, go buy somebody a cup of coffee tomorrow morning, or give a little extra in the offering at church" (p. 251). "No matter how impossible your situation may look, the good news is that God wants to turn it around and restore everything that has been stolen from you. He wants to restore ... your career. He wants to restore those broken dreams" (p. 305). And so throughout.

10. Ibid., back cover.

11. Ibid.

12. Ibid., 4.

13. The seven steps are: (1) Enlarge your vision, (2) Develop a healthy self-image, (3) Discover the power of your thoughts and

word, (4) Let go of the past, (5) Find strength through adversity, (6) Live to give, and (7) Choose to be happy.

14. Osteen, *Your Best Life Now: 7 Steps to Living at Your Full Potential*, 72.

15. Ibid., 306.

16. Ken L. Sarles, "A Theological Evaluation of the Prosperity Gospel," *BSac* 143, no. 572 (October 1986): 348, emphasis added.

17. Ibid., 347–48

18. Osteen, *Your Best Life Now: 7 Steps to Living at Your Full Potential*, 75, emphasis added.

19. Ibid., 76, emphasis added. Osteen borrows this phrase from Gene Peterson's translation of Matthew 9:29 in *The Message*. Yet, such a paraphrase—and especially Osteen's broad application of it—misses the point of the interchange between Jesus and the two men. In the context, Jesus calls on the men to *trust Him,* not some intrinsic power within themselves. The NKJV better captures the essence of Jesus' response to the men's expression of faith: "According to your faith, let it be done unto you."

20. Ibid., 310.

21. These words are used frequently throughout *Your Best Life Now*.

22. Joel Osteen, "Larry King Live," *CNN*, 20 June 2005.

23. Osteen, *Your Best Life Now: 7 Steps to Living at Your Full Potential*, 65, 67, emphasis added.

24. Ibid., 310.

25. Ibid., 81, emphasis added.

26. *The Church Report.* <http://www.thechurchreport.com/> (accessed 21 October 2006).

27. *The Potter's House.* <http://www.thepottershouse.org/> (accessed 22 February 2007).

28. Ibid.

29. Ibid., emphasis added.

30. Ibid., emphasis added.

31. E.g. Hank Hanegraaff made such a charge against Jakes in his organization's magazine, *Christian Research Journal.* See also *Watchman Fellowship.* <http://www.watchman.org/expo/ 17_2news. htm> (accessed 26 February 2007). Modalism is the anti-Trinitarian view that states there is only one person in the Godhead, variously manifested in the form or mode as Father, Son, or Holy Spirit. See Paul Enns, *The Moody Handbook of Theology* (Chicago: Moody Press, 1989), 626.

32. T. D. Jakes, *Maximize the Moment,* 2d paperback ed. (New York: Berkley Publishing Group, 2001), 43, emphasis added.

33. Ibid., 46.

34. Cf. Ibid., 165–82.

35. T. D. Jakes, *Why? Because You Are Anointed* (Lanham, Md.: Pneuma Life Publishing, 1994), 17–18, emphasis added.

36. Ibid., 18, emphasis added.

37. Ibid., 70, emphasis added.

38. Ibid., 16, emphasis added.

39. Ibid., 71, Jakes, *Maximize the Moment*, 185–89. Jakes describes *there* as a "feeling." It is "the passion that burns within you like a flaming torch. When you get 'there,' you will know it in the deepest part of your soul.... It doesn't matter where 'there' is for you, it just matters that you get there. It matters that you achieve soul satisfaction. It matters that you reach your full purpose and potential." Jakes, *Maximize the Moment*, 186–87.

40. Jakes, *Why? Because You Are Anointed*, 71.

41. T. D. Jakes, *Loose That Man and Let Him Go* (Tulsa, Okla.: Albury, 1995), 5.

42. Ibid., 8–16.

43. T. D. Jakes, *The Harvest* (Bakersfield, Calif.: Pneuma Life Publishing, 1996), 28, emphasis added.

44. See discussion of the *performance gospel* in chapter eight.

45. Jakes, *The Harvest*, 46–47, emphasis original.

46. See Kirbyjon Caldwell, Walther P. Kallestad, and Paul Sorensen, *Entrepreneurial Faith: Launching Bold Initiatives to Expand God's Kingdom* (Colorado Springs: WaterBrook Press, 2004), Kirbyjon Caldwell and Mark Seal, *The Gospel of Good Success: A Road Map to Spiritual, Emotional, and Financial Wholeness* (New York: Simon & Schuster, 1999).

47. *Kingdom Builders.* <http://kingdombuilders.com> (accessed 22 October 2006).

48. Ibid.

49. Ibid.

50. Biema and Chu, "Does God Want You to Be Rich," 56.

51. Ibid. Caldwell's reference to "clicking your heels and saying the Lord's name three times" may be a veiled reference to fellow prosperity preacher T. D. Jakes's more overt brand of "name-it-and-claim-it" theology. In the midst of an extended *Wizard of Oz* metaphor Jakes writes, "People in Oz are a lot like those in Kansas.... So you decide. Do you want to stay at home with the mediocre and milk the proverbial cows, or do you want to *click your heels on the yellow brick road*? As for me, I wear a size thirteen!" Jakes, *Maximize the Moment*, 246–47, emphasis added.

52. Caldwell and Seal, *The Gospel of Good Success: A Road Map to Spiritual, Emotional, and Financial Wholeness*, 32–33.

53. Cf. D. A. Carson, *Exegetical Fallacies*, 2d ed. (Grand Rapids: Baker Books, 1996), 27–64.

54. *Kingdom Builders.* <http://kingdombuilders.com> (accessed 22 October 2006).

55. Cf. Caldwell and Seal, *The Gospel of Good Success: A Road Map to Spiritual, Emotional, and Financial Wholeness*, 162, 202.

56. Ibid., 130–31.

57. Ibid., 130.

58. Ibid. Elsewhere, Caldwell even suggests that one should give his vision song. "Set your vision to music," such as Rocky II's *Eye of the Tiger* or *Chariots of Fire* (p. 115).

59. Ibid., 131.

60. Ibid.

61. Ibid., 57, emphasis added.

62. *Kingdom Builders.* <http://kingdombuilders.com> (accessed 22 October 2006).

63. Ibid., emphasis added.

64. Ibid.

65. Biema and Chu, "Does God Want You to Be Rich," 54.

CHAPTER 7

THE PLURALISTIC GOSPEL

We hold these truths to be *self-evident…* —from the United
States Constitution

It was suggested in chapter two that *pluralism* is one of the
defining marks of *postmodernism.* Pluralism "maintains that the
major world religions provide independent salvific access to the
divine Reality."[1] It embraces and promotes a particular view about
the relationship between the major world religions, which may be
characterized as "an egalitarian and democratized perspective that
sees a rough parity among religions concerning truth and soteriological effectiveness."[2] In essence, pluralism teaches that all religions
are equally valid pathways to heaven.[3] D. A. Carson suggests that
the evangelical expression of pluralism is *inclusivism.* Indeed, the
distinction between religious pluralism and evangelical inclusivism
is subtle. The primary distinction rests in the fact that inclusivists
maintain that "all who are saved are saved on account of the person
and work of Jesus Christ" even if they never have heard about Him,
whereas religious pluralists may have no place for Christ whatsoever
in their soteriological paradigm.[4] To put it another way, inclusivists
argue that there is one true God—the God of the Bible—but even
though "those in other religions may refuse to partake from (or not
know about) the proper religious diet, God will not let them starve."[5]
For the evangelical inclusivist, the *norm* is *Christ* as the object of

277

saving faith, but this norm is not a requirement. That is, one's faith is not *required* to be in Christ to secure eternal life.

Okholm and Phillips provide a succinct summary of the inclusivist position:

God's spirit can use positive aspects of other religions and a variety of other elements—specifically the conscience, the human religious quest, angels, social interaction—as a means of grace. The requirement for salvation is simply to trust in God—under whatever form God is known—and obedience. Perhaps some believers will receive explicit knowledge of Jesus Christ and the basis of their salvation only later, after death.[6]

In other words, inclusivism contends that Jesus Christ is the *ontological* basis for salvation but not necessarily the *epistemological* basis—one does not need to know *about Jesus* to be redeemed *by Jesus*.[7] One problem with this view, among others, is that it marginalizes Christ by making Him merely the expression or basis of God's grace rather than the instrumental object of faith as the means of salvation. It emphasizes God's general revelation but downplays or ignores altogether the significance of His special revelation, namely the incarnation of the Son of God (cf. Heb 1:1–4). As Okholm and Phillips correctly point out, "Inclusivism's inability to distinguish between God's presence and God's personal act in Jesus Christ appears to treat Jesus as just 'the sent one' and not as the actual Savior of the world."[8]

In titling this chapter *The Pluralistic Gospel*, the intent is to examine those expressions of the gospel that eschew the exclusivity of Christ as the only object of saving faith. In so doing, they violate the number one core essential of the pure gospel as discussed in chapter three above, namely: *Any gospel presentation that lacks explicit reference to Jesus Christ cannot rightly be considered the pure gospel.* This chapter examines, not religious pluralism proper, but rather *pluralistic tendencies* within evangelicalism, specifically as manifested by the coterminous ideology of inclusivism. Before examining two significant case studies of this soteriological method, a few brief anecdotes suggest that while inclusivism is not yet fully embraced by mainstream evangelicalism it is making inroads.

Joel Osteen was examined in the previous chapter in light of his tendency toward a *prosperity gospel*. There it was noted that his soteriological method fails to meet the biblical standard for several reasons. Perhaps more disconcerting, though, is his apparent affinity for the inclusivist position. As noted in chapter two, during an appearance on CNN's "Larry King Live" on June 20, 2005, Osteen was given multiple opportunities to affirm that faith in Christ is the only means of salvation, yet he steadfastly refused to do so. After a lengthy discussion regarding the salvation of Muslims, Jews and even atheists, in which he failed to articulate the gospel, Osteen responded in seeming exasperation, "You know what, I'm going to let someone—I'm going to let God be the judge of who goes to heaven and hell. I'm not going to go around telling everybody else— if they don't want to believe that that's going to be their choice."[9] To his credit, Osteen later apologized publicly to his congregation for being "unclear on the very thing in which I have dedicated my life [i.e., the gospel]," but such an apology before a hometown crowd does not undo the damage done before a television audience of millions.[10]

Using strikingly similar language, Billy Graham, when asked whether he believes "heaven will be closed to good Jews, Muslims, Buddhists, Hindus or secular people," likewise equivocated. He recently told *Newsweek* reporter Jon Meacham, "Those are decisions only the Lord will make. It would be foolish for me to speculate on who will be there and who won't. I don't want to speculate about all that. I believe the love of God is absolute. He said He gave His Son for the whole world and I believe He loves everybody regardless of what label they have."[11] It is likely that both Larry King and Jon Meacham were attempting to make their respective interviewees sound hateful toward people of other religions. But is it not possible to affirm the gospel without being hateful? One wonders why Osteen and Graham did not seize the moment to proclaim the gospel and announce that *everyone*, regardless of their religious persuasion, will miss heaven apart from explicit faith alone in Jesus Christ alone.

Before turning to the case studies, consider one final illustration of the inroads that pluralism appears to be making in mainstream evangelicalism. Ed Young, Sr. is the Senior Pastor of the largest Southern Baptist church in America, *Second Baptist Church of Houston*. During the aftermath of hurricane Katrina in 2005, Young's church hosted several training seminars for those who desired to help serve the displaced hurricane victims living in temporary shelters such as the Astrodome and the George R. Brown Convention Center. At a training seminar on September 5, 2005 attended by more than ten thousand volunteers and held in the sanctuary at Second Baptist Church, Ed Young welcomed and thanked those in attendance and then offered an invocation.[12]

He prefaced his invocation by acknowledging that many "from other faiths" were present in the audience, and encouraged everyone in attendance to pray to the god of their choice as he prayed from the pulpit. Young seemed especially concerned with not offending Muslim volunteers who were present when he specifically encouraged members of the audience to pray to "Allah," if that was their preference.[13] Following the event, the present writer, who was present on the occasion, inquired about Young's statement and whether or not his language was intentional and meant to affirm evangelical inclusivism. Young did not respond. The significance of Young's public comment seemed lost on at least one active member of Second Baptist Church, who, when asked for her response to Ed Young's assenting comments regarding the Muslim faith, seemed disinterested and replied, "But the church has excellent programs and facilities for my children."[14]

These isolated examples signal a potential shift toward an evangelical soteriological method that is no longer Christocentric. This shift is no doubt spawned, as Carson suggests, by postmodernism's "loss of objective truth" and tendency toward "extreme subjectivity."[15] A soteriology that marginalizes Christ *must*, after all, ignore or deconstruct the plain *objective truth of Scripture*. Yet, in so doing it threatens to undermine the very foundation of Christianity. The following case studies interact with two established evangelicals who are at the forefront of this inclusivist trend.

Case Study: Clark Pinnock

Noted evangelical theologian Clark H. Pinnock is well known for espousing a widening approach to the gospel.[16] Pinnock, who previously taught at such distinguished American evangelical institutions as New Orleans Baptist Theological Seminary and Trinity Evangelical Divinity School, has spent the last twenty-five years at McMaster Divinity College in Hamilton, Ontario, Canada, where he currently serves on the emeritus faculty. Pinnock contends that there is *saving faith* that is "neither Jewish nor Christian," and yet which is "nonetheless noble, uplifting, and sound."[17] Faith that makes one acceptable to God, he suggests, is sincere faith in light of the revelation one has. He continues,

When Jews and Muslims, for example, praise God as the Creator of the world, it is obvious that they are referring to the same Being. There are not two almighty creators of heaven and earth, but only one. We may assume that they are intending to worship the one Creator God that we [i.e., Christians] also serve. The same rule would apply to Africans who recognize a high God, a God who sees all, gives gifts to all, who is unchangeable and wise. If people in Ghana speak of a transcendent God as the shining one, as unchangeable as a rock, as all-wise and all-loving, how can anyone conclude otherwise than that they intend to acknowledge the true God as we do?[18]

Furthermore, in Pinnock's view, when Christians on the mission field approach individuals who have never heard about Christ, they should do so with a spirit of humility recognizing that the unevangelized may actually have a deeper relationship with God than one might think.

When we approach the man of a faith other than our own, it will be in a spirit of expectancy to find how God has been speaking to him and what new understandings of the grace and love of God we may ourselves discover in this encounter.

Our first task in approaching another people, another culture, another religion, is to take off our shoes, *for the place we are approaching is holy.* Else we find ourselves treading on men's dreams. More seriously still, we may forget that God was here before our arrival.[19]

In Pinnock's soteriological scheme, what matters in the end is one's sincerity and heart toward God (whatever "God" may mean to him). He writes, "The issue God cares about is the direction of the hcart, not the content of theology."[20]

Pinnock acknowledges the significance of the atonement as the basis for salvation for all mankind. But in his inclusivist approach, it is not necessary for one to know of Christ this side of the grave. One day, in his view, everyone will have the opportunity to reject or accept Christ at the judgment—even atheists who never acknowledged there was a God.[21] The key factor is one's basic attitude toward God. According to Pinnock, "noncognitive responses to God [i.e., ambiguous, non-specific yearnings for a higher being] count as much as cognitive responses do [i.e., explicit faith in a Savior named *Jesus Christ*]."[22]

What Pinnock fails to see, however, is that the general revelation of God that is acknowledged by those in other cultures or religions does not result in *salvation* but merely justifies their *condemnation.* Romans 1:18–22 speaks directly to this point:

For the wrath of God is revealed from heaven against all ungodliness and unrighteousness of men, who suppress the truth in unrighteousness, because what may be known of God is manifest in them, for God has shown it to them. For since the creation of the world His invisible attributes are clearly seen, being understood by the things that are made, even His eternal power and Godhead, *so that they are without excuse,* because, although they knew God, they did not glorify Him as God, nor were thankful, but became futile in their thoughts, and their foolish hearts were darkened. Professing to be wise, they became fools (emphasis added).

God's general revelation is available to all, but eternal salvation is available only to those who respond in faith to special revelation, namely, the gospel. "Nor is there salvation in any other, for there is no other name under heaven given among men by which we must be saved" (Acts 4:12).[23]

Pinnock affirms the salvific necessity of *faith*, but he ignores the essential *content* of faith that makes it salvific. He writes, "All who achieve holiness, whether in the church or outside it, achieve it not as a result of their own efforts but by the grace of God, which they receive by faith."[24] But *saving faith* for Pinnock does not require specific, essential content. It must simply have God as its object (in whatever form and by whatever name God may be known). "Faith in God is what saves, not possessing certain minimum information."[25] His evidence for the saving nature of *generic faith in God* is the biblical examples of those who were saved prior to the incarnation and Calvary. But such examples do not support Pinnock's premise, for one may reasonably conclude that Old Testament saints such as Abel, Enoch, Abraham, Noah, Moses, etc. did in fact respond to *special revelation* as the instrumental cause of salvation—not just general revelation. It is conceded—and it has been discussed already—that the *content* of saving faith changes from age to age.[26] Surely the content of the gospel in Abraham's day differs from the content of the gospel in the present age. But nevertheless Abraham believed the specific salvific revelation of God and God "accounted it to him for righteousness" (Gen 15:6). Pinnock confuses general revelation with special revelation and states plainly, "Inclusivism believes that God can use both general and specific revelation in salvific ways."[27]

Equally unconvincing is Pinnock's suggestion that God is at work salvifically in pagan religions. "For too long," he writes, "we [exclusivist evangelicals] have stared at the corrupt forms of religion mentioned in the Bible as if they represented the fullness of what religion can be according to the Scriptures, when there is more to it than that."[28] In other words, the Bible puts too negative a spin on pagan religions! We must read between the lines to see that in the Bible, God was at work "among all peoples" even those who opposed His own people.[29] In support of this notion, Pinnock again stretches the context of Scripture when he appeals to Melchizedek — an "important symbol" who shows that God was at work in the pagan Canaanite religious culture, and Cornelius — a "non-Christian" Gentile who represents the "wider hope" of the book of Acts, namely that God is at work in the non-Christian religious sphere of life. Pinnock adopts the phrase "pagan saints" to refer to those who are saved based upon their devotedness to the god of their religion even though they have never come into contact with or believed God's special revelation.

Pinnock's alleged biblical support is strained. As Carson has pointed out, "It is far from clear ... that the Bible is interested in affirming that the Queen of Sheba is among the saved[!]"[30] Bruce Demarest is correct when he concludes that just because God is at work in pagan religions does not mean that adherents to such pagan religions possess saving faith.

> On the basis of God's universal general revelation and common enabling grace, undisputed truths about God, man and sin lie embedded to varying degrees in the non-Christian religions. In addition to elements of truth, the great religions of the world frequently display a sensitivity to the spiritual dimension of life, persistence in devotion, a readiness to sacrifice, and sundry virtues both personal (gentleness, serenity of temper) and social (concern for the poor, nonviolence). But in spite of these positive features, natural man, operating within the context of natural religion and *lacking special revelation*, possess a fundamentally false understanding of spiritual truth.[31]

Thus, Pinnock draws a false conclusion based upon a correct premise. The premise that God is at work in other religions — indeed in all spheres of creation — is true. But it does not follow that He is at work *salvifically* and that one can enter into a saving relationship with God in the present age via any avenue other than faith *alone* in Christ *alone*.

Nevertheless, Pinnock insists that evangelicals "must not continue to walk the path of superiority and chauvinism" that has characterized traditional exclusivist views because "God's gracious presence" may well be in other religions. "Inclusivism," he says, "calls for a more dialogical relationship among religions."[32] Pinnock's suggestion that the traditional evangelical view of saving faith is too "narrow" and "pessimistic" represents a real and present threat to the purity of the gospel, precisely because the pure gospel *is* narrow and specific.[33] Any broadening of the gospel beyond its five-fold essence discussed in chapter three renders it false.

Case Study: John Sanders

In a similar vein is evangelical theologian John Sanders, formerly professor of religion and philosophy at Huntington University in Huntington, Indiana.[34] His defense of inclusivism has been influenced to some degree by personal experience. He writes, "... one of the three children my wife and I adopted from India asked me about the salvation of her birth parents. 'Was there any hope for their salvation?' she wondered. She did not think they had ever heard about Jesus."[35] Sanders's view on the issue is unambiguous: "People can receive the gift of salvation without knowing the giver or the precise nature of the gift."[36] For Sanders *inclusivism* is the belief that "The unevangelized may be saved if they respond in faith to God based on the revelation they have."[37] "Inclusivism," according to Sanders, "denies that Jesus must be the object of saving faith."[38] Saving faith in Sanders's view "does not necessitate knowledge of Christ in this life. God's gracious activity is wider than the arena of special revelation. God will accept into his kingdom those who repent and trust him *even if they know nothing of Jesus.*"[39]

Sanders's language stands in direct opposition to the core essence of the gospel articulated in chapter three: Saving faith is the belief in *Jesus Christ* as the Son of God who died and rose again to pay one's personal penalty for sin and the one who gives eternal life to all who trust *Him* and *Him alone* for it. How does one reconcile Sanders's statement with that of the Apostle John? "And truly *Jesus* did many other signs in the presence of His disciples, which are not written in this book; but these are written that you may believe that *Jesus* is the Christ, the Son of God, and that believing you may have life in *His name*" (John 20:30–31, emphasis added). Support for the inclusivist position must come primarily from theological extrapolation in contradistinction to clear biblical exposition.

For example, Sanders suggests that Jesus' teaching in the Olivet Discourse regarding the sheep and the goats (Matt 25:31–46) shows that some will be surprised one day to learn that they were actually saved. Evidently, they had served the Lord during their earthly life without ever realizing it![40] Such an understanding of this passage is overly simplistic and fails to consider the more complex eschatological context of the surrounding passage. The entire Olivet Discourse represents Jesus' answer to the disciples' question regarding the promised Messianic Kingdom. In Matthew 24:1–2, the disciples, with Jesus' scathing rebuke of the scribes and Pharisees still fresh in their minds (cf. Matt 23), call Jesus' attention to the temple buildings and boast about their grandeur. Jesus replies with a stunning prophecy of the destruction of Jerusalem. In Matthew 24:3, immediately after Jesus' pronouncement of judgment on Israel, the disciples (specifically Peter, James, John, and Andrew—cf. Mark 13:3) ask Jesus, "When will all of this happen—the judgment on Jerusalem, your coming and the end of the age?" Jesus answers this question in the verses that follow. Matthew 24–25 represent some of the most comprehensive, orderly teaching on end times events in all of Scripture.

In Matthew 24:4–14, Jesus begins his response by giving general signs that relate to the entire future tribulation period. That these events take place during Daniel's seventieth week (cf. Dan 9:24–27) and not the present age is seen by noting their similarity with the seal judgments in Revelation 6. Furthermore the phrase *birth pains* is used characteristically of the period of trouble that immediately precedes the Messianic age (cf. Isa 13:8; 26:17; Jer 4:31; 6:24; Mic 4:9–10). References to *the end* in verses 13–14 suggest that this passage refers to the entire seven year period and not just the first half.

In Matthew 24:15–26, Jesus discusses the most specific sign of all. When the abomination of desolation occurs, it will be clear to all that the return of Christ is very near. It will also signal the intensification of God's judgment on the earth. Those alive at the time this sign occurs should head for the hills if they want to avoid death.

Luke's account includes specific details relating to the destruction of Jerusalem which will occur at this time (cf. Luke 21:20–28). Jerusalem will experience devastation at the hands of the Gentiles for about three and one half more years until Christ returns to give Jerusalem back to Israel and establish His kingdom (Luke 21:24; Rev 11:2).

In Matthew 24:27–31, Jesus gives specific signs that *immediately will precede* his second coming. These include a number of cosmic disturbances that will be so great, no one could possibly miss his return. No one will have to wonder, "Has Christ returned yet?" It will be obvious. In Matthew 24:32–35, Jesus uses the parable of the fig tree to teach the truth that those who see all these signs He has just set forth will also see His return. In Matthew 24:36–44, Jesus gives illustrations to demonstrate that for many in the tribulation, the second coming will be completely unexpected. Even though they will know the general timeframe of His return, they will not know the precise moment. Amazingly, many during that time will be unprepared for His return in spite of all of the supernatural events occurring. The reference is to the tribulation age, not the church age.

In Matthew 24:45–51, Jesus uses the parable of the faithful and evil servant to demonstrate that for many in the tribulation, the second coming will occur sooner than expected. In Matthew 25:1–13, Jesus uses the parable of the virgins to demonstrate that for many in the tribulation, the second coming will occur later than expected. In Matthew 25:14–30, Jesus tells the parable of the talents to remind national Israel to do something with the *talent* she has received. All three servants represent Israel (cf. Isa 41:8; Luke 1:54; et al.). The focus of this parable is strictly on Israel and her preparedness for the kingdom just prior to its arrival. In view of Israel's incredible privilege as the chosen nation of God, the talent likely represents all of the resources and benefits that are hers (cf. Rom 9).[41] Finally, in Matthew 25:31–46, Jesus presents a picture of the judgment that will occur when He returns. The judgment under discussion is the judgment of the nations for the purpose of determining who will enter the Messianic Kingdom. The sheep represent those who responded favorably to the Jewish witnesses during the tribulation (i.e., accepted their message). The goats represent those who rejected the gospel of the kingdom. The proverbial "cup of cold water" is a metonym for welcoming and accepting the message of the kingdom. The passage does *not* teach that one who expresses benevolence or kindness is worthy of entrance into heaven regardless of whether he has expressed saving faith.

Sanders likewise appeals to Jesus' parable of the wedding feast (Matt 22:1–14) in support of his contention that some may be surprised to experience salvation at heaven's door even though they had no explicit knowledge of Jesus Christ or the gospel while on earth. This is because in the inclusivist scheme, even though Jesus Christ provides the *basis* for salvation (i.e., the *ontological* basis), the effects of Christ's work on the cross are not limited to those who bear the external badges of being Christians.[42] According to Sanders, "Jesus knows who is seeking God and who has faith. Hence, [inclusivists] hold that when all people stand before Christ in the eschaton, the question will not be 'Do you know Jesus?' but rather, 'Does Jesus know you (Matt 7:23)?'"[43] Sanders points to the fact that guests at the wedding feast in Jesus' parable include not only those who were invited but strangers from the highways as well. Again, however, Sanders fails to consider the context of the passage vis-à-vis Jesus' discussion of His rejection by the first century Jewish leaders as contrasted with His acceptance by sinners and tax collectors (i.e., Gentiles). The point Jesus is making in the parable and the surrounding context is two-fold. First, the makeup of the kingdom will be vastly different than the pious and self-righteous Jewish leaders presumed. Second, in light of first century Israel's rejection of Him, the kingdom will be given to a future generation of Jewish leaders who will respond appropriately in faith. The passage says nothing about gaining entrance into heaven apart from explicit faith in Christ.

The conclusion that one can be saved in the present age without explicit knowledge of Jesus Christ simply is not supported by Scripture.[44] In the words of Ronald Nash, "It is reckless, dangerous, and unbiblical to lead people to think that the preaching of the gospel (which … must contain specifics about the person and work of Christ) and personal faith in Jesus are not necessary for salvation."[45] It is reckless because it opens the door to other soteriological heresies such as universalism and annihilationism due to its foundation of faulty hermeneutics. It is dangerous because, as with any false gospel, it will not yield the fruit of salvation in those who succumb to its teaching. And it is unbiblical because it violates the clear teaching of Scripture on the essence of the gospel.

Sanders's suggestion that exclusivism is akin to *Gnosticism* is an example of the fallacy of guilt by association and does not advance his argument.[46] He suggests that traditional evangelicalism's insistence upon knowing Christ's name and believing certain propositional truths about Him in order to be saved is similar to Gnosticism's elevation of knowledge to a level of primacy. But Gnosticism—a false teaching that developed early in the history of the church (c. AD 100s)—taught that special, mystical knowledge was the basis of one's spirituality. For the Gnostics, this knowledge was *experiential* and *subjective*, not embodied in the objective standards of the apostolic corpus (i.e., the special revelation of God). The appeal of exclusivists is to the *essential gospel standards contained in the Word of God*, not to some mystical, special knowledge available only to the elite.

Like Pinnock, Sanders suggests that if salvation is available only to those who know the name of Jesus then the Old Testament patriarchs must be in hell.[47] Again, however, such reasoning fails to consider the changing nature of the content of saving faith. Ramesh Richard provides a succinct response to this argument from an evangelical dispensational point of view:

> Pre-Christ individuals have been saved without explicit knowledge of Christ. However, not having "explicit knowledge of Christ" is only part of the equation of salvation content. Dispensationalism insists that pre-Christ believers did have divinely revealed, specific content of which there had to be explicit knowledge in order to receive salvation.

> This view [i.e., that people can be saved today without explicit knowledge of Christ] disregards the content of salva-

tion at any given time and arbitrarily gives universal status to that period which yields their principle. Inclusivists jump from one half of the fact (what Old Testament believers did and could not have) to a ubiquitous means of salvation. True, people in the Old Testament have been saved without knowledge of Christ. But it is improper to conclude from this that now anyone anywhere can and will be saved in the same way. Dispensationalism insists on the critical time factor and does not permit an archetypal faith principle that claims that people can and will be saved without knowledge of Christ in this era in human history.[48]

God's salvation has always been appropriated by faith in all ages. But in the progress of revelation over the course of human history, the *specific content* of saving faith has changed. Abraham, for example, was saved by faith but his saving faith did not have as its specific content a Redeemer named "Jesus of Nazareth," as required in the present age (cf. Gen 15:6). During Jesus' earthly ministry, saving faith required the affirmation that Jesus was *Messiah*. Today, during the present church age, characterized among other distinctions by a "blindness" for Israel (Rom 11:25), saving faith does not have Christ's Messiahship as part of its core essence.[49]

The arguments advanced by Sanders in support of a pluralistic gospel are unconvincing. Like Pinnock, he interacts with the biblical text but he does so in a manner that reflects presuppositional theologizing rather than sound literal-grammatical-historical hermeneutics. Sanders's soteriological method represents a denial of the most fundamental essential of the gospel: explicit knowledge of *Jesus Christ*.

Summary of Chapter Seven

One of the defining marks of the postmodern American culture is *pluralism*. Pluralism argues that no single religion can claim to be the exclusive means of salvation. It is the view that "all religions have the same moral and spiritual value, and offer the same potential for achieving salvation, however 'salvation' be construed."[50] This ideology is pervasive in the present culture and it has found its way into evangelical thought in the form of inclusivism. *Inclusivism,* "while affirming the truth of fundamental Christian claims, nevertheless insists that God has revealed himself, even in saving ways, in other religions."[51] The pluralistic gospel, as outlined in this chapter, describes those postmodern evangelicals who suggest that one can be saved without ever affirming explicitly Jesus Christ as the object of his faith.[52] In fact, one can be saved without ever knowing that Jesus Christ exists.

Clark Pinnock and John Sanders are two leading evangelicals who espouse this view. An examination of some of their writings and biblical argumentation demonstrated significant hermeneutical as well as theological weakness. Their view is based upon an appeal to salvation in the Old Testament, which occurred apart from explicit knowledge of Christ. Yet, this argument fails to consider properly the progress of revelation and the changing nature of the precise content of saving faith. Their view is also built upon a misunderstanding of the distinction between general revelation and special revelation. General revelation is not sufficient for salvation. One must respond by faith directly to specific revelatory truth in order to be saved. Today, that truth is the essence of the gospel as contained in the New Testament.

The pluralistic gospel represents the deepest influence of postmodern thinking among any of the soteriological methods discussed thus far. It fully embraces postmodernism's disdain for certainty, absolutism, and the rejection of one, singular grand metanarrative for human history. For these reasons, it is an attractive soteriological viewpoint for many postmodern evangelicals, especially those who are ungrounded in traditional evangelical orthodoxy—and this makes it especially pernicious given its departure from the essence of the gospel.

ENDNOTES
CHAPTER SEVEN

1. Dennis L. Okholm and Timothy R. Phillips, "Introduction," in *Four Views on Salvation in a Pluralistic World*, ed. Dennis L. Okholm and Timothy R. Phillips (Grand Rapids: Zondervan, 1995), 17.

2. Harold A. Netland and Keith E. Johnson, "Why Is Religious Pluralism Fun—and Dangerous?" in *Telling the Truth: Evangelizing Postmoderns*, ed. D. A. Carson (Grand Rapids: Zondervan, 2000), 50, n. 5.

3. For further study on the subject of pluralism as it relates to the present evangelical culture see Alister E. McGrath, "The Christian Church's Response to Pluralism," *JETS* 35, no. 4 (December 1992): 487–501, Alister E. McGrath, "The Challenge of Pluralism for the Contemporary Christian Church," *JETS* 35, no. 3 (September 1992): 361–73, Harold Netland, *Dissonant Voices* (Grand Rapids: Eerdmans, 1991), Lesslie Newbigin, *The Gospel in a Pluralist Society* (Grand Rapids: Eerdmans, 1989), W. Gary Phillips, "Evangelical Pluralism: A Singular Problem," *BSac* 151, no. 602 (April 1994): 140–54.

4. D. A. Carson, *The Gagging of God: Christianity Confronts Pluralism* (Grand Rapids: Zondervan, 1996), 278. Carson further delineates two extremes of inclusivism. "Soft inclusivism," he says, "is barely distinguishable from exclusivism. It holds that people must place their faith in Jesus Christ and his redemptive work to be saved, but allows the possibility, the bare possibility, that God in his grace may save some who have never heard of Christ, assuming that in response to his grace in their lives they cast themselves in repentance and faith upon the God discernible, however dimly, in Creation" (p. 279). What he calls "hard inclusivism" refers to those who emphasize *believing* (i.e., in *something ... anything*) rather than *believing in Christ*. Thus pluralism's philosophical stance of welcoming and affirming other religions finds a home among evangelical inclusivists who, while unwilling to completely part company

with the Christological aspect of soteriology, nonetheless are like-wise unwilling to consign sincere followers of other religions to hell simply because they do not know Christ.

5. W. Gary Phillips and William E. Brown, *Making Sense of Your World* (Chicago: Moody, 1991), 160.

6. Okholm and Phillips, "Introduction," 24–25.

7. Phillips, "Evangelical Pluralism: A Singular Problem," 144. See also Carson, *The Gagging of God: Christianity Confronts Pluralism,* 279. The idea that one can wait until after death until explicitly affirming faith in Christ is a notion D. A. Carson calls *postmortem evangelism.* Carson, *The Gagging of God: Christianity Confronts Pluralism,* 299.

8. Okholm and Phillips, "Introduction," 26.

9. Joel Osteen, "Larry King Live," *CNN*, 20 June 2005.

10. See note thirty-six in chapter two.

11. Jon Meacham, "Pilgrim's Progress," *Newsweek*, August 14, 2006. Even more troubling are Graham's comments during an appearance on Robert Schuller's *The Hour of Power* television program on May 31, 1997. Graham told Schuller, "That's what God is doing today. He's calling people out of the world for His name, whether they come from the Muslim world, or the Buddhist world, or the Christian world or the non-believing world, they are members of the Body of Christ because they've been called by God. They may not even know the name of Jesus but they know in their hearts that they need something that they don't have, and they turn to the only light that they have, and I think that they are saved, and that they're going to be with us in heaven." Schuller responded, "What, what I hear you saying that it's possible for Jesus Christ to come into human hearts and soul and life, even if they've been born in darkness and have never had exposure to the Bible. Is that a correct

interpretation of what you're saying?" Graham replied, "Yes, it is, because I believe that. I've met people in various parts of the world in tribal situations that they have never seen a Bible or heard about a Bible, and never heard of Jesus, but they've believed in their hearts that there was a God, and they've tried to live a life that was quite apart from the surrounding community in which they lived." Billy Graham, "The Hour of Power with Robert Schuller," 31 May 1997. It is difficult to explain away such plain inclusivist language.

12. The present writer was in attendance at this training session. The emcee for the session announced the total number in attendance ("more than ten thousand") before introducing Ed Young for the invocation. There were approximately four to five thousand in the sanctuary itself and the rest were watching on closed circuit feed in other assembly halls throughout the sprawling Second Baptist Church complex.

13. Public statement by Ed Young at Second Baptist Church on September 5, 2005. The present writer was in the audience when the statement was made.

14. This comment was made during a private conversation between the present writer and an active member of Second Baptist Church. The implication of the woman's comment was clear: She was willing to overlook Young's conciliatory comments regarding Islam and Allah because the church had outstanding facilities that were meeting her needs and the needs of her children. Her support of the church is based on practicalities rather than principle.

15. Carson, *The Gagging of God: Christianity Confronts Pluralism*, 26.

16. See Clark Pinnock, "The Finality of Jesus Christ in a World of Religions," in *Christian Faith and Practice in the Modern World*, ed. Mark Noll and David Wells (Grand Rapids: Baker, 1988), 152–68, Clark Pinnock, "Toward and Evangelical Theology of Religions," *JETS* 33, no. 3 (September 1990): 359–68, Clark H. Pinnock, ed.,

Grace Unlimited (Minneapolis: Bethany Fellowship, Inc., 1975), Clark H. Pinnock, *Tracking the Maze: Finding Our Way through Modern Theology from an Evangelical Perspective* (San Fransisco: Harper & Row, 1990), Clark H. Pinnock, *A Wideness in God's Mercy: The Finality of Jesus Christ in a World of Religions* (Grand Rapids: Zondervan, 1992), Clark H. Pinnock, "An Inclusivist View," in *Four Views on Salvation in a Pluralistic World*, ed. Timothy R. Phillips Dennis L. Okholm (Grand Rapids: Zondervan, 1995), 95–148, Clark H. Pinnock, *Most Moved Mover: A Theology of God's Openness*, Didsbury Lectures 2000 (Grand Rapids: Baker Academic, 2001), Clark H. Pinnock and Robert Brow, *Unbounded Love: A Good News Theology for the 21st Century* (Downer's Grove: InterVarsity Press, 1994).

17. Pinnock, *A Wideness in God's Mercy: The Finality of Jesus Christ in a World of Religions*, 92.

18. Ibid., 96.

19. Ibid., 141, emphasis added. Pinnock's suggestion that followers of another religion are on *holy ground* is particularly disconcerting. The very essence of God's holiness is His distinctiveness and separation from all else.

20. Ibid., 158.

21. Ibid., 98.

22. Ibid., 164.

23. On Acts 4:12 and exclusivity see Darrell L. Bock, "Athenians Who Have Never Heard," in *Through No Fault of Their Own*, ed. William V. Crockett and James G. Sigountos (Grand Rapids: Baker, 1991). Pinnock suggests that this verse merely "makes a strong and definitively exclusive claim about the messianic, holistic salvation Jesus has brought into the world. It is a salvation that is incomparable and without rival. It is available through no other name than Jesus

the Incarnate Son of God. But the text does not exclude from eternal salvation the vast majority of people who have ever lived on earth." Clark Pinnock, "Acts 4:12—No Other Name under Heaven," in *Through No Fault of Their Own*, ed. William V. Crockett and James G. Sigountos (Grand Rapids: Baker, 1991), 107–15. The frequent calls throughout Acts to *believe explicitly* in Jesus argue against Pinnock's conclusion. Pinnock's interpretation of Acts 4:12 appears to be an example of reading one's theological presuppositions into the text. On the related issue of the salvation of infants and those who are unable to believe (as distinguished from those who have the capacity to believe but have never heard the gospel), see Robert Paul Lightner. *Safe in the Arms of Jesus: God's Provision for the Death of Those Who Cannot Believe.* (Grand Rapids: Kregel, 2000).

24. Pinnock, *A Wideness in God's Mercy: The Finality of Jesus Christ in a World of Religions*, 92.

25. Ibid., 158.

26. See discussion at note twenty-four in chapter three.

27. Pinnock, "An Inclusivist View," 117. Paul Enns defines *general revelation* as "The truths God has revealed about Himself to all mankind through nature, providential control, and conscience," and *special revelation* as "The divine revealing of truth through Jesus Christ and through the Scriptures." Paul Enns, *The Moody Handbook of Theology* (Chicago: Moody Press, 1989), 645. Prior to the written special revelation of God, which began some 1500 years before Christ when Moses recorded the Pentateuch during the wilderness wanderings, special revelation took on various forms including prophetic messages, direct conversations with God, angelic announcements, etc. Today, special revelation is limited to the truths about God as contained in Scripture.

28. Pinnock, "An Inclusivist View," 109.

29. Ibid.

30. Carson, *The Gagging of God: Christianity Confronts Pluralism*, 293.

31. Bruce A. Demarest, *General Revelation* (Grand Rapids: Zondervan, 1982), 259, emphasis added.

32. Pinnock, "An Inclusivist View," 112.

33. Cf. ibid., 123.

34. Sanders's faculty contract was not renewed for the 2005 academic year due primarily to his outspoken views on *open theism*. John Dart, "College to Close out 'Open Theism' Scholar," *Christian Century*, 28 December 2004.

35. John Sanders, "Introduction," in *What About Those Who Have Never Heard? Three Views on the Destiny of the Unevangelized*, ed. John Sanders (Downer's Grove: InterVarsity Press, 1995), 9.

36. John Sanders, *No Other Name: An Investigation into the Destiny of the Unevangelized* (Grand Rapids: Eerdmans, 1992), 255.

37. Sanders, "Introduction," 20.

38. Sanders, *No Other Name: An Investigation into the Destiny of the Unevangelized*, 265.

39. John E. Sanders, "Is Belief in Christ Necessary for Salvation?" *Evangelical Quarterly* 60 (1988): 252–53, emphasis added. Elsewhere Sanders writes, "They (inclusivists) believe that the unevangelized may be saved if they commit themselves to the God who saves through the work of Jesus. Appropriation of salvific grace can be mediated through general revelation and God's providential workings in human history. No one will be saved without Christ's atonement, but one need not be aware of that work of grace in order to benefit from it." John Sanders, "Evangelical Responses to

Salvation Outside the Church," *Christian Scholar's Review* 24, no. 1 (1994): 51–52.

40. John Sanders, "Inclusivism," in *What About Those Who Have Never Heard? Three Views on the Destiny of the Unevangelized*, ed. John Sanders (Downer's Grove: InterVarsity Press, 1995), 34. Pinnock offers the same exposition of this passage. See Pinnock, *A Wideness in God's Mercy: The Finality of Jesus Christ in a World of Religions*, 163–65.

41. The tribulation period will provide Israel with one final chance to do something with the *talent* she has been offered time and again throughout history. Those who believe the gospel of the kingdom (i.e., accept the talent rather than squandering it) will receive entrance into that kingdom. Among those who respond, there will be varying levels of faithfulness/fruitfulness. Those who make good use of their resources in spreading the gospel of the kingdom will be rewarded with positions of authority and responsibility in the kingdom. That this passage refers to Israel and not the church is confirmed by such phrases as "Enter into the joy of your lord;" (Joy is a frequent Kingdom motif [Heb 12:1–2; Rom 14:17; Isa 65:14–18; et al.]); "entering," "ruling," and "of your lord." This terminology lends support to the view that kingdom life is in view, as opposed to heaven and thus makes the passage only indirectly applicable to the church in the present day. The similar parable in Luke 19:11–27, with its different surrounding context and audience, is more directly applicable to the church in the present day.

42. Sanders, "Inclusivism," 48.

43. Sanders, "Evangelical Responses to Salvation Outside the Church," 53.

44. For a discussion of the issue of infant salvation from a non-inclusivist, evangelical perspective see Lightner, *Safe in the Arms of Jesus*.

45. Ronald Nash, *Is Jesus the Only Savior?* (Grand Rapids: Zondervan, 1994), 126.

46. Cf. Sanders, "Inclusivism," 37.

47. Ibid., 38–40.

48. Ramesh Richard, "Soteriological Inclusivism and Dispensationalism," *BSac* 151, no. 601 (January 1994): 107. See also Ramesh P. Richard, *The Population of Heaven* (Chicago: Moody Press, 1994).

49. Cf. Lewis Sperry Chafer, *Salvation* (New York: C. C. Cook, 1917), 42–53, Robert Paul Lightner, *Sin, the Savior, and Salvation: The Theology of Everlasting Life* (Nashville: T. Nelson Publishers, 1991), 158–77, Earl D. Radmacher, *Salvation*, Swindoll Leadership Library (Nashville: Word, 2000), 113–28, Charles Caldwell Ryrie, *Dispensationalism*, rev. and expanded. ed. (Chicago: Moody Press, 1995), 105–22.

50. Carson, *The Gagging of God: Christianity Confronts Pluralism*, 278–79.

51. Ibid., 27.

52. As mentioned, some inclusivists suggest that one must affirm faith in Christ after death, but all inclusivists agree that knowledge of and faith in Christ while on earth is unnecessary for salvation.

CHAPTER 8

THE PERFORMANCE GOSPEL

They say hard work never killed anyone, but I figure: why take the chance? –Ronald Reagan

"A theology that rests its salvation on one ounce of human performance is not good news; it is bad information. It is *heresy.* It is antithetical to the true message that lit the spark to the Reformation: *Sola fide*—faith alone."[1] Postmodernism's penchant for moral relativism and moral laxity, as well as a profound de-emphasis on holy living, has created a fertile ground for those who are inclined to emphasize works as part of the gospel. This chapter addresses the tendency on the part of some evangelicals to promote a soteriological method that makes man's entrance into heaven contingent to varying degrees upon his own good behavior. The *Performance Gospel* emphasizes man's good works as a either a *prerequisite* or *postrequisite* for receiving eternal life.[2] To be clear, works-oriented gospels are not a *new* approach to the gospel born out of the postmodern milieu. Indeed, the inclination on the part of man to earn his way to eternal salvation is as old as man himself. Yet the trend in postmodern American culture to accept and embrace all forms of deviant behavior with no apparent standards of morality seems to have reenergized works-based gospel models. Some well-intentioned evangelicals attempt to stem the tide of moral relativism by placing additional requirements on those who wish to gain eternal life.

For example, John MacArthur writes, "Shocking forms of open immorality have become commonplace among professing Christians."[3] He laments that the contemporary culture contains a "generation of professing Christians whose behavior often is indistinguishable from the rebellion of the unregenerate," which indicates that they "are tragically deceived" into thinking they are saved when they are not.[4] According to MacArthur one reason that this is the case is the failure to emphasize full surrender to Christ's authority as a necessary component of saving faith. He writes, "The promise of eternal life *without surrender to divine authority* feeds the wretchedness of the unregenerate heart."[5] Thus, it is apparent that the immorality so rampant in postmodernity has influenced, at least to some extent, the emphasis on good works, which characterizes this soteriological method.

The performance gospel may be subdivided into two further classifications. On the one hand, some insist that true saving faith necessarily requires a pledge of obedience and commitment on the *front end* of conversion. That is, to believe in Jesus as one's only hope of eternal life means to promise to obey Him fully. Those who hold this view are considered under the section entitled, *Performance as a Prerequisite for Eternal Life*. On the other hand, sometimes the role of performance is viewed on the *back end* of conversion as a sort of *postrequisite* to receiving eternal life. According to this line of reasoning, true saving faith is guaranteed to produce visible good behavior in every believer. An examination and critique of this view is undertaken in the section titled, *Performance as a Postrequisite for Eternal Life*. Many proponents of a performance gospel include *both* requirements in their soteriological method.

Performance as a Prerequisite for Eternal Life

The gospel standard established in chapter three is that for one to be saved, he must believe in Jesus Christ, the Son of God, who died and rose again to pay his personal penalty for sin, as the only one who can give him eternal life. Some evangelicals, however, have expanded the gospel to include the component of *personal commitment to Christ* as a prerequisite for eternal life. In their view, one must surrender to the Lordship of Christ, often couched in terms of *repentance of sins*, in order to receive eternal life.[6] John R. W. Stott provides a succinct articulation of this view:

> At its simplest Christ's call was "Follow me." He asked men and women for their personal allegiance. He invited them to learn from him, obey his words and to identify themselves with his cause.... We cannot follow Christ without forsaking sin. Repentance is a definite turn from every thought, word, deed, and habit which is known to be wrong.... To follow Christ is to renounce all lesser loyalties.... So in order to follow Christ we have to deny ourselves, to crucify ourselves, to lose ourselves. The full, inexorable demand of Jesus Christ is now laid bare. He does not call us to a sloppy half-heartedness, but to *a vigorous, absolute commitment*. He calls us to make him our Lord.[7]

For Stott and those who share his view, one cannot gain eternal life without first making a pledge of allegiance to Christ that involves forsaking all sin and following Him in unwavering obedience.

One proponent of this view even goes so far as to compare the salvation experience to a marriage ceremony in which two parties make a mutual agreement with one another. James Montgomery Boice, who is examined in more detail in the next section, uses an extended marriage metaphor to explain that eternal life is imparted only when Jesus and the would-be convert exchange vows. He even lists a suggested vow for the would-be convert to make: "I, sinner, take thee, Jesus, to be my Savior and Lord; and *I do promise and covenant*, before God and these witnesses, to be thy loving and faithful disciple...."[8] In this way, the salvation experience becomes nothing more than a contractual agreement based upon one's pledge of obedience rather than a free gift based upon faith alone in Christ alone. Yet, as the following case studies suggest, such an approach elevates one's personal performance to a level of instrumentality in obtaining eternal life and therefore contradicts the essence of the gospel message.

Case Study: John F. MacArthur (Part One)

John MacArthur is widely recognized as a leading proponent of what has come to be called *Lordship Salvation.*[9] "The Lordship Salvation debate is a debate over the gospel and, specifically, the nature of salvation, saving faith, and the relation of salvation to sanctification."[10] MacArthur and other adherents of Lordship Salvation insist on the necessity of total surrender in order to be saved. MacArthur writes,

> The saving faith in Jesus Christ that the New Testament teaches is much more than a simple affirmation of certain truths about Him.... Saving faith is *a placing of oneself totally in submission to the Lord Jesus Christ*, and it has certain indispensable elements that the New Testament clearly teaches. Saving faith in Jesus Christ involves the exercise of will. Paul told the Roman believers, "Thanks be to God that though you were slaves of sin, you became obedient from the heart to that form of teaching to which you were committed" (Rom 6:17). Salvation begins (from the human standpoint) with a person's *willful obedience in turning from sin* to follow the Lord Jesus Christ. Saving faith also involves the emotions, because, as in the verse just mentioned above, it must come from the heart as well as from the mind.[11]

MacArthur's citation of Romans 6:17 in support of the notion that willful surrender and obedience must accompany saving faith is unconvincing. To be "obedient from the heart" is simply another way of expressing what it means to believe.[12] The "form of teaching" to which Paul referred was the very teaching he had been putting forth, namely that righteousness comes by faith rather than by keeping the Mosaic Law. The verse cited says nothing about obedience vis-à-vis turning from sin and submitting to the Lordship of Christ. Furthermore, the suggestion that saving faith involves emotions, based on Paul's reference to *heart* is a strained appeal to the alleged distinction between the heart and the mind that is common among proponents of a performance gospel.[13]

Elsewhere, MacArthur writes, "The gospel call to faith presupposes that sinners must *repent of their sin* and *yield to Christ's authority.*"[14] For MacArthur, repentance of sins is defined primarily in terms of a change in behavior. He states,

> Repentance is a critical element of saving faith ... it always speaks of a change of purpose, and specifically a turning from sin. In the sense Jesus used it, repentance calls for a repudiation of the old life and a turning to God for salvation.... It is a redirection of the human will, a purposeful decision to forsake all unrighteousness and pursue righteousness instead.... Repentance is not a one-time act. The repentance that takes place at conversion begins a progressive, life-long process of confession.... Repentance has always been the foundation of the biblical call to salvation.[15]

If as MacArthur suggests, *repentance is a critical element of saving faith*; and if, as he further suggests, repentance involves the *purposeful decision to forsake all unrighteousness*, it is difficult to see how he can avoid the charge of making one's performance instrumental in salvation.

As discussed previously, the standard response to such criticism is to appeal to the regenerative work of God in producing such repentance so that the onus is removed from the one expressing faith and placed upon God Himself.[16] Since it is contended that regeneration precedes faith, and since regeneration is the sole work of God, all of the requirements of the performance gospel possess a sort of umbrella of protection from the charge of works-salvation when attached to regeneration. For example, MacArthur writes,

> Let me say as clearly as possible right now that salvation is by God's sovereign grace and grace alone. Nothing a lost, degenerate, spiritually dead sinner can do will in any way contribute to salvation. Saving faith, repentance, commit-

ment, and obedience *are all divine works*, wrought by the Holy Spirit in the heart of everyone who is saved. I have never taught that some presalvation works of righteousness are necessary to or part of salvation.... There are no human works in the saving act, but God's work of salvation includes a change of intent, will, desire, and attitude that inevitably produces the fruit of the Spirit.[17]

But such appeals to God's sovereignty are impertinent and unhelpful in that even if one holds that regeneration precedes faith, the issue at hand is what is *man's response* to the gospel? The appeal to regeneration as the instrumental first cause of all that man is allegedly guaranteed to do in order to receive eternal life makes man utterly passive in the soteriological process and contradicts more than 160 passages that require man to believe in order to be saved.[18]

MacArthur's position is untenable when examined in the light of the five-fold standard of the gospel established previously. Saving faith occurs when *faith* (assurance or confidence in an object) meets the right *object,* namely, the gospel. "The saving power resides exclusively, not in the act of faith, or the attitude of faith, or the nature of faith, but in the object of faith."[19] *Saving faith* occurs when one believes in Jesus Christ, the Son of God who died and rose again to pay one's personal penalty for sin, as the only one who can provide eternal life. By making a pledge of personal obedience a required component of saving faith, MacArthur *ipso facto* has elevated human performance to a level of instrumentality in securing salvation.

Case Study: Bill Bright

Have You Heard of the Four Spiritual Laws? is an enormously popular gospel tract that likewise reflects the tendency to elevate human performance to a key component of the gospel. The tract was written by Bill Bright, the late founder and president of *Campus Crusade for Christ.*[20] Due to the sheer size of the ministry of Campus Crusade for Christ, *The Four Spiritual Laws* has become one of the most widely-used and popular tracts over the last four decades. In fact, its use extends well beyond the ministry of Campus Crusade so that many churches, ministries and individuals have used and continue to use this tract as a primary tool for evangelism. It has a distribution of more than 2.5 billion, and has been translated into more than 200 languages.[21]

The first three sections of the tract provide a solid, biblical foundation for man's need of salvation. Section one of the tract begins with a statement affirming God's love: *God loves you and offers a wonderful plan for your life*. John 3:16 and 10:10 are cited as support for God's love. Section two states, *Man is sinful and separated from God. Therefore, he cannot know and experience God's love and plan for his life*. The passage the author cites to support the sinfulness of mankind is Romans 3:23. The passage chosen to support man's separation from God is Romans 6:23a. Both Scripture passages are well suited for their purpose in this section. In section three, the author states that *Jesus Christ is God's only provision for man's sin*. This section introduces the reader to one of the key essentials of the gospel: the death and resurrection of Christ. The supporting texts are Romans 5:8; 1 Corinthians 15:3–6 and John 14:6. Bright does an excellent job of explaining the substitutionary atonement of Christ in language that is easy to understand.

Section four explains the manner in which God's solution to man's sin problem is appropriated by the lost man. It is here that the tract begins to depart from the five-fold standard of the gospel. Citing John 1:12 and Ephesians 2:8–9, the author indicates that in order to experience God's love and plan for one's life he must *receive Christ through faith*. These verses are accurately applied and appropriate to the context. However, in attempting to support his contention that "we receive Christ through personal invitation," the author misapplies Revelation 3:20.[22] While it is true that Revelation 3:20 speaks of Christ issuing a personal invitation, in the context the invitees are *believers* from Laodicea who are invited to renew their intimate relationship with Christ through repentance from sin, *not* unbelievers who are invited to receive the free gift of eternal life. The author ignores the context of Revelation 3:20, which is unfortunate, especially in light of his apparent commitment to a context-centered hermeneutic.[23]

More troublesome than the potential confusion caused by the reference to Revelation 3:20, however, is the subsequent explanation of further conditions for salvation. "Receiving Christ," Bright says, "involves turning to God from self (repentance)" *and* "trusting Christ to come into our lives to forgive our sins and to make us what He wants us to be." Thus, additional requirements appear to be placed upon the reader who by this point quite possibly has become convinced of his need for salvation and desperately wants to know how he can receive such salvation from sin. The first additional requirement is *repentance*. If by *repentance* the author means the forsaking of sin, then the requirement is out of place as the Scripture never calls on sinners to stop sinning in order to receive eternal life. On the other hand, if by this the author means that the unbeliever must change his mind about God and recognize that only God can save him through the gift of His Son, then this additional requirement is really just a restatement of the previously stated requirement: faith in Christ.

The tract's use of an illustration clarifies that the reader should interpret the appeal to repentance as a call to make Christ Lord of one's life and thus reflects an apparent separate prerequisite for receiving eternal life. The illustration contains two circles, in which one represents a lost person and the other a saved person. Each circle contains a rudimentary drawing of a throne. In the circle representing the unbeliever, *self* (signified by an "S") is on the throne. In the circle representing the believer, *Christ* (signified by a cross) is on the throne. Bright explains that to trust Christ is to *yield to Christ* and allow him to *direct one's life and interests*. His suggested prayer for receiving eternal life encourages the reader to ask the Lord to "take control of the throne of my life." It is difficult to see how this terminology can be interpreted as anything other than calling on the unbeliever to make some type of pledge or promise to obediently serve Christ and thus it violates the standard of faith *alone* in Christ as the only means of obtaining eternal life.

Case Study: D. James Kennedy

Another widely-used tract among evangelicals similarly illustrates an emphasis on human performance as a prerequisite for receiving eternal life. *How to Know for Sure You are Going to Heaven* was written by D. James Kennedy.[24] Kennedy is the founder of Evangelism Explosion International (EE), a popular evangelism training program used by churches throughout the world. It is claimed that EE is now used in every nation on earth.[25] He has authored more than forty books, including *Evangelism Explosion* which has more than 1.5 million copies in print.[26]

Dr. Kennedy begins his tract with a familiar illustration about the college professor who is *certain* that certainty is impossible. With this illustration he introduces the reader to the fact that the present age is marked by uncertainty. "We're learning more and more about everything," he writes, "and yet we seem to know less and less for sure." He follows this assertion with a section entitled, *Know What You Know*. In this section, he points out that the followers of Jesus (presumably the twelve disciples, though he does not specify) were marked by a certainty of their belief in Christ and His teaching. "They were even willing to die for that certainty!" he writes.

He then goes on to explain that most people are not like these followers of Jesus. "Most people don't have such confidence when it comes to eternal life," he writes. This is followed by the pointed question, "Do you have certainty about eternity? Do you know for sure?" Kennedy then challenges the reader to "throw away all trust in your own goodness [and] look to the cross of Jesus Christ." After explaining that Christ paid man's penalty for sin on the cross, he once again challenges the reader to "place your trust in Him alone." The references to sin, Christ, His death and resurrection, and faith are all in keeping with the five-fold standard of the gospel. However, Kennedy's appeal to *trust* as the means of securing eternal life is clouded a bit by the suggested prayer that follows:

Lord Jesus Christ, I know I am a sinner and do not deserve eternal life. But, I believe you died and rose from the grave to purchase a place in Heaven for me. Lord Jesus, *come into my life; take control of my life*; forgive my sins and save me. I *repent of my sins* and now place my trust in You for my salvation. I accept the free gift of eternal life.[27]

Much has been said previously about the issue of repentance and this tract suffers from the same deficiency that characterizes some of the other soteriological methods already discussed. In short, by invoking the terminology *repentance of sins* and asking Jesus to *take control of one's life* in the same context, the reader is prone to conclude that such performance on his part is a separate act apart from simple faith *alone*. For that reason, Kennedy's tract fails to measure up to the standard of the pure gospel.

Case Study: David Wells

David Wells is the Andrew Mutch Distinguished Professor of Historical and Systematic Theology at Gordon-Conwell Theological Seminary in South Hamilton, Massachusetts. Wells has long been a leading critic of the collapse of evangelical theology in the face of postmodernity. He laments the absence of evangelical conviction and leadership in the face of increasing worldliness within the church. In his view, postmodern evangelicalism has capitulated to the "present worldliness" of the culture, with the result that the church is characterized by a glaring lack of morality and virtue. He writes,

Modernity is hostile to the moral world in which the biblical discussion about sin takes place. It is hostile to the idea that God is other than our sense of ourselves in our innermost feelings, that He is objective to us, that He addresses us by His Word, that He summons us to accountability before Himself.... Where Christian faith is offered as a means of finding personal wholeness rather than holiness, the church has become worldly.[28]

According to Wells, evangelicals can stem the tide of ungodliness in the church by emphasizing repentance of sin and a moral commitment to personal godliness as part of the gospel on the front end. Yet such an approach to the gospel is just as problematic as the postmodern anthropocentric approach that Wells passionately decries because it elevates human performance to an essential role in the gospel.

Wells suggests that evangelical theology properly includes three elements: (1) a confessional element, (2) reflection on this confession, and (3) the cultivation of a set of virtues that are grounded in the first two elements.[29] "Christian practice," he contends, can never be separated from the "pillars of confession," which he describes as "what the church believes."[30] After citing numerous epistolary passages regarding the importance of right belief, he elaborates,

> No one who is familiar with apostolic teaching and practice could imagine that bare, creedal orthodoxy alone is being advocated these passages. It is clear, for example, both from the structure of many of Paul's letters and from many of his specific statements, that he saw *belief and practice* as inextricably related to each other the former being the foundation of the latter and the latter being the evidence of the working of the former. This same correlation is forcefully presented in John's first epistle, in which three tests are developed for discerning the presence and authenticity of biblical spirituality: believing the right doctrine (2:18–27; 4:1–6, 13–21), *obedience to right doctrine* (2:3–6; 2:28–3:10), and giving expression to right doctrine in a life of love (2:7–11; 3:11–18; 4:7–12). Obedience and love are not substitutes for or alternatives to the doctrine, however; they are the ways—indispensable ways—in which doctrine is to be worked out in our character, attitudes, relationships, and work.[31]

It is evident that Wells elevates Christian practice to equal footing with belief. According to Wells, one cannot claim to be a Christian if his faith fails to issue forth in corresponding right behavior. Therefore, the church needs to return to an emphasis on all three components of evangelical theology. Wells's appeal to various Pauline passages does not sufficiently support his premise. For example, Paul's exhortations to "guard the faith" (2 Tim 1:13–14;

4:3) and "stand firm" in it (1 Cor 16:13), etc. do not suggest that one cannot be saved apart from a commitment to obey. While one may be able to make the connection between right belief and right action in these verses via theological linking, it does not follow that Paul is suggesting that the absence of right behavior indicates an unsaved condition. The same can be said of Wells's appeal to 1 John. As discussed previously, 1 John gives the standards of Christian fellowship, not "tests" to discern whether or not one is truly saved.

While one appreciates Wells's passionate rejection of postmodernism's disdain for doctrine, he oversteps in his critique by making performance inseparably linked to "true" saving faith. In this way and for this reason he implicitly violates the essence of the gospel which is faith *alone* in Christ alone.

Performance as a Postrequisite for Eternal Life

While some evangelicals seek to emphasize performance as an integral aspect of saving faith on the front end of conversion, still others attempt to make good works the required *result* of so-called "real" saving faith. The question of whether visible good works *must* follow saving faith in order to validate one's faith has been addressed previously in chapter three. There it was demonstrated that some evangelicals, particularly those from the Reformed tradition, insist that faith that does not produce visible good works is *spurious*—i.e., not able to save. Yet upon biblical scrutiny of this premise, it was suggested that while the manifestation of good works *should* naturally occur in the lives of believers, this is not always the case. Lack of visible good works does not necessarily indicate that one is not saved.

By requiring the presence of good works to validate one's saving faith, proponents of this view have once again elevated human performance to a level of instrumentality in securing eternal life. Although appeals are made to the sovereign work of God in regeneration (see discussion earlier in this chapter) as the source of the required good works, such argumentation is unconvincing. According to this view, at the end of the day no one will make it to heaven unless he has first produced some measure of visible good works. The following case studies illustrate this view point.

Case Study: John F. MacArthur (Part Two)

John MacArthur, about whom much has been said already, is worthy of further consideration. Not only does MacArthur suggest that human performance is vital as a prerequisite for eternal life, viz. that one must repent of his sins and surrender to the Lordship of Christ in order to be saved, he likewise insists that the absence of good works *after* one professes faith in Christ indicates he *is not truly saved.* He writes, "Faith obeys. Unbelief rebels. The fruit of one's life reveals whether that person is a believer or an unbeliever. There is no middle ground."[32] Elsewhere he asserts, "Those who cling to the *promise* of eternal life but care nothing for Christ's holiness have nothing to be assured of. Such people do not really believe."[33] This is because, in his view, "true" believers follow after holiness.

MacArthur's insistence upon the presence of good works as a requirement to validate one's saving faith is pervasive in his writings. For example, he leaves little room for misinterpreting his words when he states, "Where there are no works, we *must* assume no faith exists either.... No works, no faith. Real faith inevitably produces faith-works."[34] For MacArthur, "passive faith" devoid of the "fruits of salvation [i.e., visible good works]" is "false faith."[35] And again, "There is an inseparable relationship between obedience and faith—almost like two sides of a coin. It is impossible to detach one from the other, though many today are trying very hard to devise a doctrine of 'faith' that is disjointed from obedience."[36]

But such language begs the question, how much fruit must be evident to prove one is saved? MacArthur seems unable or unwilling to provide a quantifiable answer to the question of how much righteousness is needed to ensure salvation. He admits that Christians may commit "heinous sin" but those who live ungodly lives as a matter of "continuous practice" cannot be "genuine Christians."[37] "Those who turn away completely (not *almost* completely, or 90 percent, or 50 percent) demonstrate that they never had true faith."[38] Yet if this is the case, what value is there in insisting on a changed life to prove the genuineness of one's faith? On what basis does one determine whether his behavior is successful *enough*, *too* heinous, *too* prolonged, or represents a *complete* turning away from God?

Furthermore, such a view of saving faith encourages judgmentalism in the church. MacArthur asserts, "People have a right to be suspicious of one who says he believes in Jesus but fails to live up to that claim."[39] MacArthur's approach has been criticized because it gives individuals "the right to strip professing Christians of their claims to faith and to consign such people to the ranks of the lost."[40] In response to this criticism, MacArthur is unfazed. He suggests, "While individual Christians must never be judgmental, the church body as a whole very definitely has a responsibility to maintain purity by exposing and excommunicating those who live in continual sin or defection from the faith."[41] But how can the "church body" judge the genuineness of an individual's faith based upon his actions, without "individual Christians" taking part in this process of judging? Is not the church body made up of individuals? Perhaps MacArthur means to imply that *one believer alone* should not judge the genuineness of someone's faith but if a consensus exists, such judgmentalism is acceptable.

In the end, MacArthur's insistence upon the presence of good works in order for one rightly to be considered a Christian is an example of adding a postrequisite as a condition for receiving eternal life. The essence of the gospel is that by faith alone in Jesus Christ, the Son of God who died and rose again to pay one's personal penalty for sin, one may receive the free gift of eternal life. Good works are nowhere to be found in the essence of the gospel.

Case Study: James Montgomery Boice

A second illustration of the tendency on the part of some evangelicals to make good works a postrequisite for eternal life comes from James Montgomery Boice in his book, *The Glory of God's Grace*. In this book, Boice, well-known pastor and author from the Reformed tradition, presents a systematic discussion of the doctrine of grace. Renowned for his exegetical and theological writings, Boice delivers a detailed and orderly defense of the classic Reformed approach to

election, salvation, perseverance, and other soteriolo|
The author begins with the assertion, "Few things, I |
more greatly needed in today's nearly moribund chu|
recover an appreciation for God's grace."[42] Despite his passion for
grace, however, Boice's theological conclusions regarding the relationship between a believer's works and his eternal salvation represent a departure from the essence of the gospel.

Regarding works, Boice states, "If we are not doing them, this
is also a sign that we are not genuinely converted."[43] To support
this conclusion, he points to several of Jesus' statements in the
Gospels and claims that Jesus "insisted on changed behavior if a
person was actually following him."[44] While this is true, Boice fails
to acknowledge the distinction between the biblical call to salvation
and the biblical call to discipleship. Each of the passages cited by the
author is a call to discipleship, *not* a call to eternal salvation. Boice
is correct that Jesus demanded obedience and good works from
those who wished to be called His disciples (John 14:15; 15:14),
but being a *disciple* and being a *Christian* are two different things.
The term "disciple" means follower and refers to one who follows
the teaching of another. It is possible to be a disciple and not be a
Christian (e.g. Judas) and it is likewise possible to be a Christian and
not be a disciple (e.g. Peter on the night Jesus was betrayed). The
requirement for discipleship is obedience and good works (cf. Luke
9:23). The only requirement for eternal life is faith (cf. Acts 16:31).

As further support of his contention that every believer must
produce good works in order to validate his salvation Boice cites
Matthew 5:20, "Unless your righteousness surpasses that of the
Pharisees and the teachers of the law, you will certainly not enter the
kingdom." According to the author, by this statement Jesus meant
that one's good works must "exceed the good works of others"[45]
Paraphrasing Jesus' statement, Boice writes,

> Unless you who call yourselves Christians, who profess to be
> justified by faith alone and therefore confess that you have
> nothing whatever to contribute to your own justification—
> unless you nevertheless conduct yourselves in a way which
> is utterly superior to the conduct of the very best people who

are hoping to save themselves by their own good works, you
will not enter God's kingdom because you are not Christians
in the first place.[46]

Boice's exposition of this famous passage from the Sermon on
the Mount is puzzling. He affirms that one must be "justified by faith
alone" with "nothing whatever to contribute to [his] own justification" and yet in the same sentence suggests that one must manifest
conduct that is *superior* to the very conduct of those who are trying
to enter the kingdom on the basis of their "own good works!" Yet,
is this really what Jesus says in passage? It seems better to understand Him as eschewing *any and all self-made righteousness* (as
embodied in the pious Pharisees) in favor of the righteousness that
comes by faith (cf. Rom 9:30–10:4).

Although the author repeatedly asserts his belief that "salvation
is by faith alone," at the same time he insists that works are not
optional for those who wish to go to heaven. According to Boice
works are mandatory. Without them, there can be no assurance that
salvation has taken place. In his chapter titled *Persevering Grace,* the
author insists that all true believers will persevere in good works. He
admits that sometimes a believer may fall, but he must never fall "the
whole way."[47] If he does, it proves he was never saved to begin with.
But Boice's view suffers from the same ambiguity as MacArthur's
view in that it fails to quantify the phrase "the whole way." How far
is too far? At one point does sin in the life of a believer prove that
he is not really saved? Such a view of perseverance makes works
the determinative factor in one's eternal salvation and thus demonstrates a fatal inconsistency with the essence of the gospel.

Case Study: R. C. Sproul

Noted Reformed scholar R. C. Sproul also insists that human
performance has an essential bearing on the genuineness of one's
salvation. He writes, "*True faith shows itself in good deeds.* Thus,
said the Reformers, we are justified by faith alone, but justifying
faith is never found alone. True faith is always accompanied by non-
saving, but absolutely necessary works. True faith brings forth good

works. If there are no good works, there is no true faith."[48] It is not unreasonable to ask how good works can be "non-saving" but "absolutely necessary" at the same time. Sproul's response to such an objection, as discussed previously, is to point out that the *required* good works in his system do not originate with man himself, but rather are the guaranteed product of regeneration. According to Reformed soteriology, regeneration precedes faith and thus becomes the glue that holds the entire works-based gospel together. He writes, "Regeneration is not the fruit or result of faith. Rather, *regeneration precedes faith* as the necessary condition for faith.... God chooses to regenerate us before we will ever choose to embrace Him. To be sure, *after* we have been regenerated by the sovereign grace of God, we do choose, act, cooperate, and believe in Christ."[49] Elsewhere he adds, "In regeneration, God changes our hearts. He gives us *a new disposition, a new inclination.*"[50] Simply put, "The necessity, inevitability, and immediacy of good works are linked to the work of regeneration."[51]

For this reason, Sproul and others are content to insist on the presence of good works as a postrequisite to saving faith in order to secure eternal life. They do not view this as elevating works above faith, but rather as completing the logical process that began with regeneration.

> The relationship of faith and good works is one that may be distinguished but never separated. Though our good works add no merit to our faith before God, and though the sole condition of our justification is our faith in Christ, *if good works do not follow from our profession of faith, it is a clear indication that we do not possess justifying faith.*[52]

This line of reasoning has been addressed previously where it was suggested that an appeal to God's sovereign election does not mitigate man's obligation to respond to the call of grace and even less does it contravene the unambiguous testimony of Scripture that describes this obligatory response *only in terms of faith, not obedience or good works.*[53]

Using language similar to that of MacArthur, Sproul likewise suggests that good works may be used as the litmus test for judging the genuineness of another's salvation. "Since justification *must* result in good works, we have some ability to discern the 'root' of faith by its 'fruit.'"[54] Good works are the *proof* that someone's claim to be Christian is true. Sproul writes, "We are justified by faith alone, but not by faith that *is* alone. Good works are absolutely necessary to the Christian life, not as a means of salvation, but *as proof of it.* A man who claims to be saved by faith but who lives an immoral life is a *counterfeit believer* whose future is revealed in Matthew 7:21–23."[55] Sproul's appeal to Matthew 7:21–23 clarifies that he is referring to the appropriateness of one believer judging the genuineness of *another's* faith, not his *own*. Thus, Sproul, unlike MacArthur, does not appeal to the community standards of the church body in affirming this judgmental activity.

Furthermore, Matthew 7:21–23 actually does not help his case. After all, as discussed in chapter three, the *counterfeit believers* Jesus speaks of in this passage have sufficient good works so as to *appear outwardly like sheep.* They perform all of the appropriate actions that might cause someone to think they are believers. Indeed, this is the very point of Jesus' warning to look *beyond the outward appearance* to what is in the hearts of these false prophets. In light of the fact that they are called "false prophets" and in light of the parallel passage in Matthew 12:33–37 where "fruit" unambiguously refers to words, it seems apparent that the fruit that identifies the individuals in Matthew 7 as false prophets is the testimony of their mouths, not their behavior. In essence, Jesus says, "You cannot tell whether someone is truly a believer or not by looking at their actions." Sproul turns Jesus' statement on its head by making it say just the opposite!

Sproul's suggestion that the presence or absence of good works in the life of a believer can have a determinative factor on whether or not he is *truly* a believer is an example of adding a postrequisite as a condition for receiving eternal life. The Bible conditions eternal salvation solely upon simple faith alone in Christ alone. To express faith in Jesus is to be convinced that He has given eternal life to one who simply has believed in Him for it. No act of obedience, preceding or following faith in Jesus Christ, such as a promise to obey, repentance of sin, pledge of obedience or surrendering to the Lordship of Christ, may be added to, or considered part of, faith as a condition for receiving eternal life.

Case Study: John Piper

John Piper, like R. C. Sproul, comes from the Reformed soteriological perspective. A Baptist minister and prolific author, Piper currently serves as senior pastor of Bethlehem Baptist Church in Minneapolis, Minnesota. He has gained widespread notoriety in contemporary evangelical circles and is especially popular with the twenty and thirty-something audience who connect emotionally with his motto for life and ministry: "God is most glorified in us when we are most satisfied in him." Piper refers to those who adopt and live out this motto as *Christian Hedonists*.[56]

Piper's passion for Christ and his ardent opposition to the worldliness that characterizes the postmodern culture are akin to that of David Wells, and equally admirable. However, like Wells and other Reformed theologians, Piper elevates good works to a level of prominence that suggests good works are instrumental in determining whether or not one will go to heaven. For instance, he writes, "There is no doubt that Jesus saw some measure of real, lived-out obedience to the will of God as necessary for final salvation."[57] What is this *obedience*, exactly? Piper clarifies that the obedience Jesus demands comes in the form of outward, visible fruit. In a section entitled, *Every healthy tree bears good fruit,* he states:

We saw in *Demand #7* that being connected with Jesus by faith results in a new life of love. That's the fruit Jesus produces as he works within us: "I am the vine; you are the branches. Whoever abides in me and I in him, he it is that bears much fruit, for apart from me you can do nothing" (John 15:5). In another place he makes it clear that being a "healthy tree"—that is, being a person who *truly* believes in him—will bear good fruit: "Every healthy tree bears good fruit, but the diseased tree bears bad fruit" (Matt 7:17).

The fruit does not make the tree good. The tree makes the fruit good. Good deeds do not attach us to Jesus. *They are not the ground of our being declared righteous.* Trusting Jesus connects us with Jesus. This connection results in God's declaration that we are perfect, and this same connection releases the power that produces fruit. The reason Jesus can say, "Every tree that does not bear good fruit is cut down and thrown into the fire" (Matt 7:19) is not because the fruit is the basis of our acceptance with God—the tax collector had no fruit to offer—but because *the absence of fruit shows we are not connected to Jesus.*[58]

Once again, as with Sproul and MacArthur, the notion of *necessary* but *non-instrumental* works is evident. *Good deeds*, Piper suggests, are not the ground of one's justification. *Trusting Jesus* is what *connects one to Jesus* (i.e., justifies). Yet, once one is *connected to Jesus* he must bear the fruit of good deeds or it shows he was never *connected to Jesus* in the first place. For Piper, the discussion at hand takes place in the context of John 15 and the vine/branches analogy that Jesus uses in his Upper Room discourse with the Eleven. Piper equates *abiding in Christ* with being a Christian. If one is not abiding in Christ he is not saved. This exposition of the passage, however, makes no sense when one considers that those to whom Jesus was speaking *were already believers.* Why would He command the Eleven (Judas had already left the group) to *abide in Him* (i.e., become a Christian) if they were already Christians?

A better understanding of the passage is to see Jesus as expounding upon fellowship. Not all believers abide in Him. Jesus knew that the Eleven would face particular hardship and trials in the months and years to come. He challenged them to remain in close fellowship (Gk. μένω) with Him if they wanted to be faithful disciples and bear much fruit.[59] Jesus' discussion of the vine/branches does not support Piper's thesis that those who bear no fruit are not truly saved.

Piper further tips his hand regarding his view of the role of works in eternal salvation with the following statement: "What God will require at the judgment is not our perfection, but *sufficient*

Getting the Gospel Wrong

fruit to show that the tree had life — in our case, divine life."[60] Piper explicitly connects sufficient good deeds with God's ultimate judgment.[61] In the context "at the judgment" implies the ultimate determination of one's entrance into heaven. As with those proponents of this soteriological method considered previously, such language begs the question, how many good deeds constitute *sufficient fruit?* This tendency to make works necessary (even while insisting they are non-justifying) represents a departure from the essence of the gospel, namely, faith alone in Christ alone as the only means of securing eternal life.

Summary of Chapter Eight

It is axiomatic that postmodernism's proclivity for moral relativism has made disturbing inroads into the church. So much so, that in many cases, it is difficult to distinguish between the world and the church. Understandably, this has many evangelicals concerned about the state of the church and passionate about moral reform. Indeed *all evangelicals* should stand united in calling God's people to moral purity and godliness. In such a context, however, some evangelical leaders seem bent on adopting a soteriological method that makes man's entrance into heaven contingent to varying degrees upon his own good behavior. The case studies examined in this chapter were categorized under the heading *The Performance Gospel* because in each case man's good works are emphasized as either a *prerequisite* or *postrequisite* for receiving eternal life.

As mentioned, works-oriented gospels are not a *new* approach to the gospel born uniquely out of the postmodern milieu. Man's natural tendency to make works an instrumental part of salvation is a timeless enemy. Yet such works-based soteriological methods seem to have been reenergized in recent years by the prevalent worldliness of American postmodern culture. However well-intentioned these performance-oriented gospels may be they represent a serious infringement upon the purity of the gospel. The best way to stem the tide of immorality and make a positive impact on the world is by proclaiming the simple message that whoever believes in Jesus

Christ alone as the Son of God who died and rose again to pay his personal penalty for sin has eternal life.

ENDNOTES
CHAPTER EIGHT

1. Charles R. Swindoll, *The Grace Awakening* (Dallas: Word, 1990), 86, emphasis original.

2. The relationship between faith and works has been discussed previously in chapter three in the context of the Reformed notion of the nature of saving faith. That chapter provided a biblical and theological evaluation of the view that man's works are somehow connected to the validity of his faith. The present chapter provides additional specific examples of this soteriological approach and critiques it based upon the five-fold biblical standard established in chapter three. Some theologians already cited in chapter three are given additional attention in the present chapter.

3. John MacArthur, *The Gospel According to Jesus: What Does Jesus Mean When He Says "Follow Me"?* 1st paperback ed. (Grand Rapids: Academic Books, Zondervan, 1989), 16.

4. Ibid.

5. Ibid., emphasis added.

6. See discussion of repentance at note seventy-four in chapter three.

7. John R. W. Stott, *Basic Christianity* (London: Intervarsity Press, 1971), 109–12, emphasis added. The view that a promise of good works, or pledge of unwavering obedience, is necessary as part of the response of saving faith is gaining adherents at an alarming rate in the postmodern age. Many well-intentioned evangelicals are responding to postmodernism's disdain for standards by placing rigid, non-biblical requirements on the unbeliever who desires to be saved. Several examples will be addressed later in this chapter, but one notable adherent of this view is Ray Comfort. Comfort has amassed an enormous following, especially among Southern Baptists, with

his books *The Way of the Master* (revised edition 2006, co-authored by Kirk Cameron) and *Hell's Best Kept Secret* (expanded edition, 2004), among others. While Comfort is to be commended for his accurate portrayal of man's sinfulness, especially at a time when many evangelicals shy away from addressing sin as the essence of lost man's problem, his suggested remedy to man's sin problem is far from the biblical standard of grace.

Comfort and many like him have reshaped the gospel to include an emphasis on man's performance on the front end of the conversion experience. In order to be saved, man must completely forsake all of his sinful ways and promise to follow Christ in obedience. But, as is discussed later in this chapter, such a formula makes man's good works instrumental in securing eternal life—a fact completely at odds with the biblical teaching on salvation by grace through faith alone (c.f. Rom 3:24; 4:5; Eph 2:8–9; Titus 3:5; et. al.). For Comfort, eternal salvation becomes a self-initiated, self-accomplished transformation from a life of sinful behavior to a life of good behavior. The salvation experience requires a "commitment" that involves "repenting with all [one's] heart." Ray Comfort, *Hell's Best Kept Secret* (New Kensington, Penn.: Whitaker House, 2004), 199, 204. Comfort insists that the problem of an ineffective evangelistic enterprise in the modern church lies not with "the harvest but with the reapers." Ibid., 181. That is, by underemphasizing the high cost and commitment involved in salvation, the church naturally has produced "fruitless, lukewarm Christians" who "are not truly part of Christ's body" and will be spewed out of Christ's mouth. Ibid., 63.

Comfort's soteriological method is perhaps most clearly manifested in his book *How to Bring Your Children to Christ & Keep Them There: Avoiding the Tragedy of False Conversion* (2005). For Comfort, simple childlike faith is not enough; there must be heartfelt, steadfast, volitional commitment to stop sinning and live righteously, otherwise the conversion is deemed "false."

8. James Montgomery Boice, *The Glory of God's Grace: The Meaning of God's Grace—and How It Can Change Your Life* (Grand Rapids: Kregel Publications, 1999), 88, emphasis added.

9. His books on the issue include *The Gospel According to Jesus* (1989), *Faith Works: The Gospel According to the Apostles* (1993), and *Hard to Believe: The High Cost and Infinite Value of Following Christ* (2003).

10. S. Lewis Johnson, Jr., "How Faith Works," *Christianity Today*, September 22, 1989, 21. For detailed treatments of the Lordship Salvation debate, see R. Alan Day, *Lordship: What Does It Mean?* (Nashville: Broadman, 1993), Kenneth L. Gentry Jr., *Lord of the Saved: Getting to the Heart of the Lordship Debate* (Phillipsburg, N.J.: P & R, 1992), Zane C. Hodges, *Absolutely Free! A Biblical Reply to Lordship Salvation* (Grand Rapids: Zondervan, 1989), Charles Caldwell Ryrie, *So Great Salvation: What It Means to Believe in Jesus Christ* (Wheaton: Victor Books, 1989).

11. John F. MacArthur, *Romans* (Chicago: Moody, 1991), 204–5, emphasis added.

12. Cf. Romans 10:9–10, "that if you confess with your mouth the Lord Jesus and believe in your heart that God has raised Him from the dead, you will be saved. For with the *heart one believes unto righteousness...*" (emphasis added). See discussion of this passage at note forty-six in chapter four.

13. See discussion of *head faith* versus *heart faith* at note seventy-nine in chapter three.

14. John MacArthur, *Faith Works: The Gospel According to the Apostles* (Dallas: Word Pub., 1993), 23, emphasis added.

15. MacArthur, *The Gospel According to Jesus*, 162–67.

16. See discussion of the *ordo salutis* at note seventy-five in chapter three.

17. MacArthur, *The Gospel According to Jesus*, xiii, emphasis added.

18. See *Appendix A: 160+ Verses Demonstrating Justification By Faith Alone.*

19. Benjamin B. Warfield, "Faith," in *Biblical and Theological Studies*, ed. Samuel Craig (Philadelphia: Presbyterian and Reformed Publishing, 1952), 425.

20. *Have You Heard of the Four Spiritual Laws* is published by New Life Publications: A Ministry of Campus Crusade for Christ, 1965, 1994. Bill Bright passed away July 19, 2003.

21. *Campus Crusade for Christ.* <http://www.ccci.org/> (accessed 18 January 2007).

22. See comments regarding this verse at note ten in chapter five.

23. The tract includes a note at the bottom of the first page which instructs the reader to read all scriptural references within the tract "in context from the Bible wherever possible." This is commendable in that it signifies to the reader, who is likely to be unfamiliar with God's Word, that the passages cited are part of a larger context. Furthermore, it encourages the reader to seek out a Bible for further study. In keeping with this, on two later occasions in the tract the reader is expressly instructed to read a portion of Scripture that is not quoted within the pages of the tract.

24. *How to Know for Sure You Are Going to Heaven*, written by Dr. D. James Kennedy, copyright 2001. American Tract Society, Garland, Texas. (Tract #30849)

25. *Who Is This Jesus?* <http://whoisthisjesus.com> (accessed 21 March 2002).

26. D. James Kennedy, *Evangelism Explosion* (Wheaton: Tyndale House Publishers, 1970).

27. *How to Know for Sure You Are Going to Heaven*, emphasis added.

28. David F. Wells, "Introduction: The Word in the World," in *The Compromised Church: The Present Evangelical Crisis*, ed. John H. Armstrong (Wheaton: Crossway Books, 1998), 31.

29. David F. Wells, *No Place for Truth, or, Whatever Happened to Evangelical Theology?* (Grand Rapids: Eerdmans, 1993), 98.

30. Ibid., 99–100.

31. Ibid., 100, emphasis added.

32. MacArthur, *The Gospel According to Jesus: What Does Jesus Mean When He Says "Follow Me,"* 178. In an accompanying footnote, MacArthur clarifies that while believers do sin, they must not "continue in unbroken disobedience from the moment of conversion, without ever producing any righteous fruit whatsoever."

33. MacArthur, *Faith Works: The Gospel According to the Apostles*, 171, emphasis original.

34. Ibid., 149.

35. Ibid., 154.

36. John MacArthur, *Keys to Spiritual Growth*, rev. and expanded ed. (Tarrytown, N.Y.: F. H. Revell, 1991), 64–65. It is interesting that MacArthur employs the metaphor "two sides of a coin" to describe both the relationship between *repentance and faith* and *good works and faith*. Cf. "It has often been said that repentance and faith are two sides of the same coin.... Repentance turns from sin to Christ, and faith embraces Him as the only hope of salvation and righteousness." John MacArthur, *Faith Works: The Gospel According to the Apostles*, 77.

37. MacArthur, *Faith Works: The Gospel According to the Apostles*, 170–71.

38. Ibid., 191, emphasis original.

39. John MacArthur, *Keys to Spiritual Growth*, 64–65.

40. Hodges, *Absolutely Free! A Biblical Reply to Lordship Salvation*, 19.

41. MacArthur, *Faith Works: The Gospel According to the Apostles*, 192. It already has been pointed out that while sin or the absence of good works cannot definitively *prove* that one is not a Christian, such characteristics in the life of a professing believer certainly should be addressed by the church. But the rebuke should come in the context of Christian discipline and sanctification, not the casting of doubt upon one's profession. Unless, of course, the very testimony of the sinning church member is such that he claims by his own admission never to have trusted in Jesus Christ for salvation.

42. Boice, *The Glory of God's Grace*, xi.

43. Ibid., 72.

44. Ibid., 73.

45. Ibid., 74.

46. Ibid.

47. Ibid., 238.

48. R. C. Sproul, *Before the Face of God Book Four: A Daily Guide for Living from Ephesians, Hebrews, and James* (Grand Rapids: Baker Book House, 1994), 432, emphasis original.

49. R. C. Sproul, *Essential Truths of the Christian Faith*, paperback ed. (Wheaton: Tyndale House, 1998), 172, emphasis original.

50. R. C. Sproul, *Chosen by God*, paperback ed. (Wheaton: Tyndale House Publishers, 1994), 215, emphasis added. While it is true that regeneration gives one a new "inclination," it does not follow that the believer is now compelled to follow that inclination. Regeneration brings a new disposition but it does not bring guaranteed sanctification. It is quite possible for believers to ignore the convicting power of the Holy Spirit within and thus not bring the expected results of holiness. For Sproul, regeneration makes good works "inevitable." R. C. Sproul, *Faith Alone: The Evangelical Doctrine of Justification* (Grand Rapids: Baker Books, 1995), 26.

51. Sproul, *Faith Alone: The Evangelical Doctrine of Justification*, 26.

52. R. C. Sproul, *Essential Truths of the Christian Faith*, 191, emphasis added.

53. See *Appendix A: 160+ Verses Demonstrating Justification by Faith Alone.*

54. R. C. Sproul, *Before the Face of God Book One: A Daily Guide for Living from the Book of Romans* (Grand Rapids: Baker Book House, 1992), 147, emphasis added.

55. R. C. Sproul, *Before the Face of God Book Three: A Daily Guide for Living from the Old Testament* (Grand Rapids: Baker Book House, 1994), 86, emphasis added. Elsewhere Sproul writes, "It is possible, however, for the believer to experience a serious and radical fall. Scripture is replete with examples of believers who fell into grievous sin, such as David and Peter. Though their fall was dreadful, it was neither full nor final. Both were restored to repentance and grace. Believers can have a radical fall, but such falls are temporary and impermanent." R. C. Sproul, *Grace Unknown: The Heart of Reformed Theology* (Grand Rapids: Baker, 1997), 208.

Thus, Sproul admits that a believer may fall into serious sin even though he is unable to quantify the precise meanings of *temporary* and *impermanent*. Sproul goes on to suggest that when a believer falls into such *temporary* grievous sin, two explanations are possible. First, he may not be a believer after all—his faith was only spurious. But this view raises an entirely different set of problems regarding the nature of saving faith as discussed in chapter three. "The second possible explanation of those who make a profession of faith, give outward evidence of conversion, and then repudiate the faith, is that they are true believers who have fallen into serious and radical apostasy, but *who will repent of their sin and be restored before they die*. If they persist in apostasy until death, then theirs is a full and final fall from grace, which is evidence that they were not genuine believers in the first place." R. C. Sproul, *Grace Unknown: The Heart of Reformed Theology*, 209, emphasis added. According to this second explanation, one cannot die in a state of unrepentant, grievous sin and expect to go to heaven (because it proves he is not a true believer). Either explanation offered by Sproul for grievous sin in the life of a believer links one's performance inseparably to his ultimate salvation.

56. *Desiring God Ministries.* <http://www.desiringgod.org/> (accessed 18 February 2007).

57. John Piper, *What Jesus Demands from the World* (Wheaton: Crossway Books, 2006), 160.

58. Ibid., 161, emphasis added.

59. See discussion of μένω at note twenty-nine in chapter three.

60. Piper, *What Jesus Demands from the World*, 211, emphasis added.

61. In the quote cited earlier, Piper equates *fruit* with *good deeds*.

CHAPTER 9

SUMMARY AND CONCLUSION

Not by works of righteousness which we have done, but according to His mercy He saved us… –Titus 3:5

The present work began with a survey of the current landscape in American evangelicalism. Postmodernity has ushered in an ideology so counter to the traditional American, evangelical mindset that it has the church, in large part, scrambling to know how to respond. Postmodernism's emphasis on the supernatural realm—in contrast to modernism's dependence on rationality (i.e., science and reason)—presents a fertile ground for sharing the gospel with those who recognize that life is about more than what they can see and feel and touch. However, this awareness of the spiritual realm coupled with postmodernism's rejection of absolute truth constitutes a volatile and dangerous mixture. It is a time when "reality has crossed swords with the imagination and lost."[1] That is, reality is in the mind of the beholder. Truth is a personal creation; and with no arbiter available to police the quest for truth, individuals stand ready and eager to accept any individualized reality that is pitched as a means of bringing personal fulfillment or satisfaction.

The Impact of Postmodernism

One impact of such pluralistic thinking is a general abandon-ment of the notion of certainty. One's beliefs typically are stated in terms of individual bias or personal opinion rather than confident conviction. This reticence toward certainty is manifested within evangelicalism in the form of theologians who eschew absolute certainty when it comes to matters of orthodoxy and doctrine. And when evangelicals express uncertainty about truth, either because they have adopted postmodernism's assumptions or perhaps in a misguided effort to be accepted in the public square, it only serves to undermine confidence in the evangelical gospel as a solution to man's sin problem.

One of the more dangerous components of postmodernism is the deconstruction of language. Deconstructionism "reduces language to but a social construct mirroring the interpreter's personal perspec-tive."[2] The pluralistic mindset that dominates postmodern thought has impacted language to the extent that words, like truth, have no absolute meaning. This "loss of linguistic strength"[3] appears to have impacted the manner in which the church articulates the gospel. At the very least, the case studies in the present work suggest that multiple soteriological methods, each within the context of evan-gelical Christianity, and each in contradiction with the standard of Scripture, are being advanced. In large part, the church has been inattentive to this prevalent inconsistency among evangelicals when it comes to the precise definition of the gospel. There is a perceived indifference toward accuracy in gospel presentations, such that inherently contradictory soteriological methods are welcomed with little or no questions.

The Biblical Standard

A consistent definition of the gospel is lacking and this soterio-logical crisis within evangelicalism cannot be passed off merely as a matter of semantics. Scripture is clear regarding the gospel. Saving faith is the belief in Jesus Christ as the Son of God who died and rose again to pay one's personal penalty for sin and the one who gives eternal life to all who trust Him and Him alone for it. There is nothing magical about these particular English words; nor is it suggested that saving faith necessitates the articulation of a particular formula, verbiage or incantation. What is important to recognize is that the gospel has a particular, non-negotiable content.

The case studies in this present work were evaluated based upon the biblical standard of the gospel. This standard was expressed in terms of five non-negotiable components: (1) Jesus Christ, (2) the Son of God who died and rose again, (3) to pay one's personal penalty for sin, (4) gives eternal life to those who trust Him and (5) Him alone for it. These five essentials, however they may be expressed or articulated, must be included in the gospel and the gospel must *not* include anything that contradicts these five essentials.

Faith Versus Saving Faith

A significant aspect of the present work was a focus on the nature of saving faith. It is not enough to establish the biblical standard of the gospel if one does not understand what it means to *believe it*. It was suggested that there is a difference between *generic* faith and *saving* faith. Generic faith may be defined as the *assurance or confidence in a stated or implied truth*. This truth may be in the form of a simple *proposition*, or it may be in the form of a *person* with one or more propositions inseparably wrapped up in that person. The meaning of the word *faith* is not at all complex. When one believes in the truthfulness or reliability of someone or something, he has faith. To *believe, have faith*, and *trust* are all ways of expressing the same thing: assurance or confidence in a stated or implied truth.

Saving faith occurs when *faith meets the right object*—the gospel. "The saving power resides exclusively, not in the act of faith, or the attitude of faith, or the nature of faith, but in the object of faith."[4] Though one can and does believe many things in life, *saving faith* occurs when one believes in Jesus Christ as the Son of God who died and rose again to pay his personal penalty for sin and the one who gives eternal life to all who trust Him and Him alone for it.

The Reformed Notion of Saving Faith

It was suggested that Reformed Theology has influenced significantly evangelicalism's understanding of saving faith. Saving faith, according to Reformed soteriology, not only must be quantified (i.e., have the correct object), but *qualified* if it is to produce eternal salvation. That is, it must be the right *kind of faith* if it is going to result in eternal salvation. *Real* saving faith, it is suggested, has three components each identified by a Latin designation: A knowledge element (*notitia*), which is understanding the content of truth (i.e., mentally comprehending it); an agreement element (*assensus*), which is the mental assent to the truth (i.e., agreement that it is true); and a volitional element (*fiducia*), which is the personal determination to submit to the truth. Thus, it is said, eternal salvation is gained by acknowledging, accepting and obeying the demands of the gospel. Only when all three components are present can one be said to have *truly* believed the gospel.

The origin of the confusion regarding the nature of saving faith can be traced to the Protestant Reformation and the reaction to the Roman Catholic understanding of faith. The Reformers were concerned that Roman Catholicism was bestowing eternal salvation upon anyone who desired it even if they expressed no explicit faith in the truths of Scripture. One's self-identification with *The Church* was enough to secure eternal salvation. Often called *the baptism of desire*, this Catholic notion taught that anyone who sincerely seeks God as best he can is saved by *implicit faith*. This idea was offensive to the Reformers, and rightly so. They were correct in rejecting the Catholic idea of implicit faith. It was not saving faith. But in seeking to make faith in the gospel more *explicit* rather than *implicit*, Reformed Theology historically has appealed not just to a clearly defined, biblical *content* of faith, but to a redefinition of the meaning of *faith* itself. The problem with this approach is that it fails to consider that what makes faith deficient (i.e., unable to save) is its inaccurate content, not the qualitative nature of the faith itself. Yet this is precisely the suggestion of many evangelical theologians who perpetuate this Reformed notion of saving faith in the present age.

Spurious Faith?

Those who hold to the Reformed view of saving faith have redefined it to include various elements of personal commitment and surrender. Faith that does not involve the explicit, volitional components of a pledge of personal obedience and repentance of sins, is considered *spurious faith*. The notion of spurious faith undoubtedly developed out of the best of intentions. Evangelical pastors and leaders understandably decry the prevalence of immorality within the church. It is painful for shepherds to watch their sheep engage in conduct that reflects poorly not only on the church, but more importantly on the Lord of the church, Jesus Christ. In seeking to make sense of such behavior many evangelical theologians quite often gravitate toward the position that perhaps such pew-dwellers are not, in fact, saved after all. This would provide an easy explanation for their unchristian-like behavior. Hence, the *spurious faith* classification often is employed to describe the faith of these individuals because it is alleged that their faith lacks the elements of volitional obedience and surrender and thus will not result in eternal salvation—it is *spurious* (or so it is claimed).

But this approach, while convenient, has a definite though perhaps unintended negative implication. It makes *good works* the focus when validating one's eternal salvation and thus *ipso facto* instrumental in securing eternal life. However, it was suggested that notwithstanding the widely-respected opinions to the contrary, especially by many from the Reformed perspective, Scripture does not teach that a prolonged state of carnality or a failure to pledge oneself in total surrender to Christ prove that one is not a Christian.

The *spurious faith* category, as it is commonly defined, does not exist. Yet, it does not follow that everyone who claims to be a Christian really is saved. There *is* a category of non-saving faith. What makes their faith non-saving, however, has nothing to do with the intrinsic nature or quality of their faith; rather, what makes their faith non-saving is that it is misplaced. It is not in the correct object of saving faith. Non-saving faith describes those who, despite earnestly believing that they are saved, are not, because they have never believed the gospel.

The Purpose Gospel

In keeping with postmodernism's emphasis on ambiguity and personal experience, over and against the acceptance of universally true standards, the *purpose gospel* seeks to impact lives through an inherently individualized, relational approach. The purpose gospel lacks several essential elements of the gospel. It underemphasizes the universal problem of sin, vis-à-vis one's personal guilt and responsibility. When it is addressed, sin is often redefined and recast solely in terms of its relational impact rather than its eternal implications. It likewise underemphasizes eternal life and instead focuses primarily on this present life with its meaning, purpose, and fulfillment of dreams. The purpose gospel also fosters a lack of urgency in sharing the gospel, with many purpose driven ministries avoiding explicit gospel presentations in their marketing and promotional materials. Rick Warren is the most notable proponent of this soteriological method.

The Puzzling Gospel

The *puzzling gospel* describes those gospel presentations that lack precision, accuracy and consistency. Two famous gospel tracts were examined as well as a sampling of gospel presentations from students at a large, evangelical Bible college. These case studies demonstrate a startling *inconsistency* in evangelical soteriological methodology. Additionally, they manifest a significant degree of *imprecision and inaccuracy* when it comes to the essence of the gospel. An examination of *The Gospel According to Starbucks* uncovered perhaps the most profound example of a puzzling gospel. Not only does it lack clarity in communicating exactly what one must believe in order to have eternal life, it celebrates this lack of clarity in favor of a nebulous, experiential conversation with God, ungrounded in propositional truth.

The fog of confusion surrounding many gospel presentations manifests itself in various ways such as imprecision, inconsistency, inaccuracy, and ambiguity. It was suggested that given the ideological distinctives of postmodernity, such puzzling gospels are more likely than ever to go unnoticed and perhaps even thrive. But such confusion easily gives way to clarity when one communicates the gospel as Scripture defines it: Jesus Christ, the Son of God, died and rose again to pay one's personal penalty for sin and offers eternal life to all who simply trust Him and Him alone for it.

The Prosperity Gospel

Although the *prosperity gospel* traces its lineage to the *word of faith* movement that originated in the mid-twentieth century, it was suggested that postmodernism's experientialism and subjectivity seem to have emboldened prosperity proponents in contemporary evangelicalism. This soteriological method includes components that lie outside the scope of the pure gospel, such as the emphasis of certain present, peripheral benefits accompanying eternal salvation. These benefits usually include financial, physical and emotional well-being, in addition to spiritual salvation. Additionally, the prosperity gospel includes components that violate the essence of the gospel, such as a focus on faith as an intrinsic quality rather than an emphasis on the saving object of faith and a notable absence of the mention of sin.

Joel Osteen, T. D. Jakes, and Kirbyjon Caldwell serve as examples of this contemporary version of the prosperity gospel. Osteen's soteriological method fails to emphasize the proper meaning of sin, overemphasizes the present life to the almost complete exclusion of the eternal aspect of salvation, and elevates material blessings to a place of centrality in the gospel promise.

Both Osteen and Jakes promote an improper definition of faith. They cast faith in terms of its intrinsic quality and suggest that salvation is available only to those with the right *kind* of faith. In this scheme, the focus of saving faith is moved off of the correct object of faith and onto man and his inherent self-will and self-determination. Jakes, like Osteen, downplays *sin* and furthermore manifests a number of other theological aberrations such as a troubling view of the Trinity, belief that not all Christians are children of God and a belief in new, individual, prophetic revelation.

Caldwell's soteriological method shares the prosperity gospel's erroneous concept of faith as a positive, internal force rather than confident assurance in a stated object. Additionally, his discussion of *holistic salvation* imports non-essential elements into the salvation equation on the front end such as one's emotional and economic well-being. Caldwell's gospel includes unbiblical requirements such as following Christ for the remainder of one's life and public, verbal confession of Christ as one's Lord. Based on the established standard, the prosperity gospel, as illustrated by these three case studies, lacks the essential elements required of the pure gospel.

The Pluralistic Gospel

Pluralistic thinking has become entrenched in postmodern American culture. *Pluralism* argues that no single religion can claim to be the exclusive means of salvation. It is the view that "all religions have the same moral and spiritual value, and offer the same potential for achieving salvation, however 'salvation' be construed."[5] This ideology is manifested in *evangelical* thought in the form of inclusivism. *Inclusivism*, "while affirming the truth of fundamental Christian claims, nevertheless insists that God has revealed himself, even in saving ways, in other religions."[6] The pluralistic gospel describes those postmodern evangelicals who suggest that one can be saved without ever affirming explicitly Jesus Christ as the object of his faith. In fact, one can be saved without ever knowing that Jesus Christ exists.

Clark Pinnock and John Sanders are two leading evangelicals who espouse this view. They suggest that since individuals in the Old Testament could be saved apart from explicit knowledge of Jesus Christ, likewise those with no knowledge of Jesus Christ in the present age can receive eternal salvation. Yet, this argument fails to consider properly the progress of revelation and the changing nature of the precise content of saving faith. Advocates of a pluralistic gospel, such as Pinnock and Sanders, also fail to distinguish adequately between general revelation and special revelation. It was suggested that general revelation is not sufficient for salvation. One must respond by faith directly to specific revelatory truth in order to be saved. Today, that truth is the essence of the gospel as contained in the New Testament.

The pluralistic gospel represents significant influence of postmodern thinking. It fully embraces postmodernism's disdain for certainty, absolutism, and the rejection of one, singular grand metanarrative for human history. This makes it an attractive soteriological viewpoint for many postmodern evangelicals.

The Performance Gospel

Several case studies suggested that many evangelicals espouse a soteriological method that makes man's good works either a *prerequisite* or *postrequisite* for receiving eternal life. It was pointed out that performance-oriented gospels are not a *new* approach to the gospel born uniquely out of the postmodern age. Yet such works-based soteriological methods seem to have been reenergized in recent years by the prevalent worldliness of American postmodern culture. Postmodernism's proclivity for moral relativism has made disturbing inroads into the church, so much so, that in many cases, it is difficult to distinguish between the world and the church. In such a context, some evangelical leaders have adopted a soteriological method that makes man's entrance into heaven contingent to varying degrees upon his own good behavior in an effort to stem the tide of immorality in the church. John MacArthur, James Boice, John Piper, David Wells and R. C. Sproul are a few prominent proponents of this soteriological method.

A frequent theme of the present work was the vital importance of faith *alone* in Christ *alone* as the only means of securing eternal salvation. However well-intentioned these performance-oriented gospels may be they represent a serious infringement upon the purity of the gospel. The Bible conditions eternal salvation solely upon simple faith alone in Christ alone. To express faith in Jesus is to be convinced that He has given eternal life to one who simply has believed in Him for it. No act of obedience, preceding or following faith in Jesus Christ, such as a promise to obey, repentance of sin, pledge of obedience or surrendering to the Lordship of Christ, may be added to, or considered part of, faith as a condition for receiving eternal life.

ENDNOTES
CHAPTER NINE

1. Ravi Zacharias, "An Ancient Message, through Modern Means, to a Postmodern Mind," in *Telling the Truth: Evangelizing Postmoderns*, ed. D. A. Carson (Grand Rapids: Zondervan, 2000), 22.

2. Carl F. H. Henry, "Postmodernism: The New Spectre?" in *The Challenge of Postmodernism: An Evangelical Engagement*, ed. David S. Dockery (Wheaton: Victor Books, 1995), 39.

3. Ravi Zacharias, "The Touch of Truth," in *Telling the Truth: Evangelizing Postmoderns*, ed. D. A. Carson (Grand Rapids: Zondervan, 2000), 43.

4. Benjamin B. Warfield, "Faith," in *Biblical and Theological Studies*, ed. Samuel Craig (Philadelphia: Presbyterian and Reformed Publishing, 1952), 425.

5. D. A. Carson, *The Gagging of God: Christianity Confronts Pluralism* (Grand Rapids: Zondervan, 1996), 278–79.

6. Ibid., 27.

CHAPTER 10

SUGGESTED CORRECTIVES

For I am not ashamed of the gospel, for it is the power of
God for salvation to everyone who believes. –Romans 1:16

Identifying a problem usually is easier than solving it and such
undoubtedly is the case with the soteriological crisis identified in
the present work. The issues that have been raised are complex and
not easily resolved with the wave of a magician's wand (or a writer's pen). Yet, the issues are serious enough to warrant intentional
consideration on the part of the evangelical community. The lack
of definition, consistency and accuracy in postmodern evangelical
soteriology is a crisis of enormous proportions. The core message
of God's Word is at stake—the very message that historically has
defined evangelicalism, namely, *the gospel*. In thinking through the
various erroneous soteriological methods prevalent within postmodern American evangelicalism, several suggested correctives
come to mind.

General Suggestions

It was suggested that one of the reasons that the gospel has been
so badly marginalized in the church today is because the Bible itself
has been marginalized. That is, the Scriptures no longer occupy a
place of centrality in church ministry. Before anything else, and

above all else, if the soteriological crisis in evangelicalism today is to be resolved successfully *there must be a return to the centrality of the Scriptures in ministry.* As Carson has pointed out, "the way men and women come to know God is through his gracious self-disclosure in Scripture...."[1] If Scripture is neglected, there can be no gospel. Furthermore, to neglect the Scripture is to neglect the very thing that is profitable for improving one's life. "All Scripture is given by inspiration of God, and is *profitable for doctrine, for reproof, for correction, for instruction in righteousness*, that the man of God may be complete, thoroughly equipped for every good work" (2 Tim 3:16–17, emphasis added). According to this passage, God's Word is profitable for teaching men *what to believe* (doctrine), *what not to believe* (reproof), *how to behave* (instruction in righteousness), and *how not to behave* (correction). Given the comprehensive benefits of God's Word, the church neglects Scripture at its own peril.

The church must guard against allowing ministry programs, social initiatives, community-building, etc., to eclipse the primacy of God's Word. The church must not engage in any activities, however well-intentioned or seemingly beneficial, that "jeopardize the objectivity of the revelation God has graciously provided in his Son Jesus Christ and in the Bible."[2] When the church gathers in the weekly assembly it must gather around the Word. In commenting on the importance of biblical truth in the Christian life, Mark Dever offers an insightful analogy.

If you have any doubt that cognitive, propositional communication is at the very heart of [the Christian's] relationship [with God], let me ask this to those of you who have dogs at home: Would you say you had a good relationship with them? Probably most of you dog-owning readers of this chapter would say that, yes, you do have a good relationship with your dog. Yet even so, I predict that the quality, indeed the very nature of that relationship would change if you were to go home this evening and be greeted verbally by your dog. If your dog introduced speech into the relationship, it would change the nature of that relationship. The dog could both more fully know you and be more fully known by you. Our

God is not a mute God. Not only is he active in history, but he has spoken. And so we must care about cognitive truth. God has revealed himself as a personal God, and part of that personhood is *his communication to us of truth.*[3]

In other words, God is not a feeling to be experienced. He can be known only via His self-revelation in Scripture. One cannot hope to have a vibrant relationship with God, and even less can he hope to *enter into* a relationship with God, apart from the Word of God. The Scriptures must be central to the church's mission and ministry.

Emphasizing the centrality of Scriptures in ministry has a corollary that constitutes a second general corrective. *The church must oppose all forms of reader-response hermeneutics.* Making the Bible central in ministry is of little value if one's interpretive methodology mishandles the biblical text so as to render it meaningless. To say this another way—the Bible, *correctly handled and taught,* must occupy a place of centrality in ministry. Ultimately, many of the soteriological inaccuracies addressed in the present work may be traced to hermeneutical errors. Too often, even in the few evangelical churches that still profess to build their ministries upon the Word of God, the teaching is based upon out-of-context appeals to paraphrased Bible verses, improper cross-referencing of Scripture, and a general allegorizing of the text to suit one's homiletical topic.

Postmodernism's deconstruction of the text has spawned a hermeneutical crisis in the church. Since the prevailing hermeneutical winds insist that "there are as many meanings as there are interpreters," many evangelical leaders and pastors find themselves abandoning the notion of unequivocal meaning in the text.[4] This has a direct impact on the manner in which one preaches the gospel. In returning to the centrality of the Scriptures, the church must also return to the fundamental rules of literal-grammatical-historical hermeneutics—rules such as singularity of meaning and analytical, contextual interpretation.

Third, the church would do well *to recognize, affirm, and interact with the positive aspects of postmodernism without embracing its core values.* Not everything within the ideological framework of postmodernism is objectionable. In some small ways, postmodern thinking has improved upon modernism's ideological deficiencies and thus presents new opportunities for evangelicalism today.

> Under the regime of modernism, with its typically strident secularism, Christianity was badly bullied. The postmodern critique, however, has cut the modernist bully down to size, leaving him a lot less menacing. The breathing space is noticeable. Furthermore, the postmodern ambition to break the modernist hegemony by including marginalized and excluded voices has even at times resulted in a measured sponsorship of a Christian voice. We have found ourselves occasionally (if only reluctantly) invited to the table and allowed to articulate our story or final vocabulary. While this is by no means a homecoming, it is still, in a limited sense, a return from exile and to be acknowledged as a beneficial turn of providence.[5]

In other words, widespread pluralism has opened the door, ever so slightly, to Christianity as a viable partner in discussion. Evangelicals must be careful not to throw the baby out with the bath water in rejecting postmodernism's self-centered, experiential outlook. Worldviews contrary to the biblical worldview are nothing new in the history of the church and God has remained on the throne through it all. There are aspects of postmodern ideology that present a fertile ground for sharing the gospel. For instance, the prevalent emphasis on community can be turned into a positive if couched in terms of finding common ground with other believers through the gospel of Jesus Christ.

A fourth suggestion that may serve as a general corrective to the present soteriological crisis is: *The church must embrace certainty without apology.* Postmodernism's rejection of absolutism is not something that can be addressed tepidly. Evangelicals must continue unapologetically to teach the metanarrative of Christianity even if it is deemed naïve and intellectually offensive. To capitulate in any way to postmodernism's abandonment of certainty is to undermine the very foundation of evangelicalism, namely, the propositional truth of Scripture. Yet, in proclaiming the metanarrative of

Scripture, evangelicals must learn to communicate this metanarrative in an irenic and non-attacking manner that is effective without compromising the message of the gospel.

Suggested Correctives for the Purpose Gospel

Many of the problems identified in the purpose gospel can be mitigated simply *by emphasizing heaven and hell in presenting the gospel.* While meaning, purpose, contentment and similar decidedly earthly aspects of the Christian life are important, they are not *most important* when it comes to the issue of the gospel. "The felt need cannot be ignored, but it is important that having met on common ground, we rise to the higher ground of truth...."[6] The truth of the gospel is that anyone who trusts in Jesus Christ alone as the Son of God who died and rose again to pay his personal penalty for sin may have *eternal life.* The *sine qua non* of salvation involves being rescued from eternal damnation in hell and receiving eternal life that results ultimately in a place in heaven.[7] The primary remedy for the purpose gospel is not so much a change in the message, but an addition to it. Preach heaven and hell as part of the gospel.

At the same time, another pitfall of the purpose gospel may be avoided *by articulating clearly the notion of sin.* "Postmodern people need to grasp hold of the category of evil and wrong."[8] This involves not just theoretical knowledge of the concepts but the recognition that they are guilty themselves because of their own personal sinfulness. The church will be well-served by returning to the biblical language when discussing man's predicament. Man may be lonely, hurting, empty, purposeless, without hope and meaning—but ultimately man is guilty of sin before a holy and righteous God, and that is a core essential of the gospel. Evangelicals must not be afraid to use the word *sin.*

Finally, it will serve the church well to emphasize a more theocentric and Christocentric message rather than an anthropocentric message. The purpose-in-life approach often eclipses the important biblical truth that man's primary purpose is to glorify God, not to be happy.

Suggested Correctives for the Puzzling Gospel

While the technological advances of recent years, as well as the creativity spawned by postmodern thinking, create unprecedented opportunities to present the gospel, one must never lose sight of its simplicity and core essence. When presenting the gospel, the church needs to *keep it simple.* Sometimes creativity can be the enemy of accuracy. This does not disallow contextualized soteriological methods (cf. Acts 17:22–34), but the contextualization must not distort or cloud the essence of the gospel in any way. Evangelicals also need to *be intentional when articulating the gospel by choosing words carefully.* There is a vagueness and ambiguity that characterize many gospel presentations today. As rudimentary as it may seem, it may be helpful to stop and evaluate the gospel message *before* it is proclaimed. Are the essentials there? Is it clear? Is it accurate? Such a simple exercise may help alleviate unclear and self-contradictory gospel presentations.

Suggested Correctives for the Prosperity Gospel

In seeking to redress some of the fundamental flaws of the prosperity gospel, evangelicals must start *by emphasizing that suffering, trials, and difficulties are a normal part of the Christian life.* The Christian life is not an entitlement to prosperous living. There are many reasons why Christians may be called upon to suffer and experience circumstances that are less than prosperous.[9] This biblical teaching needs to be promoted in the church. There also must *be a marked emphasis on grace.* The prosperity gospel too often puts man in the center of the discussion, e.g. *how to have a better life, how to get a better job, how to improve one's economic standing, etc.* In shifting the focus from the supposed temporal, earthly blessings associated with salvation to the grace of God in relation to man's sinfulness, the entitlement mindset may be tempered with a measure of humility. As a practical matter, evangelicals also would be wise to *distance themselves from secular inspirational personalities,* such as talk show hosts, self-help experts, motivational speakers, media personalities, etc., and *maintain sharp lines of distinction between purveyors of secular wisdom and preachers of the gospel.* Evangelical leaders must distinguish themselves from secular motivational speakers based upon the explicit proclamation of the gospel. *Popular personalities* who may offer appealing advice from a non-Christian (or non-*decidedly* Christian) viewpoint *should not be celebrated by and promoted in the church* lest lay Christians mistakenly assume that they represent a valid evangelical soteriological method.

Suggested Correctives for the Pluralistic Gospel

Bryan Turner has suggested, "The multiplication of religious faiths in a multicultural society has in this everyday world a profoundly relativizing effect."[10] That is, the more like a melting pot American culture becomes, the more likely pluralistic thinking is to take hold.[11] Because of this, and especially because there are a "multiplicity of factors in contemporary American culture [that] converge to render this view ... intuitively appealing," the response to pluralism must be loud and firm.[12] The remedy here is rather straightforward: *Identify evangelicals who embrace and promote inclusivism and publicly challenge them.* There is no room in evangelicalism for a soteriological method that promotes salvation apart from an explicit knowledge of Jesus Christ in this life. There is a time to dialogue and there is a time to separate.[13] The church must reject inclusivism roundly, lest younger, impressionable believers be swept into the fold of the pluralistic mindset. The stakes are too high when it comes to the issue of a pluralistic gospel.

Suggested Correctives for the Performance Gospel

The performance gospel is a formidable foe. This is because it is born *not* out of a mindset that *embraces postmodernism*, but at least partly out of a passionate *opposition to postmodernism*. In this sense, those who promote the pure gospel and those who promote a performance gospel share a common enemy: postmodernism's penchant for moral relativism and the immoral behavior that it brings forth. The good intentions of the performance-oriented soteriological method often camouflage a serious error when it comes to the gospel. An effective way to unmask this error and discourage it is for evangelicals to *maintain sharp lines of distinction between discipleship and salvation in their teaching and preaching*. When confronting sin, particularly sin in the life of professing believers, the church *must deal with sinning church members as believers first*, rather than calling into question the genuineness of their salvation. Rather than encouraging ungodly church members to question their salvation, churches must emphasize various other biblical motivations for good works.[14] A renewed emphasis on principles of church discipline may serve the church more effectively than hasty accusations of so-called spurious faith.[15]

In teaching about discipleship, churches must also increase the amount of attention given to the *doctrine of eternal rewards* as a motivation for godliness, as well as to the reality of *God's temporal discipline* and the *loss of eternal rewards* as a discouragement from sin. Meanwhile, in preaching the gospel, churches must *emphasize the freeness of salvation*, even to the point of using the term *free*, to counteract the focus on man's performance that is so prevalent in many evangelical circles (cf. Rom 5:15–16; Rev 21:6; 22:17). In the face of widespread moral decay, evangelicals must resist the temptation to shy away from preaching grace for fear that it will be embraced as a license to sin. *The church must preach grace unapologetically.*

Final Thoughts

In light of (1) a prevalent inconsistency among evangelicals when it comes to the precise definition of the gospel, (2) a lack of awareness of or attentiveness to this inconsistency, and (3) perceived indifference toward accuracy in one's soteriological method, the future of American evangelicalism in this postmodern era may seem bleak. With clouds of confusion obscuring the essence of the gospel one wonders how long evangelicalism can continue in its role as the primary conduit of God's salvific message. Yet the believer is reminded that although "the grass withers, and its flower falls away, the Word of the Lord endures forever" (Isa 40:8). There are places, occasions and individual voices where the gospel message echoes forth unencumbered and pure. On a good day, one can descry (if only barely) glimmers of hope and pockets of revival. May these bright days increase.

ENDNOTES
CHAPTER TEN

1. D. A. Carson, *The Gagging of God: Christianity Confronts Pluralism* (Grand Rapids: Zondervan, 1996), 188.

2. Ibid., 191.

3. Mark E. Dever, "Communicating Sin in a Postmodern World," in *Telling the Truth: Evangelizing Postmoderns*, ed. D. A. Carson (Grand Rapids: Zondervan, 2000), 143–44, emphasis added.

4. Carson, *The Gagging of God: Christianity Confronts Pluralism*, 74.

5. Jon Hinkson and Greg Ganssle, "Epistemology at the Core of Postmodernism: Rorty, Foucault, and the Gospel," in *Telling the Truth: Evangelizing Postmoderns*, ed. D. A. Carson (Grand Rapids: Zondervan, 2000), 86–87.

6. Ravi Zacharias, "The Touch of Truth," in *Telling the Truth: Evangelizing Postmoderns*, ed. D. A. Carson (Grand Rapids: Zondervan, 2000), 40.

7. It was acknowledged previously that eternal life has both a *present* reality and a *future* reality.

8. Dever, "Communicating Sin in a Postmodern World," 148.

9. E.g. H. L. Willmington lists twenty-five reasons Christians suffer. H. L. Willmington, *Book of Bible Lists* (Wheaton: Tyndale House, 1987), 318.

10. Bryan Turner, *Orientalism, Postmodernism, and Globalism* (London: Routledge, 1994), 186.

11. The reality is America resembles more of a *stew pot* than a *melting pot*, with various individual cultures and religions retaining their distinctive and each being celebrated as valid and legitimate pathways to Truth.

12. Harold A. Netland and Keith E. Johnson, "Why Is Religious Pluralism Fun—and Dangerous?" in *Telling the Truth: Evangelizing Postmoderns*, ed. D. A. Carson (Grand Rapids: Zondervan, 2000), 64.

13. Cf. Rom 16:17; Titus 3:10–11; 2 John 10–11; Prov 14:7.

14. See *Appendix D: Biblical Motivations for the Believer to Do Good Works*.

15. Cf. R. Albert Mohler, Jr., "Church Discipline: The Missing Mark," in *The Compromised Church: The Present Evangelical Crisis* (Wheaton: Crossway Books, 1998), 171–88.

APPENDICES

Appendix A: 160+ Verses Demonstrating
Justification by Faith Alone

There are approximately 160 verses in the New Testament that indicate that salvation is based solely upon a person's belief in Jesus Christ.

Matthew 18:6
Mark 9:42
Luke 7:48–50; 8:12; 18:42
John 1:7, 12; 2:11, 23; 3:15, 16, 18, 36; 4:39; 4:41, 42; 5:24, 38, 45–47; 6:29, 35–36, 40, 47, 64; 7:5, 31, 38, 39; 8:24, 30–31, 45–46; 9:35–38; 10:24–26, 37–38, 42; 11:15, 25–27, 42, 45; 12:11, 36–38, 42, 44, 46–47; 13:19; 14:1–6, 12; 16:9; 17:20, 21; 19:35; 20:29, 31
Acts 2:44; 3:16; 4:4, 32; 5:14; 8:12–13, 37; 9:42; 10:43, 45; 11:17, 21; 13:12, 39, 48; 14:1, 23, 27; 15:5, 7, 9; 16:1, 31, 34; 17:4, 5, 12, 34; 18:8, 27; 19:4, 18; 20:21; 21:20, 25; 22:19; 24:24; 26:18; 28:24
Romans 1:16, 17; 3:22, 25, 26, 27, 28, 30; 4:3, 5, 9, 11, 13, 16, 17, 23, 24; 5:1, 2; 9:30, 32, 33; 10:4, 6, 8, 9, 10, 11, 14, 16–17; 11:20, 30–32; 13:11; 15:13
1 Corinthians 1:21; 3:5; 7:12–13; 15:2, 11; 6:15
2 Corinthians 4:4
Galatians 2:16, 20; 3:2, 5, 6, 7, 8, 9, 11, 14, 22, 24, 26; 5:5
Ephesians 1:13, 19; 2:8; 3:17
Philippians 1:29; 3:9

1 Thessalonians 1:7; 2:10; 4:14
2 Thessalonians 1:10; 2:12, 13; 3:2
1 Timothy 1:16; 3:16; 4:3, 10
2 Timothy 1:12; 3:15
Hebrews 11:6, 7, 31
James 2:23
1 Peter 1:21; 2:6, 7
1 John 5:1, 4, 5, 10, 13

Appendix B: 109 NT Occurrences of Σώζω ("save")

Meaning/Usage	References
Temporal deliverance from physical harm, sickness or danger (50 instances)	Matt 8:25; 9:21; 9:22(x2); 14:30; 16:25; 24:22; 27:40; 27:42(x2); 27:49; Mark 3:4; 5:23; 5:28; 5:34; 6:56; 8:35(1st instance); 10:52; 13:20; 15:30; 15:3(x2); Luke 6:9; 8:36; 8:48; 8:50; 9:24(1st instance); 17:19; 18:42; 23:35(x2); 23:37; 23:39; John 11:12; 12:27; Acts 4:9; 14:9; Acts 27:20; 27:31; 1 Tim 2:15; 4:16; Heb 5:7; Jas 1:21; 4:12; 5:15; 5:20; 1 Pet 3:21; 4:18; Jude 5; Jude 23
Spiritual deliverance (i.e., eternal salvation) (41 instances)	Matt 1:21; 18:11*; Mark 16:16*; Luke 7:50; 9:56*; 19:10; John 3:17; 5:34; 10:9; 12:47; Acts 2:47; 4:12; 11:14; 15:1; 15:11; 16:30; 16:31; Rom 5:9; 5:10; 8:24; 1 Cor 1:18; 1:21; 3:15; 5:5; 7:16(x2); 9:22; 10:33; 15:2; 2 Cor 2:15; Eph 2:5; 2:8; 1 Thess 2:16; 2 Thess 2:10; 1 Tim 1:15; 2:4; 2 Tim 1:9; 4:18; Titus 3:5; Heb 7:25;
Eschatological deliverance into the Messianic Kingdom (15 instances)	Matt 10:22; 19:25; 24:13; Mark 10:26; 13:13; Luke 8:12; 13:23; 18:26; Acts 2:21; 2:40; Rom 9:27; 10:9; 10:13; 11:14; 11:26;
Eschatological deliverance at the Bema Judgment (i.e., eternal rewards for temporal faithfulness) (3 instances)	Mark 8:35 (2d instance); Luke 9:24 (2d instance); Jas 2:14

* denotes instances in passages from disputed manuscripts

Appendix C: A Survey of the Biblical Usage of the Words

Repent and Repentance

1. Biblical Terms
   A. The noun *repentance* (μετάνοια) is used twenty-two times in the New Testament.
   B. The verb *repent* (μετανοέω) is used thirty-four times in the New Testament.

2. Etymological Meaning
   A. From μέτα, meaning *afterward* and νοέω, meaning *I think*
   B. The original idea was *to think afterward* or *to think again*.

3. Lexical Meaning
   A. The noun *repentance* has the following range of meanings:
      i. BDAG[1]
          o A change of mind
          o Remorse
          o Conversion
          o Turning about
          o Turning away
      ii. Louw & Nida[2]
          o A complete change of thought and attitude
          o "Though in English a focal component of repent is the sorrow or contrition that a person experiences because of sin, the emphasis in μετανοέω and μετάνοια seems to be more specifically the total change, both in thought and behavior, with respect to how one should both think and act. *Whether the focus is upon attitude or*

> *behavior varies somewhat in different contexts.*"
  iii. Vine's Change of mind or purpose[3]
  v. ALGNT: Change of opinion[4]

B. The verb *repent* has the following range of meanings:
  i. BDAG[5]
    o To change one's mind
    o To feel remorse
    o To be converted
    o To turn away from
  ii. Louw & Nida[6]
    o To change one's thought, attitude or way
  iii. Vine's: To change one's mind or purpose[7]
  iv. ALGNT: To change the way one thinks[8]

4. New Testament Usage
  A. Repent (34 times)
    o Matthew 3:2; 4:17; 11:20–21; 12:41 (5x total)
    o Mark 1:15; 6:12 (2x total)
    o Luke10:13; 11:32; 13:3, 5; 15:7, 10; 16:30; 17:3, 4 (9x total)
    o Acts 2:38; 3:19; 8:22; 17:30; 26:20 (5x total)
    o 2 Corinthians 12:21 (1x total)
    o Revelation 2:5 (2x), 16, 21 (2x), 22; 3:3, 19; 9:20, 21; 16:9, 11 (12x total)
  B. Repentance (22 times)
    o Matthew 3:8, 11 (2x total)
    o Mark 1:4 (1x total)
    o Luke 3:3, 8; 5:32; 15:7; 24:47 (5x total)
    o Acts 5:31; 11:18; 13:24; 19:4; 20:21; 26:20 (6x total)
    o Romans 2:4 (1x total)
    o 2 Corinthians 7:9, 10 (2x total)
    o 2 Timothy 2:25 (1x total)

o   Hebrews 6:1, 6; 12:17 (3x total)
o   2 Peter 3:9 (1x total)

5. Old Testament Usage (Septuagint)
   A. Repent (19x)
   "To reconsider;" "To change a plan not yet executed" (GELS)
   o   1 Samuel 15:29 (2x total)
   o   Proverbs 20:25; 24:32; 30:1 (3x total)
   o   Isaiah 46:8 (1x total)
   o   Jeremiah 4:28; 8:6; 18:8, 10; 31:19 (5x total)
   o   Joel 2:13, 14 (2x total)
   o   Amos 7:3, 6 (2x total)
   o   Jonah 3:9, 10; 4:2 (3x total)
   o   Zechariah 8:14 (1x total)
   B. Repentance (1x): Proverbs 14:15

6. Categories of New Testament Meaning
   A. Repent/repentance in the context of eternal salvation
      i. "change mind about Messiah/kingdom" (i.e., "believe the message about the Kingdom")
         o   Every reference in the Gospels *except* Luke 13:3, 5; 17:3–4; 24:47
         o   Acts 3:19; 5:31; 13:24; 19:4
      ii. "change mind about God/Christ/salvation"
         o   Luke 24:47
         o   Acts 11:18; 17:30; 20:21; 26:20 (2x)
         o   Romans 2:4
         o   Hebrews 6:1
   B. Repent/repentance in the context of sinful behavior
      i. "change your sinful behavior"
         o   Luke 13:3, 5
         o   Acts 8:22
         o   2 Corinthians 7:9, 10; 12:21
         o   2 Timothy 2:25
         o   Hebrews 6:6
         o   2 Peter 3:9

o   Every Revelation passage
ii. "change your sinful behavior so that it conforms to your new belief"
o   Acts 2:38
iii. "change your attitude about sinful behavior"
o   Luke 17:3, 4
C. Repentance in the sense of "a general change of mind" (Heb 12:17)

6. Common Misconceptions about Repentance
   A. General misconceptions
      i.   Repentance always relates to sinful behavior and thus always has the connotation of "stop sinning."
      ii. Repentance means the same thing in every context.
      iii. Repentance is always connected to sorrow, remorse, or tears.
   B. Misconceptions about repentance as it relates to eternal salvation
      i.   Repentance of sinful behavior is required in order to receive eternal life.
      ii. Repentance of sinful behavior is a necessary "first step" in order to believe the gospel and be saved.
      iii. Repentance is "the same thing as faith."
      iv. True repentance must always be evidenced by a change of behavior.
         – This is true of "repentance of sinful behavior," of course.
         – But it is not always true when repentance means a change of mind about God/Christ/Kingdom with reference to eternal salvation.

ENDNOTES
APPENDIX C

1. *BDAG*, 3d ed. (Chicago: University of Chicago Press, 2000), 640–41.

2. Johannes P. Louw and Eugene Albert Nida, *Greek English Lexicon of the New Testament: Based on Semantic Domains*, 2d edition. (New York: United Bible Societies, 1989), 1:509, emphasis added.

3. W.E. Vine and F.F. Bruce, *Vine's Expository Dictionary of Old and New Testament Words* (Old Tappan NJ: Revell, 1981), 2:280–1.

4. Timothy Friberg, Barbara Friberg and Neva F. Miller, *Analytical Lexicon of the Greek New Testament*, vol. 4, Baker's Greek New Testament library (Grand Rapids: Baker Books, 2000), 260.

5. *BDAG*, 640–41.

6. Louw and Nida, *Greek-English Lexicon of the New Testament*, 1:509.

7. Vine and Bruce, *Vine's Expository Dictionary,* 2:279-80.

8. Friberg, Friberg and Miller, *Analytical Lexicon of the Greek New Testament*, vol. 4, 260.

Appendix D: Biblical Motivations for the Believer to Do Good Works

The believer should do good works because...

1. It brings glory to God. (Matt 5:16; John 15:8; 1 Pet 2:12)
2. It demonstrates your love for God. (1 John 3:18; 4:19)
3. It is an expression of gratitude for your salvation. (Col 2:6-7)
4. It pleases the Father. (Rom 8:1-8; 1 Thess 4:1; 2 Tim 2:4)
5. It maintains fellowship and intimacy with Christ. (John 15:10; 1 John 3:24)
6. It allows you to look forward to the rapture with confidence. (1 John 2:28)
7. It encourages others to do good works. (Heb 10:24;
8. It can lead others to salvation. (1 Cor 10:32-33)
9. It strengthens your faith. (Jas 1:2-4; 2:22)
10. It brings spiritually maturity. (Heb 5:12-14; Jas 1:2-4)
11. It follows the example set by Jesus Christ. (John 10:32)
12. It is the reason you were created. (Eph 2:10)
13. It will bring God's blessings during your earthly life. (Deut 28:1-2; Prov 10:6; Matt 5:3-11; James 1:25)
14. It will prolong your life. (Prov 9:10-11; 10:27; 11:19; 12:28; 13:14; 19:16; 21:16)
15. It will deliver you from physical death. (James 1:21; 2:14)
16. It will bring rewards at the Judgment Seat of Christ. (1 Cor 3:10-15; 2 Cor 5:9-11; Rev 22:12; Col 3:23-24; 1 Tim 6:18-19)
17. It edifies others. (Rom 15:2)
18. It redeems the time. (Eph 5:15-16; Rom 13:11-14)
19. It helps defeat the enemy. (Eph 6:10-18)
20. It brings praise from those in authority over you. (Rom 13:1-5)
21. It silences the critics of Christianity. (Titus 2:6-8; 1 Pet 2:12)
22. It promotes peace. (Rom 12:17-18)
23. It vindicates the death of Christ. (Titus 2:11-15)

24. It is generally profitable in many ways. (Titus 3:8; 1 Tim 4:8)
25. It allows you to "pass the test" and be approved by God (i.e., rewarded). (Rom 12:2; Jas 1:12; 1 Pet 1:7; 2 Tim 2:15)
26. It proves the will of God in your life. (Col 4:12; Rom 12:1-2)
27. It helps prevent further stumbling. (Prov 4:12; 2 Pet 1:10)
28. It is consistent with your identity in Christ. (Eph 5:3-4)
29. It helps you overcome evil. (Rom 12:21)
30. It brings a personal sense of pride and accomplishment. (Gal 6:4)

A few popular, though unbiblical, motivations for the Christian to do good works:

Unbiblical Motivation #1: You must do good works in order to get into heaven when you die.

Unbiblical Motivation #2: You must do good works in order to keep from losing your salvation.

Unbiblical Motivation #3: You must do good works in order to prove that you are truly saved.

Unbiblical Motivation #4: You must do good works or God will not love you anymore.

GLOSSARY OF KEY TERMS

Absolutism. The belief that truth is absolute and not relative, dependent, or changeable.

Agnosticism. An intellectual perspective that holds to the uncertainty of all claims to ultimate knowledge.

Assensus. A Latin designation proposed by Reformed soteriology and referring to one of three supposed aspects of saving faith. Assensus refers to the intellectual acceptance of or assent to the truth of the gospel's content.

Assurance. The doctrine of assurance refers to the personal certainty that one has received the gift of eternal life.

Belief. A synonym for trust or faith, *belief* refers to the confidence or assurance in a stated or implied truth.

Constitutional Revisionism. An ideological mindset that seeks to interpret the United States Constitution based upon the prevailing attitudes of culture rather than the original intent of the framers.

Content of Saving Faith. The content of saving faith refers primarily to the propositional elements of the gospel which must be believed in order to secure eternal life. Often, *object of faith* (emphasizing the person of Jesus Christ) and *content of faith* (emphasizing the essential propositional truths about Him) are used interchangeably.

de facto. Latin for *in fact, in reality*.

Deconstructionism. The postmodern philosophical view of language that strips words of their meaning. Meaning in language no longer exists as an inherent end in itself but rather as the creation of the hearer or listener.

Dispensationalism. A theological perspective characterized primarily by a literal-grammatical-historical hermeneutic and an emphasis on the distinction between God's plan for national Israel and His plan for the church.

Easy-believism. A label sometimes directed at those who believe that salvation is based solely upon faith alone in Christ alone with no elements of surrender or commitment required.

Emergent Church. A movement within postmodern evangelicalism whose adherents seek to reach the unchurched by adopting many of the ideological and philosophical tenets of secular, postmodern thinking. The Emergent movement targets *Generation X* and its primary focus is on the relational *conversation* that seeks to connect with the unchurched on their level via an emphasis on dialogue rather than propositional beliefs.

Epistemology. The philosophical approach to why one believes what he believes.

Eternal Life—the present possession of all who have expressed saving faith. Eternal life has both a present and future reality. Presently, it involves the fullness or abundance of new life in Christ on earth. Ultimately, it involves spending eternity with God in the new heaven and new earth.

Etymology. The linguistic history or derivation of a word.

Evangelicalism. A broadly defined term that refers to those who, among other likely shared theological beliefs (such as belief in the

Trinity and inerrancy), believe that faith in Christ is the only means of obtaining eternal life.

Exclusivism. The view that only those who express explicit faith in Jesus Christ for salvation may be saved.

Existentialism. A philosophical outlook that emphasizes individual experience and freedom of choice as opposed to rationalism and empiricism.

Experientialism. A philosophical outlook that emphasizes personal experience as the basis for one's beliefs; similar to subjectivism.

ex post facto. Latin for *from or by subsequent action.*

Faith, Generic. A synonym for trust or belief, *generic faith* refers to the confidence or assurance in a stated or implied truth.

Faith, Non-saving. Generic faith in any object that is *not* the essence of the gospel.

Faith, Saving. Faith that results in eternal salvation. Saving faith occurs when one believes in Jesus Christ as the Son of God who died and rose again to pay one's personal penalty for sin and the one who gives eternal life to all who trust Him and Him alone for it.

Fiducia. A Latin designation proposed by Reformed soteriology and referring to one of three supposed aspects of saving faith. For some, *fiducia* involves the idea of volitional willingness to trust or follow Christ in obedience as a condition for eternal life.

Gnosticism. A false teaching that developed early in the history of the church (c. 100s AD) and taught that special, mystical knowledge was the basis of one's spirituality.

Gospel. A term used generally in Scripture to refer to any good news. With reference to salvation, it refers to the good news that one who believes in Jesus Christ alone as the Son of God who died and rose again to pay his personal penalty for sin may have eternal life.

Hermeneutics. The technique, rules and methodology of Bible study. The literal-grammatical-historical hermeneutic seeks to find the singular meaning of a given passage based on the plain, normal reading of the text in its historical and grammatical context.

Inclusivism. An evangelical expression of pluralism. Inclusivism holds that all who are saved are saved on account of the person and work of Jesus Christ but that explicit knowledge of and faith in Him in this present life are not required.

Inerrancy. The view that the Scriptures are entirely trustworthy and without error in the original manuscripts. Inerrancy is a central affirmation of conservative evangelicalism.

ipso facto. Latin for *by the fact itself.*

Messianic Kingdom. The future earthly reign of Jesus Christ over the earth in fulfillment of God's promises. The first one thousand years of the kingdom will be on the old earth (referred to as the millennium) and then the kingdom will continue for all eternity in the new heaven and new earth.

Metanarrative. The all-encompassing story or plotline of human history as contained in the Bible.

Notitia. A Latin designation proposed by Reformed soteriology and referring to one of three supposed aspects of saving faith. *Notitia* refers to the facts or data of the gospel.

Object of Saving Faith. Ultimately, Jesus Christ. The object of saving faith refers to the propositional and personal elements of the gospel which must be believed in order to secure eternal life. Often, *object of faith* (emphasizing the person of Jesus Christ) and *content of faith* (emphasizing the essential propositional truths about Him) are used interchangeably.

Ontological. Relating to the essence of being or existence.

Performance Gospel. A soteriological method that emphasizes man's good works as a either a prerequisite or postrequisite to saving faith.

Perseverance of the Saints. A classic Reformed soteriological doctrine that has been variously understood as referring to (1) the view that once one is saved he can never again be lost—a view commonly phrased, *once-saved-always-saved,* or (2) the notion that believers will persist in visible good works throughout their lives. According to this second understanding of perseverance of the saints, a failure to persist in good works proves that one's faith was spurious, since, according to this view, God's salvation necessarily brings with it the guarantee of both positional justification and practical sanctification.

Pluralism. The view that the major world religions each provide independent roads to salvation.

Pluralistic Gospel. A soteriological method in which salvation is deemed possible apart from explicit knowledge of Jesus Christ in this present life.

Postmodern. The adjective *postmodern* is employed to indicate a person or viewpoint characterized by the underlying ideologies of postmodernism.

Postmodernism. The term *postmodernism* refers to the philosophical mindset and general attitude pervasive throughout the present American culture. This worldview rejects any broad, grand, universally applicable truth claims and challenges the fundamental underpinnings of historic Christianity as expressed in the Bible.

Postmodernity. The term *postmodernity* refers to the present age— an age characterized by the philosophy of postmodernism.

Postrequisites for Salvation. Additional requirements posited by some evangelicals that must be performed *after* one's expression of saving faith in order to have eternal life.

Prerequisites for Salvation. Additional requirements posited by some evangelicals that must be performed *before* or at the same time as one's expression of saving faith in order to have eternal life.

Prosperity Gospel. A soteriological method that connects the gospel with the promise of earthly blessings such as wealth and good health.

Purpose Gospel. A soteriological method that expresses the gospel in terms of personal fulfillment and meaning in this present life with little or no emphasis on sin and its eternal consequences.

Puzzling Gospel. A soteriological method in which the gospel is expressed using terms that are imprecise, vague or inconsistent.

Relativism. A philosophical viewpoint in which criteria of judgment vary with individuals and their environments.

Reformed Soteriology. A view of salvation that emphasizes a tripartite notion of saving faith that includes *notitia, assensus* and *fiducia*. A distinguishing mark of reformed soteriology is the belief that one must surrender his life in full commitment to Christ as a part of saving faith. The name *Reformed* comes from the supposed connection of this view to the teachings of theologians during the Protestant Reformation, especially John Calvin.

Repentance. The word itself means *a change of mind*. In Reformed soteriology, it is defined as a willingness to stop sinning and surrender to the Lordship of Christ and usually is considered a required part of saving faith. Others suggest that repentance relates to salvation only to the extent that it refers to a complete change in one's thinking about God and Christ.

Semantics. Pertains to the meaning, or interpretation of the meaning, of a word or phrase. Often disagreements are said to be based upon semantic differences rather than substantive differences.

sine qua non. Latin for *an indispensable condition or element* (literally *without which [something] is not).*

Soteriological Method. Describes the means by which one obtains eternal life.

Soteriology. The study of salvation.

Spurious Faith. A phrase often used by proponents of Reformed soteriology to characterize as *non-saving,* the faith of professing believers whose behavior is unrighteous.

Subjectivism. The view that the basis for truth is one's personal experiences; similar to experientialism.

Trust. A synonym for faith or belief, *trust* refers to the confidence or assurance in a stated or implied truth.

Vis-à-vis. French for *in relation to* (literally *face to face).*

Viz. The abbreviation for the Latin word *videlicet,* meaning *namely* or *that is.*

Zeitgeist. A German word referring to the *spirit of the times* (i.e., the general mindset or feelings characteristic of a particular era).

BIBLIOGRAPHY

Monographs

Barna, George. *Evangelism That Works: How to Reach Changing Generations with the Unchanging Gospel.* Ventura, Cal.: Regal Books, 1995.

Barton, David. *Original Intent: The Courts, the Constitution & Religion.* Aledo, Tex.: WallBuilder Press, 1996.

Berkhof, Louis. *Systematic Theology.* 2d rev. and enl. ed. Grand Rapids: Wm. B. Eerdmans Publishing Co., 1941.

Boice, James Montgomery. *The Glory of God's Grace: The Meaning of God's Grace and How It Can Change Your Life.* Grand Rapids: Kregel Publications, 1999.

Bork, Robert H. *The Tempting of America: The Political Seduction of the Law.* New York: Collier Macmillan, 1990.

————. Slouching Towards *Gomorrah: Modern Liberalism and American Decline.* New York: Regan Books, 1996.

Bowman, Robert M. *The Word-Faith Controversy: Understanding the Health and Wealth Gospel.* Grand Rapids: Baker, 2001.

Brookes, James H. *How to Be Saved or the Sinner Directed to the Saviour*. Grand Rapids: Baker Book House, 1967.

_____. *The Way Made Plain*. Grand Rapids: Baker Book House, 1967.

Caldwell, Kirbyjon, Walther P. Kallestad, and Paul Sorensen. *Entrepreneurial Faith: Launching Bold Initiatives to Expand God's Kingdom*. Colorado Springs: WaterBrook Press, 2004.

_____, and Mark Seal. *The Gospel of Good Success: A Road Map to Spiritual, Emotional, and Financial Wholeness*. New York: Simon & Schuster, 1999.

Calvin, John. *Institutes of the Christian Religion*. Translated by John Allen. Vol. 1. 7th American ed. Philadelphia: Presbyterian board of Christian education, 1928.

Carson, D. A. *Exegetical Fallacies*. 2d ed. Grand Rapids: Baker Books, 1996.

_____. *The Gagging of God: Christianity Confronts Pluralism*. Grand Rapids: Zondervan, 1996.

Chafer, Lewis Sperry. *Salvation*. New York: C. C. Cook, 1917.

_____. *Systematic Theology*. Vol. 3 Soteriology. 8 vols. Dallas: Dallas Seminary Press, 1948.

Chantry, Walter J. *Today's Gospel: Authentic or Synthetic*. Carlisle, Pa.: Banner of Truth Trust, 1970.

Chay, Fred, and Correia, John. *The Faith that Saves: The Nature of Faith in the New Testament*. Scottsdale, Az.: Grace Line, Inc., 2008.

Clark, Gordon Haddon. *What Is Saving Faith?* Jefferson, Md.: Trinity Foundation, 2004.

Comfort, Ray. *Hell's Best Kept Secret.* New Kensington, Penn.: Whitaker House, 2004.

Cunningham, William, James Buchanan, and James Bannerman. *The Reformers and the Theology of the Reformation.* London: The Banner of Truth Trust, 1967.

Day, R. Alan. *Lordship: What Does It Mean?* Nashville: Broadman, 1993.

Demarest, Bruce A. *General Revelation.* Grand Rapids: Zondervan, 1982.

Derickson, Gary, and Earl Radmacher. *The Disciplemaker.* Salem, Ore.: Charis Press, 2001.

Dever, Mark, and Paul Alexander. *The Deliberate Church: Building Your Ministry on the Gospel.* Wheaton: Crossway Books, 2005.

Dillow, Joseph C. *The Reign of the Servant Kings.* Hayesville, N.C.: Schoettle Publishing Co., 1992.

Dockery, David S., ed. *The Challenge of Postmodernism: An Evangelical Engagement.* Wheaton: Victor Books, 1995.

Enns, Paul. *The Moody Handbook of Theology.* Chicago: Moody Press, 1989.

Fee, Gordon. *The Disease of the Health and Wealth Gospels.* 3d paperback ed. Beverly, Mass.: Frontline Publishing, 1985.

_____, and Douglas K. Stuart. *How to Read the Bible for All It's Worth: A Guide to Understanding the Bible*. 2d ed. Grand Rapids: Zondervan, 1993.

Gentry, Jr., Kenneth L. *Lord of the Saved: Getting to the Heart of the Lordship Debate*. Phillipsburg, N.J.: P & R, 1992.

Guinness, Os. *God in the Dark: The Assurance of Faith Beyond a Shadow of Doubt*. Wheaton: Crossway Books, 1996.

Hanegraaff, Hank. *Christianity in Crisis*. Eugene, Ore.: Harvest House, 1993.

Henrichsen, Walter A., and Gayle Jackson. *Studying, Interpreting, and Applying the Bible*. Grand Rapids: Lamplighter Books, 1990.

Hodges, Zane C. *Dead Faith: What Is It?* Dallas: Redencion Viva, 1987.

_____. *Absolutely Free! A Biblical Reply to Lordship Salvation*. Grand Rapids: Academie Books/Zondervan Pub. House, 1989.

_____. *Harmony with God: A Fresh Look at Repentance*. Dallas: Redencion Viva, 2001.

Ironside, Harry A. *Except Ye Repent*. New York: American Tract Society, 1937.

_____. *God's Unspeakable Gift*. London: Pickering & Inglis, 1908.

Jakes, T. D. *Why? Because You Are Anointed*. Lanham, Md.: Pneuma Life Publishing, 1994.

————. *Loose That Man and Let Him Go.* Tulsa, Okla.: Albury, 1995.

————. *The Harvest.* Bakersfield, Calif.: Pneuma Life Publishing, 1996.

————. *Maximize the Moment.* 2d paperback ed. New York: Berkley Publishing Group, 2001.

Johnson, Elliott E. *Expository Hermeneutics: An Introduction.* Grand Rapids: Academie Books, 1990.

Kendall, R. T. *Calvin and English Calvinism to 1649.* New York: Oxford University Press, 1979.

Kennedy, D. James. *Evangelism Explosion.* Wheaton: Tyndale House Publishers, 1970.

Lightner, Robert Paul. *Sin, the Savior, and Salvation: The Theology of Everlasting Life.* Nashville: T. Nelson Publishers, 1991.

————. *Safe in the Arms of Jesus: God's Provision for the Death of Those Who Cannot Believe.* Grand Rapids: Kregel, 2000.

MacArthur, John. *The Gospel According to Jesus: What Does Jesus Mean When He Says "Follow Me"?* 1st paperback ed. Grand Rapids: Academic Books Zondervan Pub. House, 1989.

————. *Keys to Spiritual Growth.* Rev. and expanded ed. Tarrytown, N.Y.: F.H. Revell, 1991.

————. *Faith Works: The Gospel According to the Apostles.* Dallas: Word Pub., 1993.

————. *The Gospel According to Jesus: What Does Jesus Mean When He Says "Follow Me"?* Rev. and exp. ed. Grand Rapids: Zondervan, 1994.

_____. *Hard to Believe: The High Cost and Infinite Value of Following Christ.* Nashville: Thomas Nelson, 2003.

McConnell, D. R. *A Different Gospel.* Updated ed. Peabody, Mass.: Hendrickson Publishers, 1995.

McLaren, Brian D. *A Generous Orthodoxy: Why I Am a Missional, Evangelical, Post/Protestant, Liberal/conservative, Mystical/poetic, Biblical, Charismatic/contemplative, Fundamentalist/Calvinist, Anabaptist/Anglican, Methodist, Catholic, Green, Incarnational, Depressed-Yet-Hopeful, Emergent, Unfinished Christian.* Grand Rapids: Zondervan, 2004.

Murray, John. *Collected Writings of John Murray.* Vol. 2. Carlisle, Pa.: Banner of Truth Trust, 1978.

Nash, Ronald. *Is Jesus the Only Savior?* Grand Rapids: Zondervan, 1994.

Netland, Harold. *Dissonant Voices.* Grand Rapids: Eerdmans, 1991.

Newbigin, Lesslie. *The Gospel in a Pluralist Society.* Grand Rapids: Eerdmans, 1989.

Osteen, Joel. *Your Best Life Now: 7 Steps to Living at Your Full Potential.* New York: Warner Books, 2004.

Packer, J. I. *Concise Theology: A Guide to Historic Christian Beliefs.* Wheaton: Tyndale House, 1993.

Packer, J. I., and Thomas C. Oden. *One Faith: The Evangelical Consensus.* Downer's Grove: InterVarsity Press, 2004.

Pentecost, J. Dwight. *Design for Discipleship.* Grand Rapids: Zondervan Publishing House, 1971.

Phillips, W. Gary, and William E. Brown. *Making Sense of Your World*. Chicago: Moody, 1991.

Pierson, Arthur T. *The Heart of the Gospel: Sermons on the Life-Changing Power of the Good News*. Grand Rapids: Kregel Publications, 1996.

Pinnock, Clark H. *Grace Unlimited*. Minneapolis: Bethany Fellowship, Inc., 1975.

_____. *Most Moved Mover: A Theology of God's Openness*. Grand Rapids: Baker Academic, 2001.

_____, and Robert Brow. *Unbounded Love: A Good News Theology for the 21st Century*. Downer's Grove: InterVarsity Press, 1994.

_____. *Tracking the Maze: Finding Our Way through Modern Theology from an Evangelical Perspective*. San Fransisco: Harper & Row, 1990.

_____. *A Wideness in God's Mercy: The Finality of Jesus Christ in a World of Religions*. Grand Rapids: Zondervan, 1992.

Piper, John. *What Jesus Demands from the World*. Wheaton: Crossway Books, 2006.

Portmann, John. *In Defense of Sin*. New York: Palgrave Macmillan, 2003.

Radmacher, Earl D. *Salvation*. Nashville: Word, 2000.

Richard, Ramesh P. *The Population of Heaven*. Chicago: Moody Press, 1994.

Rokser, Dennis. *Seven Reasons Not to Ask Jesus into Your Heart*. Duluth, Minn.: Duluth Bible Church, 1998.

Ryrie, Charles Caldwell. *So Great Salvation: What It Means to Believe in Jesus Christ.* Wheaton: Victor Books, 1989.

_____. *Dispensationalism.* Rev. and expanded. ed. Chicago: Moody Press, 1995.

_____. *Basic Theology: A Popular Systemic Guide to Understanding Biblical Truth.* Chicago: Moody Press, 1999.

Sanders, John. *No Other Name: An Investigation into the Destiny of the Unevangelized.* Grand Rapids: Eerdmans, 1992.

Sproul, R. C. *Before the Face of God Book One: A Daily Guide for Living from the Book of Romans.* Grand Rapids: Baker Book House, 1992.

_____. *Before the Face of God Book Four: A Daily Guide for Living from Ephesians, Hebrews, and James.* Grand Rapids: Baker Book House, 1994.

_____. *Before the Face of God Book Three: A Daily Guide for Living from the Old Testament.* Grand Rapids: Baker Book House, 1994.

_____. *Chosen by God.* Paperback ed. Wheaton: Tyndale House Publishers, 1994.

_____. *Essential Truths of the Christian Faith.* Paperback ed. Wheaton: Tyndale House, 1998.

_____. *Faith Alone: The Evangelical Doctrine of Justification.* Grand Rapids: Baker Books, 1995.

_____. *Getting the Gospel Right: The Tie That Binds Evangelicals Together.* Grand Rapids: Baker Books, 1999.

_____. *Grace Unknown: The Heart of Reformed Theology.* Grand Rapids: Baker, 1997.

Stackhouse, John Gordon. *Evangelical Futures: A Conversation on Theological Method.* Grand Rapids: Baker Books, 2000.

_____. *No Other Gods before Me? Evangelicals and the Challenge of World Religions.* Grand Rapids: Baker Academic, 2001.

Stanley, Charles. *Eternal Security: Can You Be Sure?* Nashville: Oliver Nelson, 1990.

Stott, John R. W. *Basic Christianity.* London: Intervarsity Press, 1971.

Sweet, Leonard. *The Gospel According to Starbucks.* Colorado Springs: WaterBrook Press, 2007.

Swindoll, Charles R. *The Grace Awakening.* Dallas: Word Pub., 1990.

Turner, Bryan. *Orientalism, Postmodernism, and Globalism.* London: Routledge, 1994.

Vanhoozer, Kevin J. *Is There a Meaning in This Text? The Bible, the Reader, and the Morality of Literary Knowledge.* Grand Rapids: Zondervan, 1998.

Warren, Rick. *The Purpose Driven Life.* Grand Rapids: Zondervan, 2002.

Wells, David F. *No Place for Truth, or, Whatever Happened to Evangelical Theology?* Grand Rapids: W.B. Eerdmans, 1993.

_____. *God in the Wastelands: The Reality of Truth in a World of Fading Dreams.* Grand Rapids: Eerdmans, 1994.

Wilkin, Robert N. *Confident in Christ: Living by Faith Really Works.* Irving, Tex.: Grace Evangelical Society, 1999.

Willmington, H. L. *Book of Bible Lists.* Wheaton: Tyndale House, 1987.

Articles and Essays

Adams, Jay E. "Perseverance of the Saints." In *Distinctives of Reformed Theology: After Darkness, Light: Essays in Honor of R. C. Sproul*, ed. R. C. Sproul Jr., 173–88. Phillipsburg, N.J.: P & R Publishing Company, 2003.

Anderson, David R. "The Nature of Faith." *Chafer Theological Seminary Journal* 5, no. 4 (September 1999): 2–26.

_____. "Repentance Is for All Men." *Journal of the Grace Evangelical Society* 11, no. 1 (Spring 1998): 3–20.

Andrus, Michael P. "Turning to God: Conversion Beyond Mere Religious Preference." In *Telling the Truth: Evangelizing Postmoderns*, ed. D. A. Carson, 153–162. Grand Rapids: Zondervan, 2000.

Biema, David Van, and Jeff Chu. "Does God Want You to Be Rich?" *TIME*, September 18, 2006, 48-56.

Bigalke, Jr., Ron J. "The Latest Post-Modern Trend: The Emerging Church." *Journal of Dispensational Theology* 10, no. 31 (2006): 19–39.

Bing, Charles C. "The Cost of Discipleship." *Journal of the Grace Evangelical Society* 6, no. 1 (Spring 1993): 33–52.

_____. "The Condition for Salvation in John's Gospel." *Journal of the Grace Evangelical Society* 9, no. 1 (Spring 1996): 25–36.

_____. "Why Lordship Faith Misses the Mark for Salvation." *Journal of the Grace Evangelical Society* 12, no. 1 (Spring 1999): 21–35.

_____. "How to Share the Gospel Clearly." *Journal of the Grace Evangelical Society* 7, no. 1 (Spring 1994): 51–65.

Blauvelt, Jr., Livingston. "Does the Bible Teach Lordship Salvation?" *BSac* 143, no. 569 (January 1986): 37–45.

Bock, Darrell L. "A Review of *The Gospel According to Jesus.*" *BSac* 146, no. 581 (Jan 1989): 21–40.

_____. "Athenians Who Have Never Heard." In *Through No Fault of Their Own*, ed. William V. Crockett and James G. Sigountos, 117–24. Grand Rapids: Baker, 1991.

Butcher, J. Kevin. "A Critique of *The Gospel According to Jesus.*" *Journal of the Grace Evangelical Society* 2, no. 1 (Spring 1989): 27–43.

Brookes, James H. "A Voice from the Past: Self-Examination as It Relates to Assurance." *Journal of the Grace Evangelical Society* 6, no. 2 (Autumn 1993): 53–55.

Carson, D. A. "Reflections on Christian Assurance." *WTJ* 54, no. 1 (Spring 1992): 1–29.

Congdon, Philip F. "Evangelical/Roman Catholic Agreement on the Doctrine of Justification and Its Ramifications for Grace Theologians." *Journal of the Grace Evangelical Society* 13, no. 1 (Spring 2000): 11–23.

Darby, J. N. "Operations of the Spirit of God," in *The Collected Writings of J. N. Darby*, edited by William Kelly. Reprint, 1972 (Winschoten, Netherlands: H. L. Heijkoop), 3:76.

Dart, John. "College to Close out 'Open Theism' Scholar." *Christian Century*, December 28, 2004.

Davy, Keith A. "The Gospel for a New Generation." In *Telling the Truth: Evangelizing Postmoderns*, ed. D. A. Carson, 352–68. Grand Rapids: Zondervan, 2000.

Derickson, Gary. "Viticulture and John 15:1–6." *Journal of the Grace Evangelical Society* 18, no. 1 (Spring 2005): 23–43.

Derrida, Jacques. "Signature Event Context." *Glyph* 1 (1977): 172–198.

Dever, Mark E. "Communicating Sin in a Postmodern World." In *Telling the Truth: Evangelizing Postmoderns*, ed. D. A. Carson, 138–52. Grand Rapids: Zondervan, 2000.

Dillow, Joseph C. "Abiding Is Remaining in Fellowship: Another Look at John 15:1–6." *BSac* 147, no. 585 (Jan 1990): 44–53.

Dockery, David S. "Millard J. Erickson: Baptist and Evangelical Theologian." *JETS* 32, no. 4 (December 1989): 519–532.

Dykman, Jackson, Kathleen Adams, Jeremy Caplan, Kristina Dell, and Coco Masters. "America by the Numbers." *TIME*, October, 30 2006, 41–54.

Farstad, Art. "The Words of the Gospel: Believe/Faith." *Grace In Focus*, June 1991.

Fernando, Ajith. "The Urgency of the Gospel." In *Telling the Truth: Evangelizing Postmoderns*, ed. D. A. Carson, 371–83. Grand Rapids: Zondervan, 2000.

Grossman, Cathy Lynn. "This Evangelist Has a 'Purpose'." *USA Today*, 21 July, 2003.

Guiness, Os. "I Believe in Doubt: Using Doubt to Strengthen Faith." In *Doubt and Assurance*, ed. R. C. Sproul, 31–35. Grand Rapids: Baker Book House for Ligonier Ministries, 1993.

Hart, John F. "The Faith of Demons." *Journal of the Grace Evangelical Society* 8, no. 2 (Autumn 1995): 39–54.

_____. "How to Energize Our Faith: Reconsidering the Meaning of James 2:14–26." *Journal of the Grace Evangelical Society* 12, no. 1 (Spring 1999): 37–66.

Henry, Carl F. H. "Postmodernism: The New Spectre?" In *The Challenge of Postmodernism: An Evangelical Engagement*, ed. David S. Dockery. Wheaton: Victor Books, 1995.

Hinkson, Jon, and Greg Ganssle. "Epistemology at the Core of Postmodernism: Rorty, Foucault, and the Gospel." In *Telling the Truth: Evangelizing Postmoderns*, ed. D. A. Carson, 68–89. Grand Rapids: Zondervan, 2000.

Hixson, J.B. "Dan's Dilemma." *Grace In Focus*, Jan-Feb 2002.

_____. "Review of *the Purpose Driven Life* by Rick Warren." *Journal of Ministry and Theology* 8, no. 1 (Spring 2004): 134–39.

Hodges, Zane C. "Problem Passages in the Gospel of John Part 2: Untrustworthy Believers-John 2:23–25." *BSac* 135, no. 538 (April 1978): 135–52.

_____. "We Believe In: Assurance of Salvation." *Journal of the Grace Evangelical Society* 3, no. 2 (Autumn 1990): 3–17.

_____. "Calvinism Ex Cathedra: A Review of John H. Gerstner's Wrongly Dividing the Word of Truth." *Journal of the Grace Evangelical Society* 4, no. 2 (Autumn 1991): 59–70.

_____. "Light on James Two from Textual Criticism." *BSac* 120, no. 480 (October 1963): 341–50.

_____. "Post-Evangelicalism Confronts the Postmodern Age." *Journal of the Grace Evangelical Society* 9, no. 1 (Spring 1996): 3–14.

_____. "Assurance: Of the Essence of Saving Faith." *Journal of the Grace Evangelical Society* 10, no. 1 (Spring 1997): 3–17.

_____. "How to Lead People to Christ Part 1: The Content of Our Message." *Journal of the Grace Evangelical Society* 13, no. 2 (Autumn 2000): 3–12.

_____. "How to Lead People to Christ Part 2: Our Invitation to Respond." *Journal of the Grace Evangelical Society* 14, no. 1 (Spring 2001): 9–18.

Holloway, Paul. "A Return to Rome: Lordship Salvation's Doctrine of Faith." *Journal of the Grace Evangelical Society* 4, no. 2 (Autumn 1991): 13–21.

Jensen, Robert. "Getting Religion: Why This Atheist Is a Christian (Sort of)." *Houston Chronicle*, 11 March, 2006.

Johnson, Jr., S. Lewis. "How Faith Works." *Christianity Today*, September 22, 1989, 21–25.

Keathley, Ken. "Does Anyone Really Know If They Are Saved? A Survey of the Current Views on Assurance with a Modest Proposal." *Journal of the Grace Evangelical Society* 15, no. 1 (Spring 2002): 37–60.

Kent, Homer A. "Review Article: *The Gospel According to Jesus.*" *Grace Theological Journal* 10, no. 1 (Spring 1989): 67–77.

Kilpatrick, Ron. "Assurance and Sin." In *Doubt and Assurance*, ed. R. C. Sproul. Grand Rapids: Baker Book House for Ligonier Ministries, 1993.

Llewellen, Thomas G. "Has Lordship Salvation Been Taught Throughout Church History?" *BSac* 147, no. 55 (1990): 54–68.

Longfellow, Henry Wadsworth. "A Psalm of Life." In *One Hundred and One Famous Poems*, ed. Roy J. Cook. Chicago: The Reilly & Lee Co., 1958.

MacArthur, John F. "Faith According to the Apostle James." *JETS* 33, no. 1 (March 1990): 13–34.

McGrath, Alister E. "The Christian Church's Response to Pluralism." *JETS* 35, no. 4 (December 1992): 487–501.

_____. "The Challenge of Pluralism for the Contemporary Christian Church." *JETS* 35, no. 3 (September 1992): 361–73.

McQuilkin, Robertson, and Bradford Mullen. "The Impact of Postmodern Thinking on Evangelical Hermeneutics." *JETS* 40, no. 1 (March 1997): 69–82.

Meacham, Jon. "Pilgrim's Progress." *Newsweek*, August 14, 2006.

Mitchell, C. Ben. "Is That All There Is? Moral Ambiguity in a Postmodern Pluralistic Culture." In *The Challenge of Postmodernism: An Evangelical Engagement*, ed. David S. Dockery, 267–80. Wheaton: Victor Books, 1995.

Mohler, Jr., R. Albert. "Church Discipline: The Missing Mark." In *The Compromised Church: The Present Evangelical Crisis*, ed. John H. Armstrong, 171–88. Wheaton: Crossway Books, 1998.

Myers, Jeremy D. "The Gospel Is More Than 'Faith Alone in Christ Alone'." *Journal of the Grace Evangelical Society* 20, no. 2 (Autumn 2006): 33–56.

Niemela, John. "The Message of Life in the Gospel of John." *Chafer Theological Seminary Journal* 7, no. 3 (July 2001): 2–20.

Okholm, Dennis L. and Phillips, Timothy R. "Introduction." In *Four Views on Salvation in a Pluralistic World*, ed. Dennis L. Okholm and Timothy R. Phillips, 7–26. Grand Rapids: Zondervan, 1995.

Phillips, W. Gary. "Evangelical Pluralism: A Singular Problem." *BSac* 151, no. 602 (April 1994): 140–54.

Pinnock, Clark. "The Finality of Jesus Christ in a World of Religions." In *Christian Faith and Practice in the Modern World*, ed. Mark Noll and David Wells, 152–68. Grand Rapids: Baker, 1988.

_____. "Acts 4:12-No Other Name under Heaven." In *Through No Fault of Their Own*, ed. William V. Crockett and James G. Sigountos, 107–15. Grand Rapids: Baker, 1991.

_____. "Toward and Evangelical Theology of Religions." *JETS* 33, no. 3 (September 1990): 359–68.

_____. "An Inclusivist View." In *Four Views on Salvation in a Pluralistic World*, ed. Timothy R. Phillips Dennis L. Okholm, 95–148. Grand Rapids: Zondervan, 1995.

Proctor, Mark. "Faith, Works, and the Christian Religion." *The Evangelical Quarterly* 69, no. 4 (1997): 307–32.

Pyne, Robert A. "Review of *Faith Works: The Gospel According to the Apostles*." *BSac* 150, no. 600 (October 1993): 497–99.

Radmacher, Earl D. "First Response to 'Faith According to the Apostle James' by John F. Macarthur, Jr." *JETS* 33, no. 1 (March 1990): 35–41.

Reid, W. Stanford. "Justification by Faith According to John Calvin." *WTJ* 42, no. 2 (Spring 1980): 290–307.

Richard, Ramesh. "Soteriological Inclusivism and Dispensationalism." *BSac* 151, no. 601 (January 1994): 85–108.

Rodgers, Ann. "Pastor Urges Anglicans to Unite and Care for Poor." *Pittsburgh Post-Gazette*, 12 November, 2005.

Sanders, John. "Evangelical Responses to Salvation Outside the Church." *Christian Scholar's Review* 24, no. 1 (1994): 51–55.

_____. "Inclusivism." In *What About Those Who Have Never Heard? Three Views on the Destiny of the Unevangelized*, ed. John Sanders, 21–70. Downer's Grove: InterVarsity Press, 1995.

_____. "Introduction." In *What About Those Who Have Never Heard? Three Views on the Destiny of the Unevangelized*, ed. John Sanders, 7–20. Downer's Grove: InterVarsity Press, 1995.

_____. "Is Belief in Christ Necessary for Salvation?" *Evangelical Quarterly* 60 (1988): 241–59.

Sapaugh, Gregory P. "A Response to Hodges: How to Lead People to Christ, Parts 1 and 2." *Journal of the Grace Evangelical Society* 14, no. 2 (August 2001): 21–29.

Sarles, Ken L. "A Theological Evaluation of the Prosperity Gospel." *BSac* 143, no. 572 (October 1986): 329–52.

Shockley, Paul R. "Postmodernism as a Basis for Society?" In *The God of the Bible and Other Gods: Is the Christian God Unique among World Religions?* Robert Paul Lightner, 197–209. Grand Rapids: Kregel Publications, 1998.

_____. "The Postmodern Theory of Probability on Evangelical Hermeneutics." *Conservative Theological Society Journal* 4, no. 11 (April 2000): 65–82.

Smith, Colin S. "The Ambassador's Job Description." In *Telling the Truth: Evangelizing Postmoderns*, ed. D. A. Carson, 175–91. Grand Rapids: Zondervan, 2000.

Sproul, R. C. "The Anatomy of Doubt." In *Doubt and Assurance*, ed. R. C. Sproul, 15–19. Grand Rapids: Baker Book House for Ligonier Ministries, 1993.

Stackhouse, John Gordon. "Preface." In *What Does It Mean to Be Saved? Broadening Evangelical Horizons of Salvation*, ed. John Gordon Stackhouse, 9–11. Grand Rapids: Baker Academic, 2002.

Stallard, Mike. "Justification by Faith or Justification by Faith Alone?" *Conservative Theological Society Journal* 3, no. 8 (April 1999): 53–73.

_____. "The Tendency to Softness in Postmodern Attitudes About God, War, and Man." *Journal of Ministry and Theology* 10, no. 1 (Spring 2006).

Stegall, Tom. "The Tragedy of the Crossless Gospel: Parts 1–5." *The Grace Family Journal* 2007.

Thorson, Stephen. "Tensions in Calvin's View of Faith: Unexamined Assumptions in R.T. Kendall's *Calvin and English Calvinism to 1649*." *JETS* 37, no. 3 (September 1994): 413–26.

Veith, Gene Edward. "A Postmodern Scandal." *World Magazine*, February 21, 1998, 24.

Warfield, Benjamin B. "Faith." In *Biblical and Theological Studies*, ed. Samuel Craig, 404–44. Philadelphia: Presbyterian and Reformed Publishing, 1952.

Webster, John. "What's Evangelical About Evangelical Soteriology?" In *What Does It Mean to Be Saved? Broadening Evangelical Horizons of Salvation*, ed. John Gordon Stackhouse, 179–84. Grand Rapids: Baker Academic, 2002.

Wells, David F. "Introduction: The Word in the World." In *The Compromised Church: The Present Evangelical Crisis*, ed. John H. Armstrong, 19–34. Wheaton: Crossway Books, 1998.

Wilkin, Robert N. "Head Faith, Heart Faith, and Mind Games." *Grace In Focus*, May-June 2001.

_____. "The So-Called So-Called Brother—1 Corinthians 5:11." *The Grace Evangelical Society News*, October 1991.

_____. "The High Cost of Salvation by Faith-Works: A Critique of John F. MacArthur, Jr.'s 'Faith Works: The Gospel According to the Apostles'." *Journal of the Grace Evangelical Society* 6, no. 2 (Autumn 1993): 3–24.

_____. "When Assurance Is Not Assurance." *Journal of the Grace Evangelical Society* 10, no. 2 (Autumn 1997): 27–34.

_____. "Another View of Faith and Works in James 2." *Journal of the Grace Evangelical Society* 15, no. 2 (Autumn 2002): 3–21.

_____. "A Review of John MacArthur's *Hard to Believe: The High Cost and Infinite Value of Following Jesus*." *Journal of the Grace Evangelical Society* 17, no. 33 (Autumn 2004): 3–9.

_____. "The Subtle Danger of an Imprecise Gospel." *Journal of the Grace Evangelical Society* 10, no. 1 (Spring 1997): 41–60.

_____. "How Deep Are Your Spiritual Roots? Luke 8:11–15." *Journal of the Grace Evangelical Society* 12, no. 1 (Spring 1999): 3–19.

_____. "Beware of Confusion About Faith." *Journal of the Grace Evangelical Society* 18, no. 1 (Spring 2005): 3–14.

_____. "Does Your Mind Need Changing? Repentance Reconsidered." *Journal of the Grace Evangelical Society* 11, no. 1 (Spring 1998): 35–46.

Young, William. "Historic Calvinism and Neo-Calvinism (Part One)." *WTJ* 36, no. 1 (Fall 1973): 48–64.

_____. "Historic Calvinism and Neo-Calvinism (Part Two)." *WTJ* 36, no. 2 (Winter 1974): 156–73.

Zacharias, Ravi. "An Ancient Message, through Modern Means, to a Postmodern Mind." In *Telling the Truth: Evangelizing Postmoderns*, ed. D. A. Carson, 19–29. Grand Rapids: Zondervan, 2000.

_____. "The Touch of Truth." In *Telling the Truth: Evangelizing Postmoderns*, ed. D. A. Carson, 30–43. Grand Rapids: Zondervan, 2000.

Commentaries

Barrett, C. K. *The First Epistle to the Corinthians*. Peabody, Mass.: Hendrickson Publishers, 1993.

Beasley-Murray, George R. *John*. Word Biblical Commentary. Vol. 36. Dallas: Word, 1998.

Blomberg, Craig. *Matthew*. The New American Commentary, Vol. 22. Nashville: Broadman and Holman, 1992.

Blum, Edwin A. "John." In *The Bible Knowledge Commentary*. Vol. 2, ed. John F. Walvoord and Roy B. Zuck, 267–348. Wheaton: Victor Books, 1983.

Borchert, Gerald L. *John 1–11*. The New American Commentary. Vol. 25a. Nashville: Broadman & Holman, 1996.

Brunner, Frederick Dale. *Matthew: Volume 1 The Christbook*. Dallas: Word, 1987.

Carson, D. A. "Matthew." In *The Expositor's Bible Commentary*. Vol. 8, ed. Frank E. Gaebelein and J. D. Douglas. Grand Rapids: Zondervan, 1984.

Constable, Thomas L. *Expository Notes on First Corinthians*. Garland, Tex.: Sonic Light, 2005.

_____. *Expository Notes on John*. Garland, Tex.: Sonic Light, 2005.

_____. *Expository Notes on Luke*. Garland, Tex.: Sonic Light, 2005.

_____. *Expository Notes on James*. Garland, Tex.: Sonic Light, 2006.

Fung, Ronald Y. K. *The Epistle to the Galatians*. International Commentary on the New Testament. Grand Rapids: Wm. B. Ecrdmans Publishing Co., 1988.

Harrison, Everett F. *John the Gospel of Faith.* Everyman's Bible Commentary. Chicago: Moody Press, 1962.

Hendriksen, William. *A Commentary on the Gospel of John.* 3d ed. London: Banner of Truth Trust, 1964.

Hodge, Charles. *Commentary on the Epistle to the Romans.* Grand Rapids: Eerdmans, 1967.

Hodges, Zane C. *The Epistle of James: Proven Character through Testing: A Verse by Verse Commentary.* Irving, Tex.: Grace Evangelical Society, 1994.

_____. *The Epistles of John: Walking in the Light of God's Love.* Irving, Tex.: Grace Evangelical Society, 1999.

Larkin, William J. *Acts.* The IVP New Testament Commentary Series, Vol. 5, ed. Grant Osborne. Downer's Grove: InterVarsity Press, 1995.

Longenecker, Richard N. "The Acts of the Apostles." In *The Expositor's Bible Commentary,* vol. 9, ed. Frank E. Gaebelein and J. D. Douglas. Grand Rapids: Zondervan Pub. House, 1981.

MacArthur, John F. *Mathew.* MacArthur New Testament Commentary. Chicago: Moody, 1989.

MacDonald, William, and Arthur L. Farstad. *Believer's Bible Commentary: A Complete Bible Commentary in One Volume.* Nashville: Thomas Nelson Publishers, 1995.

Martin, John A. "Luke." In *Bible Knowledge Commentary.* Vol. 2, ed. John F. Walvoord and Roy B. Zuck, 197–265. Wheaton: Victor Books, 1983.

Morris, Leon. *The Gospel According to John: The English Text with Introduction, Exposition and Notes.* Grand Rapids: Eerdmans, 1971.

Showers, Renald E. *The Most High God: A Commentary on the Book of Daniel.* Bellmawr, N.J.: The Friends of Israel Gospel Ministry, Inc., 1982.

Stein, Robert H. *Luke.* The New American Commentary, Vol. 24. Nashville: Broadman & Holman, 1992.

Tenney, Merrill C. "The Gospel of John." In *The Expositor's Bible Commentary*, vol. 9, ed. Frank E. Gaebelein. Grand Rapids: Zondervan, 1981.

Toussaint, Stanley D. "Acts." In *Bible Knowledge Commentary*, vol. 2, ed. John F. Walvoord and Roy B. Zuck, 349–432. Wheaton: Victor Books, 1983.

Towns, Elmer. *The Gospel of John: Believe and Live.* Twenty-First Century Biblical Commentary Series, ed. Mal Couch and Ed Hindson. Chattanooga, Tenn.: AMG Publishers, 2002.

Walvoord, John F. *Daniel: The Key to Prophetic Revelation.* Chicago: The Moody Bible Institute, 1971.

Whitacre, Rodney A. *John.* The IVP New Testament Commentary Series, vol. 4, ed. Grant Osborne. Downer's Grove: InterVarsity Press, 1999.

Reference Works

Bultmann, Rudolf. "Πιστεύω, etc." in *TDNT*, ed. Gerhard Kittel, Gerhard Friedrich, and Geoffrey William Bromiley. (Grand Rapids: Eerdmans, 1985), 6:173–228.

Danker, Frederick W., Walter Bauer, and William Arndt. *BDAG*. 3d ed. Chicago: University of Chicago Press, 2000.

Friberg, Timothy, Barbara Friberg and Neva F. Miller. *Analytical Lexicon of the Greek New Testament*. Vol. 4. Grand Rapids: Baker Books, 2000.

Louw, J. P. and Eugene Albert Nida. Greek-English Lexicon of the New Testament; Based on Semantic Domains. 2d ed. New York: United Bible Societies, 1989.

Strong, James, and John R. Kohlenberger. *The New Strong's Complete Dictionary of Bible Words*. Nashville: Thomas Nelson Publishers, 1996.

Vine, W. E., F. F. Bruce and W. E. Vine. *Vine's Expository Dictionary of Old and New Testament Words*. Old Tappan, N.J.: F.H. Revell Co., 1981.

Vine, W. E., Merrill Frederick Unger, and William White. *Vine's Complete Expository Dictionary of Old and New Testament Words with Topical Index*. Nashville: T. Nelson, 1996.

Wallace, Daniel B. *The Basics of New Testament Syntax: An Intermediate Greek Grammar*. Grand Rapids: Zondervan Pub. House, 2000.

Electronic Sources

Billy Graham Evangelistic Association. http://www.billygraham. org. Accessed 1 March 2007.

Campus Crusade for Christ. http://www.ccci.org. Accessed 18 January 2007.

Child Evangelism Fellowship. http://www.cefonline.com. Accessed 19 September 2006.

The Church Report. http://www.thechurchreport.com. Accessed 21 October 2006.

Community of Faith. http://www.cofonline.org. Accessed 18 September 2006.

Crosspoint Community Church, Mission. http://www.crosspointcc. net/crosspoint/

mission___values. Accessed 21 October 2006.

Crosspoint Community Church, Mission and Values. http://www. crosspointcc.net/

crosspoint/mission___values. Accessed 3 December 2006.

Crosspoint Community Church, What We Believe. http://www. crosspointcc.net/

crosspoint/what_we_believe. Accessed 3 December 2006.

Desiring God Ministries. http://www.desiringgod.org. Accessed 18 February 2007.

Evangelical Theological Society. http://www.etsjets.org. Accessed 2 September 2006.

Fellowship of the Woodlands. http://www.fotw.org. Accessed 1 October 2006.

Fellowship of the Woodlands, About Us. http://www.fotw.org/ aboutus/whatwepractice.asp Accessed 1 October 2006.

Fellowship of the Woodlands, What We Believe. http://www.fotw. org/aboutus/

whatwebelieve.asp. Accessed 1 October 2006.

Gotlife Ministries. http://www.gotlifeministries.com/index.cfm. Accessed 14 November 2006.

Gotlife.Org. http://www.gotlife.org/intro.html. Accessed 14 November 2006.

Joel Osteen Ministries. http://www.joelosteen.com/sitc/PageServer. Accessed 13 July 2005.

Kingdom Builders. http://kingdombuilders.com. Accessed 22 October 2006.

McMaster Divinity College. http://www.macdiv.ca/home.php. Accessed 20 October 2006.

National Association of Evangelicals. http://www.nae.net/index. cfm?FUSEACTION=nae.statement_of_faith. Accessed 28 February 2007.

The Potter's House. http://www.thepottershouse.org. Accessed 22 February 2007.

Purpose Driven. http://www.purposedriven.com/en-US/Home.htm. Accessed 15 September 2006.

Purpose Driven Life. http://www.purposedrivenlife.com/rickwarren. aspx. Accessed 15 November 2006.

Reclaiming the Mind Ministries. http://www.ttpstudents.com/ content/. Accessed 2 October 2006.

The Theology Program. http://www.ttpstudents.com/content/ttp/ about. Accessed 2 October 2006.

Theology Unplugged Archives. http://www.ttpstudents.com/content/ tup/archive. Accessed 21 October 2006.

Watchman Fellowship. http://www.watchman.org/expo/17_2news. htm. Accessed 26 February 2007.

Wikipedia, Purpose Driven Life. http://en.wikipedia.org/wiki/The_ Purpose_Driven_Life. Accessed. 15 November 2006.

Who Is This Jesus? http://whoisthisjesus.com. Accessed 21 March 2002.

Miscellaneous Sources

"Donald P. Roper, Superintendent, Potosi Correctional Center, Petitioner V. Christopher Simmons." United States Supreme Court, 2005.

Graham, Billy. "The Hour of Power with Robert Schuller," 31 May 1997.

Osteen, Joel. "Larry King Live." *CNN*, June 20, 2005.

_____. "Larry King Live." *CNN*, December 22, 2006.

Warren, Rick. "Dateline." *NBC*, May 23, 2005.

Wilkin, Robert N. "Why Is Certainty Objectionable among Evangelical Scholars?" Valley Forge, PA: 57th Annual Meeting of the Evangelical Theological Society, 2005.

_____. "Repentance as a Condition for Salvation" (Th.D. diss., Dallas Theological Seminary, 1985).

EPILOGUE

Do you know for certain that you will go to heaven when you die? This is a very important question that everyone must answer. Life's ultimate statistic is the same for all of us: 1-out-of-1 will die. Have you taken the time to contemplate your eternal destiny? Perhaps after reading this book, you have come to realize that you have never truly understood the gospel message. Quite possibly, like so many others throughout the centuries, you have been attempting to gain a right relationship with God through all the wrong means. Maybe you are counting on your good works or righteous deeds to get you into heaven. Maybe you are hoping that your family heritage or church affiliation will gain your acceptance before God in the hereafter.

But at the end of this life, none of that matters. The reality is: every one of us is a sinner. "For all have sinned and fall short of the glory of God" (Rom 3:23). And the penalty for our sin is eternal separation from God in a literal place of torment called hell. No matter how good we are, or how good we try to be, no amount of good works can remedy our sin problem. That is because entrance into heaven requires *perfect righteousness*. But the good news is, God has given us an indescribable gift. "But God demonstrates His own love toward us, in that while we were yet sinners, Christ died for us" (Rom 5:8). God provided for our salvation when He sent His Son, Jesus, to die in our place on the cross. Jesus' work on the cross paid the penalty for our sin. This is what the Bible calls, *the Gospel* (or *good news*).

Today, all who trust Jesus, the Son of God, and Him alone, to forgive their sins and give them the free gift of eternal life will be saved. The Bible says that the gospel message of Jesus Christ and His work on the cross saves those who believe it. "God was well-pleased through the foolishness of the message preached to save those who believe" (1 Cor 1:21). When we believe the gospel message, Christ's perfect righteousness covers our sin and grants us entrance into heaven.

Let me encourage you, right now, in the best way you know how, to trust in what Jesus has done on the cross for you as being all you will ever need to take away your sins and assure you a place in heaven. If you have trusted Christ for eternal life, or for more information on how to have eternal life, please contact Dr. J. B. Hixson at: **281-989-9813** or **jb@notbyworks.org**.

FREE GRACE ALLIANCE

The mission of the Free Grace Alliance (FGA) is to connect, encourage and equip the body of Christ to advance the grace message throughout the world. As members of the Evangelical Tradition, we affirm the Bible alone, and the Bible in its entirety, is the inspired Word of God and is therefore inerrant in the autographs. Furthermore, God is a Trinity, Father, Son, and Holy Spirit, each an uncreated person, one in essence, equal in power and glory. As members of this tradition, we are concerned about the clear understanding, presentation, and advancement of the Gospel of God's Free Grace.

If you are interested in hosting a FGA conference, or if you would like to have Dr. Hixson speak at your church, please contact us at **281-989-9813** or **jb@freegracealliance.com**. For more information about the Free Grace Alliance please visit **www.freegracealliance.com**.

LOGOS BIBLE SOFTWARE

Dr. J. B. Hixson is pleased to partner with Logos Bible Software. Logos is the premier Bible study tool in the world. Almost all of the exegetical and theological research for *Getting the Gospel Wrong* was done using Logos. Logos is the choice of over 600 Bible colleges and seminaries and thousands of pastors, evangelical leaders, and lay people alike. This amazing tool is available to anyone who is serious about studying God's Word. If you are interested in purchasing Logos Bible Software at a special discount price, or to learn more about Logos, please contact Dr. Hixson at **281-989-9813** or **jb@notbyworks.org**. To view a demo of this software, please visit www.logos.com/demo.